Studies on Interdisciplinary Economics and Business - Volume III

Özer ÖZÇELİK (ed.)

Studies on Interdisciplinary Economics and Business – Volume III

PETER LANG

Bibliographic Information published by the Deutsche Nationalbibliothek
The Deutsche Nationalbibliothek lists this publication in the Deutsche Nationalbibliografie; detailed bibliographic data is available online at http://dnb.d-nb.de.

Library of Congress Cataloging-in-Publication Data
A CIP catalog record for this book has been applied for at the Library of Congress.

Printed by CPI books GmbH, Leck

ISBN 978-3-631-81903-6 (Print)
E-ISBN 978-3-631-83211-0 (E-PDF)
E-ISBN 978-3-631-83212-7 (EPUB)
E-ISBN 978-3-631-83213-4 (MOBI)
DOI 10.3726/b17417

Peter Lang – Berlin · Bern · Bruxelles · New York · Oxford · Warszawa · Wien

This publication has been peer reviewed.

www.peterlang.com

Foreword

Researchers from various universities and institutions provided support for the third volume of the book Interdisciplinary Economics and Business which its first volume was published in 2018 and the second was released in 2019. Most of the studies in this volume consisted of economics and business administration branches. Studies have been specifically made for Turkey and generally made on a global scale. Conceptual and analytical studies are summarized as follows:

In their study Kırca and Ozer attempted to estimate the relationship between international tourism demand and sectoral income. Mere and Masca studied the gravity model in international trade flows. Şengür and Obiero tried to estimate the relationship between income inequality and economic growth in Kenya. In their study, Altıner and Bozkurt focused on the effects of economic freedom on foreign direct investments. In his study, Vardari analyzed active portfolio management in emerging markets. Guler made an analysis to fix inflation expectations for vulnerable economies under open inflation targeting strategy. In their study, Türedi and Yavuz analyzed the relationship between remittances and economic growth in scale of Turkey. Canbay and Mercan focused on the application and operation of the interest rate corridor. In his study, Gokce created an energy security flaw index for the European Union and for Turkey. Belke and Özel analyzed the relationship between inflation and growth in developing countries. Güney estimated the impact of the geopolitical risks on the stock market dynamics in Turkey. Topçuğlu and Buladi Cubukcu observed the state policies for promoting tourism in Turkey according to the provinces. Durmaz examined the Tekirdağ industry in the first years of the Republic. Kasa analyzed the relationship between domestic violence against women and economic development. Akinci examined the privatization revenues in Turkey in the period between 1986 and 2020. Aytekin analyzed the tax amnesties implemented in Turkey. In his study, Tüzüntürk focused on The Applications of Two-Sample Hotelling's T2 Test and One-Way Multivariate Analysis of Variance (MANOVA) Test. Hacıhasanoğlu examined the impact of climate change on financial risks. Çelik analyzed the financial performance of the paper products, printing and publishing companies traded at BIST. In his study, Yunus Düğer investigated the effects of COVID-19 (Coronavirus) on human rights. Kestane researched the role of internal control system in strengthening the corporate management in banks. In their study, Özbek and Altınbay examined the effects of organizational and professional commitment on the behavior of auditors working in independent audit companies. Tamer studied communication issues in health institutions. Yavuz Selim Düğer examined the issue of deliberate blindness in effective leadership and discussed whether this difficulty would be overcome. Tirgil and Acar studied on mental illness, gender, and labor supply. In her study, Koçyiğit examined the continuation of competition advantage in industry 4.0 era. Varışlı discussed the importance of strategic human sources management in creating a culture of competition and innovation. In their study, Eroğlu, Özsoy and Esen examined the expectation of the industries from the designers. Dülgeroğlu studied the sales issue with NLP. Göçmen made an investigation for discovery problem solving method in the solution of management problems. Bayar examined the importance of managers' attitudes and behaviors against cultural differences observed in organization. Kırpık made a literature review on "decision fatigue".

All publishing rights of the published book chapters belong to the publisher, and the content responsibility of the published articles belongs to the author. The opinions in the book chapters are the personal opinions of the authors; it is not an official opinion of any institution or organization.

I express my gratitude to the authors of the book chapters that contributed to the book "Studies on Interdisciplinary Economics and Business – Volume III" without losing their research spirit in spite of the Covid-19 epidemic, which is on the global agenda.

Özer Özçelik
Kütahya/Türkiye

Table of Contents

List of Contributors

Yasin Acar
Ph.D., Assist. Prof., Bilecik Şeyh Edebali University, Department of Public Finance, Bilecik, Turkey. yasin.acar@bilecik.edu.tr, orcid: 0000-0002-0847-1902

Adil AKINCI
Ph.D., Assoc. Prof., Bilecik Seyh Edebali University, Department of Public Finance, adilakinci@gmail.com, orcid: 0000-0002-2181-6952

Ali ALTINBAY
Ph.D., Assist. Prof., Kütahya Dumlupinar University, Faculty of Economics and Administrative Sciences, Department of Accounting and Finance, ali.altinbay@dpu.edu.tr, orcid: 0000-0003-3128-0669

Ali Altıner
Ph.D., Assoc.Prof., Recep Tayyip Erdogan University, Faculty of Economics and Administrative Sciences, Department of Economics, ali.altiner@erdogan.edu.tr, orcid:0000-0001-7362-8198

İkrabin AYTEKİN
Ph.D., Independent Accountant and Financial Consultant, tekinmusavirlik@gmail.com., orcid: 0000- 0001-9662-6195.

Münevver BAYAR
Ph.D. Manager, Social Security Institution, munevverbayar@hotmail.com, orcid: 0000-0002-8077-2160

Murat Belke
Ph.D., Assist.Professor, Burdur Mehmet Akif Ersoy University, Faculty of Economics and Administrative Sciences, Department of Economics, muratbelke@gmail.com, orcid: 0000-0002-3299-7162

Eda Bozkurt
Ph.D., Assoc. Prof., Ataturk University, Faculty of Open Education, Department of Foreign Trade, edabozkurt@atauni.edu.tr, orcid: 0000-0001-7158-8049

Şerif Canbay
Ph.D., Assist. Prof., Duzce University, Faculty of Political Sciences, Department of Economic, canbay.serif@gmail.com, orcid: 0000-0001-6141-7510

Pelin ÇELİK
Ph.D., Assist. Prof., Bayburt University, Faculty of Applied Sciences, Department of Management Information Systems, pelincelik@bayburt.edu.tr, orcid: 0000-0002-2234-2656

Özge Ceylan Esen
Ph.D., Candit., Mimar Sinan Fine Arts University, ozgecey@yahoo.com.tr, orcid: 0000-0002-4450-7079

Betül Buladi Çubukcu
Ph.D., Assist. Prof., Atatürk University, Erzurum Vocational School, Hotel, Department of Restaurant and Catering Services, betul.cubukcu@atauni.edu.tr, orcid: 0000-0003-1535-3071

Yunus Düger
Ph.D., Lecturer, Bilecik Seyh Edebali University, Osmaneli Vocational School, Department of Foreign Trade. yunus.duger@bilecik.edu.tr, orcid: 0000-0003-3077-6793

Yavuz Selim Düger
Ph.D., Assist. Prof., Kütahya Dumlupinar University, Faculty of Economics and Administrative Sciences, Department of International Trade and Finance, yselim.duger@dpu.edu.tr, orcid: 0000-0003-3523-9671

İsmail DÜLGEROĞLU
Ph.D., Assist. Prof., Kırklareli University, Faculty of Economics and Administrative Sciences, Department of Business Administration, ismail.dulgeroglu@klu.edu.tr, orcid: 0000-0002-0153-2514

Edip DURMAZ
Ph. D., Assist. Prof. , Kırklareli University, Department of History, edipdurmaz@klu.edu.tr

Ilgım Eroğlu
Ph.D., Assist. Prof. ,Mimar Sinan Fine Arts University, ilgim.eroglu@msgsu.edu.tr, ilgimeroglu@gmail.com, orcid: 0000-0001-8181-3334

İbrahim Ethem Güney
Ph.D., Doha Representative, Central Bank of the Republic of Turkey, ethem.guney@tcmb.gov.tr, orcid: 0000-0001-6890-205X

Didem GÖÇMEN
Ph.D., Assist. Prof., University of Turkish Aeronautical Association, dgocmen@thk.edu.tr, orcid: 0000-0002-3939-441X

Cem GÖKCE
Ph.D, Assist. Prof., Afyon Kocatepe University, Faculty of Economics and Administrative Sciences, Department of Economy, cgokce@aku.edu.tr, orcid: 0000-0001-7805-6977

Aslı GÜLER
Ph.D., Assist. Prof., Ordu University, Faculty of Economics and Administrative Sciences, Department of Economics, asliguler@odu.edu.tr, orcid: 0000-0002-2900-1184

Yavuz Selim Hacıhasanoğlu
Ph.D. Economist, Central Banf of the Republic of Turkey, yavuz.selim@tcmb.gov.tr. The views in this chapter are only those of the author and should not be interpreted as reflecting those of the Central Bank of the Republic of Turkey.

Hicran KASA
Ph.D., Assist. Prof., Türk Hava Kurumu University, hkasa@thk.edu.tr,orcid: 0000-0001-7266-0313

Ali Kestane
Ph.D., Research Assist., Kilis 7 Aralık University, FEAS, Department of Business Administration, alikestane@kilis.edu.tr, orcid: 0000-0002-7049-0354

Mustafa Kırca
Ph.D., Assist. Prof., Düzce University, Akçakoca Bey Faculty of Political Sciences, Department of Economics, mustafakirca52@gmail.com, orcid: 0000-0002-5630-7525

Gülşen Kırpık
Ph.D., Assist. Prof., Adiyaman University, Pharmacy Faculty, Department of Pharmacy Management, gkirpik@adiyaman.edu.tr, orcid: 0000 0003 4785 9624

Yeşim Kaya Koçyiğit
Ph.D., Assist. Prof., Istanbul Gelisim University, Faculty of Economics, Administrative and Social Sciences, Department of Business Administration (English), yesimkocyigit@gmail.com, ykocyigit@gelisim.edu.tr, orcid: 0000-0003-2192-8492

Mahmut MASCA
Ph.D., Prof., Afyon Kocatepe University, Faculty of Economics and Administrative Sciences, Department of Economics, mmasca@aku.edu.tr, mmasca@aku.edu.tr

Derya Mercan
Ph.D., dmercan@gmail.com, orcid: 0000-0003-3011-4423

Murat MERE
Ph.D., Lect., Afyon Kocatepe University, Başmakçı Vocational High School, Department of Foreign Trade, meremurat@aku.edu.tr, orcid: 0000-0002-8511-2583

Wilkista Lore OBIERO
Eskisehir Osmangazi University, Institute of Social Sciences, Department of Economics, lwilkista@gmail.com., orcid: 0000-0002-0498-3142

Ali ÖZBEK
Ph.D., Türmob, smmmaliozbek@gmail.com, orcid: 0000-0001-9183-6513

Emrah Özel
Ph.D Candidate., Research Assist., Burdur Mehmet Akif Ersoy University, Faculty of Economics and Administrative Sciences, Department of Economics, eozel@mehmetakif.edu.tr, orcid:0000-0002-3970-3622

Mustafa Özer
Ph.D., Prof., Anadolu University, Faculty of Economics Administrative Sciences, Department of Economics, muozer@anadolu.edu.tr, orcid: 0000-0001-9852-8441

Mehmet Şengür
Ph.D. Assistant Professor, Eskisehir Osmangazi University, Faculty of Economics and Administrative Sciences, Department of Economics, msengur@ogu.edu.tr, orcid: 0000-0002-2173-9977

Gülay Tamer
Ph.D., Assist. Prof., İstanbul Gelişim University, Scholl of Health Sciences, Department of Healthcare Management,gtamer@gelisim.edu.tr., orcid: 0000-0002-7897-1603

Abdullah Tirgil
Ph.D., Assist. Prof., Ankara Yildirim Beyazit University, Department of Public Finance, Ankara, Turkey, atirgil@ybu.edu.tr., orcid: 0000-0002-4491-4459

Özlem Topçuoğlu
Ph.D., Assist. Prof., Atatürk University, Erzurum Vocational School, Department of Foreign Trade, ozlemgunduz@atauni.edu.tr, orcid: 0000-0002-9821-5856

Salih Türedi
Ph.D., Assoc. Prof., Recep Tayyip Erdogan University, Faculty of Economics and Administrative Sciences, Department of Economics, salih.turedi@erdogan.edu.tr, orcid: 0000-0001-6294-1007

Selim Tüzüntürk
Ph. D., Assoc. Prof., Bursa Uludağ University, Department of Econometrics, selimtuzunturk@uludag.edu.tr., orcid: 0000-0002-8987-2280

Luan VARDARI
Ph.D., Assist. Prof., "Universum" College, Faculty of Business and Management, Kosovo, luan.vardari@gmail.com, orcid: 0000-0003-3212-5783

Nuran Varışlı
Ph.D., Expert, Republic of Turkey Social Security Institution, gulmennuran@hotmail.com

Vildan Yavuz
Ph.D., Assist. Prof., Recep Tayyip Erdogan University, Faculty of Economics and Administrative Sciences, Department of Economics, vildan.yavuz@erdogan.edu.tr, orcid: 0000-0003-3232-8265

Çiğdem Yılmaz Özsoy
Ph. D., Istanbul University, cigdemyilmazozsoy@gmail.com, orcid:0000-0002-7436-7273

Mustafa Kırca & Mustafa Özer

Structural Breaks and Cointegration Analysis of the Relationship between International Tourism Demand and Sectoral Incomes in Turkey[1]

1 Introduction

According to the Unbalanced Growth Theory developed by Hirschman (1958), there are forward and backward linkages among the sectors of an economy. A backward link indicates the sector's relative importance as user input from non-primary economic activities, while forward links point out sector's relative importance as a supplier to the other sectors in the economy. The existence of forward and backward linkages also proves the existence of an input-output relations among economic activities or sectors. Well known contributions of the tourism sector to overall economy are the creation of output and income, foreign exchange earnings, increasing government revenues, creation of employment and business opportunities, inducing of investment in infrastructure and contribution to regional development.

Also, it is widely argued that the contribution of the services sector, particularly tourism and hospitality, to economic revitalization by creating more labor income is considered greater than even that of agricultural and manufacturing industries. Creating more impacts on value-added, employment entails and output, the economic impact of the tourism and hospitality sector greatly outweigh those of agricultural- or manufacturing-related industry (Kim and Kim, 2015). The tourism sector has close input-output linkages with related sectors such as accommodation management, travel management, food-beverages management as well as other sectors such as agriculture and industry. Furthermore, any positive contributions of tourism incomes for a region or country's economy also impact the industry, agriculture and services sectors. Also, an increase in tourism expenditure may lead to additional activity in related industries and

1 This section is derived from the PhD thesis which is written under the supervision of Prof. Dr. Mustafa Özer by Mustafa KIRCA in Anadolu University, Eskişehir, Turkey. Title of the Thesis: "The Econometric Analysis of the Relationships Between Selected Macroeconomic Variables and Tourism in Turkey"

causing a greater rise in spending than an initial increase in spending. Thus, as (Cernat and Gourdon, 2012) indicated, one of best ways to indicate economic benefits is to integrate tourism into the national economy by establishing strong linkages between tourism and other economic sectors such as agriculture, fisheries, manufacturing, construction and other service industries, such as culture, arts, entertainment, recreation, and sport. We know that when the tourism sector makes use of products and services produced within the local economy or sectors of the economy, it will contribute to strengthen of these other sectors and provide additional income through the multiplier effect of the tourism sector on the overall economy. In addition to having interaction with other sectors through its input-output relations, the tourism sector creates also a multiplier effect. According to this effect, an increase in the tourism sector's income will increase the incomes of other sectors. The effects of the incomes generated by the tourism sector are generally divided into three main groups: direct, indirect and (additionally) adapted effects (Coltman, 1989; Vellas and Bécherel, 1995; Page, 2009; Dwyer, Forsyth and Dwyer, 2010).

The direct effects mentioned herein indicates the expenses tourists made by directly buying goods and services from businesses such as hotels, restaurants and transportation services. Indirect effects are effects that arise due to tourism businesses, particularly hotels, purchasing goods and services from local suppliers. Finally, adapted effects are those that are generated through the expenses made for goods and services bought by the personnel employed in the tourism businesses with their salaries. Therefore, a one-unit increase in income generated by the tourism sector has the capacity to generate more than a one-unit increase in incomes of other sectors. Thus, rise in income of the tourism sector is expected to increase the incomes of other sectors. But, this expectation should be supported by empirical studies. Also, the contribution and impacts of tourism to a country's economy are generally by examining its effect on the economic growth of the country. According to most of these studies, international tourism has a positive effect on economic growth and these positive effects of tourism on growth are multiple. As Blake et al. (2006) concludes, the tourism plays a crucial role in rising income and human capital, and in fostering efficiency and competitiveness. But, it is hard to see rich literature particularly investigating sectors' relationships with the incomes of other sectors, even though as the tourism industry is growing in many countries, the causal relationship between international tourism demand and incomes of various sectors is becoming important for policy makers.

Thus, this section aims to investigate the relationships between international tourism demand and the selected sectoral incomes in Turkey by using quarterly data between the first quarter of 1998 and the last quarter of 2013. We use Kapetanios (2005) multiple break unit root test, Maki (2012) multiple break cointegration test, and cointegration parameter estimation methods.

2 Literature Review

There are many studies that investigate the relationships between the tourism sector and other sectors. Gül (2013) conducted a study by using input-output analysis methodology for the purpose of investigating the effects of increases in tourism income in Turkey. By generating a "social accounts matrix", inter-sectoral income multipliers were derived. The empirical findings of the study indicate that the demand-oriented shocks in the tourism sector may be utilized for revitalizing the economy and handling unemployment issues.

Kadiyali and Kosova (2013) conducted a study on the distribution of employment that is provided by the development of tourism for other sectors in the USA. Data pertaining to 43 states of the USA covering the period between the years 1987 and 2006 were utilized in the study, and the researchers reached the conclusion in the result of the study that 100 rooms booked daily cause around 2–5 new employment opportunities in other sectors. It was underlined that this situation is reflected most in the sectors of construction, retail, health, and vocational and technical services.

Kweka et al. (2001) investigated whether or not there is a relationship between tourism and other sectors in Tanzania, focusing on employment and tax incomes by using Input-Output Analysis. They reached the conclusion that tourism had an impact on the production of sectors due to its robust link with other sectors. However, it was mentioned that the income impact brought by tourism is found out to be not significant. The reason behind that was explained as low added-value products being produced in the tourism sector. Despite this situation, it was indicated that tourism is the sector that has the potential to make a positive impact on economic growth.

Telfer and Wall (1996) conducted a study that investigated the relationships between tourism and food production in Lombok Island in Indonesia. Authors revealed that these two sectors benefited from each other. They highlighted particularly the link between the agriculture sector and the tourism sector. It was observed that there were potentials towards increasing the backward links between tourism and local food production. They mentioned that local production would increase with the development of tourism demand, and thus local production would develop in parallel to this. However, they also pointed out that there are challenges required to be overcome in order to strengthen such links.

A study that explores the correlation between the tourism sector and agriculture sector was conducted by Torres (2003). Torres interviewed many groups such as tourists, tourism sector employees, farmers and migrants at important tourism destinations of Mexico. Through such interviews, the researcher tried to perceive the link between agriculture and tourism. In the result of the study, it was indicated that the intertwinement of the two sectors caused an increase in local production and thus tourism incomes would also increase. With the development of tourism, there are certain benefits that rural communities may receive from tourism. At the same time, it was pointed out that different agricultural products are produced due to tourists being willing to try different products.

Çıkın et al. (2009) conducted a study that investigated the importance of the tourism sector within Turkey's economy and the effect of tourism on other sectors. In the light of the analyzes conducted, the authors mentioned that the development of the agricultural sector is linked with the development of the tourism sector. According to the research, it was indicated that agriculture and tourism were sectors that are in constant and close interaction and that they complemented each other. Furthermore, they expressed that most of the inputs to tourism are provided from the agriculture sector due to tourism being a sector of food and beverages. Another important finding from the study was the observation that the development of agricultural tourism in response to tourism meant also the development of both the tourism and agriculture sectors. In addition, it was mentioned in the study that Turkey possessed many natural, seasonal and sociocultural superiorities compared to many competing countries in global tourism markets. It was highlighted at the conclusion of the study that due to such superiorities it was possible for the country to receive a larger share of the tourism sector market throughout the world and for an integrated growth to be realized in the agriculture sector that entails intensive agricultural activities in rural regions. Other studies that explored the links between agriculture, food production, and tourism sector were conducted by Bélisle (1983) and Rogerson (2012). In the study conducted by Bélisle (1983) specific to the Caribbean region, it was expressed that tourism demand boosted food import and thus decreased the positive economic effect of the tourism sector. Furthermore, Bélisle expressed that the links between tourism and local food production were not defined in full. On the other hand, Rogerson (2012) in his study highlighted that the links between the tourism sector and agriculture sector are of significance for maximizing the economic effects of tourism sector particularly in developing countries.

Khadaroo and Seetanah (2007) conducted a study that investigated the correlations between the development level of transportation infrastructure and tourism. In this study realized specific to Mauritius island, overall tourism demand was modeled. In conclusion of the study that utilized dynamic panel data analysis, it was observed that the tourists visiting from Europe/America and Asia were sensitive against the transportation infrastructure of the island. It was also revealed through tourism demand equation that the tourism demand is dependent on tourist's income, distance and price. These results indicate that the tourism sector is correlated with the development of transportation infrastructure. Infrastructure works affect many sectors.

Literature review shows that there is a lack of studies examining the sectoral linkages of tourism in terms of its effect on other sector incomes. Thus, we study its effects on the selected sectoral incomes in Turkey.

3 Methodology

To investigate the dynamic linkages between international tourism demand and sectoral incomes, we first examine the time-series properties of variables by using the multiple breaks unit root test developed by Kapetanios (2005) due to several structural breaks observed in the series over the study period. And then, we use the multiple breaks cointegration test developed by Maki (2012). Finally, we estimate the coefficients of cointegrating regression.

According to Perron (1989), in the presence of structural break(s) in variables, the traditional unit root tests[2] produce results subject to criticism. Thus, in this case, the structural breaks unit root tests should be used to determine the degree of integration of variables. There are many tests that take into consideration of structural breaks.[3] However, every test possesses both advantages and disadvantages. Kapetanios (2005) developed multiple breaks unit root test eliminating the drawbacks of these tests. To carry out the Kapetanios (2005) tests, we consider the following regressions[4]:

$$y_t = \mu_0 + \mu_1 t + \alpha y_{t-1} + \sum_{i=1}^{m} \gamma \Delta y_{t-i} + \sum_{i=1}^{m} \varphi DU_{i,t} + \sum_{i=1}^{m} \psi DT_{i,t} + \varepsilon_t \quad (1)$$

2 Such as Augmented Dickey-Fuller (ADF), Phillips-Perron (PP), Kwiatkowski-Phillips-Schmidt-Shin (KPSS).

3 Such as Perron (1989), Zivot and Andrews (1992), Lumsdanie and Papell (1997), Lee and Strazicich (2003, 2008).

4 Since first test equation includes both constant and trend, and not applicable for cases where only constant should be included, Gómez-Zaldívar , Ventosa-Santaulària, and Wallace (2013:1355) revised the test equation only allowing break in constant.

and

$$y_t = \mu_0 + \alpha y_{t-1} + \sum_{i=1}^{m} \gamma \Delta y_{t-i} + \sum_{i=1}^{m} \varphi DU_{i,t} + \varepsilon_t \tag{2}$$

Where DU and DT are dummy variables that represent breaks for the constant term and on the trend respectively; μ_0 indicates the constant, μ_1 indicates the coefficient of the trend, φ indicates the differential constant term, ψ indicates the differential coefficient of the trend, and ε_t indicates the error term (disturbance). Similar to many structural breaks time series analyzes, DU and DT are defined as follows; $DU_{i,t} = \begin{cases} 1 \textit{ when } t > T_{b,i} \\ 0 \textit{ when } t \leq T_{b,i} \end{cases}$ *and* $DT_{i,t} = \begin{cases} t - T_{b,i} \textit{ when } t > T_{b,i} \\ 0 \textit{ when } t \leq T_{b,i} \end{cases}$. Where $Tb_{,i}$ indicates break date and "i" takes on values as i=1,2,. . .m.

As Kapetanios (2005:127) also expressed clearly, the method developed by Bai and Perron (1998) is used when determining break dates in this test. Furthermore, the number of breaks is also decided through this method. In order to carry out the test, following null and alternative hypotheses are tested: H_0: Variable has unit root (α=1, $\mu_1 = \varphi_1 = \ldots = \varphi_m = \psi_1 = \ldots = \psi_m = 0$) and H_1: m is stationary with the breaking (α<1, $\varphi_{i+1} = \psi i +_1 = \ldots = \psi_m = 0$, (i= 1,. . .,m)).

Kapetanios (2005:129) calculated critical values referring to 5 breaks by using Monte Carlo simulation method. In order to determine whether or not variables are stationary with the structural break, the calculated values of the test statistic and the table values are compared: when the sample value of the test statistic (t statistic value) is greater than the table value, H_0 is rejected and it is concluded that the variable Y is stationary with "m" number of breaks.

After determining the degree of integration of the variables, we determine the existence of cointegration by using multiple breaks cointegration test developed by Maki (2012), since in the presence of structural breaks, traditional cointegration tests[5] are most likely produce biased results. Even though there are other cointegration tests take into account of structural break, such as Gregory and Hansen (1996a, 1996b) and Hatemi-J (2008), we preferred Maki test due to the fact that better results will be generated in cases where the number of breaks is not known and that it allows for four different model estimations. These models are as shown Maki's (2012:2011–2012) article. In the article Model 0, 1, 2, and 3 represents Equation 1, 2, 3, and 4, respectively.

5 Such as Engle and Granger (1987), Johansen (1988, 1991), and Johansen and Juselius (1990).

Maki (2012:2012) determines both the number of breaks and break dates by using Bai and Perron (1998) test. The only difference is that both the number of breaks and break dates of the residual terms ($\hat{u}_t$) are determined based on the following equation:

$$\Delta \hat{u}_t = \rho \hat{u}_{t-1} + \sum_{j=1}^{\rho} \alpha_j \Delta \hat{u}_{t-j} + \varepsilon_t \tag{3}$$

The residual terms in Equation (3) obtained from Model 0,..,3. For the first breakpoint, "t" statistics belonging to the hypothesis of H_0: ρ=0 (H_1: ρ<0) for all possible break dates are obtained and the minimum t statistic is recorded as τ^1 and break date is determined based on minimum RSS. The hypotheses belonging to this test are as follows; *H_0: ρ=0, there is no cointegration between variables with structural breaks and H_1: ρ<0, there is cointegration between variables with structural breaks.*

Maki (2012:2013) calculated the critical values for each model we explain above with five breaks. When the calculated value of test statistic is greater than the critical value, H_0 is rejected and it is concluded that there is a cointegration between variables with structural breaks.

After determining the existence of cointegration, we use three fully efficient estimation methods of cointegrating regression of Fully Modified Least Squares (FMOLS) estimator developed by Phillips and Hansen (1990), Canonical Cointegrating Regression (CCR) estimator developed by Park (1992), and finally Dynamic Least Square (DOLS) estimator developed by Stock and Watson (1993). These three estimators are known as fully efficient estimators and allow us to estimate the coefficients of cointegrating regression and provides unbiased estimates of the coefficients.

4 Data and Empirical Results

To investigate the impacts of international tourism demand on sectoral incomes by using the quarterly time series between 1998 and 2013. We extract the sectoral income series from the Central Bank of Republic of Turkey (CBTR) (2014) Electronic Data Delivery System (EVDS) system and number of foreign tourist as a measure of international tourism demand (LNYZ) from Turkish Statistics Institute (2014) (TurkSTAT). All income series are expressed in constant prices of 1998 and logarithmic values of variables are used in the analysis. Sectors that included in the study are Culture, arts, entertainment, recreation and sports activities (LNKSEDS), Agriculture, forestry and aquaculture (LNTOB), Real estate activities (LNGF), Accommodation and Food Service Activities (LNKHY) and Activities of households as employers (LNHIV). Figure 1 represents the time series plots of variables.

The time series plots of variables show that all variables exhibit strong seasonality and structural breaks. Thus, to focus on other components of time series, we remove the seasonal components of variables by using Census X12 method and use seasonally adjusted variables in our empirical analysis.

In this section of the study, first, we present the results of unit root and cointegration tests and then coefficient estimates. Table 1 presents the results of the Kapetanios (2005) unit root tests for all variables.

According to results in Table 1, each variable is first difference stationary with structural breaks. The first break date for LNKYH 1999Q3 caused by the earthquakes of 1999. Second break date is 2003Q4 caused by terror attacks in Istanbul (15 November 2003, a bomb attack at synagogue; 20 November 2003 attack at HSBC Bank). Third break date is 2008Q1 caused by Global Crisis initiated in late 2007 in the USA. The last break date is 2010Q1 caused by announcement İstanbul as "European Culture Capital" in the year 2010 (Istanbul Metropolitan Municipality, 2009). The only significant break date for LNYZ is 2004Q4 influenced by European Union (EU) deciding on December 2004 to commence negotiations with Turkey on 3 October 2005 (Ministry of European Union Affairs, 2016). The first break date of LNTOB is 2001Q1 caused by unexpected drought throughout Turkey in the year 2001. The second break date is 2004Q4 initiated by commencing negotiations between the EU and Turkey. The third break date is 2007Q1 influenced by the "Communiqué on Making Direct Income Support Payment" published in the year 2007. The significant structural break dates for LNKSEDS, based on a model with constant and trend, are 2001Q4 caused by the economic crisis in 2001 and 2005Q1 period may have occurred due to the membership negotiations commenced with the EU. Also, the test results based on a model with a constant term indicate the significant breaks in 2005Q4. The significant structural break dates LNGF are 1999Q4, most probably caused by 1999 earthquakes, 2002Q1 following the economic crisis of 2000 and 2001, 2003Q2, influenced by the Law no. 4916 adopted on the date 3 July 2003 that allows sales of real estate to foreigners, 2006Q2 and 2010Q3 caused by the changes made to the Real Estate Tax Law no. 1319. The significant structural break dates of LNHIV are 2001Q4 followed by the crisis in 2001, 2008Q4 caused by the global crisis of 2008. Also, only considering the model with constant, the break dates are 1999Q4 caused by earthquakes in 1999. The

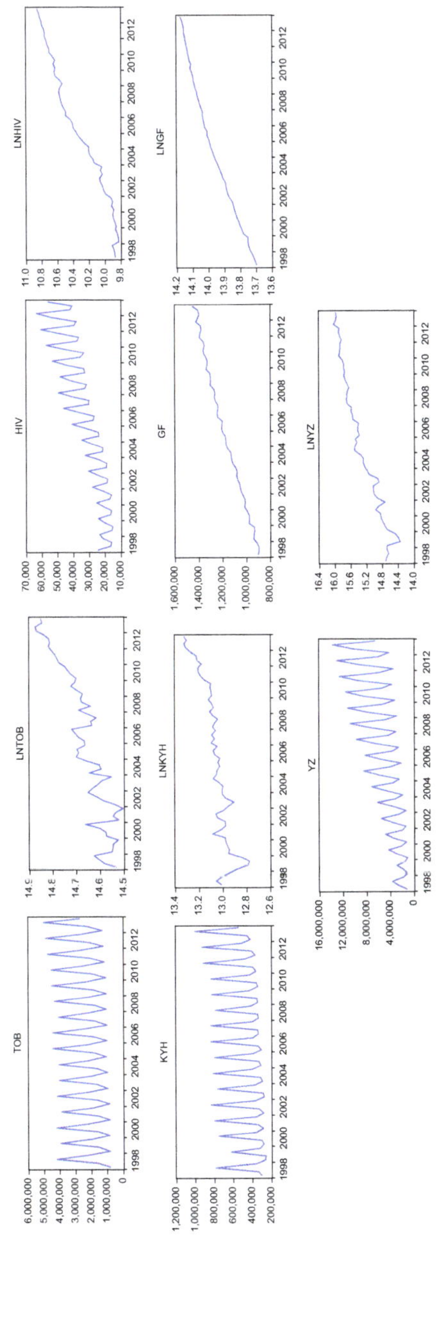

Figure 1. Time Series Plots of Variables

Table 1. Kapetanios Unit Root Test Results

Sector Name	Constant Model (Test Statistics)	Break Dates – Constant Model					First Difference (Test Statistics)
LNKYH	-7.3264	1999Q1	2000Q3	2002Q3	2008Q1	2012Q1	-9.2627*
LNTOB	-7.2636	2001Q1	2004Q4	2007Q1	2010Q4	2012Q3	-7.8205*
LNKSEDS	-5.7640	2000Q2	2001Q4	2003Q4	2005Q4	2007Q2	-12.4882*
LNGF	-6.0592	1999Q4	2002Q1	2003Q2	2010Q3	-	-8.0253*
LNHIV	-5.8125	1999Q4	2003Q1	2005Q1	2008Q4	2012Q1	-10.9836*
LNYZ	-5.9106	2000Q1	2001Q4	2004Q2	2005Q3	2011Q2	-7.6558*
Sector Name	**Constant and Trend Model (Test Statistics)**	**Break Dates – Constant and Trend Model**					**First Difference(Test Statistics)**
LNKYH	-6.3047	1999Q3	2010Q1	2011Q2	2012Q3	-	-8.2250*
LNTOB	-9.1341*	2000Q2	2002Q2	2004Q4	2006Q2	2008Q1	-
LNKSEDS	-6.1388	2001Q4	2003Q1	2005Q1	-	-	-12.3805*
LNGF	-5.6692	1999Q4	2006Q3	-	-	-	-12.7041*
LNHIV	-7.1064	2001Q4	2005Q1	2006Q4	2011Q3	-	-11.6366*
LNYZ	-3.9681	2004Q4	-	-	-	-	-7.1519*

* Indicates stationarity according to 5 % significance. Critical values were taken from the article of Kapetanios (2005, p. 129) and Gomez-Zaldivar, Ventosa-Santaulària and Wallace'in (2012, p. 1358)

results in Table 1 indicate that LNYZ has the break date of 2004Q4 influenced by European Union (EU) deciding on December 2004 to commence negotiations with Turkey on 3 October 2005. Table 2 presents the results of Maki tests.

The results in Table 2 indicate that there is cointegration relationship between them at 5 % significance with 1 break according to Model 0, at 5 % significance with 2 breaks according to Model 1, at 1 % significance with 3 breaks according to Model 2, and finally at 1 % significance with 3 breaks according to Model 3. In other words, there is a long-run relationship between LNKYH and LNYZ with a structural break. When the results of the Maki cointegration tests between LNTOB and LNYZ in Table 2 are examined, it is observed that there is a cointegration between them at 5 % significance with 5 breaks according to Model 0, at 1 % significance with 5 breaks according to Model 1, at 5 % significance with 1 break according to Model 2, and finally at 1 % significance with 4 breaks according to Model 3. In other words, LNYZ has a significant effect on LNTOB in the long-run. Maki cointegration tests results in Table 2 also show that there is cointegration between them at 1 % significance with 3 breaks according to

Table 2. Results of Maki Test

Maki Cointegration Test Result between LNKYH and LNYZ							
Model	**Test Statistic**	**Number of Breaks**	**Break Dates**				
0	-5.2387**	1	2010Q4	-	-	-	-
1	-5.2470**	2	2002Q3	2008Q4		-	-
2	-7.0639*	3	2001Q4	2004Q4	2011Q2	-	-
3	-7.6677*	3	2002Q3	2007Q3	2009Q4	-	-
Maki Cointegration Test Result between LNTOB and LNYZ							
Model	**Test Statistic**	**Number of Breaks**	**Break Dates**				
0	-5.6695**	5	2004Q3	2006Q4	2009Q1	2010Q3	2012Q2
1	-6.3124*	5	1999Q3	2001Q3	2003Q4	2006Q4	2010Q4
2	-5.1554**	1	2008Q2	-	-	-	-
3	-8.2846*	4	2000Q4	2003Q2	2006Q4	2010Q4	-
Maki Cointegration Test Result between LNKSEDS and LNYZ							
Model	**Test Statistic**	**Number of Breaks**	**Break Dates**				
0	-5.9970*	3	2002Q1	2004Q2	2005Q4	-	-
1	-4.8730	3	2003Q3	2007Q2	2011Q4	-	-
2	-8.7748*	5	2000Q1	2001Q4	2004Q2	2005Q4	2008Q2
3	-6.1659	3	2001Q4	2003Q4	2008Q1	-	-
Maki Cointegration Test Result between LNGF and LNYZ							
Model	**Test Statistic**	**Number of Breaks**	**Break Dates**				
0	-5.4627**	5	2000Q3	2003Q4	2005Q2	2008Q2	2011Q2
1	-4.9622	5	2000Q3	2003Q2	2006Q3	2008Q4	2011Q4
2	-7.6069*	4	2000Q3	2006Q2	2010Q2	2012Q2	-
3	-6.6579	5	2001Q1	2002Q4	2006Q4	2008Q3	2011Q1
Maki Cointegration Test Result between LNHIV and LNYZ							
Model	**Test Statistic**	**Number of Breaks**	**Break Dates**				
0	-6.8088*	5	1999Q4	2002Q4	2005Q4	2008Q2	2011Q2
1	-4.3541	4	2001Q4	2003Q4	2007Q2	2009Q2	-
2	-6.5392**	4	1999Q3	2002Q4	2004Q4	2006Q3	-
3	-5.6043	4	2003Q4	2005Q4	2008Q4	2010Q4	-

***, **,* Shows Maki Cointegration Relationship according to 10 %, 5 % and 1 % significances. Critical values were taken from Maki (2012) article. The optimal lag length was defined by using "t" statistic value.

Model 0, and with 5 breaks according to Model 2 between LNKSEDS and LNYZ. In other words, LNYZ has a significant effect on LNKSEDS in the long-run. When the results of the Maki cointegration analysis between LNGF and LNYZ in Table 2 are examined, it is observed that there is a cointegration between them at 5 % significance with 5 breaks according to Model 0, and at 1 % significance with 4 breaks according to Model 2. In other words, LNYZ has a significant effect on LNGF in the long-run. Finally, the results in Table 2 indicate that there is evidence of cointegration between LNHIV and LNYZ with structural breaks. For example, there is cointegration between them at 1 % significance with 5 breaks according to Model 0, and at 5 % significance with 4 breaks according to Model 2. Thus, we can conclude that LNYZ has a significant effect on LNHIV in the long-run. Table 3 gives the cointegrating coefficient estimates.

Based on Model 0 estimates, three methods provide significant coefficient estimates. Besides, the estimates indicate the same break date of 2010Q4 as Maki cointegration analysis. According to coefficient estimates, 1 % increase in LNYZ increases LNKYH by approximately 0.15 %. Thus, we can conclude that the impact of the rising number of foreign tourists on the incomes of sectors of Accommodation and Food Service Activities is relatively small.

The coefficient estimates of cointegrating regression of LNYZ on LNTOB are significant for all models, but we only use the estimates based on Model 0. All break dates determined through Maki cointegration analysis are found to be statistically significant. According to the cointegrating coefficient estimate, a %1 increase in LNYZ increases the LNTOB by approximately 0.06 %.

The cointegrating coefficient estimates for the relationship between LNYZ and LNKSEDS are all significant and close to each other. The break dates are all significant as well. A 1 % increase in LNYZ cause an increase in LNKSEDS by approximately 0.18 %.

The estimation results of coefficients of cointegrating regression between LNYZ and LNGF in Table 2 shows that the coefficients are significant for all models and all breaks are found to be significant. Thus, we can conclude that a 1 % increase in LNYZ creates approximately 0.14 % increase in LNGF. Finally, when we examine the results of cointegrating regression between LNYZ and LNHIV based on the Results in Table 2, we can conclude that the cointegrating confidents and break dates are all significant for all models. A 1 % increase in LNYZ leads to approximately 0.42 % increase in LNHIV.

Based on the estimated values of cointegrating coefficients, we can conclude that the impact of international tourism demand (LNYZ) is highest for Activities of households as employers (LNHIV) followed by Culture, arts, entertainment, recreation and sports activities (LNKSEDS), Accommodation

Table 3. Cointegrating Coefficient Estimates

Cointegration Model Estimates between LNKYH and LNYZ			
LNKYH	**FMOLS**	**DOLS**	**CCR**
Constant Term	10.7912 (0.0001)*	10.6977 (0.0001)*	**10.7999 (0.0001)***
LNYZ	**0.1462 (0.0001)***	**0.1526 (0.0001)***	0.1456 (0.0001)*
D2010Q4	0.1291 (0.0001)*	0.1139 (0.0001)*	0.1299 (0.0001)*
$\overline{R^2}$	0.8450	0.8420	0.8447
Cointegration Model Estimates between LNTOB and LNYZ			
LNTOB	**FMOLS**	**DOLS**	**CCR**
Constant Term	13.7148 (0.0001)*	13.4595 (0.0001)*	13.7210 (0.0001)*
LNYZ	**0.0583 (0.0400)****	**0.0754 (0.0070)***	**0.0579 (0.0467)****
D2004Q3	0.0715 (0.0014)*	0.0631 (0.0036)*	0.0729 (0.0025)*
D2006Q4	-0.0425 (0.0212)**	-0.0458 (0.0112)**	-0.0432 (0.0171)**
D2009Q1	0.0507 (0.0113)**	0.0487 (0.0126)**	0.0508 (0.0113)**
D2010Q3	0.0701 (0.0011)*	0.0683 (0.0011)*	0.0702 (0.0011)*
D2012Q2	0.0526 (0.0122)**	0.0509 (0.0129)**	0.0526 (0.0122)*
$\overline{R^2}$	0.8948	0.8960	0.8948
Cointegration Model Estimates between LNKSEDS and LNYZ			
LNKSEDS	**FMOLS**	**DOLS**	**CCR**
Constant Term	7.7161 (0.0001)*	7.5392 (0.0001)*	7.7222 (0.0001)*
LNYZ	**0.1768 (0.0001)***	**0.1885 (0.0001)***	**0.1764 (0.0001)***
D2002Q1	0.1206 (0.0001)*	0.1209 (0.0001)*	0.1207 (0.0001)*
D2004Q2	0.0665 (0.0039)*	0.0624 (0.0116)**	0.0669 (0.0044)*
D2005Q4	0.1814 (0.0001)*	0.1778 (0.0001)*	0.1813 (0.0001)*
$\overline{R^2}$	0.9848	0.9838	0.9848
Cointegration Model Estimates between LNGF and LNYZ			
LNGF	**FMOLS**	**DOLS**	**CCR**
Constant Term	11.7510 (0.0001)*	11.7490 (0.0007)*	11.7444 (0.0001)*
LNYZ	**0.1369 (0.0001)***	**0.1367 (0.0001)***	**0.1373 (0.0001)***
D2000Q3	0.06517 (0.0001)*	0.0712 (0.0003)*	0.0659 (0.0002)*
D2003Q4	0.0350 (0.0608)***	0.0321 (0.1550)	0.0348 (0.0809)***
D2005Q2	0.0445 (0.0024)*	0.0474 (0.0073)*	0.0445 (0.0024)*
D2008Q2	0.04315 (0.0018)*	0.0418 (0.0113)**	0.0430 (0.0027)*
D2011Q2	0.0336 (0.0081)*	0.0335 (0.0284)**	0.0335 (0.0093)*
$\overline{R^2}$	0.9796	0.9772	0.9796

(continued on next page)

Table 3. Continued

Cointegration Model Estimates between LNKYH and LNYZ			
Cointegration Model Estimates between LNHIV and LNYZ			
LNHIV	**FMOLS**	**DOLS**	**CCR**
Constant Term	3.6184 (0.0001)*	3.7575 (0.0001)	3.6048 (0.0001)*
LNYZ	**0.4287(0.0001)***	**0.4189 (0.0001)***	**0.4286 (0.0001)***
D1999Q4	-0.0558 (0.0212)**	-0.0511 (0.0341)**	-0.0556 (0.0181)**
D2002Q4	0.0562 (0.0202)*	0.0618 (0.0148)**	0.0556 (0.0276)**
D2005Q4	0.2000 (0.0001)*	0.2035 (0.0001)*	0.1996 (0.0001)*
D2008Q2	0.0479 (0.0207)**	0.0501 (0.0209)**	0.0477 (0.0228)**
D2011Q2	0.0952 (0.0001)*	0.0969 (0.0001)*	0.0950 (0.0001)*
$\overline{R^2}$	0.9878	0.9877	0.9878

***, **, * Show significance compared to 10 %, 5 % and 1 %, respectively.

and Food Service Activities (LNKHY) and Real estate activities (LNGF). Unlike to expectations, the least effect of international tourism demand (LNYZ) is on Agriculture, forestry, and aquaculture (LNTOB). Thus, it is fair to conclude that the impacts of international tourism demand are limited, small and contradicts to the expectations that it will create significant additions to incomes of sectors of Turkey.

6 Conclusion

In this study, we study the impacts of international tourism demand on the incomes of selected sectors of Turkey including culture, arts, entertainment, recreation, and sports activities, Agriculture, forestry and aquaculture, Real estate activities, Accommodation and Food Service Activities and Activities of households as employers. To estimate the long-run effects of international tourism demand on the incomes of selected sectors of Turkey, we first determine the degree of integration of variables by using Kapatinos multiple breaks unit root test and Maki's cointegration tests with breaks.

The results of the former tests indicate that all variables are stationary with multiple breaks and the latter tests results reveal that there is cointegration between international tourism demand on the incomes of selected sectors of Turkey. Also, the estimates of cointegrating coefficient tell us that the impact of international tourism demand on the incomes of selected sectors of Turkey varies across sectors; but, they are unexpectedly small, especially Agriculture, forestry and aquaculture. While the largest effect of international tourism demand is on the income of activities of households as employers, the smallest effect on the Agriculture, forestry, and aquaculture.

If we use these results as an indicator of linkages between international tourism demand and sectoral incomes of Turkey, unfortunately, it is hard to claim that the sector's backward and forward linkages are high and strong. Thus, the results of the study should be considered as an alarming bell and should be taken cautiously to evaluate the importance of the tourism sector for the development of Turkey's economy. Moreover, sector representatives, policymakers and academics should focus on how to increase the sector's sectoral income contribution, since increasing these contributions can be crucial for policymakers to decrease the regional income differences and to increase the well-being of citizens of Turkey. As a future study, the reasons for this low-income contribution of tourism to sectors of Turkey's economy should be investigated fully.

References

Bai, J. & Perron, P. (1998). Estimating and Testing Linear Models with Multiple Structural Changes. Econometrica, 66(1), 47–78.

Bélisle, F. J. (1983). Tourism and Food Production in the Caribbean. Annals of Tourism Research, 10(4), 497–513.

Blake, A., Durbarr, R. & Eugenio-Martin, J. L. et al. (2006). Integrating Forecasting and CGE Models: The Case of Tourism in Scotland. Tourism Management, 27(2), 292–305.

Central Bank of the Republic of Turkey (TCMB). (2014). Electronic Data Delivery System (EVDS). https://evds2.tcmb.gov.tr/index.php? (14.12.2014).

Cernat, L. & Gourdon, J. (2012). Paths to Success: Benchmarking Cross-Country Sustainable Tourism. Tourism Management, 33(5), 1044–1056.

Çıkın, A., Çeke, H. & Uçar, M. (2009). The Effect of Tourism on Agriculture Sector, Agro-Tourism and Its Economical Results. Tarım Ekonomisi Dergisi, 15(1), 1–8.

Coltman, M. M. (1989). Introduction to Travel and Tourism: An International Approach. New York: Van Nostrand Reinhold.

Dwyer, L., Forsyth, P. & Dwyer, W. (2010). Tourism, Economics and Policy. Bristol: Channel View Publications.

Engle, R. F. & Granger, C. W. J. (1987). Co-integration and Error Correction: Representation, Estimation, and Testing. Econometrica, 55(2), 251–276.

Gómez-Zaldívar, M., Ventosa-Santaulària, D. & Wallace, F. H. (2013). The PPP Hypothesis and Structural Breaks: The Case of Mexico. Empirical Economics, 45(3), 1351–1359.

Gregory, A. W. & Hansen, B. E. (1996a). Residual-Based Tests for Cointegration in Models with Regime Shifts. Journal of Econometrics, 70(1), 99–126.

Gregory, A. W. & Hansen, B. E. (1996b). Tests for Cointegration in Models with Regime and Trend Shifts. Oxford Bulletin of Economics and Statistics, 58(3), 555–560.

Gül, H. (2013). Economic Impacts of an Increase in the Foreign Tourism Receipts: A Sam-Based Income Multiplier Analysis for Turkey. Advances in Hospitality and Tourism Research, 1(1), 17–36.

Hatemi-J. A. (2008). Tests for Cointegration with Two Unknown Regime Shifts with an Application to Financial Market Integration. Empirical Economics, 35(3), 497–505.

Hirschman, A. O. (1958). The Strategy of Economic Development. New Haven and London: Yale University Press.

Istanbul Metropolitan Municipality. (2009). http://www.ibb.gov.tr/sites/ks/tr-TR/0-Istanbul-Tanitim/Pages/2010_Avrupa_Kultur_Baskenti_Istanbul.aspx (10.01.2016).

Johansen, S. (1988). Statistical Analysis of Cointegration Vectors. Journal of Economic Dynamics and Control, 12(2–3), 231–254.

Johansen, S. (1991). Estimation and Hypothesis Testing of Cointegration Vectors in Gaussian Vector Autoregressive Models. Econometrica, 59(6), 1551–1580.

Johansen, S. & Juselius, K. (1990). Maximum Likelihood Estimation and Inference on Cointegration – With Applications to the Demand for Money. Oxford Bulletin of Economics and Statistics, 52(2), 169–210.

Kadiyali, V. & Kosová, R. (2013). Inter-industry Employment Spillovers from Tourism Inflows. Regional Science and Urban Economics, 43(2), 272–281.

Kapetanios, G. (2005). Unit-Root Testing Against the Alternative Hypothesis of Up to M Structural Breaks. Journal of Time Series Analysis, 26(1), 123–133.

Khadaroo, J. & Seetanah, B. (2007). TransportInfrastructure and Tourism Development. Annals of Tourism Research, 34(4), 1021–1032.

Kim, H. & Kim, B.-G. (2015). Economic Impacts of the Hotel Industry: An Input-Output Analysis. Tourism Review, 70(2), 132–149.

Kweka, J., Morrissey, O. & Blake, A. (2001). Is Tourism a Key Sector in Tanzania? Input-Output Analysis of Income, Output, Employment and Tax Revenue. Christel DeHaan Tourism and Travel Research Institute, 1.

Lee, J. & Strazicich, M. C. (2003). Minimum Lagrange Multiplier Unit Root Test with Two Structural Breaks. Review of Economics and Statistics, 85(4), 1082–1089.

Lumsdaine, R. L. & Papell, D. H. (1997). Multiple Trend Breaks and the Unit-Root Hypothesis. Review of Economics and Statistics, 79(2), 212–218.

Maki, D. (2012). Tests for Cointegration Allowing for an Unknown Number of Breaks. Economic Modelling, 29(5), 2011–2015.

Ministry of European Union Affairs. (2016). http://www.ab.gov.tr/index.php? (26.01.2016).

Page, S. J. (2009). Tourism Management. Oxford: Butterworth-Heinemann.

Park, J. Y. (1992). Canonical Cointegrating Regressions. Econometrica, 60(1), 119–143.

Perron, P. (1989). The Great Crash, the Oil Price Shock, and the Unit Root Hypothesis. Econometrica, 57(6), 1361.

Phillips, P. C. B. & Hansen, B. E. (1990). Statistical Inference in Instrumental Variables Regression with I(1) Processes. The Review of Economic Studies, 57(1), 99–125.

Rogerson, C. M. (2012). Strengthening Agriculture-Tourism Linkages in the Developing World: Opportuniyies, Barries and Current Initiatives. African Journal of Agriculture Research, 7(4), 616–623.

Stock, J. H. & Watson, M. W. (1993). A Simple Estimator of Cointegrating Vectors in Higher Order Integrated Systems. Econometrica, 61 (4), 783–820.

Telfer, D. J. & Wall, G. (1996). Linkages between Tourism and Food Production. Annals of Tourism Research, 23(3), 635–653.

Torres, R. (2003). Linkages between Tourism and Agriculture in Mexico. Annals of Tourism Research, 30(3), 546–566.

Turkish Statistics Institutc. (2014). http://www.tuik.gov.tr/ (14.12.2014).

Vellas, F. & Bécherel, L. (1995). International Tourism: An Economic Perspective. Basingstoke, UK: Macmillan.

Zivot, E. & Andrews, D. W. K. (1992). Further Evidence on the Great Crash, the Oil-Price Shock, and the Unit-Root Hypothesis. Journal of Business and Economic Statistics, 10(3), 251–270.

Murat Mere & Mahmut Masca

The Gravity Model in International Trade Flows

1 Introduction

Gravity Model is a model that empirically explains foreign trade flows and is increasingly being used recently. The starting point of the model is based on the law of gravity developed by physicist Isaac Newton in 1687. The model is the application of Newton's general law of gravity to bilateral trade relations. According to this law, the force between the two bodies interacts positively with the masses of the objects and negatively interacts with the distance between the objects. The masses of objects are the economic size of the countries expressed by national income. The distance between objects is the geographical distance between countries. In the studies carried out, the distance between either the capitals of the countries or the most developed cities as commercial potential is generally used as geographical distance. In this study, the contributions made to the model from J. Tinbergen (1962), who used the gravity model for the first time in international trade trends, will be handled in general, and information will be given about the application areas of the gravity model in the economy.

2 Theory and Historical Development of Gravity Model

The drafting model has a long history, based on the flow between different locations and the relationship between the weight of these places and the opposite of distance by many authors. The first logical formulation of the gravity model can be seen in the article on migration by Ernest Ravenstein, published in 1885. In this study by Ravenstein, he stated that migration flows continue with the merging of trade and industrial centers, but they are decreasing at a specific rate with distance. He also stated that, in the first half of the 20th century, classical trading models neglected the relationship between trade and geographical location by Ohlin. In their study in Isard and Peck (1954), empirically demonstrated that trade and distance are a typical tool kit in the trade economy and the negative effect of distance for different models of both domestic and international transport. Isard (1954) approached to formulate the gravity equation. However, the physicist used a slightly different electrical potential than Newton's law of gravity (Bergeijik and Brakman, 2010: 4). The electrical potential is the electrical potential energy per unit electrical charge at any point within an electrical field. It is a scalar size, indicated by the U symbol, and its unit is volt. The electrical potential at point A within the area of the charge Q is formulated as follows;

$$UA = k * \left(\frac{Q}{rA}\right) \tag{1}$$

In Equation (1);

UA: Potential of point A (volts)
k: Coefficient depending on the unit system used
Q: Electric charge
rA: Distance of point A to Q charge (meters)
Isard (1954) formulated the income potential as follows;

$$\dot{I}V = \sum_{j=1}^{n} \dot{I}Vj = \sum_{j=1}^{n} k\frac{Yj}{d_{ij}^{a}} \tag{2}$$

Y_j: income of the nation j
d_{ij}: distance between i and j nations
a: constant power raised by d_{ij}
k: similar constant for gravity constant
ivj: income potential generated by the j nation above the nation i
iv: It refers to the income potential generated by all nations above the nation i.

The income potential generated by any nation above the nation i changes inversely with the distance between two nations. Industrial and institutional structures of the two nations with similar resources, those close to the nation i will have stronger ties with the nation i. This will be reflected in the high-income potential generated by the nation i (Isard, 1954: 308). Isard has examined some of the concepts that the attraction model is based on, including the commercial agreement, the effect of cultural factors on trade and distance (Bergeijik and Brakman, 2010: 4).

Although there are many pioneers of the gravity model, Jan Tinbergen was the first to publish the model's empirical application and mathematical formulation (Bergeijik and Brakman, 2010: 5). The basis of the model that Tinbergen has applied is based on Newton's law of gravity.

The universal law of gravity proposed by Isaac Newton in 1687 was formulated as follows (Head, 2000; 2);

$$F_{ij} = G\frac{MiMj}{d_{ij}^2} \quad (3)$$

In the equation (3);

F_{ij}: the magnitude of the gravitational force between the masses i and j

M_i: the size of the mass i

M_j: the size of the mass j

d_{ij}: the distance between the masses i and j

G: universal gravitational constant.

According to the gravitational force, the masses of the objects affect positively as the mass increases, and negatively as the distance between the objects increases. Briefly, the gravitational force between the two masses is directly proportional to the masses of the objects and inversely proportional to the distance of the objects to each other. In his work in 1962, Tinbergen adapted Newton's law of attraction to the field of economy in order to analyze international trade flows.

The purpose of presenting Tinbergen's analysis is to decide on the regular and standard model of international trade, which prevails in the absence of trade barriers. In his study, he aimed to statistically test the main factors regulating the trade volume between any country pair and to estimate the expected foreign trade values of many countries in the light of this information. He attributes the importance of the deviation between the realized and calculated trade to the accuracy and reliability of the theoretical values of the trade volume calculated by econometric methods. A better standardized international trade model defines reality. Tinbergen was interested in deviations in trading models and investigated which countries showed significant negative deviations. These deviations are indicative of barriers to the optimum flow of international trade (Tinbergen, 1962: 262). In his study, Tinbergen (1962), by adapting Newton's law of gravity to international trade, defined the trade flow equation as simple as follows by replacing the masses of the objects in equation (3) with the economical size of the countries and the geographical distance between the countries instead of the distance between the objects;

$$E_{ij} = \propto_0 Y_i^{\propto 1} Y_j^{\propto 2} D_{ij}^{\propto 3} \quad (4)$$

In the equation (4);

E_{ij} : the trade flow in country i to country j

Y_i :: GDP of country i

Y_i : GDP of country j

D_{ij} :: the distance between country i and country j
$\propto_0$: the gravitational constant
Symbols $\propto_1$, $\propto_2 and \propto_3$ show the parameters of the model (Tinbergen, 1962: 264).

Tinbergen explained the main factors that determine the size of the trade flow between any country pair as follows (Tinbergen, 1962: 263);

i. The export amount of a country depends on its economic size.
ii. The export level of a country depends on the economic size of the importing country.
iii. Trade volume depends on transportation costs. This situation can be explained roughly by the geographical distance between the two countries. The effect of the distance on trade flows will be negative.

Tinbergen first tested the hypothesis of three explanatory variables for a limited number of countries with similar economic structures, using 1958 data from 18 developed countries. Then, using the dummy variables, whether the country couples are or are not members of the Commonwealth of Nations, whether they are Benelux countries and whether they are neighboring countries or not, has achieved the following equation;

$$E_{ij} = \propto_0 Y_i^{\propto 1} Y_j^{\propto 2} D_{ij}^{\propto 3} N^{\propto 4} P_C^{\propto 5} P_B^{\propto 6} \qquad (5)$$

He obtained the equation (6) by taking the logarithm of both sides;

$$logE_{ij} = \propto_1 logY_i + \propto_2 logY_j + \propto_3 logD_{ij} + \propto_4 log_N + \propto_5 log_{PC} + \propto_6 log_{PB} + \propto_0' \qquad (6)$$

In the equation (6);
In the equation (6);

N: shows the dummy variable for neighboring countries. Accordingly, if the country couples are neighbors, the dummy variable takes any positive value, while the country couples are not neighbor, the dummy variable takes the value zero.

Pc: shows the dummy variable for the Commonwealth of Nations. According to this situation, if the country pairs are members of the Commonwealth of Nations, the dummy variable takes any positive value. In contrast, if the country pairs are not members of the Commonwealth, the dummy variable takes the value zero.

P_B: shows the dummy variable for Benelux countries. According to this situation, if the country pairs Benelux country, the dummy variable takes any positive value, if the country pairs are not Benelux country, the dummy variable takes the value zero.

According to the test results of the model (6), only the dummy variable representing the Commonwealth of Nations made a statistically significant contribution in the explanation of the export flow. These results show the dominant role of three fundamental variables, such as export and import, growth, and distance (Tinbergen, 1962: 265–266).

At the end of his study, Tinbergen emphasized that the current analysis is the first step in an exciting and promising approach to the study of world trade flows. He emphasized that detailed studies to be carried out in the future will contribute to the formation of a more accurate model of world trade flows and that they can produce more precise results about the geographical location with the effect of trade barriers (Tinbergen, 1962: 293).

On the other hand, Linnemann (1966) expanded the model of gravity by including the population size in addition to the economic size of the countries. The extended gravity model is defined as follows;

$$T_{ij} = \beta_0 \, GDP_i^{\beta 1} \, GDP_j^{\beta 2} \, POP_i^{\beta 3} \, POP_j^{\beta 4} \, d_{ij}^{\beta 5} \tag{7}$$

In the equation (7);

T_{ij} : Trade flow between countries i and j

β_0 : Constant

GDP_i : GDP of country i

GDP_j : GDP of country j

POP_i : population of country i

POP_j : population of country j

d_{ij} : refers to the distance between countries i and j (Genç, 2011: 99).

The gravity model was criticized for its lack of theoretical economic background when it started to be used to explain trade flows. The first theoretical explanation of the gravity model started with the work of Anderson (1979), and many studies have been carried out since that date, examining the institutional infrastructure of the gravity model and contributing to its development. Anderson concluded in his study that the gravity model could be derived from the characteristic of the spending system. He assumed that the tariff and transportation costs preventing the trade were zero. Also, he assumed that the preference function for all countries has constant elasticity of substitution (CES) function and that countries produce different goods according to the country where the production takes place.

Fratianni (2007) stated that the gravity equation in international trade began to be used as an empirical proposal to explain bilateral trade flows without a theoretical basis in the sixties. This equation became legitimate in the late seventies with studies showing that the basic gravity equation is consistent with various commercial flow models. Over time, empirical practices have been extended to cover issues such as the effect of regional trade agreements, national borders, and foreign exchange unions on trade. According to the author, the development of the gravity equation is undoubtedly due to the empirical success of the equation. The gravity equation has been very successful in explaining real trading models.

3 Application Areas of the Gravity Model

3.1 Application of Gravity Model to Explain International Trade Flows

Filippini and Molini (2003) analyzed the bilateral trade flows between industrialized eastern Asian countries, including China, and some developed countries using the gravity model. Their work covers the period 1970–2000 and 26 countries. Export flow in the year t was used as the dependent variable. Exports, GDP, population, distance, and technological distance in the t-1 period were used as independent variables. As a result of their studies, they found that GDP affects trade positively and that rich countries trade more, and the population variable affects bilateral trade negatively. Geographical distance and technological distance have a negative relationship in bilateral trade flows. These two types of distances are considered as obstacles to international trade.

In their study, Kimura and Lee (2006) investigated the relationship between the bilateral service trade and bilateral goods trade between 10 OECD countries and non-member countries, for 1999 and 2000, using the standard draft model. They used bilateral trade flows as dependent variables, GDP, distance, GDP per capita as the independent variable, regional trade regulation index, world economic freedom index and language as dummy variables. The gravity model performs in international service trade better than goods trade. There are also some differences between service trade and commodity trade in terms of the flexibility of the explanatory variables. Geographic distance is more important in service trade than in commodity trade. In their study, they found that the border dummy variable has a more significant effect on bilateral commodity trade than the bilateral trade on services. They also found that joint membership in regional trade regulations had a significant impact on both service and commodity trade. The effect of economic freedom is higher in service trade. As a result, they concluded that the service trade would play a more critical role in the global economy as it grows faster than the trade of goods.

3.2 Application of the Gravity Model to the Theory of Human Migration and Tourism Movement

Buluk and Duran (2018), in their study, analyzed the foreign travel potential of Turkey by a panel gravity model. They have used cross-sectional data obtained from 103 different countries of the tourists who visited Turkey in 2016 in the study. They used the number of tourists coming to Turkey as the dependent variable. GDP per capita of tourists sending country, GDP of tourists sending country, the distance between the capital cities of tourist sending country and Turkey were used as independent variables. Whether the tourist sending countries has ethnic, cultural, and historical similarity with Turkey, whether they are neighbors with Turkey, whether they are Muslim countries, and whether they are European countries, were used in the model as dummy variables. As a result of their study, they found that incoming tourists were positively affected by the economic size factor of their own country and negatively by the distance factor. They found that population density did not have an impact on the tourist flow. They also concluded that having a common border, historical, cultural, and ethnic ties increase the number of tourists, and the fact that the country is Muslim reduces the number of tourists.

In their study, Ramos and Surinach (2013), using the gravity model, analyzed the past and future trends of bilateral migration relations between the EU and the European Union neighboring countries and major countries for 200 countries between 1960 and 2010. As the dependent variable, they used migration flows between countries. They used the population of the countries, the distance between the capitals of the countries, the difference between the GDP per capita in the country pairs as independent variables. They used geographic size of the countries, whether the countries are neighbors, the use of the common official language, sharing a language spoken by at least 9 % of the population, whether it had a colonial bond, whether there was a colonial relationship after 1945, relative differences in GDP per capita among country couples as the dummy variables. They estimated the model using the variables mentioned above. As a result of their studies, while the population in the countries that are the source of migration has a positive and important effect on the amount of migration, they showed that there is a negative relationship between the population and the migration in the countries receiving the migration. Geographical distance affects migrant movements negatively and found that having a common language and colonial relationship significantly increases migrant movements. They also concluded that there is a positive relationship between migration movements and per capita GDP, that is, better economic opportunities positively affect migration.

3.3 Application of Gravity Model to Formations of Regional Economic Integrations

In their study, Antonucci and Manzocch (2006), using data from the 1967–2001 period, estimated by the gravity model if there is an exclusive commercial relationship between the EU and Turkey. They made estimation using exports or imports of goods as the dependent variable, and the sum of GDP of both exporting and importing countries, size similarity at a certain value, relative factor equipment, the distance between capitals as independent variables, and also EU membership, development of relations with the EU in time, Customs Union, trade agreement and common border as dummy variables. As a result of their work, they found the total GDP of the countries positive. This showed that it tends to make more trade with Turkey's largest economy. They found that similarity in size had a positive effect on the trade flow. The relative factors endowment coefficient shows the factor of similarity, and it encourages the export of Turkey. However, relative factor endowment was not statistically significant in the import equation. They have found no evidence that the establishment of the Customs Union with the EU increases the trade between Turkey and the EU.

In his study, Sandalcılar (2012), using yearly data between 2002 and 2009, estimated the trade potential of Turkey with BRIC countries by panel gravity model. He used trade volume between countries as the dependent variable and multiplying the GDP values of countries, multiplying the population values of countries, geographical distance between countries as independent variables, and the shared border as a dummy variable. As a result of the study, he found that the increase in the GDP and population of the BRIC countries and Turkey and having a shared border effects foreign trade positively and increasing the distance between the countries affects the foreign trade negatively.

3.4 Application of the Gravity Model for Foreign Direct Investment

In her study, Christie (2003) analyzed the foreign direct investments, which were directed to five South Eastern European countries from nine selected Western

European countries, using the data from the 1990–1998 period, using the five Central European countries as a control group, by gravity model. He made estimations by using foreign direct investment as a dependent variable, GDP values of countries, GDP per capita, foreign direct investment flow value, total GDP, and geographic distance values as independent variables. As a result of his study, he determined that foreign direct investment flow values and total GDP values are positive and significant, per capita GDP and distance values are negative and significant.

In their study, Quere, Coupet and Mayer (2007) made a cross-sectional analysis for 2000 and panel data analysis for the period 1985–2000, using data from the period 1985–2000 for 123 countries. In their studies, they used foreign direct capital stock as the dependent variable, and actual GDP of countries, planned GDP, per capita GDP, planned GDP per capita, distance as independent variables, and, use of common language, the neighborhood of countries, protection of property as dummy variables in their model.

As a result of their studies, according to both cross-sectional and panel data analysis, actual GDP, planned GDP, actual GDP per capita, planned GDP per capita, common language, neighboring countries, and protection of property rights are the variables that affect the direct foreign capital investments. The distance affects the direct foreign capital investments negatively and significantly, as expected in the gravity model.

3.5 Application of Gravity Model for Developments in Communication Technology and Internet Usage

In their study, Freund and Weinhold (2000) analyzed the effects of the internet on foreign trade for the 56 countries with the data of 1995–1999 by the gravity model. In their studies, they used the total trade volume as a dependent variable, and GDP of the exporting and importing countries, the population of the exporting and importing countries, the distance between the exporting and importing countries, the number of hosts in the exporting and importing countries as independent variables and having a common language, the presence of colonial ties, whether they are members of free trade areas as dummy variables. As a result of their studies, the impact of GDP data on foreign trade is positive and significant, the impact of population data on foreign trade is negative and significant for the year 1995, while it is negative and insignificant for other years, the effect of distance variable on foreign trade is negative and significant, common language and colonial ties values in foreign trade is positive and significant, the effect of being a member of a common union on foreign trade was positive and insignificant, while the number of hosts owned had a positive and insignificant effect on foreign trade for the year 1995, and had a positive and meaningful effect in the other years. They concluded that the number of hosts, especially in 1998–1999, had a higher degree of positive and significant impact.

Şeker (2017), in his study, with data of the 2005–2014 period, investigated the effect of the number of Internet users on trade volume between Turkey and 25 EU member states. In his study, he used the total foreign trade volume of Turkey as the dependent variable. GDP of the country, population, the distance between the capital cities, internet usage rates of the countries, rate of change of imports and exports totals to GDP, and rate of change of civil liberties in the countries as independent variables. As a result of his study, he found that the effects of GDP of the country, population, internet usage rates of the countries, rate of change of imports and exports totals to GDP on Turkey's total foreign trade volume of the variable positive and significant, the effect of distance variable on Turkey's total foreign trade volume of negative and significant, and the effect of rate of change of civil liberties in the countries on Turkey's foreign trade volume is negative and insignificant.

4 Conclusion and Assessment

Tinbergen was the first to publish the empirical application of the gravity model. Tinbergen's model is based on Newton's law of gravity. In his work in 1962, Tinbergen adapted Newton's law of gravity to the field of economy to analyze international trade flows. In this way, he aimed to statistically test the main factors affecting the trade volume between the country pairs and to estimate the expected foreign trade values of many countries in the light of the results obtained. Thus, the first step of an exciting and promising approach has been taken in the study of world trade flows. However, the Gravity Model was criticized for its lack of a theoretical economic background when it started to be used to explain trade flows. Anderson made the first theoretical explanation of the model in his work in 1979, and many studies were conducted that examine the theoretical infrastructure of the gravity model and contribute to its development. Today, besides the explanation of the international trade flows, the Gravity Model has been applied to human migration and tourism mobility between countries, the explanation of regional economic integrations in foreign trade, foreign direct investment, developments in communication technology, and internet use.

References

Anderson, J. (1979). A Theoretical Foundation for the Gravity Equation. American Economic Review, 69, 106–116.

Antonucci, D. & Manzocchi, S. (2006). Does Turkey Have a Special Trade Relation with the EU? A Gravity Model. Approach Economic Systems, 30, 157–169.

Bergeijik, P. A. G. & Brakman S. (2010). The Gravity Model in International Trade Advances and Applications. Cambridge University Press.

Buluk, D. & Duran, E. (2018). Türkiye'ye Yönelik Dış Turizm Potansiyelinin Panel Çekim Modeli İle Analizi [Analysis of Foreign Travel Potential of Turkey by a Panel Gravity Model]. Anatolia: Turizm Araştırmaları Dergisi, Cilt 29, Sayı 1, Bahar: 51 – 62.

Christie, E. (2003). Foreign Direct Investment in Southeast Europe. wiiw Working Papers No. 24, 1–31.

Freund, C. ve Weinhold, D. (2000). On the Effect of the Internet on International Trade. Board of Governors of the Federal Reserve System International Finance Discussion Papers, 693, 1–42.

Fratianni, M. (2007). The Gravity Equation in International Trade. Working Papers 2007 – 17, Indiana University, Kelley School of Business, Department of Business Economics and Public Policy.

Filippini, C. & Molini, V. (2003). The Determinants of East Asian Trade Flows: A Gravity Equation Approach. Journal of Asian Economics, Elsevier, 14(5), 695–711.

Genç, M. C. (2011). Bölgeselleşme ve Bölgeselleşmenin Ticaret Akımları Üzerindeki Etkisinin Çekim Modeli İle Analizi [Regionalization and Analysis of the Effect of Regionalization on Trade Flows by the Gravity Model]. (Doktora Tezi). Karadeniz Teknik Üniversitesi, Trabzon.

Head, K. (2000). Gravity for Beginners.

Isard, W. (1954). Location Theory and Trade Theory: Short-run Analysis. Quarterly Journal of Economics, 68, 305–20.

Isard, W. and Peck, M. J.(1954). Location Theory and International and Regional Trade Theory. Quarterly Journal of Economics, 68(1), 97–114.

Kimura, F. ve Lee, H. H. (2006). The Gravity Equation in International Trade in Services. Review of World Economics, 142(1), 92–121.

Quere, B. A., Coupet, M. ve Mayer, T. (2007). Institutional Determinants of Foreign Direct Investment. The World Economy, 764–782. doi: 10.1111/j.1467-9701.2007.01022.

Ramos, R. ve Surinach, J. (2013). A Gravity Model of Migration between ENC and EU. IZA Discussion Paper No. 7700.

Sandalcılar, A. E. (2012). Türkiye'nin BRIC Ülkeleriyle Ticari Potansiyeli: Panel Çekim Modeli Yaklaşımı [Turkey's Commercial Potential with the BRIC Countries: a Panel Gravity Model Approach]. Journal of Yaşar University, 25(7), 4164–4175.

Şeker, A. (2017). Uluslararası Ticarette İnternet Kullanımının Rolü: Türkiye Örneği [Role of Internet Use in International Trade: The Case of Turkey]. Ege Akademik Bakış, Cilt: 17, Sayı: 1, 75–88.

Tinbergen, J. (1962). Shaping the World Economy: Suggestions for an International Economic Policy. New York: Twentieth Century Fund.

Mehmet Şengür & Wilkista Lore Obiero

The Relationships between Income Inequality and Economic Growth: The Case of Kenya

1. Introduction

Income inequality is a term that refers to considerable differences in the quantity earned and wealth owned by the people with higher income status as compared to those with low income status. This means that most of the money circulating in the economy only belongs to the few people who are rich. Income inequality is not a desirable feature in the economy because it is a symbol of many people surviving on barely sufficient income that cannot fulfil all the needs and wants present while the rich minority are able to afford all the luxuries. The widely accepted measure of income inequality is by the use of a Gini coefficient. A coefficient value of zero indicates perfect equality in the country while a coefficient of 100 indicates existence of perfect inequality.

Economic growth refers to increase in the value and quantity of the goods in the economy which is reflected in a higher gross domestic product of the country, reduced disparities in the different income levels and even increased connection with other countries in terms of trade and investment levels. It is important for policy makers to come up with ways of ensuring sustained growth in the economy and one of the widely accepted ways of measuring the extent of achieved growth or comparing the levels of different countries is by the use of Gross Domestic Product (GDP).

Many economists seek to find the nature of the relationship existent between disparities in income and economic advancement in the country. This type of research has intensified in the current years following the proposition put forward by Kuznets (1955) that during the early years of economic development, inequality is very high but as development progresses, inequality reduces. This characteristic is expressed in the form of an inverted U curve. Studies have been conducted on in a bid to prove or disapprove the Kuznets hypothesis some of which have been included in the literature review section of the paper. The main result arrived at by reviewing the current literature is that not all the economies follow the hypothesis put forward by Kuznets (1955).

The main contribution of this paper is that it will provide an up to date information to the already existing literature on income disparity and growth in

Kenya. Kenyan data reveal the existence of high levels of disparities in income evidenced by a current Gini index of 42.5. Further studies by Wanyangathi (2016) reveal that 10 % of the rich people in Kenya own more than half of the total income in the country while the remaining 90 % of the population is left to share the remaining percentage.

Growth rate in Kenya is not constant, it keeps fluctuating with the average figure being 5 %. There are various factors that have been contributing to this rate of growth and these include the value of trade with other countries, the proportion of GDP spent on health, education, capital spending and the proportion that is saved. All these factors have been included as control variables alongside disparities in income and their effect on growth measured.

The subsequent parts of the paper are organized as follows: The second part provides a brief explanation on Kuznets inverted U curve, the third section is on the literature review, the fourth section describes the data used and the results obtained from the analysis while the last part presents the conclusion and the policy implications of the paper.

2. Theoretical Framework

Stability in growth is one of the desired goals of every economy. The GDP of a country is one of the popular means of measuring economic growth. For economic growth to occur certain institutions must be involved including the markets, monetary exchange systems and property rights. The markets provide the buyers and sellers with the existing information of the products and services giving room for trade to occur. For the markets to run effectively property rights have to be in place as these govern the acquisition use and final abandonment of all the factors in the market. When people have clearly established property rights then they can have faith in their market and thus invest more. All these factors help in creating a favorable environment for growth in the economy (Mishkin, 2014).

For growth to be persistent, people must purchase new capital investments like machines because these help to increase productivity in firms. Skills and knowledge of human beings must also increase which can be through an increase in education levels and an increase in research and development. Technological discoveries also help to facilitate the process of economic development in different economies because, with more efficient technologies, productivity increases and the economy becomes better (Sellgren et al., 1999).

GDP remains the most popular measure of economic growth and from the GDP equation, the following factors influence the level of economic growth in a country;

i. Consumer led growth; as the economy expands, population expansion will also be experienced and this increase will lead to an increase in the value of goods and services consumed in the economy. This further increases GDP and thus growth will occur in the economy.
ii. Export-led growth; when the value of exports from a country increases with no change in import value, the GDP will increase and thus economic growth will occur as a result.
iii. Investment led Growth; an increase in the number of investments will affect the GDP positively and thus lead to economic growth.

This refers to the theories which help in explaining the cause and effect of growth in the economy. They are universal and can be applied by both developed and underdeveloped economies. They help explain how underdeveloped economies can become even richer (Parkin et al., 2005).

Classical Growth Theory: Also known as the Malthusian theory because it was developed by Robert Thomas Malthus. This theory states that growth in real GDP is only temporary and that as time grows there will be an increase in population which will help in reducing the growth in real GDP per person. Malthus suggests that with an increase in technology levels of productivity will increase, firms will be able to produce more output at low costs and their income will increase leading to an improvement in the economy but the improvement in the economy will soon be accompanied with an increase in population forcing the economy to adjust. The adjustment will lead to canceling out of the previous increase in GDP (Dornbusch and Fischer, 1994).

Neo-Classical Growth Theory: This theory was developed by Robert Solow as a result of the shortcomings of the classical growth theory. They suggested that with economic growth, the population did not explode as earlier suggested in the classical growth theory explained by the concept of opportunity cost which would arise between working and having children. In their argument, as the rate of birth increases so does the rate of death improved technology in the medical industry notwithstanding and soon after birth and death rates cancel out in the long run. According to this theory, economic growth comes about due to advances in technology which create opportunities for growth and profit. This leads to growth and prosperity in the economy although it states that for the economy to keep advancing further, technology must also be advancing (Heijdra, 2002).

New Growth Theory: States that people, due to the choices they make in their daily life influence the GDP level of the economy. People make discoveries but these discoveries depend on the level of research and development in place. Knowledge was ascertained to be a public good and that when people make a profit out of their knowledge, they are motivated to constantly seek out new ways. As opposed to the classical and neoclassical growth theories which are all subject to diminishing productivity, this theory is not subject to diminishing returns since knowledge is available for everyone and can always be increased through conducting more research. Growth according to this theory is indefinite and depends on the choices made and how they affect technology (Parkin et al., 2005).

It's a curve showing how inequality varies with growth as put forward by Kuznets (1955). During initial stages of development, the interaction between market forces will lead to worsened inequality situation. However, later as development progresses, the same market forces will lead to improvements in welfare and decline in the general societal inequality. This rise and fall situation in inequality levels with changes in income is known widely as Kuznets U shaped hypothesis. Kuznets contends that during the early stages of development in a country, investment opportunities multiplies for money holders but the wage rate cannot rise because of the existence of cheap labor which arises as many people move to the urban centers from the rural areas. Modeling various countries data to fit the idea put forward by Kuznets (1955) is important in determining the level of development of a country because the economies which are just picking up their development process will be characterized in the first part of the curve before the turning point and with this information, appropriate economic and structural policies which in turn will fasten the development process. The curve is also important in connecting economic position of a country based on the industrialization position and the environmental issues that should be addressed since during economic transition, people often move from rural to urban areas in search of better pastures and with the increase in urban population comes the problem of environmental conservation. It is therefore important to fit the data in order to adopt the relevant policies.

Income can also refer to the satisfaction obtained from making use of the assets one possesses. These may include profits from investments, salaries earned and wages received by investing labor. The level of development of a country is best shown by the value of total GDP per annum, when this total figure is divided by the number of people in the country then it is possible to obtain the average income per person which is a representation of what every person would earn were the incomes to be distributed equally. In practical economies however, this is rarely the case because some people receive much higher income than others. This difference in earnings is what is referred to as income inequality. It differs from one country to another and is measured by use of a Lorenz curve although the use of Lorenz curve has often been criticized for failing to take into consideration some types of incomes like incomes from capital gains. This inequality is caused by factors like differences in the level of education, hours spent in productive labor, skills possessed and the years of experience. These are factors directly linked to productivity and output. However, inequality sometimes arises from factors like racial differences and sexual orientation which do not directly relate to output levels. There are different economic models that have been brought up by neoclassical economists to help explain the different types of discrimination and their effects on the society (Rycroft, 2014).

Samy (2014), suggests that inequality needs to be addressed because it has significant impacts on every economy. There are various debates across the world on whether the policies should focus on encouraging economic growth or on reducing income inequality. The paper further suggests that care should be taken when using Kuznets theories to analyze inequalities because other factors other than the ones put forward by Kuznets (1955) may be responsible for inequality levels and growth relationship in the economy. The paper states that the relationship between these two variables will always hold as long as industrialization is a direct determinant of growth keeping all other factors constant.

This study explores this relationship for the Kenyan economy to help explain its development characteristics currently and provide suggestions on how it can be improved without negatively influencing the environment.

3 Model, Data and Findings

The explanatory variables used in the study include: Kenya's Gini coefficient, GDP, Trade values as a percentage of GDP, The square of GDP per capita, Government investment, Capital investment, Gross savings value and the value of net education. These are presented in Table 1 as shown below:

To check for the viability of this data, the following diagnostic tests were conduct in Table 2. The data is free from heteroscedasticity and autocorrelation, the data is also normal and so the results obtained are trustable. To obtain the relationship between disparity in wages and growth in Kenya, the following model will be used.

$$GINI = \beta_0 + \beta_1 lnGDP_t + \beta_2 trade_t + \beta_3 lnGDP2_t + \beta_4 Gvt_t + \beta_5\ Capital_t + \beta_6 Gsav_t + \beta_7 Netedu_t + \mu_t$$

Table 1: Variables Descriptions

Variable	Measurement	Source
GINI	Country's GINI coefficient	World Development Indicators(2018)
GDP	Country's GDP base year2010	World Development Indicators(2018)
Trade	Percentage of trade on GDP	World Development Indicators(2018)
GDP^2	Square values of GDP	World Development Indicators(2018)
Gvt	Government expenditure values	World Development Indicators(2018)
Capital	Percentage of constant capital on GDP	World Development Indicators(2018)
Gsav	Percentage of Savings on GDP	World Development Indicators(2018)
Netedu	Percentage of net education on GDP	World Development Indicators(2018)

Source: http://datatopics.worldbank.org/world-development-indicators, Author's compilation

Where t= 1. . . 12 (1995–2011)

GINI; is the country's Gini coefficient. **GDP;** is the natural logarithm of the GDP per capita of the country as a proxy for economic growth. **Trade;** is the percentage of trade in the GDP. **GDP2;** is the square values of the natural log of the per capıta GDP. **Gvt;** is the value of Government expenditure Capital is the percentage of capital expenditure in the GDP. **Gsav;** is the percentage of gross saving in the GDP. **Netedu**; is the percentage of net education in the GDP.

The author expects that: β_(1 >) 0,β_3 <0, β_7,β_2 <0,

The results of stationarity test are displayed in Table 3. In order to prevent the possibility of spurious regression, the data values have to be tested for stationarity (Dickey and Fuller, 1979). First the test is carried out at the level, then first difference and if still stationarity has not been obtained, the second difference is also obtained. In all the cases, first the test is done at intercept only and then later at intercept and trend. The table shown below gives the stationarity test results for the data.

The effect of Gini on growth rate can be decomposed as follows:

GINI=0.128159lnGDP-0.01673lnGDP2
(Δ GINI)/(Δ lnGDP) =0.128159-0.01673lnGDP
LnGDP*= (0.128159)/(-0.01673) = -7.6604

OLS results reported as shown in Table 4. From the results, when GDP increases, the level of wages disparity as measured by the Gini coefficient also increases and attains maximum where the GDP growth rate is at 7.6604. Trade is positively related to Gini coefficient indicating that when trade increases, the economy will perform better, GDP will increase and thus income inequality will also increase.Government expenditure is negatively related to Gini coefficient

Table 2: Results from the Diagnostic Tests

	F/ Jacque Berra	Prob
Heteroscedasticity	0.375184	0.8551
Autocorrelation	1.98214	0.1999
Normality	1.376887	0.502357

Source: Authors compilation

which indicates that as government expenditure increases in the Kenya, income inequality is reduced. The rate of fixed capital stock as a percentage of GDP was found to be negative indicating that as more of GDP goes to fixed capital stock, income inequality declines. Gross savings were found to have a positive relationship with Gini coefficient indicating that as people saved more, then inequality would increase. Net education was found to have a negative relationship with GDP indicating that as more people obtained education, the İncome inequality gap was reduced.

4 Conclusion

To determine the validity of Kuznets curve in Kenya, data values belonging to the period 1995–2011 was investigated by the use of OLS test. The log of the value of GDP was first obtained then squared to obtain a quadratic model. To avoid the possibility of spurious data being used, stationarity test was conducted and the results were tabulated in the study. The estimated turning point was at 7.6604. Similar results were found by Chen (2003) and Morrisson and Snyder (2000) who conducted the same study using data for France.

The coefficient of lnGDP is positive while the coefficient of the square of lnGDP is negative and all were significant at 10 % level. Thus the Kuznets curve is found to hold in Kenya based on the data used because when these figures are plotted then the curve obtained will be inverted U shaped. Kenyan economy should therefore adopt applicable policies for growth given that they are still transitioning into higher levels of development.

Trade was found to have a positive impact on inequality indicating the presence of unbalanced trade in the country. The conditions put in place and the existing tax systems could be the limiting factor to many lower income earners leading to increased income gap when the trade values increase. The presence of a negative relationship between government expenditure and income inequality indicates that when the government intervenes in the Kenyan economy through

Table 3: Results of Stationarity Test

Variables	Lvl		1st Diff		2st Diff
	Int	Int & Trend	Int	Int & Trend	Int
GINI	……	………	…………	-3.034877*	…………
LNGDP	…….	……...	………...	…………	-4.22*
LNGDP2	……...	……...	………	………..	-4.2316*
TRADE	…….	……...	……….	-3.0566*	………..
GVT	……...	………	……….	………..	-3.68*
CAPITAL	……...	………	……….	-3.5168**	………
GSAV	……...	………	……….	-3.98939**	………..
NETEDU	……….	………	………...	…………	-2.95*

*,**, indicate 10 and 5 % level of significance respectively. Data covers the period 1995–20
Source: Authors compilation

Table 4: OLS Results

Variable	Coefficient	Std. Error	t-Statistic	Prob.
GDP	0.128159	0.016236	7.893481	0.0000
Trade	0.000172	6.8605	2.506029	0.0311
GDP^2	-0.008365	0.002467	-3.390429	0.0069
GVT	-2.0305	4.3006	-4.712316	0.0008
Capital	-0.000403	0.000262	-1.535667	0.1556
G Sav	0.00138	0.000118	1.17165	0.2685
Net Edu	-0.000565	0.000528	-1.069931	0.3098

Source: Authors compilation

introducing progressive tax systems and tax rebates or through providing free services in some parts of the economy then the gap of wages differentials is likely to be lower.

Increasing the percentage of capital stock in GDP was found to be effective in reducing the wage differentials this indicates that encouraging capital stock creation by adopting lower interest rate levels is important in the economy and should be encouraged. Gross savings were found to be less effective in closing the huge wage differential in the economy and this can be explained using economic theory whereby increasing savings by all members in the economy would lead to lower consumption in the economy which would in turn lead to decrease in national output implying a backward movement away from the desired level of income to a region characterized by high inequality (Ahiakpor, 1995).

As the literacy levels increase in the economy, more people move to the cities where they are either employed or are able to create their own jobs. This is an important factor because it is in line with the postulations put forward regarding the nature of economies such as Kenya. This study is important in analysis of the development level of an economy and in coming up with policies to encourage growth.

References

Ahiakpor, J. C. W. (1995). A Paradox of Thrift or Keynes's Misrepresentation of Saving in the Classical Theory of Growth? Southern Economic Journal, 62(1), 16.

Chen, B. L. (2003). An Inverted-U Relationship between Inequality and Long-Run Growth. Economics Letters, 78(2), 205–212.

Dickey, D. A., & Fuller, W. A. (1979). Distribution of the Estimators for Autoregressive Time Series with a Unit Root. Journal of the American Statistical Association, 74(366), 427.

Dornbusch, R., & Fischer, S. (1994). Macroeconomics. New York: McGraw-Hill.

Heijdra, B. J. (2002). Foundations of Modern Macroeconomics. USA: Oxford University Press.

Kuznets, S. (1955). Economic Growth and Income Inequality. The American Economic Review, 45(1), 1–28.

Mishkin, F. S. (2014). Macroeconomics: Policy and Practice. London: Pearson.

Morrisson, C., & Snyder, W. (2000). The Income Inequality of France in Historical Perspective. European Review of Economic History, 4(1), 59–83.

Parkin, M., Powell, M., & Matthews, K. (2005). Economics, 6th Edition. London: Pearson.

Rycroft, R. (2014). The Economics of Inequality, Discrimination, Poverty and Mobility. New York: Routledge.

Samy, Y. (2014). Globalization, Income Inequality and Deindustrialization: The Case of South Korea. Korea. Economic Institute of America (KEI) Academic Paper Series.

Sellgren, A. W., Doepke, M., & Lehnert, A. (1999). Macroeconomics. Illinois: University of Chicago Publish.

Wanyangathi, A. M. (2016). Income Inequality and Economic Growth in Kenya. Kenya: University of Nairobi School of Economics.

https://www.reuters.com/article/us-kenya-economy/kenyas-economy-to-grow-at-a-faster-pace-next-year-world-bank-idUSKBN1X92K7, Retrieved: 15.12.2019.

http://datatopics.worldbank.org/world-development-indicators, Retrieved: 15.12.2019.

Ali Altıner & Eda Bozkurt

The Effects of Economic Freedom on Foreign Direct Investment

1 Introduction

According to the general approach in the literature on development, the foreign direct investments (FDI) significantly contribute to the capital accumulation, technological capacity, employment power, management knowledge, and balance of payment in country. For this reason, various policies are implemented in many countries in order to draw FDI that are seen as the driving force of growth.

In recent years, multinational companies have been in search of productivity for investment, rather than search for market and source. Thus, the importance of traditional factors such as the level of wages and infrastructure for the FDI decreased, while the importance of several non-traditional factors such as corporate quality and economic freedom (EF) increased (Dunning, 2002; Subasat and Bellos, 2011: 697). In parallel with this, the number of theoretical and empirical studies on the relationship between EF and FDI gradually increases. The increasing importance of EF for FDI is the main motivation for such studies.

In the present study, the effect of EF on FDI was theoretically investigated. For this purpose, the FDI are analyzed in detail within the conceptual frame in the first section. In the second section, the concept of "EF" is explained and its relationship with FDI is revealed. Then, a comprehensive literature summary is presented. In the fourth section, the historical change in FDI and EF between the countries and income groups is explained. Finally, the study is completed with a general review on the subject. This study aims to contribute to the literature through detailed conceptual examinations, explaining the relationships in historical process by making use of tables and diagrams, and providing a comprehensive literature review.

2 Conceptual Frame of FDI

The international movements are classified as public and private capital movements. The public capital movements are performed though the capital transfers between the states in the form of subsidy and credits. The international private capital movements are, however, performed in 3 main forms: foreign bank credits, portfolio investments, and FDI. Thanks to their advantages, FDI are the most desired type of international investment for any country. First of them is the "Green Field Investments", in which a foreign investor builds a factory in the host country. The second one is the "Brown Field Investments" in the form of merging or takeover, in which the assets of domestic companies are bought by foreign investors (Chang and Grabel, 2005: 142).

FDI is very important since it offers advantages of decreasing the production costs and increasing the competitive power and profitability. Besides that, there are many factors influencing the decision of direct investment such as the economic, political, corporate, social, and cultural structure of the host country. In the World Investment Report, which was published by the United Nations in year 1998, these factors have been specified in detail. Accordingly, the ***political factors*** are the economic, political, and social stability, rules about the market, standards for the transactions of foreign partners, policies about the structure and functioning of market, international agreements related with FDI, privatization policies, and trade and tax policies. The ***factors related to investment environment*** are the investment incentives, the status of corruption and administrative efficiency, and social opportunities such as quality of life. The ***economic factors*** are classified into those related to market, source, and efficiency. The *market-related factors* are size of market, income per capita, opportunities for access to the global and regional markets, consumer preferences, and market structure. The *source-related factors* are raw materials, low-wage and unqualified labor force, qualified labor force, technologic, innovative, and other assets, and physical infrastructures such as roads, harbors, and communication. The *efficiency-related factors* are the cost of assets, sources, labor productivity, other input costs, and regional integration agreement memberships (UNCTAD, 1998: 91). Based on these explanations, it can be stated that the countries with no political intervention from the state to the market, providing freedom of trade, having a low level of corruption, high level of investment incentives, and large production capacity, having sufficient and productive production factors, and using these factors at low cost could draw FDI more. Given all these factors, it can be stated that EF, details of which are explained below, is very important for foreign investors in making an investment decision.

2.1. Economic Freedom and Its Relationship with FDI

One of two leading institutions publishing statistics about the world economic freedom index (EFI), Fraser Institute defines the concept "EF" as *"individuals' ability to perform their economic activities without any intervention from the state"*. The Heritage Association defines the EF as *"the relationship of individual who can independently manage his/her labor and property with state and other organized groups without any state restriction*". Similar to these definitions, the scientists investigating the EF have made the definition of EF concept over several subjects. In one of these studies, Alston (1990) defined the EF as enjoying the economic rights, freely establishing and joining commercial unions, and protecting the property rights. Friedman (2002) related the EF to the protection of property rights, the production factors belonging to private capital, and the free trade under perfect competition market conditions.

Regarding measuring the EF, there are 3 indices: Freedom House Index, Fraser Institute Index, and Heritage Association Index. However, it was emphasized in the majority of previous studies that EFI developed by the Heritage Association is more inclusive when compared to the other 2 indices. According to this index, EF includes 12 qualitative and quantitative freedom types under 4 subcategories. Accordingly, the subcategory of "*rule of law*" consists of property rights, government integrity, and judiciary efficacy. The *size of public sector* consists of public expenses, tax burden, and fiscal health components. *Regulatory efficiency* consists of freedom of business, freedom of labor, and monetary freedom components. Finally, the "*open markets*" subcategory consists of trade freedom, investment freedom, and financial freedom components. Each of 12 EF components in 4 subcategories is rated between 0 and 100. The general score of each country is calculated as the average of 12 components (each having the same weight). The index value of 100 indicates that the country is completely freedom from the economic aspect, whereas the index value of 0 indicates suppression (Heritage, 2020: 489–500). According to this calculation, the level of EF increases as the index value increases. In other words, an improvement in the property rights, government integrity, and judiciary efficacy, the fiscal stability through reducing the public expenses and tax burden, the increase in business, labor, and monetary freedom, and the increase in trade, investment, and financial freedom also increase the level of EF.

Given the factors determining FDI, it can be stated that they largely overlap with the components of EFI from various aspects because EF includes many fundamental rights and freedom such as the protection of property rights, the absence of state intervention in production and consumption in the economy, and the individuals' freedom of trading, working, and investing in any way. Quazi (2007) emphasized that the level of EF reflects the investment climate in a country, whereas Azman-Saini et al. (2010) advocated that it indicates a country's capacity of attracting FDI and adopting new technologies. In general, it can be stated that EF affects FDI in 4 different ways. The first of them is that EF offers many opportunities for multinational companies to explore their own sources and use them efficiently. The second one is that judicial independence and protection of intellectual property rights in the host country would secure the efficiency of legal frame. Thus, the country would warrant the revenues to be obtained through foreign investors' trust in the legal system. Therefore, in absence of EF, multinational companies limit their investments in foreign countries. The third one is that EF creates a stable macroeconomic environment that is suitable for investments. For instance, large-scale volatility in exchange rates negatively affects the investment decisions of multinational companies. Finally, the fourth one is that EF has the business, credit, and labor markets, which are necessary for the proper functioning of international trade, to be regulated. For instance, the laws on flexible working and the easy access to money are one of the important determinants of finance sector FDI (Anwar and Mughal, 2012: 2994–2995; Azman-Saini et al. 2010: 1086–1087; Campa, 1993: 614; UNCTAD, 1995: 287).

3 Literature

Together with the gradually increasing mobility of individuals, goods, services, and capital regardless of the level of development, the countries became more dependent on each other. With the effects of increasing globalization since 1990s, the economic activities started to pass beyond the borders. The international economic activities forced the countries to be liberal not only politically but also economically. Since it became possible to measure EF of countries by using various indices, the relationship between economic variables and economic freedom started to be investigated theoretically and empirically. In the "literature" section, these studies are summarized.

4. EF and FDI by the Developmental Status of Countries

The most frequently used method in categorizing the countries by their developmental status is the Atlas classification method of the World Bank. Using the data of World Bank (2020), the countries having income per capita equal to or lower than $1.025 are categorized as low-income countries, those having income per capita between $1.026 and $3.995 are categorized as lower-middle-income countries, those having income per capita between $3.996 and $12.375 as upper-middle-income countries, and those having income per capita higher than $12.376 as high-income countries. In general, the countries at the middle-income level are called developing countries. In this section, the course of FDI and EF series is discussed separately. FDI series were examined using $ inputs in World Bank World Development Indicators (WDI) database,

Table 1. Literature on the Relationship between FDI and EF

Author(s)/Year	Country(s)/ Period	Method	Result
Bengoa and Sanchez-Robles/2003	18 Latin America Countries /1970–1999	Static Panel Estimation	Positive effect
Savaşan and Dursun/ 2006	Low, lower-middle, middle, upper-middle, and high-income non-OECD and OECD countries /1996–1998	One-Way Variance Analysis and T-test	Countries with higher EF scores receive more FDI.
Kapuria-Foreman/2007	Several developing countries /1990–1998	Regression Analysis	Positive relationship
Quazi/2007	7 Southeastern Asia Countries /1995–2000	Static Panel Data Analysis	EF is an important determinant of FDI
Caetano and Caleiro/2009	MENA countries /1999–2001 and 2004–2006/	Fuzzy Logic Clustering	Positive relationship
McGowan/2011	100+ countries /1997–2001	Linear Regression	Significant relationship
Subasat and Bellos/2011	39 countries/1990–2005	Panel Attraction Model	Significant relationship for several countries
Türen et al./2011	70 countries /2002–2010	Multiple Linear Regression	EF explains 51.9 % of FDI.
Pearson et al./2012	50 states in the USA /1987–2007	Static Panel Data	Positive effect
Azman-Saini et al./2013	75 countries /1981–2005	GMM	EF is important for FDI
Tunçsiper and Biçen/2014	Turkey and 7 Balkan countries /1994–2012	Static Panel Data	Trade freedom is effective
Sambharya and Rasheed/2015	95 Developed and Developing Countries /1995–2000	GLS	Economic and politic freedom are effective
Hossain/2016	179 Developing Countries /1998–2014	Cointegration, GLS, GMM	EF is important in FDI inflows
Moussa et al. /2016	156 countries /1995–2013	Static Panel Data	Positive effect
Vogiatzoglou/2016	13 Asian countries /1995–2014	GMM	Trade freedom is an effective component

(*continued on next page*)

Table 1. Continued

Author(s)/Year	Country(s)/ Period	Method	Result
Badri and Sheshgelani/2017	10 Developing Countries /2001–2013	Static Panel Data	Significant relationship and positive effect
Habibi and Hidayet/2017	ASEAN/2004–2015	Static Panel Data	Trade freedom has a positive effect
Imtiaz and Bashir/2017	South Asia /1995–2014	Static Panel Data	Fiscal and commercial freedom is significant
Kazemi and Azman-Saini/2017	87 countries /1981–2010	GMM	Significant relationship and positive effect
Sovbetov and Moussa/2017	156 countries /1995–2016	Static Panel Data	1 unit improvement in EF increases FDI by 1.15 units
Muslija/2018	34 OECD countries/1997–2016	GMM, Granger Causality, and ARDL	Positive and two-way causality in short-term and
Şahin/2018	BRICS-T /1995–2014	Kónya (2006) Bootstrap Panel Causality	Causality for Turkey
Şenalp/2018	Theoretical		Positive effect
Akkaya/2019	12 Developing Countries /1995–2016	Dynamic Panel Data	No relationship
Kamacı/2019	15 Developed Countries, 15 Developing Countries, 10 Underdeveloped Countries/2000–2017	FMOLS and DOLS	Positive relationship except for Underdeveloped Countries
Sofuoğlu et al./2019	Top 10 FDI-receiving countries /1995–2015	Pedroni Cointegration FMOLS and DOLS	Positive relationship

and EF was examined using the Economic Freedom Index (EFI) series used by the Heritage Association. Since the beginning and ending dates of variables were different, the data between 1970 and 2018 were used for FDI and those between 1995 and 2020 were used for EFI. In the analysis based on income classification, the same datasets were used by taking the year 1995 as the

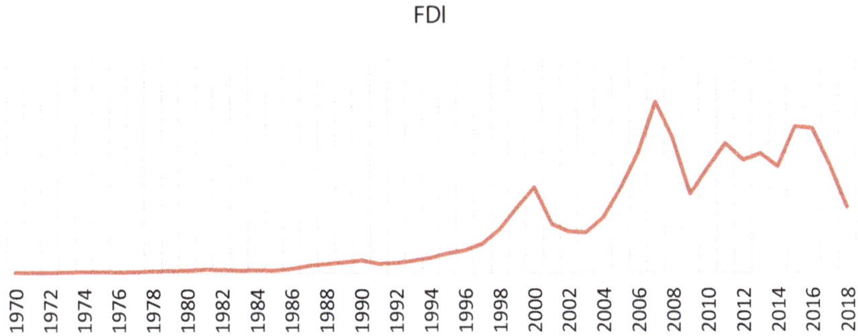

Figure 1. Trend of FDI in the world

beginning year. Since there was no data for the income groups in the database of the Heritage Association, the calculations were performed within the scope of this study. Moreover, in order to better reveal the change in FDI inflows, an FDI index was created. The year 2010 was taken as the base year for FDI index (2010=100).

It can be seen that FDI series, development course of which is seen in Figure 1, followed a wavy structure. The increase in FDI began in the late 1980s and then has become more remarkable since the 1990s. An important point in the FDI series is the increase in FDI value of year 2018 to more than 95 folds of the value of year 1970. There is no doubt that globalization has an important effect on this increase. The economic freedom enabling the free mobilization of production factors enabled the investors to perform new activities in new markets. However, the interesting point in the diagram is that the FDI inflows, which tended to increase after the global crisis in 2008, have dramatically decreased since 2015. According to UNCTAD (2018), the reasons for this negative trend are the political uncertainties arising from the overseas operations and the decrease in return rates of FDI. Accordingly, the return rate of FDI in 2012 was 8.1 % and, as a result of constant decrease, it decreased to 6.7 % in 2017. Besides these reasons, it can also be stated that the risk of a trade war between the USA and China might have decreased FDI.

The trend of EFI variable in the world is presented in Figure 2. Despite the small deviations, the trend of increase continued and the index increased from 57.6 points in 1995 to 60 points in 2020. FDI and EFI values show similar movements. Given the theoretical and empirical literature on this subject, it can be stated that the FD has effects increasing the FDI.

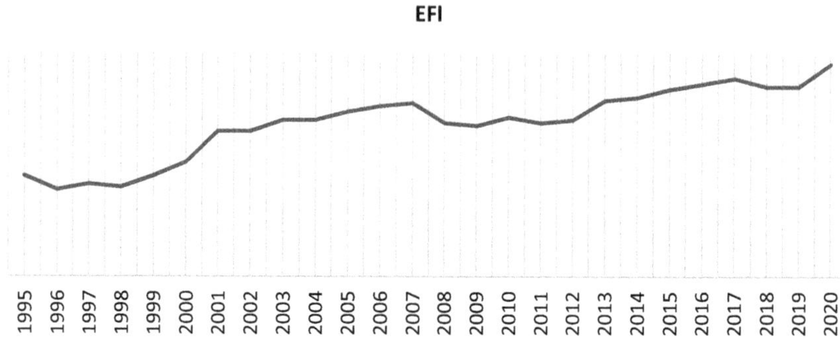

Figure 2. Trend of EFI in the world

Although EF and FDI are increasing throughout the world, is the case the same for the country groups? Figure 3 should be analyzed to answer this question. It can be said for all the country groups that EFI generally moved in direction of increase. The index value of year 1995 was found to be 68 for high-income countries, 57 for upper-middle-income countries, 50 for lower-middle-income countries, and 48 for low-income countries. In year 2020, the same parameter's value is 72 for high-income countries, 59 for upper-middle-income countries, 55 for lower-middle-income countries, and 51 for low-income countries. The highest level of freedom is in high-income countries and the lowest level is in low-income countries. Actually, it can be said that economic freedom increases together with an increase in developmental status. However, the important point here is the index increase performances of country groups from 1995 to 2020. The increase was 4 points in high-income countries, 2 points in upper-middle-income countries, 5 points in lower-middle-income countries, and 3 points in low-income countries. The most remarkable increase was 5 points observed in lower-middle-income countries.

Similar to EFI series, the highest level of increase in FDI variable was observed in lower-middle-income country group. The increase in comparison to the base year was 140 % in year 2018. The increase rate was 111 % for low-income countries, 86 % for upper-middle-income countries, and 46 % in high-income countries.

Considering EFI and FDI series together, it can be seen that the economic freedom of lower-middle-income countries increased and FDI inflows increased, too. It can be said that the same applies to all country groups, except for high-income countries.

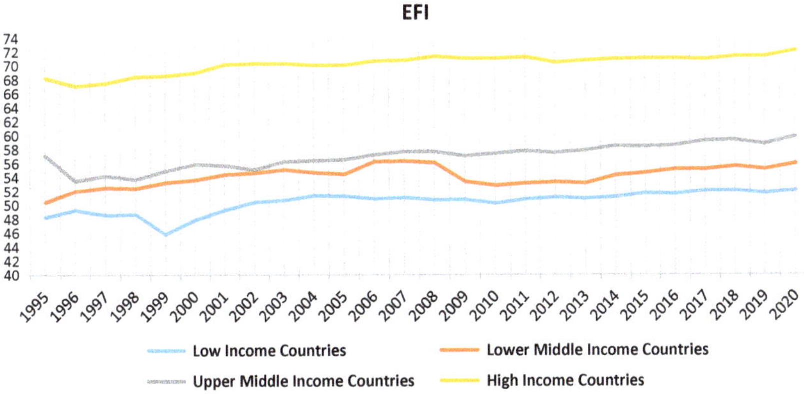

Figure 3. Trend of EFI in country groups

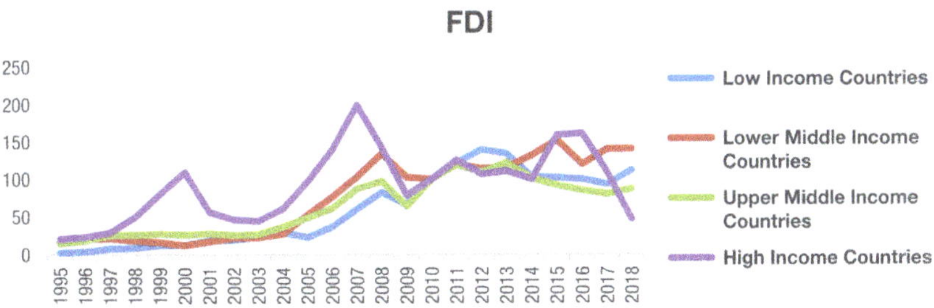

Figure 4. Trend of FDI in country groups

5 Conclusion

From the aspect of development economics, it can be stated that the foreign direct investments are of significant importance for the development of a country. For this reason, many studies have been carried out in order to determine the factors affecting the foreign direct investments. In these studies, it was generally emphasized that the variables considered as economic freedom indicator had a significant effect on the foreign direct investment inflows. For instance, it is stressed that the improvements in economic freedom indicators such as decrease in state intervention to economy, protection of property rights, and free national and international trade are also useful for drawing more foreign direct investment.

Given the findings in the literature, it can be seen in many studies carried out on different regions, countries, periods, and methods that the economic freedom increases the foreign direct investments. From the aspect of this study, the interesting result of the relationship between economic freedom and foreign direct investments is that the increase in economic freedom increased in lower-middle-income countries and foreign direct investments accompanied this increase. Although the level of economic freedom is higher in high-income countries, foreign capital investments are observed to move towards developing countries. In order to reduce the production costs of high-income countries, they mainly prefer low-income countries that are rich especially in natural sources and labor supply. The increasing trend of foreign direct investments in countries having a lower level of income cannot be explained solely with the "economic freedom" concept. However, an improvement in economic freedom increases such countries' ability to draw investment.

In order for the countries to draw foreign direct investments, they need to focus on subcomponents of economic freedom and make up for the lack of these subcomponents. Some of the measures to be taken are to ensure economic stability, to expand financial liberalization, to decrease bureaucracy, to ensure ease of operation, and to establish an effective market system. Moreover, the improvements in the rule of law, level of democracy, and corruption would increase the investment inflows.

References

Akkaya, M. (2019). Gelişen Piyasalarda Doğrudan Yabancı Sermaye Yatırımı, Ekonomik Özgürlük ve Ekonomik Büyüme İlişkisi, TESAM Akademi Dergisi, 6(1), 283–303.

Alston, P. (1990). U.S. Ratification of the Covenant on Economic, Social, and Cultural Rights: The Need for an Entirely New Strategy. The American Journal of International Law, 84(2), 365–393.

Anwar, A., & Mughal, M. (2012). Economic Freedom and Indian Outward Foreign Direct Investment: An Empirical Analysis. Economics Bulletin, AccessEcon, 32(4), 2991–3007.

Azman-Saini, W. N. W., Tun, Y.-L., & Ibrahim, S. (2013). International Evidence on the Link between Foreign Direct Investment and Economic Freedom, MPRA Working Paper 65894, 1–21.

Badri, A., & Sheshgelanib, A. (2017). Economic Freedom and FDI in Selected Developing Countries. International Journal of Economics and Financial Research, 2(5), 82–87.

Bengoa, M., & Sanchez-Robles, B. (2003). Foreign Direct Investment, Economic Freedom and Growth: New Evidence from Latin America. European Journal of Political Economy, 19(2003), 529–545.

Caetano, J., & Caleiro, A. (2009). Economic Freedom and Foreign Direct Investment: How Different are the MENA Countries from the EU, Universidade De Evora, Documento De Trabalho, 2009/02.

Campa, M. (1993). Entry by Foreign Firms in the United States under Exchange Rate Uncertainty. The Review of Economics and Statistics, 75(4), 614–622.

Chang, H. J., & Grabel, I. J. (2005). Kalkınma Yeniden: Alternatif İktisat Politikaları Elkitabı. İmge Kitabevi.

Dunning, J. (2002). Relational Assets, Networks, and International Business Activities. In F. Contractor & P. Lorange (Eds.), Cooperative Strategies and Alliances (pp. 569–593). Amsterdam: Pergamon.

Friedman, M. (2002). Economic Freedom Behind the Scenes. In J. Gwartney, R. Lawson, C. Edwards, W. Park, V. Rugy, ve S. Wagh (Eds.), Economic Freedom of the World: 2002 Annual Report. Vancouver: The Fraser Institute.

Habibi, A., & Hidayat, R. W. (2017). Analisis Pengaruh Economic Freedom Terhadap Foreign Direct Investment Di Negara Asean. Jurnal Ekonomi Pembangunan, 15(1), 87–100.

Heritage Foundation. (2020). Index of Economic Freedom. Available at: http://www.heritage.org (10.03.2020).

Hossain, Md. S. (2016). Foreign Direct Investment, Economic Freedom and Economic Growth: Evidence from Developing Countries. International Journal of Economics and Finance, 8(11), 200–214.

Imtiaz, S., & Bashir, M. F. (2017). Economic Freedom and Foreign Direct Investment in South Asian Countries. Theoretical and Applied Economics. XXIV(2017). 2(611), Summer, 281–294.

Kamacı, A. (2019). Ekonomik Özgürlüklerin Dış Ticaret ve Doğrudan Yabancı Yatırımlara Etkisi. Business & Management Studies: An International Journal, 7(2), 1097–1116.

Kapuria-Foreman, V. (2007). Economic Freedom and Foreign Direct Investment in Developing Countries. The Journal of Developing Areas, 41(1), 143–154.

McGowan, C. B. Jr. (2011). The Relationship between Political and Economic Openness and Foreign Direct Investment. Southwestern Economic Review. Spring (2004), 177–187.

Morteza, K., & Azman-Saini, W. N. W. (2017). Foreign Direct Investment, Economic Freedom and Democracy. International Journal of Economics and Management, 11(1), 1–15.

Moussa, M., Çaha, H., & Karagöz, M. (2016). Review of Economic Freedom Impact on FDI: New Evidence from Fragile and Conflict Countries. Procedia Economics and Finance, 38, 163–173.

Muslija, A. (2018). Foreign Direct Investments and Economic Freedom in OECD Countries. International Journal of Economic Studies, 4(4), 52–59.

Pearson, D., Nyonna, D., & Kim, K. J. (2012). The Relationship between Economic Freedom, State Growth and Foreign Direct Investment in US States. International Journal of Economics and Finance, 4(10), 140–146.

Quazi, R. (2007). Economic Freedom and Foreign Direct Investment in East Asia. Journal of the Asia Pacific Economy, 12(3), 329–344.

Sahin, D. (2018). BRICS-T Ülkelerinde Ekonomik Özgürlükler ve Doğrudan Yabancı Sermaye Yatırımları Arasındaki İlişki: Bootstrap Panel Nedensellik Testi, Bingöl Üniversitesi Sosyal Bilimler Enstitüsü Dergisi, 8(16), 285–294.

Sambharya, R., & Rasheed, A. (2015). Does Economic Freedom in Host Countries Lead to Increased Foreign Direct Investment? Competitiveness Review, 25(1), 2–24.

Savaşan, F., & Dursun, I. (2006). Ekonomik Özgürlükler ve Doğrudan Yabancı Yatırımlar: İstatistiksel Bir Analiz. Sosyal Ekonomik Araştırmalar Dergisi, 6(12), 29–52.

Senalp, B. (2018). Foreign Direct Investment, Economic Growth and Economic Freedom: A Literature Survey. Istanbul Journal of Economics, 68(2), 301–336.

Sofuoğlu, E., Kızılkaya, O., & Uysal, D. (2019), Ekonomik Özgürlükler ve Doğrudan Yabancı Yatırımlar Arasındaki İlişki: Panel Eşbütünleşme Analizi, Business and Economics Research Journal, 10(2), 341–355.

Subasat, T., & Bellos, S. (2011). Economic Freedom and Foreign Direct Investment: A Panel Gravity Model Approach. The Empirical Economics Letters, 10(7), 697–704.

Türen, U., Gökmen, Y., & Dilek, H. (2011). Ekonomik Özgürlük Endeksinin Yurt Dışına Doğrudan Yabancı Yatırım Yapan Türk Sermayesinin Ülke Seçim Kararına Etkisi Var mıdır?, Maliye Dergisi, 161(Temmuz –Aralık), 298–325.

UNCTAD. (1995). World Investment Report 1995: Transnational Corporations and Competitiveness, United Nations, New York and Geneva.

UNCTAD. (1998). World Investment Report 1998: Trends and Determinants, United Nations, New York and Geneva.

UNCTAD. (2018). World Investment Report 1998: Investment and New Indutrial Policies, United Nations, New York and Geneva.

Vogiatzoglou, K. (2016). Free Market Institutions and FDI Performance in Emerging Asian Economies. The Journal of Developing Areas, 41(1), 143–154.

Worldbank. https://datahelpdesk.worldbank.org/knowledgebase/articles/906519-world-bank-country-and-lending-groups, (12.03.2020).

Luan Vardari

The Analysis of Active Portfolio Management in Emerging Markets: Markowitz Modern Portfolio Method

1 Introduction

Portfolio performance formation is the determination of the success level of the portfolio in terms of various indicators. Portfolio performance is generally measured by two methods. In this measurement, the risk and return of the portfolio are used. Before 1950, portfolio managers and investors measured portfolio performance by rate of return. During this time, they realized that risk is a very important variable in determining the investment success. Considering the results obtained, if the result is positive, it is concluded that performance has a positive effect on the portfolio diversification and the targeted goal has been achieved, if the result is negative, the effect of portfolio diversification on performance is negative and a correct diversification has not been made.

Markowitz, who put forward the modern portfolio theory, stated that "*it is not possible for the investor who invests a certain amount in securities to know the money that he can obtain at the end of the period*" and that he can make some predictions by taking advantage of the past performance of the stock. In Modern Portfolio Theory, there are two stages in portfolio selection. The first stage is to gain knowledge and experience about the future performance of the security. The second stage is the selection of portfolios as a result of the information received (Markowitz, 1952). Capital asset pricing model of William Sharpe and John Litner marks the birth of asset pricing theory. The appeal of the capital assets pricing model advocates how to measure risk and make power predictions of the relationship between expected return and risk.

Treynor (1965) is the first researcher to develop the idea that portfolio performance is a composite measure. It measured portfolio risk with beta and calculated portfolio market risk premium, and then in 1966, Sharpe developed a composite index similar to the Treynor criterion. The only difference is the use of standard deviation instead of beta.

In 1967, the Sharpe index evaluated fund performance based on both rate of return and diversity, but for a fully diversified portfolio, the Treynor and Sharpe indices will give the same ranking. In 1968, Jensen tried to establish a measure based on the Securities market line and showed the difference between the expected return rate of the portfolio and the expected return of a comparison portfolio to be positioned on the line in the security market.

According to Spermann, "*Portfolio measurement is important not only to inform about the quality of a portfolio performance, but also to distinguish and analyse the success factors of a portfolio*" (Kallberg et al., 1984).

2 Emerging Markets: Definition and Features

Although the word "Emerging market" is a frequently used word in the international trade literature, most researchers do not have a common general definition of emerging markets. Without a clear market definition, only a country that meets the following criteria can be recognized as a developing market (Meyer et al., 2004):

- Low level of economic development, expressed in GDP per capita (less developed country);
- Transition economy (and society): The state is constantly undertaking economic reforms. These; It should increase the impact on growth politically, economically and democratically, together and integrated.
- The high growth rate stemming from the government's attempt to create a market economy can be expressed in the GDP growth rate (at least 5 % per year);
- The difference between the level of economic development achieved (purchasing power parity is also used as a criterion) and the average GDP of developed countries causes a great economic phenomenon in the future.

The driving force of every emerging market is a quality of economic (and political) reforms, which is also a very risky area (Meyer et al., 2004).

In his study in 1987, Çavuşgil described the emerging markets as follows: "*Emerging Markets are countries with high growth potential, offering attractive business opportunities for western firms*".

Miller's idea for emerging markets in 1988 is as follows: "*Despite individual differences, future growth potentials of all emerging markets are similar*". "*Compared to a developed economy, less developed economies are seen as investment opportunities in the future*". "*Such economic incentives (new technologies, foreign investments or attracting foreign participation in commercial businesses) and leading policies have a positive impact on growth.*"

Miller listed some features of emerging markets in 1998. Although each developing market is unique, its most common features can be summarized as follows:

- Physical characteristics, insufficient commercial infrastructure and inadequate all other aspects of physical infrastructure (communication, transportation, energy production);
- Social and political features, including political instability, inadequate legal framework, weak social discipline and (unique) cultural characteristics as well as reduced technological levels;
- Limited personal income, the effective role of government in economic activities.

Comparison is required in developing markets (developing economies) and developing countries. The reason why developing economies are so important for the world economy is more clearly seen in the irrelevant categories of these countries.

It is very important to recognize whether a country is a developing economy or a developed economy, especially for multinational companies. From the point of view of the countries in question, it can be questioned whether countries such as Israel, South Africa, Hong Kong or Singapore are in emerging markets or developed economies. Many sources see the mentioned countries as developing countries, but these countries are defined as follows. Each has a high GDP and a stable economic system with fully developed institutions of the market economy. From this point of view, these countries can only be considered as developed countries with a great market potential (with the awareness of the transition economy, the most important part of this line) that separates the developing markets from the developed markets (Civi, 2010).

3 Portfolio Performance Measurement

Portfolio is a new asset that investors who want to achieve certain goals have, are related to each other and have self-measurable qualities. Economic conditions that change over time require that portfolios be bought and sold (Demirtaş & Güngör, 2004). The main purpose of creating a portfolio is to allocate investment funds to different financial assets and to try to minimize especially non-systematic risk through diversification or optimization. Therefore, it is of great importance to provide diversification above all in the process of creating a portfolio. Portfolio management, on the other hand, is a dynamic investment management process that aims to share the funds held by the investor among the available financial asset alternatives in a way to ensure the highest return at a certain risk level or to provide the lowest risk at a certain return level (Bayramoğlu & Yayalar, 2017).

Modern portfolio management is an approach that aims to objectively measure the individual risks and returns of the assets, while also considering the quantitative relationship between the assets in portfolio creation. Modern portfolio theory is based on the fact that the returns of assets do not move together perfectly. With the help of the correlation coefficient, which is a measure of the tendency to act together, it has been shown that the assets with negative correlations acting independently can be reduced in portfolio without sacrificing returns (Okuyan & Deniz, 2017).

The measurement of portfolio performance begins with the evaluation of each security in the portfolio. Then, the return of the portfolio and portfolio manager (selectivity, timing ability) is calculated. These results are compared with the returns of a market index or other sample portfolios. The risk assumed while obtaining these returns is calculated both absolute and relative. Returns are adjusted for risk and made comparable. In the next step, the contributions of portfolio managers to portfolio performance are determined. Finally, the results obtained are reported in accordance with current legal regulations and announced to savings owners (Feibel, 2003).

The main elements in the evaluation of portfolio performance are listed as the suitability of the indicator preferred for comparison, the effect of market timing and the internalization of transaction costs. In this context, it is stated that rational investment decisions and collaterals are accepted as reference when they are affected by fund performance (Omağ, 2010).

"*The method of choosing a portfolio is divided into two stages,*" says Markowitz. *The first phase begins with observation and experience and ends with expectations about the future performance of existing securities. The second phase starts with expectations about future performances and ends with the selection of the portfolio*". This article is about the second stage (Markowitz, 1952) and it is accepted that he made a modern and ground breaking start to portfolio theory with his article "Portfolio Selection". What Markowitz emphasizes is the fact that diversification is not sufficient alone in increasing the expected return, but it is very useful in keeping the portfolio at the lowest level (Stephen, 1995).

4 Analysis of Data

This section consists of 3 main topics. First, eight indices selected from the emerging markets between 2000 and 2017 were analyzed using the Markowitz portfolio optimization model with the Microsoft Excel 2019 program.

Optimal weights for assets in a portfolio are those that maximize the portfolio's Sharpe ratio.

$$S_p = \frac{E_{(rp)} - r_f}{\sigma_p}$$

Table 1. Description Statistics

DESCRIPTION STATISTICS								
	MSCI	**EEM**	**FEM**	**IEMG**	**JFAM**	**LZEM**	**SCHE**	**VWO**
N	216	216	216	216	216	216	216	216
Mean	9.36	31.4	19.2	32.5	16.8	15.7	21.5	35.8
Mean S.E.	0.0907	0.886	0.518	0.874	0.502	0.355	0.324	0.593
Median	9.61	36.0	21.5	37.3	19.5	17.2	21.9	37.7
Standard Error	1.33	13.0	7.61	12.8	7.37	5.21	4.76	8.71
Minimum	6.43	8.40	6.20	9.18	3..36	5.99	8.87	21.0
Maximum	12.3	55.7	37.5	55.7	31.4	28.3	30.6	58.6

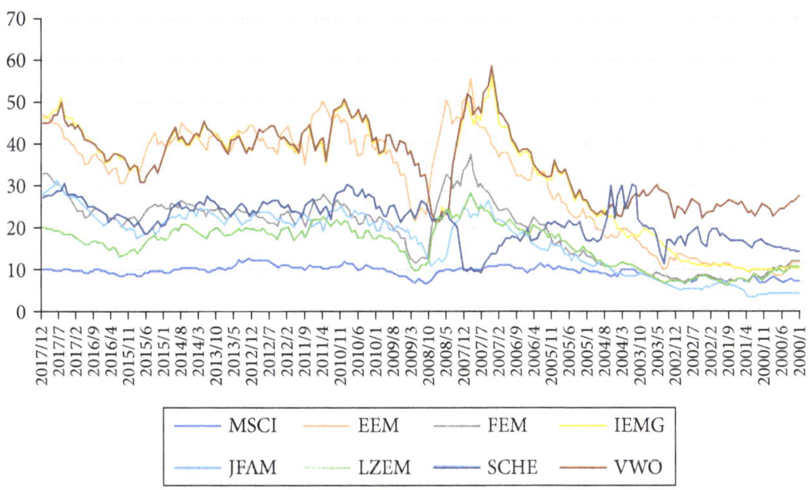

Graph 1. *DESCRIPTION STATISTICS*

Calculation of emerging indices according to this calculation system is as in Table 7.

Eight indices seem to be the most profitable in MSCI. We can say that the MSCI index has spread over the years, between 5 % and 10 %. There are some reasons for this, MSCI index seems to have the highest trading volume among other portfolios. As it can be seen in the EEM index chart, expected returns in the index range between 15 % and -20 %. The FEM index ranges between 20 % over the years.

The MSCI index provides an average return of 10 % between 2000 and 2017. The EEM index provides an average return of 20 % between 2000 and 2017. The FEM index provides an average return of 20 % between 2000 and 2017. The IEMG index provides an average return of 15 % between 2000 and 2017. The JFAM index provides an average return of 20 % between 2000 and 2017. The LZEM index provides an average return of 10 % between 2000 and 2017. The SCHE index provides an average return of 20 % between 2000 and 2017. The VWO index provides an average return of 15 % between 2000 and 2017.

The effective limit of Markowitz is the basis of the modern portfolio. This enables us to identify the risks that are widely used in the Capital Asset Pricing model and the risks. The portfolio with the highest average among the indices is the JFAM index as seen in the table. The index has an average of 1.0826 %. This is a higher average than other Indices. The portfolio with the lowest average is the MSCI index with a rate of 0.2556 %. It is seen that the SCHE index is the highest in calculating the variance and standard deviation of the portfolio. The variance of the SCHE index is 0.008651 % and its standard deviation is 0.093012 %. In the standard deviation calculation, the index closest to zero and the least deviating index is MSCI 0.04535 % index. As with the expected returns, the MSCI index is the index with the highest trading volume, and its standard deviation seems to be the index closest to zero.

As can be seen in Table 3, monthly and annual returns and variances of the indices are calculated. Considering these calculations, the index with the highest return as monthly return is JFAM index with 1.082 % ratio. The SCHE index achieves the highest return with an annual average rate of return of 0.8869 %. Considering the monthly and annual variance rates, the highest monthly variance rate is SCHE index with the rate of 0.86 %. The SCHE index is the highest with an annual variance rate of 10,430 %. Looking at the table in general, the SCHE index appears to have the highest return and variance rates.

As seen in Equal Weight Portfolio Analysis, portfolios have an equal share. The share of each portfolio is determined as 0.125, which is calculated as 0.125x8 =

Table 2. Effective Limit Values

	MSCI	EEM	FEM	IEMG	JFAM	LZEM	SCHE	VWO
Mean	0,255 %	0,860 %	0,688 %	0,893 %	1,082 %	0,510 %	0,705 %	0,428 %
Variance	0,00205	0,00410	0,00424	0,00351	0,00415	0,0040118	0,00865	0,003874
Standard Error	0,04535	0,06409	0,06511	0,05926	0,06444	0,0633391	0,09301	0,062245

Table 3. Returns and Variance Rates of Indices (Monthly/Annual)

	MSCI	EEM	FEM	IEMG	JFAM	LZEM	SCHE	VWO
Monthly Average Return	0,2556 %	0,8602 %	0,6887 %	0,8930 %	1,0826 %	0,5100 %	0,7055 %	0,4282 %
Monthly Variance	0,2067 %	0,4127 %	0,4260 %	0,3529 %	0,4172 %	0,4031 %	0,8692 %	0,3893 %
Average Annual Return	3,0671 %	10,3228 %	8,2643 %	10,7158 %	12,9908 %	6,1205 %	8,4665 %	5,1389 %
Annual Variance	2,4801 %	4,9524 %	5,1121 %	4,2348 %	5,0066 %	4,8367 %	10,4301 %	4,6711 %

1. Portfolio return calculated according to this distribution is expected to be 8.14 %. Sharp ratio, on the other hand, seems to be 11.16 % even though the portfolio diversification distributions are equal.

The expected return of portfolios is seen in the JFAM index with a maximum rate of 12.99 %. As a result of the analysis made here, Sharp Ratio has a ratio of 0.4601. Since the index is based on USD (US dollar), American Central Bank indicator interest rate is taken as 3 % for 2018.

As it can be seen in Table 5, the indexes with the highest weights are MSCI and EEM with 0,015 ratio and MSCI-FEM 0,0202 indices.

Table 4. Portfolio Return

	Portfolio return
MSCI	3,0671 %
EEM	10,3228 %
FEM	8,2643 %
IEMG	10,7158 %
JFAM	12,9908 %
LZEM	6,1205 %
SCHE	8,4665 %
VWO	5,1389 %
Risksiz Oran	3,00 %
A	10
Sharp Ratio	0,46010751

Table 5. Portfolio Variance – Covariance Matrix

	MSCI	EEM	FEM	IEMG	JFAM	LZEM	SCHE	VWO
MSCI	0,002057126	0,01532721	0,0202083	-0,0011265	0,00064477	0,01941238	0,00043385	-0,002385
EEM	0,015327205	0,04929352	0,04121077	-0,0039473	-0,0006213	0,03886058	0,00385702	-0,002166
FEM	0,020208298	0,04121077	0,05088356	-0,0034627	-0,000464	0,04647005	-0,0029489	-0,0058473
IEMG	-0,001126461	-0,0039473	-0,0034627	0,04215125	0,00779822	-0,002387	-0,0003785	0,03756541
JFAM	0,000644772	-0,0006213	-0,000464	0,00779822	0,04983267	0,00149127	-0,0097194	0,00798356
LZEM	0,019412384	0,03886058	0,04647005	-0,002387	0,00149127	0,0481422	-0,0003843	-0,0053009
SCHE	0,000433854	0,00385702	-0,0029489	-0,0003785	-0,0097194	-0,0003843	0,10381553	0,00224796
VWO	-0,00238501	-0,002166	-0,0058473	0,03756541	0,00798356	-0,0053009	0,00224796	0,04649359

Table 6. Optimal Risk Portfolio/Capital Allocation Line

Optimal Risk Portfolio	
MSCI	0,703
EEM	0,003
FEM	0,021
IEMG	0,130
JFAM	0,117
LZEM	0,015
SCHE	0,050
VWO	0,210
Total	1
Expected return	6,87 %
Standard deviation	8,70 %
Sharp ratio	0,44453753
y'	0,510789977

Table 7. Equal-Weighted and Markowitz Optimization Model Returns

	Equal-weighted portfolio return	**Markowitz optimal portfolio return**
Expected Return	8.14	6.87
Standard Deviation	11.16	8.70
Sharpe Ratio	0.46	0.44

In Table 6, data were obtained using the Optimal Risk Portfolio analysis used in my modern portfolio method of Markowitz. The expected return of portfolios is here as 6.87 %. This shows us that total portfolios' expected returns are higher than 6 %. The most important analysis for us in this analysis is the Sharp rate. Here, this ratio seems to be 0.4445. Sharp rate is the ratio that shows us what the portfolio's return is according to the risk. The Sharp rate is found by subtracting the risk-free interest rate from the portfolio's return and dividing it by total risk. As can be seen in the table, the total index is 1. The portfolio with the highest share here is the MSCI 0,703 portfolio. This is followed by VWO 0,210 and IEMG 0,130. Here y shows us the risk aversion rate. This ratio seems to be 0.510.

As can be seen in Table 7, there is the return of equal-weighted portfolios in the left section and Markowitz's optimal portfolio returns in the right section. When we read the results of the table, while the portfolios distributed equally in terms of the expected return provided a return of 8.14, the portfolio return in distributed weights according to the Markowitz ratio was 6.87. Standard deviation rates and Sharp ratio were higher in equally distributed portfolios.

5 Result

In this study, emerging markets were analyzed by using emerging market indices data between 2000 and 2017 as historical data for active portfolio management review. The indices used in the analysis are MSCI, EEM, FEM, IEMG, JFAM, LZEM, SCHE and VWO developing market indices. These indices, which were selected first, were analyzed according to the equal portfolio distribution, and then analyzed according to the Markowitz portfolio distribution. According to the equal and Markowitz distributions analyzes, risk is compared as results as minimum return and maximum return. Portfolio risks were taken at risk exposure (0.95 confidence interval). When looking at portfolio risks, genetic algorithm optimization reaches the lowest value when analyzed according to the Markowitz model. Both the equally weighted portfolio distribution and the Markowitz portfolio distribution provide the opportunity to compare the actual values with the value at risk and portfolio returns. According to historical data analyzed for emerging market indices, it has been determined that the Markowitz portfolio function reaches the lowest risk value when operated with genetic algorithm optimization.

References

Bayramoğlu, M. F. (2017). "Portföy Seçiminde Toplam Riski Temel Alan Portföy Performans Ölçütlerinin Değerlendirilmesi", AİBÜ Sosyal Bilimler Enstitüsü Dergisi, Cilt:17, Yıl:17, Sayı: 1, pp: 1–28.

Çavusgil, S. T. (1997). "Measuring the Potential of Emerging Markets: An Indexing Approach". Business Horizons, 40(1), 87–92.

Civi, E. and Sunje, A. (2010). "Emerging markets: A review of conceptual frameworks". Challenges for business administrators in the new millennium. 202–216. Availbel at: http://www.opf.slu.cz/vvr/akce/turecko/pdf/sunje.pdf

Demirtaş, Ö. and Güngör Z. (2004). "Portföy yönetimi and portföy seçimine yönelik uygulama". Havacılık andUzay Teknolojileri Dergisi, 1(4), 103–109.

Deniz, D. and Okuyan, H. A. (2017). "Geleneksel andModern Portföy Yönetiminin Ampirik Sonuçlarının Karşılaştırılması: BİST Uygulaması", Uluslararası Katılımlı 21. Finans Sempozyumu/18 – 21 Ekim-Balıkesir.

Feibel, B. J. (2003). "Investment Performance Measurement". Hoboken, New Jersey: Wiley Finance, John Wiley & Sons, Inc.

Kallberg, J. G. and Ziemba, W. T. (1984). "Mis-specification in Portfolio Selection Problems," in G. Bamberg and K. Spremann (Eds.), Risk and Capital: Lecture Notes in Economics and Mathematical Systems. New York: Springer-Verlag.

Markowitz, H. M. (1952). "Portfolio Section". Journal of Finance, 7(1), 77–91.

Meyer, R. L., Richard, R. R. and Adam, M. (2004). "Developing Rural Financial Markets in Uganda: The Way Forward," Financial Systems Development Programme. Bank of Uganda, Kampala, Oct.

Miller, M. and Scholes, M. (1972). "Rates of Return in Relation to Risk: A Reexamination of Some Recent Findings," in Michael C. Jensen (Ed.), Studies in the Theory of Capital Markets (pp. 47–78). New York: Praeger.

Omağ, A. (2010). "Türkiye'de A Tipi ve B Tipi Yatırım Fonlarının 2000–2008 Dönemi Performans Analizi", Istanbul Ticaret Üniversitesi Sosyal Bilimler Dergisi Yıl:9 Sayı:17, pp. 235–250.

Sharpe, W. F. (1966). "Mutual fund performance". Journal of Business,39(1), Part 2: Supplement on Security Prices (Jan., 1966), 119–138.

Spremann, K. and Pascal, F. (2000). "Approaches to Modern Performance Measurement". Journal of Portfolio Management, 12, 48–62.

Stephen, J. B. (1995). "Performance Persistence." The Journal of Finance, 2, 679–698.

Terzioğlu, M. K. (2018). "Riske Maruz Değer Kavram ve Uygulamalar". Gazi Kitabevi. Ankara.

Treynor, J. L. (1965). "How to Rate Management of Investment Funds". Harvard Business Review, 43(1), 63–75.

Treynor, J. L. and Ferguson, R. (1985). "In Defense of Technical Analysis". Journal of Finance, 40(3), 757–773.

https://www.msci.com/documents/1296102/1362201/GlobalIndexes-cbr-en.pdf/ed3a08b3-84bb-4e71-8d2e-8b267213cb44

www.theice.com/products/Futures-Options/Financials/MSCI-Indexes

http://www.calamos.com/~/media/FA/Documents/Products/MF/Papers/Evolving%20World%20Paper.aspx

http://www.investopedia.com/terms/e/emergingmarketsindex.asp#ixzz4cLSF5bVP

https://www.invesco.com/static/us/investors/contentdetail?contentId=b029e01e98630410VgnVCM10000046f1bf0aRCRD

Aslı Güler

The Anchoring of Inflation Expectations under Explicit Inflation Targeting Strategy: Panel ARDL Analysis for Fragile Economies[1]

1 Introduction

Although the criticism suggesting that inflation targeting is not a flexible system has increased after the financial crisis, these discussions actually have started before the crisis. According to those who oppose inflation targeting on grounds that it is a strict system, in the presence of external or financial shocks, central banks will not be able to fight macroeconomic instability while keeping inflation under control. They argue that the flexibility of monetary policy would be significantly reduced because having a legal numerical inflation target of the central bank requires intense inflation oriented (Kohn, 2005: 338; Galindo & Ros, 2009: 158). Despite these criticisms, many views suggest that inflation targeting is not a strict monetary policy system. For example, Bernanke et al. (1999) and Svensson (1997, 1999) portray inflation targeting as a flexible monetary policy system where central banks can adapt their monetary policy against macroeconomic fluctuations while maintaining price stability. In this system, monetary policy can be maintained as a rule (targeting rule), which can be adjusted according to the situation. In this sense, inflation targeting is a monetary policy system that includes "disciplined discretionary". According to King (1997: 87; 1999: 15), inflation targeting is described as "the combination of an inflation target set at the beginning of the period and a response strategy to be expected against unexpected shocks".

The main problem here is the question of the trade-off between the flexibility and reliability of monetary policy. Because a disciplined and reliable monetary policy is needed to achieve the announced inflation targets. On the other hand, in order to stabilize macroeconomic fluctuations, especially in times of crisis, monetary policy needs to be flexible. In this case, the following question is faced: Could the inflation targeting be a strict strategy to achieve the main target price stability, but also a flexible strategy to ensure output stability? (Kuttner and Posen, 2011: 1). Apparently these two situations contradict each other. A number

1 This study is derived from my Ph.D. thesis entitled "Flexibility of Inflation Targeting in Combating Real Economic Instability: Dynamic Panel Analysis on Fragile Economies".

of theories have been put forward on how monetary policy can have both reliability and flexibility conditions by providing coordination between these two situations within the same monetary policy system. According to one of these, the inflation targeting system gives the central bank the flexibility to combat macroeconomic fluctuations thanks to its ability to *anchor inflation expectations*. In this sense, whether inflation targeting has a flexible monetary policy system can be measured through its ability to anchor its expectations.

On the other hand, there is a great deal of criticism arguing that most of the success in the field of anchoring of inflation should be attributed to the stable macroeconomic environment, not to inflation targeting system itself. (Clark and Nakata, 2008: 17–18). This study aims to empirically question whether the inflation expectations have been under the anchor in the 2008 crisis period in fragile economies implementing inflation targeting and to evaluate whether the monetary policy can be flexibly applied to combat recession in the light of the data obtained. Accordingly, the rest of the study organized as follows: The next section focused primarily on the relationship between the degree of anchor of inflation expectations and the flexibility of monetary policy. Then, the results of the empirical studies on this subject are summarized in the literature review section. Finally, the degree of the sensitivity of 12 months ahead inflation expectations to inflation rates and inflation targets in fragile economies for pre-crisis and crisis periods are analyzed by using a dynamic panel method. In the conclusion part, an evaluation has been made about the flexibility of inflation targeting by comparing the results obtained from two periods, and policy suggestions are recommended.

2 Relationship between Anchoring Effect and Flexibility of Monetary Policy

According to Walsh, the policy pursued by the central bank is a good policy if the monetary strategy implemented can provide a strong nominal anchor and reduce economic instability (Walsh, 2008: 21). The anchoring effect is that inflation targets become the main indicator that is taken as a reference when being built inflation expectations. The stronger the anchoring effect, the weaker the relationship between inflation expectations and past inflation rates and other macroeconomic developments. This means that even if the central bank applies expansionary policies in the short term to eliminate the stagnation, inflation expectations are not updated upwards. Thus, the anchored inflation expectations provide central bankers with a certain maneuver area where monetary policy can be used flexibly to tackle short-term real and financial instability (Pétursson, 2004: 57).

In this point of view, most economists think that inflation targeting is a flexible monetary policy system and derives its flexibility from its robust ability to anchor inflation expectations (Siklos, 2010: 60–61). However, it is not sufficient to announce inflation targets alone so that expectations can be anchored. In order for expectations to be anchored to inflation targets, the central bank and the inflation targets it declares must be found reliable by economic actors. Therefore, the key element of the system is credibility. Only under a reliable monetary policy system inflation expectations not be adapted to macroeconomic developments and not be revised upwards even if the monetary policy is implemented for the purpose of short-term real stability. In order for the announced inflation targets to be a guide for inflation expectations, an effective communication strategy have to be followed by the central bank to create credibility. Considering that the credibility is the main factor that provides the feature of being an anchor to inflation targets, it is a realistic approach to evaluate well-anchored inflation expectations as an indicator of confidence (Valdés, 2007: 18).

3 Literature Review

In empirical studies conducted for fragile economies, it was found that inflation expectations were generally not under anchor. In addition, it is another common result obtained from studies in which past inflation rates in these economies are the most important determinant of inflation expectations. Accordingly, there is strong inflation inertia in fragile economies.

Lee (1994) examined the process of the expectation building process of economic units' regarding prices and cost inflation for the period of 1972–1989 with the expectation series obtained from the responses of surveys of nine industry sectors covering the manufacturing sector in England. According to the findings, while inflation expectations are updated upwards much more rapidly in periods when inflation rates are rising, the rate of adjustment of inflation expectations is much slower in decreasing periods.

Castelnuovo et al. (2003) investigated whether the degree of anchor for long-term inflation expectations for the fifteen industrial countries has strengthened in the period after 1990. As a result of the panel data analysis conducted for the period of 1990–2002, it was found that long-term inflation expectations were well anchored in countries other than Japan, especially in the last ten years.

In their study, Kim and Park (2006) investigated the degree of inflation dependence of inflation expectations for Korea before and after the adoption of inflation targeting. According to the regression results obtained, the degree of sensitivity of inflation expectations to changes in actual inflation rates is much higher in the pre-inflation targeting period.

Bevilaqua et al. (2007) investigated whether inflation expectations in Brazil show a systematic deviation from inflation targets after the 2002 crisis using regression analysis for the period 2000: m1–2006: m8. According to the results of the study, while the effects of inflation targets on inflation expectations weakened in crisis periods, the strength of inflation targets on expectations increases when the crisis period is excluded.

Clark and Davig (2008) empirically tested the degree of anchor of inflation expectations for the US economy discussed for 1982: a q3-2008q2 period using the VAR model. The result of the study indicates that changes in CPI make it difficult to anchor short and long term inflation expectations to inflation targets.

Cerisola and Gelos (2009) examined what were the main macroeconomic determinants of inflation expectations in the period since 1999, when Brazil started to apply EH, by the Johansen cointegration test, GMM and OLS methods. The study found that the inflation target and the ratio of the consolidated primary surplus to GDP were effective in shaping expectations. In addition, it has been determined that since 2004, inflation expectations were shaped less retrospectively and better anchored to the inflation target.

Baskaya, Gulsen, and Orak (2010), examined the changes in the effect of inflation targets on 12 and 24 months ahead inflation expectations after the revision of the inflation target made on June 12, 2008, in Turkey. It was revealed in the study that after the revision of the target, the determination of inflation targets on inflation expectations increased and the role of past inflation realizations in expectation formation decreased.

Wimanda et al. (2011) analyzed the degree of adaptation of inflation expectations to past inflation rates and inflation targets using the GMM method for the period 1980: m1–2008: m12 for Indonesia, which has been implementing EH since 1999. According to the results obtained, inflation expectations are mostly shaped by past inflation rates.

Binal Yilmaz (2012), investigated the determinants of 12 months ahead inflation expectations for two sub-periods 2002–2011 and 2006–2011 by using Johansen and Jeselius cointegration techniques. As a result of the cointegration analysis, it was determined that the change value of the CPI compared to 12 months ago continued to be an important determinant of the 12-month ahead inflation expectations, and the effect of inflation targets on expectations increased after 2006.

Table 1: Definitions of the Variables

Variable	Definition	Sources
π^e_{t+12}	12 month ahead inflation expectations	CBRT for Turkey, Chile Statistic Data Base for Chile, and Central Bank of Brazil for Brazil.
π_t	CPI inflation (%,yoy)	OECD
π^T	Inflation targets (	Central Banks of countries

4 Data Set and Sampling

Fragile economies (Turkey, Brazil, and Chile) that are implementing inflation targeting and publish 12 months ahead inflation expectations series on a regular basis are the samples of this study[2]. Analyzes in this study were conducted for two sub period: one of them is the period of 2002: 1–2008: 1 named as the pre-crisis period in which macroeconomic uncertainty is relatively low, and the other is the period of 2008: 10–2014: 1 named as the crisis period. The data set was created on a monthly frequency. The dependent variable of the analysis is the 12-month ahead inflation expectations. The independent variables of the analysis are past inflation rates and inflation targets. Annual CPI change rates were used to measure the sensitivity of 12 months ahead inflation expectations to inflation realizations. Inflation targets were transformed to monthly frequency using the linear interpolation method. Data definitions and resources are presented in Table 1.

5 Econometric Method: Panel ARDL

In this study, the short and long-term adaptation of 12 months ahead inflation expectations to the inflation rates and the inflation targets both in the pre-crisis period and in the crisis period were estimated by the panel autoregressive delay distributed model (panel ARDL) developed by Pesaran et al. (1999). Pesaran et al. (1999) developed two estimators for the panel ARDL model: one of them is "Average Group Estimator (MG)" and the other is "Pooled Mean Group Estimator (PMG)". One of the modeling problems here is the choice between these two alternative estimators. Pesaran et al. (1999) suggested that the

2 Indonesia and South Africa could not be included in the analysis since the 12-month ahead inflation expectation series could not be reached at the desired intervals.

homogeneity test of long term parameters should be done with the Hausman test. Although PMG and MG are consistent estimators under the assumption of long-term homogeneity, only PMG is an effective estimator (Erdem et al. 2010: 375–76; Mamun et al. 2013: 570). The models in the analysis were estimated separately for the periods 2002: 1–2008: 8 and 2008: 10–2014: 1. The models are as follows:

$$\pi^e_{t+12} = \mu_i + \sum_{j=1}^{pi} \lambda_{ij}\pi^e_{t+12\,i,t-j} + \sum_{jo}^{qi} \delta_{ij}\ \pi_{ti,t-j} + \ \varepsilon_{it} \qquad (1)$$

$$\pi^e_{t+12} = \mu_i + \sum_{j=1}^{pi} \lambda_{ij}\pi^e_{t+12\,i,t-j} + \sum_{jo}^{qi} \delta_{ij}\ \pi^T{}_{i,t-j} + \ \varepsilon_{it} \qquad (2)$$

Equations were re-parameterized as follows, as suggested by Pesaran et al. (1999);

$$\pi^e_{t+12\,it} = \mu_i +_i \pi^e_{t+12\,i,t-1} + \beta\prime_i \pi_{ti,t} + \sum_{j=1}^{p-1} \lambda^*_{ij}\pi^e_{t+12\,i,t-j} + \sum_{j=0}^{q-1} \delta^*_{ij}\pi_{ti,t-j} + \varepsilon_{\mathrm{it}} \qquad (3)$$

$$\pi^e_{t+12\,it} = \mu_i +_i \pi^e_{t+12\,i,t-1} + \beta\prime_i \pi^T{}_{i,t} + \sum_{j=1}^{p-1} \lambda^*_{ij}\pi^e_{t+12\,i,t-j} + \sum_{j=0}^{q-1} \delta^*_{ij}\pi^T{}_{i,t-j} + \varepsilon_{\mathrm{it}} \qquad (4)$$

In the equations above; i=3, t=2001:1,. . . . . ..2008:8 and t=2008:10,. . . . .2014:1, ε_{it} is error correction term distributed independently between i and t. π^e_{t+12} denotes 12 months ahead inflation expectations, whereas π_t denotes past inflation rates, and π^T represents inflation targets. ϕ_i represents the error correction coefficient. Error correction coefficient ϕ_i, is a measure of the convergence rate of y_{it} towards the long-term equilibrium value following the change in x_{it}. If the condition $\phi_i < 0$ is met it can be mentioned that there is a long term relationship between variables.$\beta\prime_i$ denotes the long-term coefficients of the explanatory variables in the model, whereas λ_{ij},the short-term coefficient of 12 month ahead inflation expectations lags and δ_{ij} the short-term coefficients of the explanatory variables. The analyzes in this study were carried out with Gauss 20, Stata 11 and Eviews 10 econometrics programs.

Variables to be used in the panel ARDL model should be stationary utmost at first order. For this reason, before the analysis, "Im, Pesaran and Shin" panel unit root tests developed by Im et al. (2003) were used to determine the stationarity

Table 2: Unit Root Test Results

Variable	2002:1–2008:8				2008:10–2014:1	
	Level		First Difference		Level	
	Constant	Constant& Trend	Constant	Constant& Trend	Constant	Constant& Trend
π^e_{t+12}	-1.52***	-0.55	-6.14*	-6.76*	-1.90**	-3.0*
π_t	-1.74**	-1.73**			-2.10**	-2.35*
π^T	-1.41***	-			-5.06*	-1.45**

Note: *, **, *** indicate 1 %, 5 % and 10 % statistical significance levels, respectively.

of the variables. Unit root test results for 2002: 1–2008: 8 and 2008: 10–2014: 1 periods are presented in Table 2.

According to the results of the unit root test for 2002:1–2008:8 period, the 12-month-ahead inflation expectation variable (π^e_{t+12}) , could not be found stable at its level value but became stationary at first difference. Other variables were found stationary at their levels. According to the results of the unit root test for the period 2008:10–2014:1, all variables are stationary in their level values.

6 Findings

The sensitivity of inflation expectations to past inflation realizations and inflation targets provides important evidence about the degree of anchoring of inflation expectations. When the relationship between inflation expectations and inflation realizations weakens significantly, volatility in inflation expectations becomes dependent largely on confidence in the announced inflation targets. Besides, in cases where the announced inflation targets are not trusted inflation expectations become more volatile depending expectations about the future course of monetary policy (Levin et al. 2004: 3).

Findings obtained from PMG and MG estimators for the relationship between 12 month ahead inflation expectations and past inflation rates are presented in Table 3. First, the negative and significant error correction coefficients (φ) obtained from the models indicate the existence of a cointegration relationship between 12 month ahead inflation expectations and the past inflation rates in both periods. When the short term coefficients obtained from PMG and MG estimators are examined, it is seen that the coefficients of the past inflation rates (π_t) are statistically significant at 1 % in both periods. Accordingly, past inflation rates meaningfully affect 12 month ahead inflation expectations both pre-crisis

Table 3: The Effect of the Past Inflation Rates on the 12 Month Inflation Expectations: Results of PMG and MG Estimators

	2002:1–2008:8			**2008:10–2014:1**		
	PMG	**MG**	**H.Test Testi**	**PMG**	**MG**	**H.Test**
Long Term Coefficient						
π_t	-0.073*	-0.043	1.23	0.168*	0.192*	1.12
Error Correction Term						
φ	-0.464*	-0.817**		-0.829*	-0.808*	
Short Term Coefficients						
π_t	-0.034*	-0.018		0.139*	0.149*	
π^e_{t+12} (-1)	-0.037	0.185		0.071	0.050	
π^e_{t+12} (-2)	-0.026	0.111		0.000	0.000	
π_t	0.052***	0.047***		-0.130*	-0.138*	
π_t (-1)	-0.035	-0.024		-0.076**	-0.080	
π_t (-2)	0.00	0.000		0.000	0.000	
Sabit	0.212*	0.157		-0.002	-0.002	

Note: The optimal lag length was determined via Akaike information criterion. PMG estimates are calculated with back-substitution algorithm. (*) 1 %, (**) 5 % and (***) 10 % indicate significance levels. H Test: Hausman Test.

and crisis periods. Nevertheless, it is possible to say that the level of sensitivity of inflation expectations to past inflation rates increased during the crisis.

When the long-term coefficients obtained from PMG and MG estimators are analyzed, it is understood that the short-run relationship between the past inflation rates and 12-month ahead inflation expectations continues. As in the short term, the inflation rate coefficient (π_t) for the period 2008: 10–2014: 1 has received an absolutely high value than the pre-crisis period. As a result of the Hausman test conducted to test whether long-term parameters are homogeneous, the null hypothesis that assumes long-term homogeneity could not be rejected. Therefore, it has been decided that the PMG estimator, which is efficient and consistent under the long-term homogeneity assumption, is an appropriate estimator. Findings indicate that 12 month inflation expectations are more sensitive to inflation realizations in the crisis period.

Table 4: Effect of Inflation Targets on 12 Month Ahead Inflation Expectations: Results of PMG and MG Estimators

	2002:1–2008:8			2008:10–2014:1		
	PMG	**MG**	**H. Test**	**PMG**	**MG**	**H. Test**
Long Term Coefficient						
π^T	-0.046*	-0.049*	0.12	-0.032**	-0.037*	1.32
Error Correction Term						
φ	-0.382*	-0.408*		-0.876*	-0.875*	
Short Term Coefficients						
π^T	-0.018*	-0.020*		-0.028*	-0.030*	
π^e_{t+12} (-1)	0.142*	0.157*		0.040	0.040	
π^e_{t+12} (-2)	0.000	0.000		0.076	0.077	
π^T	-0.014	-0.014		-0.003	-0.002	
π^T (-1)	-0.026	-0.026		0.022	0.023	
π^T (-2)	0.000	0.000		0.049	0.049	
Constant	0.004	0.023		-0.008	-0.003	

Note: The optimal lag length was determined via Akaike information criterion. PMG estimates are calculated with back-substitution algorithm. (*) 1 %, (**) 5 % and (***) 10 % indicate significance levels. H Test: Hausman Test.

The results of from PMG and MG estimators for short and long term relationships between 12-month ahead inflation expectations and inflation targets are summarized in Table 4.

First of all, error correction terms (φ) that are negative and statistically significant at 1 % level in both periods indicate that there is a cointegration relationship between inflation targets and 12-month ahead inflation expectations. When the short-term coefficients obtained from PMG and MG estimators, it is seen that the coefficients for inflation targets (π^T) are statistically significant in both periods. Accordingly, inflation targets in the short term have an impact on 12-month ahead inflation expectations in both pre-crisis and crisis periods. However, when compared with the effect of past inflation rates on expectations, the effect of inflation targets on expectations seems very limited. On the other hand, the long-term coefficient of inflation targets may provide clearer evidence for the degree of anchoring of expectations. Long term inflation target coefficients (π^T) obtained from PMG and MG estimators are statistically significant at 1 % in both periods. Accordingly, the announced inflation targets affect the inflation

Table 5: Effect of the Inflation Rates on the 12 Months Ahead Inflation Expectations: Diagnostic Test Results

2002:1–2008:8								
	PMG				**MG**			
	χ^2_{SC}	χ^2_{HE}	$\bar{R}^2$	LL	χ^2_{SC}	χ^2_{HE}	$\bar{R}^2$	LL
Turkey	0.85	0.83	0.40	-54.64	0.35	0.80	0.40	-54.37
Chile	3.15	7.99	0.19	13.90	3.89	1.47	0.41	25.97
Brazil	3.55	0.17	0.54	-37.66	1.80	0.08	0.55	-37.29
2008:10–2014:1								
	PMG				**MG**			
	χ^2_{SC}	χ^2_{HE}	$\bar{R}^2$	LL	χ^2_{SC}	χ^2_{HE}	$\bar{R}^2$	LL
Turkey	0.38	10.92	0.45	23.22	0.68	10.82	0.45	23.27
Chile	5.85	9.04	0.41	34.64	6.10	9.58	0.41	34.65
Brazil	0.96	30.38	0.26	47.17	0.55	27.63	0.27	47.74

Note: χ^2_{SC}:Breusch –Godfrey auto-correlation test statistics,χ^2_{HE}:White heteroscedasticity test statistics, $\bar{R}^2$:Corrected R^2, LL: logLikelihood.

expectations in the long run. However, although the long-term coefficients of inflation targets do not differ significantly in size as of 2002: 1–2008: 8 and 2008: 10–2014: 1, anchoring effect of inflation targets on expectations are appears to weaken as of 2008: 10–2014: 1 $(\pi^T_{2002:1-2008:8} > \pi^T_{2008:8-2014:1})$. The null hypothesis that assumes long-term homogeneity was not rejected as a result of the Hausman Test. In this case, it was decided that the PGM estimator is an appropriate estimator.

Diagnostic test results for the models are shown in Tables 5 and 6. According to the results, autocorrelation and heteroscedasticity problems were not found in individual equations.

7 Conclusion

In this study, it was questioned whether inflation targeting could maintain the degree of anchoring of inflation expectations during the periods of macroeconomic crisis, and therefore, it could gain monetary policy ability to act flexibly while applying measures for the crisis thanks to well-anchored inflation expectations. For this purpose, the long and short-run dynamic relations between 12 month ahead inflation expectations and past term inflation ratios and inflation targets were analyzed for a group of the country which represents fragile economies during 2002:1–2008:8 and 2008:10–2014:1 periods using the

Table 6: Effect of the Inflation Targets on the 12 Months Ahead Inflation Expectations: Diagnostic Test Results

2002:1–2008:8								
	PMG				**MG**			
	χ^2_{SC}	χ^2_{HE}	$\bar{R}^2$	LL	χ^2_{SC}	χ^2_{HE}	$\bar{R}^2$	LL
Turkey	6.89	2.01	0.20	-44.38	6.97	2.36	0.20	-44.09
Chile	0.48	1.06	0.19	-3.04	0.15	0.85	0.21	-2.26
Brazil	1.44	5.47	0.04	-42.19	1.85	4.91	0.04	-42.06
2008:10–2014:01								
	PMG				**MG**			
	χ^2_{SC}	χ^2_{HE}	$\bar{R}^2$	LL	χ^2_{SC}	χ^2_{HE}	$\bar{R}^2$	LL
Turkey	1.86	0.11	0.42	49.18	1.87	0.13	0.42	49.18
Chile	0.09	3.86	0.38	57.87	0.10	3.84	0.38	57.89
Brazil	3.89	0.02	0.35	54.14	3.70	3.84	0.35	54.17

Note: χ^2_{SC}:Breusch –Godfrey auto-correlation test statistics,χ^2_{HE}:White heteroscedasticity test statistics, $\bar{R}^2$:Corrected R^2, LL: logLikelihood.

panel ARDL method. By measuring the change in the sensitivity level of inflation expectations to past inflation rates and inflation targets between the pre-crisis period and crisis period, it was questioned whether the anchoring degree of inflation expectation deteriorated in the crisis period. Thus, it was evaluated whether the inflation targeting system in fragile economies gains the flexibility to central banks to fight against the crisis without disturbing the inflation expectations thanks to its ability to anchor inflation expectations.

Negative and statistically significant error correction terms obtained from panel ARDL models indicate that there is a cointegration relationship between 12 month ahead inflation expectations and past term inflation ratios and inflation targets. However, estimated long and short-run coefficients reveal that the dynamic relationships among the variables change across the pre-crisis and crisis periods. Accordingly, it is understood that during the crisis period, the sensitivity of the 12 month ahead inflation expectations to past inflation rates has increased and whereas the sensitivity to inflation targets has decreased significantly. This result indicates that in the countries sample representing fragile economies, inflation expectations were formed based on past inflation rates rather than inflation targets. When the findings obtained from PMG and MG estimators are evaluated together, it was concluded that inflation targeting in the period of 2008: 10–2014: 1 failed to anchor the 12 month ahead inflation expectations. Accordingly, it seems hard for the central bank to use the monetary policy flexibly in order to eliminate the effects of the crisis on the real economy without disrupting inflation expectations.

The fact that inflation expectations moved apart from the targets, as of the crisis period indicates that there is a strong credibility gap regarding the inflation targets in the countries. The lack of confidence in monetary policy prevents the announced inflation targets from acting as an anchor for inflation expectations. In this context, the problem of the credibility gap needs to be eliminated in order to combat short-term real instabilities flexibly and effectively by anchoring inflation expectations to announced inflation targets. Overshooting inflation targets continuously is the main reason for the credibility gap. For this reason, the first step in the credibility facility should be to make realistic revisions of unreachable targets. Then inflation targets should be supported by a strong commitment. The monetary policies required to achieve inflation targets in line with the commitment made should be implemented with the support of an effective communication strategy including greater transparency and accountability.

References

Baskaya, Y. S., Gulsen, E., & Orak, M. (2010). 2008 Hedef Revizyonu Öncesi ve Sonrasında Enflasyon Beklentileri, TCMB Ekonomi Notları, 2010–1, 1–6.

Bernanke, B. S., Laubach, T., Mishkin, F. S., & Posen, A. S.(1999). Inflation Targeting: Lessons from the International Experience. Princeton University Press: Princeton, New Jersey.Bevilaqua, A. S., Mesquita, M., & Minella, A. (2007). Brazil: Taming Inflation Expectations, Central Bank of Brazil Working Paper Series, 129, 1–39.

Binal Yılmaz, C. (2012). Türkiye'de Enflasyon Beklentilerini Belirleyen Makroekonomik Unsurlar, Yayımlanmamış Uzmanlık Tezi, Türkiye Cumhuriyet Merkez Bankası.

Castelnuovo, E., Nicoletti Altimari, S., & Rodriguez-Palenzuela, D. (2003). Definition of Price Stability, Range and Point Inflation Targets: The Anchoring of Long-Term Inflation Expectations, ECB Working Papers, 273, 1–51.

Cerisola, M., & Gelos, R. G. (2009). What Drives Inflation Expectations in Brazil? An Emprical Analysis. Applied Economics, 41, 1215–1227.

Clark, T. E., & Davig, T. (2008). An Emprical Assesment of the Relationship Among Inflation and Short and Long Term Expectations, The Federal Reserve Bank of Kansas City Working Papers, 05, 1–48.

Clark, T. E., & Nakata, T. (2008). Has the Behavior of Inflation and Long-Term Inflation Expectations Changed?. Economic Review, 93(1), 17–49.

Erdem, E., Guloglu, B., & Nazlioglu, S. (2010). The Macroeconomy and Turkish Agricultural Trade Balance with the EU Countries: Panel ARDL Analysis. International Journal of Economic Perspectives, 4(1), 371–79.

Galindo, L. M., & Ros, G. (2009). Alternatives to Inflation Targeting in Mexico, in Gerald A. Epstein & A. Erinç Yeldan (Ed.), Beyond Inflation Targeting: Assessing the Impacts and Policy Alternatives, içinde (pp. 158–178). USA: Edward Elgar Publishing.

Im, K. S., Paseran, M. H., & Shin, Y. (2003). Testing for Unit Roots in Heterogeneous Panels. Journal of Econometrics, 115, 53–74.

Kim, S., & Park, Y. C. (2006). Inflation Targeting in Korea: A Model of Success?. BIS Papers, 31, 140–164.

King, M. (1997). Changes in UK Monetary Policy: Rules and Discretion in Practice. Journal of Monetary Economics, 39, 81–97.

King, M. (1999). Challenges for Monetary Policy: New and Old, 1–57, http://www.kansascityfed.org/publicat/sympos/1999/s99king.pdf (12.3.2011).

Kohn, D. L. (2005). Comment on Marvin Goodfriend's Inflation Targeting in United States?, in B. S. Bernanke & M. Woodford (Eds.), The Inflation Targeting Debate (Vol. 32, pp. 337–350). Chicago ve London: University of Chicago Press.

Kuttner, K. N., & Posen, A. S. (2011). How Flexible Can Inflation Targeting Be and Still Work, Peterson Institute for International Economics Working Papers, 11–15, 1–32.

Lee, K. C. (1994). Formation of Price and Cost Inflation Expectations in British Manufacturing Industries: A Multi-sectoral Analysis. The Economic Journal, 204(423), 372–385.

Levin, A. T., Natalucci, F. M., & Piger, J. M. (2004). The Macroeconomic Effects of Inflation Targeting. Review-Federal Reserve Bank of Saint Louis, 86(4), 51–8.

Al Mamun, M., Sohog, K., & Akhter, A. (2013). A Dynamic Panel Analysis of the Financial Determinants of CSR in Bangladeshi Banking Industry. Asian Economic and Financial Review, 3(5), 560–578.

Pesaran, M. H., Shin, Y., & Smith, R. P. (1999). Pooled Mean Group Estimation of Dynamic Heterogeneous Panels. Journal of the American Statistical Association, 94(446), 621–634.

Pétursson, T. G. (2004). Formulation of Inflation Targeting Around the World. Monetary Bulletin 2004/1, 57–84.

Siklos, P. L. (2010). Inflation Targeting: It's Not Broke, It Doesn't Need Fixing, But Can It Survive?. Journal of International Commerce, Economics and Policy, 1(1), 59–80.

Svensson, L. E. O. (1997). Inflation Forecast Targeting: Implementing and Monitoring Inflation Targets. European Economic Review, 41, 1111–1146.

Svensson, L. E. O. (1999). Inflation Targeting as a Monetary Policy Rule. Journal of Monetary Economics, 43(3), 607–654.

Valdés, R.(2007). Inflation Targeting in Chile: Experience and Selected Issues, Economic Policy Papers, 22, 1–23.Walsh, C. E.(2008). Inflation Targeting: What have We Learned?, Prepared for International Experience with the Conduct of Monetary Policy under Inflation Targeting, Bank of Canada, July 22–23.

Wimanda, R. E., Turner, P. M., & Hall, M. J. (2011). Expectations and the Inertia of Inflation: The Case of Indonesia. Journal of Policy Modelling, 33, 426–438.

Salih Türedi & Vildan Yavuz

Remittances and Economic Growth: A Causality Analysis for Turkey

1 Introduction

In order to achieve economic growth, countries need to translate their sources into investments in productive fields. However, it might sometimes not be possible to create these sources through domestic savings and, thus, many countries have to apply to external sources. From this aspect, as stated by Barajas et al. (2010), the remittances have become a non-ignorable external funding source for developing countries in achieving the sustainable growth thanks to the advantages they offer such as not creating repayment obligation as foreign debts do, as well as the stability it offers. According to the estimations of the World Bank, the remittances in developing countries increased from 28.6 Billion USD in 1990 to 74.7 Billion USD in 2000 and 526 Billion USD in year 2018. Thus, approx. 18 folds increase in the remittances in the last 30 years drew the attention of economists and the macroeconomic outcomes of the remittances became one of the most discussed subjects especially in the recent period. The relationship between remittances and economic growth is widely discussed in the literature from this aspect.

In the theoretical literature, there are two prominent opinions about the relationship between these variables. According to the first one, the remittances create positive effects on economic growth by increasing the consumption, savings, and investments (Dridi et al., 2019: 7). Within this context, the remittances that are an additional income for the households in the recipient country contribute to the improvement of the level of welfare by reducing the income inequality and, consequently, the poverty. On the other hand, through the positive multiplier effect they create by increasing the consumption expenses that are an important component of total demand in the economy, they support the total demand and economic growth (Gupta et al., 2009: 105; Ratha, 2003: 164; Eggoh et al., 2019: 2). Besides that, the remittances (if stable and at a significant level) increase the level of savings, besides the consumption, and create an important source for funding the investments, which are one of the main determinants of growth (Barajas et al., 2009: 5; Yiheyis and Woldemariam, 2016: 247). This positive effect of remittances on economic growth is stronger in countries, in which the financial system is not developed enough, because both the financial system cannot fulfill its role as an intermediary and the access to the credits is limited due to the lack of savings and capital accumulation. From this aspect, the remittances reduce the credit constraints, accelerate the investments, and contribute to the economic growth (Lartey, 2013: 1039; Abbas, 2019: 93; Jongwanich, 2007: 5–6).

According to the second opinion, the effect of remittances on economic growth is negative. In theoretical literature, this negative effect is explained with "*Moral Hazard*" and "*Dutch Disease*" arguments. According to the Moral Hazard argument, the remittances, which are considered as a non-labor income, might encourage households in the recipient country to work less and to demand more leisure time (Sutradhar, 2020: 276). It might undermine the economic growth by reducing the efforts to join the labor market and labor supply in the recipient country (Chami et al., 2008: 60). Finally, sustained and significant remittances negatively affect the economy by creating a situation like Dutch Disease. According to this argument, the increase in disposable income due to the increase in remittances causes an increase in demand/price of non-commercial goods. This process resulting in the appreciation of the national currency and, consequently, increase in the real exchange rate negatively affect the growth by reducing the export performance of the recipient country (Catrinescu et al., 2009: 82; Ahortor and Adenutsi, 2009: 3277; Muratoğlu, 2017: 461).

In the present study, the long-term causality relationship between remittances and economic growth was investigated. For this purpose, the time-series data of Turkey for the period between 1974 and 2018 were used. As a result of the empirical analysis, the evidences indicating that there is a significant and one-way causality relationship from remittances to economic growth in Turkey were obtained. Thus, it can be stated that remittances might play an important role as an external funding source in establishing the sustainable economic growth in Turkey.

2 Literature Review

The "Relationship between Remittances and Economic Growth" is an important and actual subject investigated not only in theoretical researches but also in empirical studies. In empirical studies carried out in different countries and different periods by using econometric methods, it can be stated that the evidences indicating that this relationship can be positive, negative, or insignificant depending on the level of financial development and institutional infrastructure in recipient countries, as well as on how these incomes were used. For instance, using the panel co-integration test, Ramirez and Sharma (2008) estimated that remittances positively affected the economic growth in Latin America and Caribbean countries. Stating that there is no consensus in the literature about the effect of remittances on the growth, Catrinescu et al. (2009) emphasized in a panel data analysis for 162 countries that the remittances created positive effects on the economic growth but this effect was stronger in countries having high-quality political and economic policies and institutions. In their VAR-VECM analysis carried out on Bangladesh by using time-series data for the period of 1976–2005, Ahmed and Uddin (2009) found a one-way causality relationship from remittances to economic growth. Stating that remittances are an important external financing source for developing countries, Bjuggren et al. (2010) determined in an analysis of 79 developing countries that remittances accelerated the growth via investments. According to the results of Granger's causality test conducted on Bangladesh, India, and Sri Lanka, Siddique et al. (2012) reported that there was no significant relationship between these variables in India. Researchers also reported a one-way causality relationship from remittances to economic growth for Bangladesh and a two-way causality relationship between the variables for Sri Lanka. Investigating the causality relationship between remittances and growth in Tunisia, Jouini (2015) reported a two-way causality relationship between the variables in the short-term and one-way causality relationship from remittances to economic growth in the long-term. Emphasizing that the remittances are important for the countries having insufficient savings, Karamelikli and Bayar (2015) used ARDL test and determined that remittances have a positive effect on growth in Turkey. Stating that remittances affect the growth through consumption, savings, and investments, Meyer and Shera (2016) carried out an analysis on 6 countries having a high-level of remittance (Albania, Bulgaria, Macedonia, Moldova, Romania, and Bosnia Herzegovina) and reported that remittances contributed to the economic growth in these countries. In GMM estimation using the data of 1980–2012 for 4 MENA countries (Tunisia, Morocco, Algeria, and Egypt), Zghidi et al. (2018) found a positive relationship between remittances and growth. In another study, in which the GMM method was used, Eggoh et al. (2019) determined that remittances increased the growth in 49 developing countries. Abduvaliev and Bustillo (2019) reported that 1 % increase in remittances increased the economic growth by 0.25 % and reduced the poverty by 2 % in the Commonwealth of Independent States.

In their study on 13 Latin America and Caribbean countries, Amuedo and Pozo (2004) revealed that remittances had a negative effect on export industries by decreasing the competitive power of these countries. In their panel data analysis on 113 countries, Chami et al. (2005) reported that there was a negative correlation between remittances and economic growth and, consequently, the remittances did not contribute to the economic growth. As a result of their study on 84 countries by using the annual data for the period 1970–2004, Barajas et al. (2009) showed that remittances had no significant effect on economic growth. Thus, the researchers suggested that other policies should be implemented instead of increasing the remittances in order to increase the growth. In a regression analysis on Turkey by using data of the period between 1970 and 2005, Karagöz (2009) showed that the remittances had a negative and significant effect on the economic growth. In a time-series analysis carried out on Bangladesh, Ahmed (2010) reported that the remittances negatively affected the growth. Kaphle (2018) tested the short- and long-term relationships between remittances and economic growth in Nepal by using time-series methods such as co-integration and error-correction model. According to the results obtained, there was no significant short-term relationship between these variables, whereas there was a significant relationship in the long-term. Using a balanced panel data series for 1977–2016, Sutradhar (2020) investigated the effect of remittances on economic growth in 4 South Asian countries. According to the results, the remittances affected the growth positively in India and negatively in Bangladesh, Pakistan, and Sri Lanka.

3 Dataset and Descriptive Statistics

In the present study examining the causality relationship between remittances and economic growth, the annual data of Turkey for the period between 1974 and 2018 were used. In the estimation models, [GDPpc: Gross Domestic Product per capita] refers to the economic growth and [REM] refers to the remittances. Calculated using the prices of year 2010 in USD, [GDPpc] variable was obtained from the World Bank's World Development Indicators [WDI] database. Moreover, [REM] variable obtained from [WDI] database and the Electronic Data Distribution System of the Central Bank of the Republic of Turkey was realized using GDP deflator (2010=100). The variables were used with logarithmic values in the analysis. The descriptive statistics of the variables are presented in Table 1.

It can be seen that the mean remittance in Turkey for the period between 1974 and 2018 was $2.940 Billion. The year with the lowest remittance was 2018 with $0.329 Billion, whereas the highest remittance value was achieved in 1988 with $6.838 Billion. Mean GDPpc in Turkey was calculated to be $8281. The lowest GDPpc value was achieved in 1974 with $4744.4, whereas the highest value was found to be $15069 in 2018. According to the results of the Jarque-Bera normality test, the (J-B) test statistic was found to be [5.3238] for GDPpc and [2.6284] for

REM. The test statistics < 5.99 (or p-values > 0.05) indicate that both series have a normal distribution.

Table 1. Descriptive Statistics (1974–2018)

Variables	**GDPpc [year]**	**REM [year]**
Mean	8281	2.940
Maximum	15069 [2018]	6.838 [1988]
Minimum	4744.4 [1974]	0.329 [2018]
Jarque-Bera (J-B) test statistic	5.3238	2.6284
J-B (p-value)	0.0698	0.2686
Number of observations	45	45

4 Econometric Methodology and Findings

In econometric analyzes, if the variables contain unit-root should be examined primarily in order to achieve reliable findings. For this purpose, it was first investigated if the LGDPpc and LREM variables were stable by using (ADF), (PP), and (DF-GLS) tests. In this test, which was conducted using the level values of variables, it was determined that both variables were non-stationary. Then, by taking the first differences of variables, the tests were repeated. The null hypothesis that the series include unit root was rejected and it was determined that both series were stationary at the first difference. Thus, it was found that $[d_{max} = 1]$ for LGDPpc and LREM.

Table 2. The Results of Unit-Root Tests

Variables	**ADF**	**PP**	**DF-GLS**
LGDPpc	-1.9268	-1.9958	-1.9345
LREM	-2.3441	-1.1967	-2.4654
ΔLGDPpc	-4.9595***	-6.5670***	-4.3480***
ΔLREM	-4.5338***	-5.4605***	-4.1533***

Notes: The constant-trend model was used in the tests. *** refers to statistical significance at 1 %.

4.1. Toda-Yamamoto and Bootstrap Toda-Yamamoto Causality Tests

Toda-Yamamoto [TY] causality test is a test that can be conducted regardless if the series are stationary or co-integrated. In the first step of the test, the unit root tests are used for determining the variables' maximum degree of integration

[d_{max}]. Then, the optimal lag (p) of VAR model is determined. In the final step, a VAR model at (p+d_{max}) degree is estimated. The first (p) of calculated coefficients is subjected to MWALD test. The null hypothesis that the independent variable coefficients are equal to zero in MWALD test with asymptotic χ^2 distribution was tested against an alternative hypothesis stating that the coefficients are not equal to zero. If it is found that the coefficients are not equal to zero, then the null hypothesis is rejected and it is accepted that there is causality between the variables (Kónya, 2004: 84; Zombe et al., 2017: 174–175; Michael and Emmanuel, 2016: 76). The same procedure is applied with Bootstrap [TY] test recommended by Hacker and Hatemi-J (2006). On the other hand, Hacker and Hatemi-J (2006) reported that having an ARCH error process in asymptotic standard χ^2 distribution yields greater distortions but these distortions are not significant while using bootstrap distribution (Hacker and Hatemi-J, 2006: 1499). Thus, emphasizing that the [TY] test would not provide reliable results in presence of above mentioned problems, Hacker and Hatemi-J (2006) recommended using MWALD test, which has bootstrap distribution, instead of asymptotic χ^2 distribution (Tülümce and Zeren, 2017: 304). In the present study, besides the standard [TY] test, also the Bootstrap [TY] test was applied in order to achieve more robust findings.

In [TY] causality test, after determining the optimal lag length (p=3) for models (1) and (2) as seen in Table 3, VAR(4) model was estimated using SUR model according to the principle of VAR (p+d_{max}). As seen in Table 4, it was found that the calculated MWALD χ^2 test statistic was statistically significant for Model (1) at 10 % but insignificant for Model (2). This finding empirically suggests the presence of one-way and significant causality relationship from remittances to economic growth.

Table 3. Optimal Lag Lenght of the VAR Model

Lags	LR	FPE	AIC	SIC	HQ
0	NA	0.025423	2.0036	2.0880	2.0341
1	204.2261	0.000125	-3.3159	**-3.0626***	**-3.2243***
2	4.0929	0.000136	-3.2329	-2.8107	-3.0802
3	**9.8427***	**0.000123***	**-3.3311***	-2.7400	-3.1174
4	2.0411	0.000142	-3.1970	-2.4370	-2.9222
5	5.2195	0.000147	-3.1770	-2.2481	-2.8411

* indicates optimal lag lenght.

Table 4. The Results of Toda-Yamamoto [TY] Test

Models	χ^2 statistic		Result
Model (1): LGDPpc = f(LREM) [H_0: LREM does not Granger cause LGDPpc]	**7.378** [0.0608]*	H_0 Reject	LREM → LGDPpc
Model (2): LREM = f(LGDPpc) [H_0: LGDPpc does not Granger cause LREM]	3.630 [0.3042]	H_0 Accept	

Notes: [] refers to the probability values of test statistics and * refers to statistical significance at 10 % levels.

The results of bootstrap [TY] test are presented in Table 5. It can be seen that MWALD χ^2 test statistic was higher than bootstrap critical values for Model (1) at the level of 5 % but lower than bootstrap critical values for Model (2). For this reason, the null hypothesis was rejected for Model (1) but could not be rejected for Model (2). In conclusion, in corroboration with the results of [TY] test, the results of bootstrap [TY] test showed the presence of a statistically significant one-way causality from remittances to economic growth.

Table 5. The Results of Bootstrap Toda-Yamamoto [TY] Test

		Bootstrap Critical Values				
Models	**χ^2 statistic**	**1 %**	**5 %**	**10 %**		**Result**
Model (1): LGDPpc = f(LREM)] [H_0: LREM does not Granger cause LGDPpc]	**4.593****	7.41	4.15	2.83	H_0 Reject	LREM → LGDPpc
Model (2): LREM = f(LGDPpc) [H_0: LGDPpc does not Granger cause LREM]	1.129	7.58	4.13	2.84	H_0 Accept	

Notes: Optimal lag length was calculated using HJC criterion. ** refers to statistical significance at 5 %. The number of bootstraps is 10.000.

5 Conclusion

In theoretical and empirical literature, there are many studies investigating the relationship between remittances and economic growth. In these studies, it can be seen that different findings were achieved and there is still no consensus on this subject. The present study aims to reveal which type of relationship there is between remittances and economic growth by providing new evidences. Within this context, by using the time-series data of Turkey for the period between 1974 and 2018, the Toda-Yamamoto and Bootstrap Toda-Yamamoto causality tests were conducted. The empirical findings yielded evidences proving the presence of one-way significant relationship from remittances to economic growth. Considering that the remittances increase the level of welfare by increasing the consumption and accelerate the economic growth by expanding the access to credit opportunities in countries with a lack of savings and capital accumulation, it can be stated that remittances might play an important role in Turkey's growth process. From this aspect, for the macroeconomic policymakers in Turkey, it might be recommended to develop policies aiming to increase the level of remittances and canalizing these revenues to productive areas.

References

Abbas, S. (2019). Workers' Remittances and Domestic Investment in South Asia: A Comparative Econometric Inquiry. International Migration, 57(5), 89–104.

Abduvaliev, M. & Bustillo, R. (2019). Impact of Remittances on Economic Growth and Poverty Reduction amongst CIS Countries. Post-Communist Economies, 1–22.

Ahmed, A. H. & Uddin, S. G. (2009). Export, Imports, Remittance and Growth in Bangladesh: An Empirical Analysis. Trade and Development Review, 2(2), 79–92.

Ahmed, S. (2010). Migrant Workers Remittance and Economic Growth: Evidence from Bangladesh. ASA University Review, 4(1), 1–13.

Ahortor, K. R. C. & Adenutsi, E. D. (2009). The Impact of Remittances on Economic Growth in Small-Open Developing Economies. Journal of Applied Sciences, 9(18), 3275–3286.

Amuedo, D. C. & Pozo, S. (2004). Workers' Remittances and the Real Exchange Rate: A Paradox of Gifts. World Development, 32(8), 1407–1417.

Barajas, A., Chami, R., Hakura, S. D. & Montiel, P. (2010). Workers' Remittances and the Equilibrium Real Exchange Rate: Theory and Evidence, IMF Working Paper 10/287, 1–42.

Barajas, A., Gapen, M. T., Chami, R., Montiel, P. ve Fullenkamp, C. (2009). Do workers' remittances promote economic growth?, IMF Working Paper, No:153.

Bjuggren, P., Dzansi, J. ve Shukur, G. (2010). Remittances and investment. In CESIS Electronic Working Paper Series, No. 216.

Catrinescu, N., Ledesma, L. M., Piracha, M. & Quillin, B. (2009). Remittances, Institutions, and Economic Growth. World Development, 37(1), 81–92.

Chami, R., Barajas, A., Cosimano, T., Fullenkamp, C., Gapen, M. & Montiel, P. (2008). Macroeconomic Consequences of Remittances, IMF Occasional Paper 259, 1–84.

Chami, R., Fullenkamp, C. ve Jahjah, S. (2005). Are Immigrant Remittance Flows a Source of Capital for Development?, IMF Staff Papers, 52(1), 55–81.

Dridi, J., Gürsoy, T., Saiz, P. H. & Bari, M. (2019). The Impact of Remittances on Economic Activity: The Importance of Sectoral Linkages, IMF Working Paper 19/175, 1–37.

Eggoh, J., Bangake, C. ve Semedo, G. (2019). Do Remittances Spur Economic Growth? Evidence from Developing Countries. The Journal of International Trade & Economic Development, 28(4), 391–418.

Gupta, S., Pattillo, A. C. & Wagh, S. (2009). Effect of Remittances on Poverty and Financial Development in Sub-Saharan Africa. World Development, 37(1), 104–115.

Hacker, S. R. & Hatemi-J. A. (2006). Tests for Causality between Integrated Variables Using Asymptotic and Bootstrap Distributions: Theory and Application. Applied Economics, 38(13), 1489–1500.

Jongwanich, J. (2007). Workers' Remittances, Economic Growth and Poverty in Developing Asia and the Pacific Countries, UNESCAP Working Paper 01, 1–20.

Jouini, J. (2015). Economic Growth and Remittances in Tunisia: Bi-directional Causal Links. Journal of Policy Modeling, 37, 355–373.

Kaphle, R. R. (2018). Relationship between Remittance and Economic Growth in Nepal. Tribhuvan University Journal, 32(2), 249–266.

Karagöz, K. (2009). Workers' Remittances and Economic Growth: Evidence from Turkey. Journal of Yasar University, 4(13), 1891–1908.

Karamelikli, H. & Bayar, Y. (2015). Remittances and Economic Growth in Turkey. Ecoforum, 4(2), 33–40.

Kónya, L. (2004). Unit-Root, Cointegration and Granger Causality Test Results for Export and Growth in OECD Countries. International Journal of Applied Econometrics and Quantitative Studies, 1(2), 67–94.

Lartey, K. K. E. (2013). Remittances, Investment and Growth in Sub-Saharan Africa. The Journal of International Trade & Economic Development: An International and Comparative Review, 22(7), 1038–1058.

Meyer, D. ve Shera, A. (2016). The Impact of Remittances on Economic Growth: An Econometric Model. Economia, 18(2), 147–155.

Michael, O. E. & Emmanuel, N. (2016). Granger Causality between Private Domestic Savings and Economic Growth in Nigeria: Toda-Yamamoto Approach. Journal of Economics and Sustainable Development, 7(24), 71–79.

Muratoglu, G. (2017). Economic Impacts of Workers' Remittances: The Case of Latin America, In İ. Şiriner, A. Ş. Koç & H. Yıldız (Eds.), Current Debates in Economics & Econometrics (Vol. 1, pp. 457–480) London: United Kingdom.

Ramirez, M. D. ve Sharma, H. (2008). Remittances and Growth in Latin America: A Panel Unit Root and Panel Cointegration Analysis. Working Papers, 51, Yale University, Department of Economics.

Ratha, D. (2003). Workers' Remittances: An Important and Stable Source of External Development Finance, Global Development Finance, World Bank, 157–175.

Siddique, A., Selvanathan, A. E. & Selvanathan S. (2012). Remittances and Economic Growth: Empirical Evidence from Bangladesh, India and Sri Lanka. Journal of Development Studies, 48(8), 1045–1062.

Sutradhar, R. S. (2020). The Impact of Remittances on Economic Growth in Bangladesh, India, Pakistan and Sri Lanka. International Journal of Economic Policy Studies, 14, 275–295.

Tülümce, Y. S. & Zeren, F. (2017). Türkiye'de Kamu Harcamaları ve Ekonomik Büyüme Arasındaki İlişkinin Asimetrik Nedensellik Testi ile Analizi. Uluslararası Yönetim İktisat ve İşletme Dergisi, 13(2), 299–310.

World Bank. Available at: https://www.worldbank.org/en/topic/migration-remittances diaspora issues/brief/ migration-remittances-data (30.03.2020).

Yiheyis, Z. & Woldemariam, K. (2016). The Effect of Remittances on Domestic Capital Formation in Selected African Countries: A Comparative Empirical Analysis. Journal of International Development, 28, 243–265.

Zghidi, N. Sghaier, I. M. ve Abida, Z. (2018). Remittances, Institutions, and Economic Growth in North African Countries. Journal of the Knowledge Economy, 9(3), 804–821.

Zombe, C., Daka, L., Phiri, C., Kaonga, O., Chibwe, F. & Seshamani, V. (2017). Investigating the Causal Relationship between Inflation and Trade Openness Using Toda–Yamamoto Approach: Evidence from Zambia. Mediterranean Journal of Social Sciences, 8(6), 171–182.

Şerif Canbay & Derya Mercan

Implementation and Functioning of the Interest Rate Corridor (IRC)

1 Introduction

Capital flows to developing countries was gaining momentum and liberating their financial markets in the 1990s, immediately after the financial liberalization that began in the 1980s, together with the changes in the structure of capital flows. During this process, capital flows to developing countries have become short-term, and capital movements pursuing speculative profits have gained considerable importance. Similarly, the same years have been the years of intensive capital movements also in Turkey. While some of these increased capital movements were the direct capital movements, the more significant part was speculative, and short-term capital flows based on a fixed exchange rate with high real interest. However, developing countries, which provided the necessary financing for economic growth through the international flow of capital in this process, experienced serious financial crises since they could not take measures to slow down the sudden inflows and outflows of capital into the market. In the 1990s and early 2000s, in which globalization was expanding rapidly, these sudden inflows and outflows of capital movements caused the financial crises, especially in East Asia, East-Central Europe and Latin America. The increase in financial actors and the inevitable financial crises that occur during this process also leads to a financial crisis that can cause global instability. After the 2000s, the central banks of some countries that have this kind of experience considered it necessary to take some measures and began to pay more attention to monetary policies by focusing on the goal of price stability, together with financial stability.

The central banks of some countries, including the Central Bank of the Republic of Turkey (CBRT), which reacted against the economic crisis that began in the United States in 2008 and then became global, have had to implement alternative monetary policy instruments that are different from previous customary practices. Immediately after the 2000s, the central banks of some countries have included especially the overnight interest rates among the monetary policy instruments (Whitesell, 2006, 1177–1178). The interest rate corridor (IRC) is one of the instruments recently included in the monetary policy instruments implemented to guide the total demand by controlling short-term interest rates under the control of the central bank. The application of the IRC has been one of the alternative instruments implemented to reach both price and financial stability with regard to monetary policies.

Many central banks have implemented an IRC system, even at least temporarily, especially during the 2008 financial crisis (Bernhardsen and Kloster, 2010:1). Some of the central banks that implemented the IRC system include Australia, Canada, New Zealand and the European Central Bank (ECB) (Berentsen and Monnet, 2008:3). As of the end of 2010, the CBRT has included the IRC within the monetary policy instruments for financial stability.

2 Definition of the Interest Rate Corridor

Controlling and directing the relationship between short-term interest rates and bank interest rates known as the traditional interest rate channel is an essential tool among the monetary policy channels, determined and implemented by the central banks, which affect the economy. The extent to which these short-term interest rate changes are reflected in banks' credit and deposit interest rates may be decisive in the effect of monetary policy on aggregate demand to control changes in the short-term interest rates in the economy since ensuring interest rate stability is among the critical monetary policy objectives of the central banks (Binici et al., 2016:2).

Capital flows from developed countries to emerging market economies were in question because of monetary easing, more liquidity and undetermined status for all economies. This situation leads to fluctuations in exchange rates and credit growth in developing country economies. To reduce risks arising from global imbalances, central banks implement new tools to intervene in the markets combining macro-financial as an additional goal of financial stability. For this purpose, one of the new tools evolved within the context of this is the interest rate corridor (IRC). It consists of a margin between the overnight lending rates and deposit rates of the central bank. The IRC system guides the short term market interest rates towards the central bank policy rate. IRC system is different from the traditional inflation targeting regime. The interest rate corridor is symmetric and narrow in the traditional system. It just enables the short term interest rates to be close to the official rate. The corridor is a passive tool in this system. Bu oppositely in the IRC system, the corridor is an asymmetric and wideband, so can be actively used as a monetary tool (Binici et al., 2013:2).

The distance between the ceiling and floor set for the interest corridor is also the difference between the credit and deposit interest of the country implementing the system. When we look at the countries implementing this

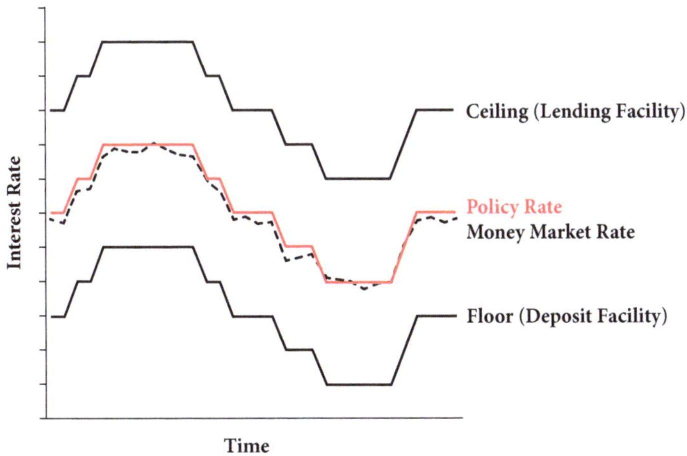

Figure 1: Stylised Interest Rate Corridor
Source: Bank of Philippines (2016:1)

system, it is seen that varying rates are used between the ceiling and the floor of the interest rate corridor, and the policy interest rate is determined based on the center of the IRC (Yücememiş et al., 2015:453).

As shown in Figure 1, the IRC can be expressed as the band between the borrowing interest rate and the lending deposit rate of central banks to other banks in line with the framework of the most common liquidity management operations in the market (Bernhardsen and Kloster, 2010:1). The IRC tries explicitly to keep the overnight interest rate on the money market close to the target interest rate (Berentsen and Monnet, 2008:3). While the upper limit of the IRC band set by the central bank is the overnight lending interest rate, the lower limit is the borrowing interest rate. In an IRC application, the lending interest rate is the interest rate that a bank is willing to borrow and repay in the short-term from the central bank in the event of a temporary liquidity shortage. Borrowing interest rate is the rate when a bank deposits its excess liquidity to the central bank to gain interest (Vural, 2013:63). The corridor system can change and manage liquidity policy and interest rate policy in a mostly independent way. For example, while official interest rates can be introduced against speculative attacks towards the exchange rate, they can also protect and even improve market interest rates by limiting the liquidity of the internal financial system at the lower limit of the corridor (Goodhart, 2011:22).

As can be seen in Figure 1, there is also a policy interest rate other than the lower and upper limit of the interest corridor band. Usually, in the IRC concept, the central bank sets the target policy interest rate between the lower and upper limits of the corridor and it is at the same distance from these limits. This rate serves as the primary signal of the central bank's policy attitude (Kahn, 2010:26). The policy interest rate reflects the central banks' position in the face of macroeconomic changes as a critical policy tool. If inflationary pressure is present in an economy, the policy interest rate is raised to prevent the overall level of prices from rising. In the event of a recession, the policy interest rate is reduced to trigger economic activities. The interest rate between the lower and upper limit of the IRC is the policy interest rate of the central banks. At this point, the IRC system ensures that the interest rate stays within these limits, preventing the market interest rate from deviating significantly from the policy interest rate (Üzar and Başoğlu, 2017:137). There is a consistent relationship between short-term interest rates in the market and policy interest rates in liquidity management. Central banks adjust the IRC to keep the overnight interest rate on the money market close to the target interest rate (Berentsen and Monnet, 2008:3).

3 Purpose of the Interest Rate Corridor System

The interest rate corridor, one of the new instruments of monetary policy aimed primarily at eliminating uncertainties in the economy, is a practice aimed at getting close to the overnight interest rate set in the money markets. Central banks try to stabilize the exchange rate by changing the distance between the IRC ceiling and the floor. While providing liquidity to the market through this practice, central banks have the opportunity to react rapidly to the difference between perceptions in the face of constantly changing situations and to be more flexible about the interest rates they will apply (Vural, 2013:31).

It is aimed to reduce the average return on short-term interest rates by widening the distance between the ceiling and the floor of the interest rate corridor. In such a case, such capital inflows into the market are discouraged by increasing interest rate fluctuations and reducing the yield/risk ratios of speculative-oriented short-term instruments. To briefly explain the operation of the interest rate corridor, central banks reduce the overnight debt interest rates that they have given to banks by pulling down the floor of the interest rate corridor. One of the aims here is to reduce the inflow of speculative short-term capital into the markets. The central bank aims to slow down capital outflow by proposing to borrow at higher interest rates by raising the ceiling of the corridor to discourage foreign exchange exit from the market (Gökalp, 2016:138). In particular, it allows developing countries to control and discourage the speculative movements of short-term capital through the IRC system.

Theoretically, besides reducing fluctuations in policy interest rates, the IRC system can keep the policy interest rate close to the targeted interest rate in many countries. In IRC, the central bank conventionally sets the target for the overnight policy interest rate according to the inflation and economic growth aims. In this system, the interest rate floor is set below the overnight interest rate. Interest rate floor has two aspects. Firstly, the excess reserves can be deposited at a fixed interest rate per night by the depository institutions. Similarly, with the discount rate, the central bank can also set deposit rates below target policy rates. Such a case encourages depositors to invest their surplus funds in interbank markets rather than the central bank. On the other hand, the floor can often be seen like the interest rate paid from reserves, that is usually set below the target interest rate. Interest rate corridor reduces the fluctuations of the official interest rates via the interest rate ceiling and floor. When the required reserve balances held on short, the depository institutions will not have to pay a rate higher than the overnight borrowing interest rate discount rates, and when the held excess balances, they will not have to accept a rate lower than the deposit interest rate. Also for the interest rates between the ceiling and the floor, it encourages the depository institutions which has insufficient resources for borrowing from overfunded institutions as well as promoting the formation of an active private market for overnight liquidity. Consequently, whatever the supply of reserves, the overnight funds' interest rates are controlled by the central bank (Kahn, 2010:12–13).

The central bank can also shift its reserve supply while keeping policy interest rates under control with the help of IRC. As supply gradually increases, policy interest will eventually fall to its lower limit of zero. However, in the IRC system, the decrease in the policy interest rate is limited through the corridor's floor point, that is the interest rate on excess reserves (Kahn, 2010:16).

In the IRC system, central banks offer two proposals to banks to adjust interest rates more flexibly. These are the interest rate it pays for the deposits deposited with it and the interest rate it applies through lending. When lending, central banks supply the banks with the liquidity, they need overnight over a determined debt interest rate, while in borrowing, they pay interest in exchange for excess reserves of the banks at a specific interest rate. The interest rate that the central bank pays for the excess reserves of the banks is the floor of the corridor, while the interest rate that it applies when lending to the banks is the ceiling of the corridor. The policy interest rate is a ratio between this base and the ceiling. The main objective of the corridor system is to ensure that the overnight interest rate in the money markets is within the band range set by the central bank and close to the specified target. When the central bank wants to make a change in policy, it changes the ceiling and floor of the corridor (Tokucu, 2013:10).

The primary rationale for implementing an IRC system is to prevent short-term capital movements from causing fragility and volatility in the market. The review shows that there is a positive relationship between IRC bandwidth and interest rate volatility (Bindseil and Jablecki, 2011:6). The primary purpose of the IRC system is to prevent market interest rates from deviating significantly from policy interest rates. The gap between the ceiling and the floor of the IRC is generally wide during the periods of economic recession, where banks have to implement tight monetary policy, which reduces the supply of credit. During periods of economic expansion, however, the gap between the ceiling and the floor of the IRC becomes narrower (Bernanke et al. 1994:14; Yücememiş et al. 2015:453).

The application of the IRC allows the central bank to affect the economy through changes in the lower and upper bands rather than directly changing the policy rate. Also, while determining the lower and upper bands of the central banks of the interest rate corridor, it takes into consideration the compliance of the policy rate targeted as the midpoint of the corridor with the inflation and economic growth targets of the bank. At the same time, the central bank aims to limit the volatility in policy interest through the application of the interest rate corridor, and this goal is in line with the central bank's target to reduce uncertainties in the economy. Finally, the fact that the IRC application has a flexible structure and provides considerable convenience in controlling interest rates has directed the central banks globally to this application, and the application of IRC as a policy tool has been used by many central banks (Emirkadı, 2008:473).

4 Operation of the Interest Rate Corridor System

Central banks were the first to implement inflation targeting and also the first to implement the interest rate corridor. The first central banks that have implemented the IRC system were the central banks of New Zealand, Canada, the United Kingdom, and Norway. In Turkey, the IRC system has been implemented as a new monetary policy tool since November 2010 (Tokucu, 2013:8). Before the global financial crisis in 2008, the ECB and the central banks of Australia, Japan, England, Sweden, Canada, Norway and New Zealand used various methods to manage interest rate fluctuations and market expectations. However, with the recent global crisis, the ECB, the central banks of Japan, Britain, Canada and Norway have switched to using the base system. In contrast, the central banks of other countries have tended to keep policy interest rates near the center of

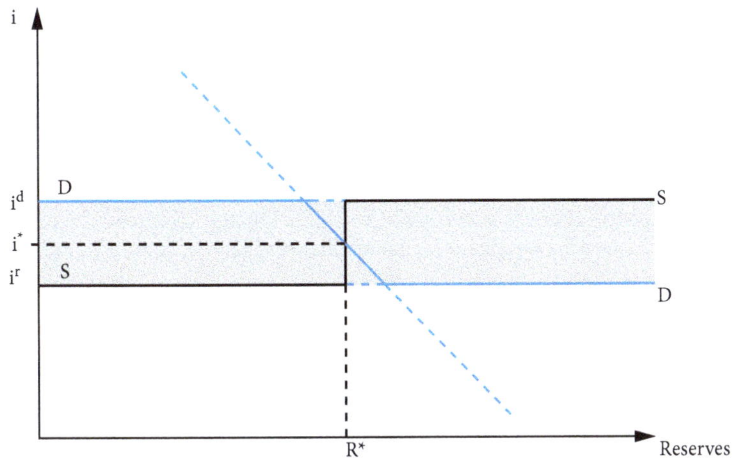

Figure 2. The Corridor Operating Framework
Source: Kahn (2010:15)

the corridor. In general, as a result of the studies, it is showed that IRC system helps central banks to limit overnight interest rate fluctuations and to provide significant liquidity for the banking system during financial crises as well (Kahn, 2010:18–22). For these reasons, the central banks of Indonesia, Iceland, Hungary, Poland, Romania, Serbia and Turkey chose to use this system after the 2008 global crisis (Vural, 2013:44).

The operation of the IRC system, which is one of the new monetary policy instruments implemented by many central banks in recent years, is explained in Figure 2.

In Figure 2, i on the vertical axis refers to the overnight interest rates, and R on the horizontal axis refers to the number of reserves. The value D, demand for reserves, is fully elastic at the level of discount rate i^d. This is because no deposit institution wants to borrow from the rate higher than the central bank's rates in the interbank market. Demand D is also sufficiently flexible at the level of i^r, interest rates on reserve surplus. That's because no institution will be willing to lend to interbank markets for a lower rate than the central bank is willing to pay. Reserve demand line between the upper i^d and lower i^r points of the IRC tends towards the negative, that is downwards. This is because the opportunity cost associated with holding reserves arises when interest rates decrease or increase. In this region, deposit institutions have to maintain a balance between the cost of having excess reserves and having scarce reserves and to hold the required rate for transactions. As the rates of overnight funds drop, the cost of holding excess reserves drops as well. In such a case, the demand curve has a downward slope. The supply of reserves is called S. R* is the vertical section of the supply curve. The central bank sets this amount and can change it with open market operations. Buying from the open market increases the reserves, and this operation replaces the vertical section to the right. On the contrary, open market sales shift the vertical section to the left. The position of the horizontal section to the left of the R* is determined by the deposit rate or reserve surplus rate. This rate creates a floor below the overnight interest rate for central bank balances, regardless of how much demand will fall. The position and discount rate of the horizontal section to the right of the R* is assigned by i^d. As demand for central bank balances increases, the payments demanded central bank lending services and the increases in rates in interbank transactions are restricted. When this rate is tested, the central bank fulfils the excess demand for reserves with its loans. It is since deposit institutions will not pay a higher rate than the central bank has set. The balance interest rate in the interbank market occurs at the point where supply and demand lines intersect. In Figure 2, this intersection occurs at the i* interest rate and R* reserve balances. The volatility of demand does not matter since overnight interest rate fluctuates in the range between i^r to i^d. As a result, central banks are able to keep overnight interest rate fluctuations more tightly controlled through open market transactions. With this method, the target rate can be controlled and maintained fairly tightly (Kahn, 2010:14–15, Bernhardsen and Kloster, 2010:1).

5 Conclusion

This study is a conceptual evaluation of the IRC system, which began to be adopted in the 1990s as a monetary policy instrument and became more critical for many countries with the global financial crisis of 2008. Especially the quantitative easing policies implemented by developed countries to overcome the global financial crisis in 2008 generate a liquidity surplus, and this surplus capital acts as a catalyst short-term capital inflows towards developing countries, including Turkey. At this point, measures to prevent the negative effects of the speculative money flow or to directly control the short-term capital inflow come to the fore. Thus, one of these measures is the IRC system applied by the central banks.

The interest rate corridor, one of the new instruments of monetary policy aimed primarily at eliminating uncertainties in the economy, is a practice aimed at achieving stability in the exchange rates by changing the bandwidth between the ceiling and the floor, which is determined by the central banks, as well as approaching to the overnight interest rate set in the money markets. In this way, central banks have the opportunity to discourage such capital inflows into the market by widening the distance between the ceiling and the floor in the IRC and reducing the average return on short-term interest rates, as well as reducing the return/risk ratios of short-term instruments for speculative purposes, and to keep the financial system under control more effectively and rapidly. The IRC practice has the power to ensure both financial systems and price stability, especially in developing countries such as Turkey, which are trying to attract foreign capital. As in every country included in the globalized world economy, the Turkish economy can be adversely affected by the decisions taken by the central banks of other countries. For example, the conclusion of the central bank of a country to increase interest rates may affect accelerating capital outflows in some countries that do not have economic depth, resulting in some negative economic consequences, such as the depreciation of the domestic currency and inflation in the economy. The IRC system, which allows rapid control and softens the mood of panic caused by successive economic consequences, should be used more effectively as an important monetary policy tool at hand, by the central banks of developing countries in particular.

References

Bank of Philippines. (2016). http://www.bsp.gov.ph/downloads/publications/FAQs/IRC.pdf, Access Date: 10/03/2020.

Berentsen, A. & Monnet, C. (2008). Monetary Policy in a Channel System, Journal of Monetary Economics, 55(6), 1067–1080.

Bernanke, B., Gertler, M. & Gilchrist, S. (1994). The Financial Accelerator and the Flight to Quality, The Review of Economics and Statistics, 78(1), 1–15.

Bernhardsen, T. & Kloster, A. (2010). Liquidity Management System: Floor or Corridor, Norges Bank Staff Memo, 4.

Bindseil, U. & Jablecki, J. (2011). The Optimal Width of the Central Bank Standing Facilities Corridor and Banks' Day-To-Day Liquidity Management, ECB Working Paper, 1350.

Binici, M., Erol, H., Kara, A. H., Özlü, P. & Unalmis, D. (2013). Interest Rate Corridor: A New Macroprudential Tool? CBT Research Notes in Economics No: 2013–20, Research and Monetary Policy Department, Central Bank of the Republic of Turkey.

Binici, M., Kara, H. & Özlü, P. (2016). Faiz Koridoru ve Banka Faizleri: Parasal Aktarım Mekanizmasına Dair Bazı Bulgular, TCMB Çalışma Tebliği, 16/8, 1–36.

Clews, R., Salmon, C. & Weeken, O. (2010). The Bank's Money Market Framework. Bank of England, Quarterly Bulletin, 50(4), 292–301.

Emirkadı, Ö. (2008). 2008 Global Crisis and Changing Monetary Policy: The Practise of Interest Rate Corridor in the World and Turkey, Karadeniz Sosyal Bilimler Dergisi, 9(2), 465–486.

Goodhart, C. A. E. (2011). The Changing Role of Central Banks, Financial History Review, 18(2), 135–154.

Gökalp, B. T. (2016). The Effect of Monetary Policy Decisions on Stock Prices, Suleyman Demirel University Journal of Faculty of Economics & Administrative Sciences, 21(4), 1379–1396.

Kahn, G. A. (2010). Monetary Policy under a Corridor Operating Framework, Economic Review-Federal Reserve Bank of Kansas City, 95(4), 5–34.

Tokucu, E. (2013). Para Politikalarının Uygulanmasında Faiz Koridoru Sistemi ve Kanada, İngiltere ve Yeni Zelanda Deneyimleri, Finans Politik & Ekonomik Yorumlar, 50(581), 7–24.

Üzar, U. & Başoğlu, A. (2017). Central Banking and New Quests: Nominal GDP Targeting and Developmental Central Banking Discussions, KTÜ Sosyal Bilimler Enstitüsü Sosyal Bilimler Dergisi, 123–145.

Vural, U. (2013). Geleneksel Olmayan Para Politikalarının Yükselişi, TCMB Uzmanlık Yeterlilik Tezi, Ankara.

Whitesell, W. (2006). Interest Rate Corridors and Reserves, Journal of Monetary Economics, 53(6), 1177–1195.

Yücememiş, B. T., Alkan, U. & Dağıdır, C. (2015). Interest Corridor as a New Money Policy Instrument: Effect of the Interest Decisions of the Monetary Policy Board on Inflation in Turkey, Finansal Araştırmalar ve Çalışmalar Dergisi, 7(13), 449–478.

Cem Gökce

A Different View on Energy Supply Security: Energy Vulnerability Index for the European Union and Turkey[1]

1 Introduction

In this study, empirical applications will be conducted concerning the problem of energy supply deficit, which is an important problem for the European Union and Turkey. As the energy supply deficit of countries has grown to a great extent, which has turned into a vulnerability, countries such as Turkey and the European Union have tried to find ways to cope with this deficit through various energy policies and even economic policies. Particularly with the concern about depletion of fossil resources, serious steps have been taken towards the solution of this problem recently. Through the method to be used in this study, certain information will be given in order to reveal the current state of energy supply deficit and the resulting vulnerability.

Developed countries have started to take serious steps since 1980s about energy supply security, whose significance was understood particularly after the 1970s. In this regard, the European Union has taken various measures, and is still supporting these measures with various policies today. In Turkey, the significance of the issue has been understood a little later and studies have started to be conducted on this issue in the 2000s.

2 Literature Review

There are numerous research studies in the literature on measuring the vulnerability created by foreign dependency in the energy field as a result of the energy supply deficit and the increase of this deficit to great extents. In this section, energy supply deficit and econometric models created against the risks posed by

1 This study was derived from the doctoral thesis named "Energy Supply Deficit and Energy Fragility in the European Union and Turkey" written by Cem GÖKÇE under the supervision of Prof.Dr. İsmail AYDOĞUŞ and Assoc. Dr. Harun ÖZTÜRKLER in Afyon Kocatepe University, Institute of Social Sciences.

this deficit will be examined and information will be given about the model of this study. This model will then be evaluated together with its results.

It is obvious that the risk posed by high energy supply shortages also leads to a security problem in countries. There are many studies in the literature on how energy supply security can be measured. Many of the studies attempted to measure energy security by creating various indexes. Some of these indexes are oil vulnerability index, energy vulnerability index, supply/demand index, energy policy index, Shannon-Wiener index, Herfindahl-Hirschman Index, etc. All of these studies were investigating for a method to measure the energy security.

In this section of the study, some previous studies will be presented and examined in terms of their contents. In the report published by the European Commission Joint Research Center and written by Badea (2010), energy security indicators were explained. This report describes energy security indicators in three groups. These are simple indicators, diversification indicators and composite indicators. Energy intensity, energy dependence in terms of energy resources, reserve-production ratio and energy prices are among the basic indicators. Energy (fuel) type, geographical source and suppliers are included in the diversification indicators. The Supply/Demand index, oil vulnerability index and vulnerability indexes are among the composite indicators according to the report.

A similar report was published by Delgado (2011). In this study, indicators of energy security were attempted to be determined. The study discusses energy safety indicators in six groups. These are indicators of dependence, vulnerability, connectivity, resources availability, sustainability and market. In creating these indicators, the study uses many variables, from import dependence to energy intensity and from stock capacity to energy prices.

In another study conducted on the measurement of energy supply security, Löschel, Moslener and Rübbelke (2010) approached energy supply security from a different perspective, reporting that the concept of energy security can be measured with two groups of indicators as ex-post and ex-ante indicators. Ex-post indicators represent realized indicators, while ex-ante indicators represent projected indicators. In this study, price and volume components were used as the explanatory variables of ex-post indicators, while market saturation and diversification of fossil fuels were used as explanatory variables of ex-ante indicators.

In order to measure energy supply security, Jansen, Arkel and Boots (2004) created a diversification index using the Shannon index. Jansen et al., reports that there are four different aspects of long-term energy supply security. These variables are the diversification of energy sources covered in the energy supply, supplier diversification in imported sources, long-term political stability, and the resources in the regions of countries. Some of the indicators used to create indexes in the study are energy import dependency, long-term political stability, the ratio of primary energy sources within the primary energy supply, and the diversity of primary energy sources.

Another important method for measuring energy supply security is the creation of an energy vulnerability index. Some of the important studies on this subject were conducted by Gupta (2008), Gnansounou (2008) and Christos, Alexandros and Psarras (2009). What these studies have in common is that they all attempt to measure energy security by creating an index of vulnerability. Among these studies, the root mean square method was used in Gnansounou (2008), while Gupta (2008) and Christos et al. (2009) used the principal component analysis as the method. The oil vulnerability index was created by Gupta (2008), based on 26 oil importing countries for the year 2004. Christos et al. (2009) created an oil vulnerability index for 27 European Union countries for the period of 1995–2007. In Gnansounou's study (2008), the energy vulnerability index was created for 37 industrialized countries for the year 2003. While these studies used similar variables to form the index of vulnerability, it was seen that they added different variables to the model. Moreover, Gupta (2008) and Christos et al. (2009) created the oil vulnerability index, while Gnansounou (2008) incorporated natural gas into the index, creating the energy vulnerability index. As the conclusion of Gupta's study (2008), countries were classified according to their vulnerability degrees concerning the oil vulnerability index. Christos et al. (2009) examined how the vulnerability index changed in terms of EU-27 countries in the 1995–2007 period. In Gnansounou's study (2008), energy vulnerability was classified as low, medium and high grades and this classification was evaluated for 37 industrialized countries.

3 Dataset and Application

The method to be applied in this study is the Principal Components Analysis (PCA). This method is used in many studies and it will be based on in this study for the creation of the energy vulnerability index.

3.1 Principal Components Analysis (PCA)

The origin of principal components analysis is quite old. It is written in the literature that principal components analysis has been studied since the early 1900s.

Accordingly, Jolliffe (2002) states that the history of this technique dates back to the early 1900s.

Principal components analysis is one of the most frequently used methods in the literature for multivariate data analysis. In the simplest terms, principal components analysis is a variable reduction analysis. In this analysis, each variable is converted to another variable whose mean value is 0 and standard deviation value is 1. This process is called standardization. Through the standardized series, all variables will be expressed in the same unit. As was reported in the study of Öztürk and Türkmen (2013), the standardization process is carried out as follows: firstly, the mean and standard deviation are calculated for each time series. Secondly, the mean of each series, as seen in Equation (1), is first subtracted from the value of each period and then divided into the standard deviation of the series. Thus, each time series is transformed into a new time series with a mean of 0 and a standard deviation of 1.

$$\forall \mathcal{X}_i = \frac{\mathcal{X}_i - Ort.(\mathcal{X}_i)}{Std.S.(\mathcal{X}_i)} \qquad (1)$$

Subsequent to the standardization of the series, the weights of these variables are calculated that will be used in the formation of the index. These weights are determined with the help of principal components analysis. After these determined weights are standardized, the created index will again have a mean of 0 and a standard deviation of 1. As a result, weights in the principal components analysis will show the effect of a standard-deviation change on the index in terms of standard deviation.

Principal components analysis is a method of analysis that can explain a relationship, which can be explained through a large number of variables with correlations (in other words, with linear relationship) in between, by means of fewer variables than the original series and with variables that have no correlation in between. Sevinç (2012) explained principal components analysis from a different standpoint, as an analysis that redefines the relationship, which can be expressed with the data sources at hand, through vertical axes that are sorted by their explanation rates for the linear relationship between these series.

By means of this analysis, various relationships can be explained without changing the length of the data set, but with variables that have less and no correlation in between. According to Holland (2008), one of the key points in this analysis is that the first principal components calculate the largest variance in the data set.

3.2 Energy Vulnerability Index

The vulnerability index is a practice that can be applied to many macro-economic variables in many areas of the economy today. In the simplest terms, vulnerability can be defined as the response of variables to various negative changes. Today, vulnerability index has been created in many economic areas, but vulnerability index has a particular place in the literature concerning the energy resources. Similar to the above definition, the World Energy Council WEC (2007, 4) and Gnansounou (2008, 3735) defined the energy vulnerability as follows: "The vulnerability of an energy system is the extent to which this system is unable to cope with certain unwanted events".

Emerging as a result of energy supply deficit, energy vulnerability is an indicator for measuring energy supply security. Concerning the significance of energy vulnerability, Christos et al. (2009) reported that one of the major factors affecting a country's energy security is the level of vulnerability, which indicates the main fuel in the primary energy supply in those countries.

A supply/demand-oriented vulnerability index was created in some of the studies in the literature, while some others created vulnerability indexes based on only oil among the energy resources. In this study, a separate vulnerability index will be created for each of the oil, natural gas and coal, all of which are called fossil fuels. The main reason for measuring the vulnerability of these three fossil sources is that these three sources have a high potential to represent energy systems since they cover a very large proportion of the energy consumption of both Turkey and the European Union.

The main purpose of this section is, by using the variables that are thought to determine the energy vulnerability, to create a new series (vulnerability index) that explains an important part of the variation in the vulnerability, and to analyze the behavior of this series.

3.3 Variables of the Model, Dataset and Period

In this study, benefiting from the principal components analysis described above, the Oil Vulnerability Index (OVI), Natural Gas Vulnerability Index (NVI) and Coal Vulnerability Index (CVI) will be created both for Turkey and for the European Union. A common data set was used for these three vulnerability indexes.

In the process of creation of the vulnerability index, a total of five variables were used in the study and a total of four ratios were obtained from these variables. These variables are primary energy consumption, primary energy production, reserve amount, industrial production index and import amount of related resource. Although GDP is generally used as a measure of economic performance in the literature, in this study, the industrial production index was used concerning the economic performance since this study contained monthly data.

These variables were obtained from the Statistical Office of the European Union (Eurostat), the U.S. Energy Information Administration, and the Turkish Ministry of Energy and Natural Resources (MENA), and the Turkish Statistical Institute (TURKSTAT).

When calculating these ratios, each variable that makes up the ratio was calculated by converting it into the same unit. In other words, even if the ratios are in different units, the variables representing each ratio are expressed in the same unit. In addition, the increase in the rate, which resulted from the change in each variable, was included in the index to increase the vulnerability. The four ratios used in this study are described below.

$\frac{\textit{Primary Energy Consumption}}{\textit{Primary Energy Production}}$ (C/P Ratio): This ratio is the proportion of the country's energy consumption to its energy production. An increase in this ratio indicates increased foreign dependency. Therefore, an increase in this ratio increases the vulnerability.

$\frac{\textit{Primary Energy Consumption}}{\textit{Reserves}}$ (C/R Ratio): This ratio shows the number of periods, for which the country has enough reserves, based on its consumption at that period. Therefore, an increase in this ratio increases the vulnerability.

$\frac{\textit{Primary Energy Consumption}}{\textit{Industrial Production Index}}$ (C/IPI Ratio): This ratio is called energy intensity in the literature. It shows how many units of energy must be used to obtain a unit of output. Therefore, an increase in this ratio increases the vulnerability.

$\frac{\textit{Imports}}{\textit{Industrial Production Index}}$ (IMP/IPI Ratio): This ratio is the proportion of imports of the relevant energy source to industrial production index. An increase in this ratio indicates increased foreign dependency for the particular resource. Therefore, an increase in this ratio increases the vulnerability.

In this study, a total of 60 observations were used on a monthly basis covering the 2008–2012 period in line with the availability of data. This study covers the period between January 2008 and December 2012.

4 Application Results

For the estimation of the principal components analysis method applied in this study, initially, the data was standardized to a mean value of "0" and standard deviation "1". These ratios will now be expressed with an S at the beginning of the definitions (SC/P, SC/R, SC/IPI and SIMP/IPI), in other words, they will be expressed as "standardized" variable. Thus, each of the variables will be expressed in the same unit.

In this section of the study, based on the standardized form of the four variables described in the previous section, primarily, OVI, NVI and CVI will be created for Turkey and the results of principal component analysis will be interpreted. Subsequently, using the same method, OVI, NVI and CVI will be created for the European Union.

4.1 PCA Results of Turkey's Energy Vulnerability Index

The principal components analysis results of the oil vulnerability index for Turkey are presented in Table 1. In this table, the cumulative ratio shows the explanation rate of the principal components for the total variance. The first principal component (PC 1) explains about 88 % of the total variance in Turkey. This is a quite high ratio. The figure 96 % shown below points that the first principal component and the second principal component (PC 2) together explain 96 % of the total variance. Eigenvectors indicate the weights of the variables used in the analysis on the first, second, third and fourth principal components, respectively. For Turkey's oil vulnerability index, the weight of the SC/P ratio is 0.50, the SC/R ratio is 0.47, the SC/IPI ratio is 0.50 and the SIMP/IPI ratio is 0.50. It should be noted here that as the explanation rate of the principal component for the total variance increases, the success of the model increases.

The principal components analysis results of the natural gas vulnerability index for Turkey are presented in Table 2. According to the results, the first principal component explains about 82 % of the total variance. This figure indicates that the model is quite successful. Another important point here is that the variables are positive. In other words, the variables are positively correlated with the vulnerability index.

The principal components analysis results of the coal vulnerability index for Turkey are presented in Table 3. According to the analysis results, the first principal component explains about 61 % of the total variance. This ratio suggests that the model is quite successful. As a general evaluation for Turkey, it can be mentioned that all three vulnerability indexes have achieved quite successful results.

4.2 PCA Results of the EU's Energy Vulnerability Index

In this section, the principal components analysis results of the vulnerability indexes created for the European Union will be given. Three types of vulnerability indexes were created for the European Union as oil, natural gas and coal vulnerability indexes.

Eigenvalues/ Number	Value	Difference	Proportion	Cumulative Value	Cumulative Proportion
1	3,516638	3,188374	0,8792	3,516638	0,8792
2	0,328264	0,228069	0,0821	3,844902	0,9612
3	0,100195	0,045292	0,025	3,945097	0,9863
4	0,054903	---	0,0137	4	1
Eigenvectors	Variables	PC 1	PC 2	PC 3	PC 4
	STU	0,509938	0,223649	-0,830585	-0,008508
	STR	0,477439	0,728748	0,488898	0,044241
	STSUE	0,508048	-0,426331	0,204494	-0,719939
	SITHSUE	0,503887	-0,486981	0,17114	0,692574

Eigenvalues/ Number	Value	Difference	Proportion	Cumulative Value	Cumulative Proportion
1	3,274303	2,780509	0,8186	3,274303	0,8186
2	0,493794	0,311944	0,1234	3,768098	0,942
3	0,18185	0,131798	0,0455	3,949948	0,9875
4	0,050052	---	0,0125	4	1
Eigenvectors	Variables	PC 1	PC 2	PC 3	PC 4
	STU	0,480839	0,575941	0,659302	0,049062
	STR	0,511034	-0,493142	0,005697	0,704005
	STSUE	0,494702	0,444252	-0,74576	-0,041876
	SITHSUE	0,512747	-0,477224	0,095562	-0,707259

Table 1: OVI of Turkey **Table 2:** NVI of Turkey

Eigenvalues/ Number	Value	Difference	Proportion	Cumulative Value	Cumulative Proportion
1	2,441313	1,589638	0,6103	2,441313	0,6103
2	0,851675	0,221819	0,2129	3,292988	0,8232
3	0,629856	0,5527	0,1575	3,922844	0,9807
4	0,077156	---	0,0193	4	1
Eigenvectors	Variables	PC 1	PC 2	PC 3	PC 4
	STU	0,587889	-0,067069	-0,430168	0,681794
	STR	0,347081	0,831913	0,429627	0,053627
	STSUE	0,410066	-0,549404	0,726252	0,050586
	SITHSUE	0,604787	-0,039717	-0,320832	-0,72782

Eigenvalues/ Number	Value	Difference	Proportion	Cumulative Value	Cumulative Proportion
1	1,984783	0,880196	0,4962	1,984783	0,4962
2	1,104586	0,194219	0,2761	3,089369	0,7723
3	0,910367	0,910103	0,2276	3,999736	0,9999
4	0,000264	---	0,0001	4	1
Eigenvectors	Variables	PC 1	PC 2	PC 3	PC 4
	STU	0,173468	0,919983	0,076717	0,343009
	STR	0,283377	-0,13157	0,949936	-0,002889
	STSUE	0,690258	0,14069	-0,188507	-0,684262
	SITHSUE	0,642767	-0,341362	-0,237068	0,643523

Table 3: CVI of Turkey **Table 4:** OVI of the EU

The principal components analysis results of the oil vulnerability index for EU are presented in Table 4. According to this table, the first basic component explains about 50 % of the total variance. This rate is also considered a sufficient rate. Considering the weights of the variables within the European Union's oil vulnerability index, it could be seen that the energy intensity and the IMP/IPI ratio had greater weights.

Another table is Table 5, where the principal components analysis results of the natural gas vulnerability index for the EU are presented. The remarkable point in the table is that the first principal component explains about 91 % of the total variance. Considering the weights of the variables in the natural gas vulnerability index, it could be observed that all variables took weights close to each other.

According to the Table 6, where principal components analysis results of the coal vulnerability index for the EU are presented, the first principal component explains about 60 % of the total variance. Considering the weights of the variables in the coal vulnerability index, it could be observed that the C/R ratio is less weighted than the other three variables. As a general evaluation for the European Union, it can be said that all three indexes have achieved successful results in the model.

5 Evaluation of the Analysis Results

In this section, the charts of the energy vulnerability indexes, whose application results were given in the previous sections, will be presented with the charts of the Industrial Production Index (IPI) and evaluated together with the economic vulnerability. Thus, the reality of the vulnerability indexes created for Turkey and the European Union will be discussed.

The comparison of the OVI for Turkey and the Industrial Production Index is presented in Chart 1. Here, the Industrial Production Index was standardized like other variables and expressed in the same units as the vulnerability indexes. An index value below 0 indicates that vulnerability is low, while a value above 0 indicates that vulnerability is high. Evaluating the chart for Turkey, it can be mentioned that the vulnerability was quite high in 2008, when the global crisis was intense. The vulnerability index, which started to fall towards the end of 2008, started to increase again in 2009. Despite the recent economic recovery, the vulnerability index was still above 0 in 2011 and 2012. Although the vulnerability of the last two years was not as much as the vulnerability of 2008, it is a reality that there is a vulnerability in terms of oil.

Eigenvalues/ Number	Value	Difference	Proportion	Cumulative Value	Cumulative Proportion
1	3,653088	3,47576	0,9133	3,653088	0,9133
2	0,177329	0,025412	0,0443	3,830417	0,9576
3	0,151917	0,134251	0,038	3,982334	0,9956
4	0,017666	---	0,0044	4	1
Eigenvectors	Variables	PC 1	PC 2	PC 3	PC 4
	STU	0,489316	0,829414	0,124086	0,239259
	STR	0,50395	-0,387704	-0,511041	0,578409
	STSUE	0,515303	-0,026015	-0,354651	-0,779749
	SITHSUE	0,490985	-0,401349	0,773087	-0,013759

Eigenvalues/ Number	Value	Difference	Proportion	Cumulative Value	Cumulative Proportion
1	2,387603	1,423177	0,5969	2,387603	0,5969
2	0,964426	0,580433	0,2411	3,352028	0,838
3	0,383992	0,120013	0,096	3,736021	0,934
4	0,263979	---	0,066	4	1
Eigenvectors	Variables	PC 1	PC 2	PC 3	PC 4
	STU	0,183335	0,972798	0,121965	0,071956
	STR	0,549627	-0,180973	0,772158	-0,262547
	STSUE	0,571371	0,008786	-0,596339	-0,563772
	SITHSUE	0,581235	-0,144348	-0,18242	0,779777

Table 5: NVI of the EU **Table 6:** CVI of the EU

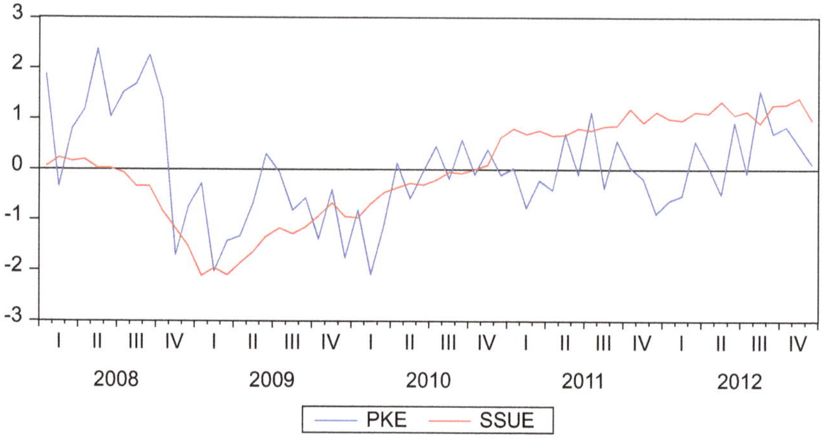

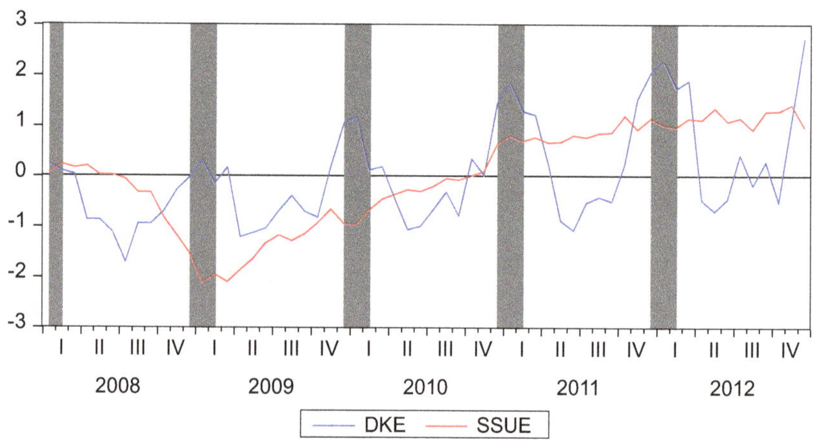

Chart 1 and 2: OVI-IPI Comparison and NVI-IPI Comparison of Turkey

In Chart 2, dark columns indicate the winter months. As can be seen from the chart, NVI rises considerably during the winter months, which can be due to increased demand during the winter months. Besides the seasonal effect, it can be seen that NVI responded to the 2008 global crisis later than oil. Another remarkable point in the chart is that vulnerability increases with each passing winter. From here, it can be mentioned that the vulnerability in natural gas is increasing.

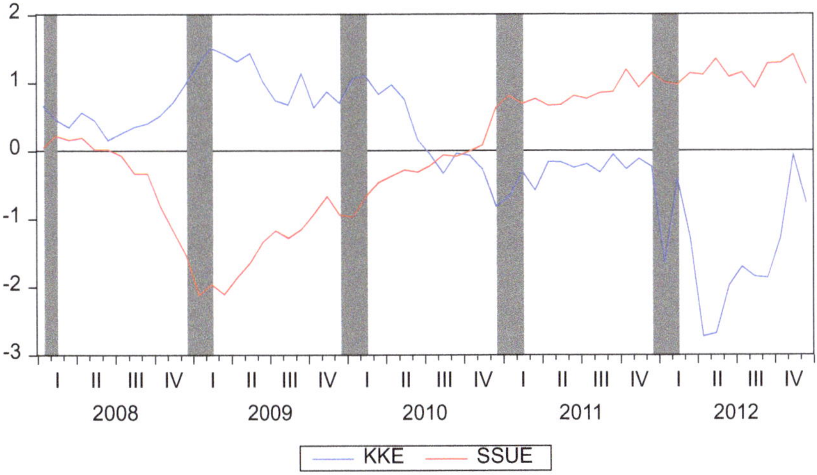

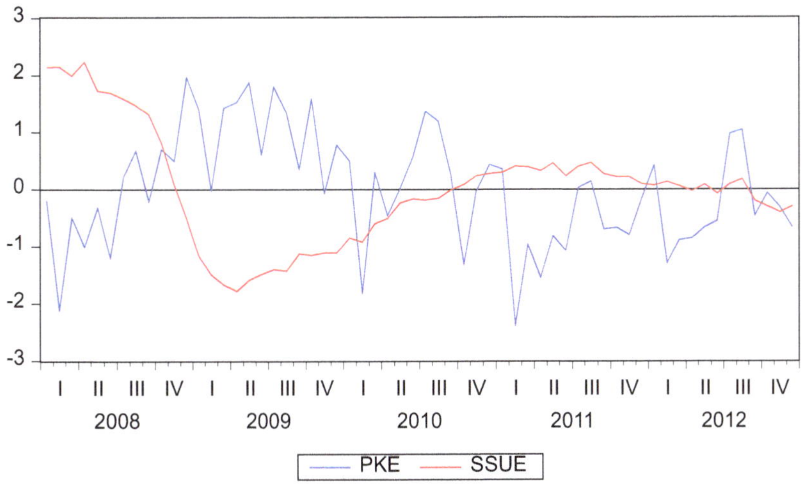

Chart 3 and 4: CVI-IPI Comparison of Turkey and OVI-IPI Comparison of the EU

The comparison of CVI and IPI for Turkey is presented in Chart 3. As can be seen clearly from the chart, there is an inverse proportion between Turkey's CVI and IPI. In the 2008–2009 period, when there was economic contraction, CVI increased above 0 and pointed increased vulnerability. In the following period, the vulnerability of coal began to decrease as the IPI increased with the economic recovery. As a matter of fact, in the last two years, while IPI rose above 0, CVI pointed that vulnerability decreased by going below 0.

The comparison of the OVI and IPI for Europe is presented in Chart 4. As can be expected in the chart, there is an inverse relationship between OVI and IPI. This indicates that oil vulnerability of the EU increased during periods of economic pressure and contraction. On the contrary, during periods of economic growth, vulnerability was observed to decrease.

Chart 5 shows the relationship between the NVI and IPI of the EU. Remarkable point here is the seasonal effect, similar to the situation in Turkey. Vulnerability rises in the winter and decreases in the summer. However, in contrast to Turkey, the NVI decreases even more in each passing winter. At this point, it is worth noting that natural gas purchases are subject to contracts and these are long-term contracts including quantity and price commitments. Therefore, it can be said that there may be no significant interaction between the Industrial Production Index and the NVI.

Examining at the overall trend of the EU's CVI, it can be seen that it is different from Turkey. The seasonal effect is quite dominant in CVI. Apart from the seasonal effect, a negative relationship can be mentioned between the IPI and CVI. Despite the seasonal effect, it was observed that CVI was quite high and the vulnerability increased during the contraction phase as of the end of 2008.

6 Conclusion and Recommendations

Examining the results of the method of this study in general, it is observed that energy vulnerability indexes sound alarm during periods of economic contraction, increasing the vulnerability. Ignoring the seasonal effects in the natural gas vulnerability index, it can be thought that energy vulnerability indexes could form a prediction for policymakers. However, the seasonal effects experienced at this point have a cyclical meaning in terms of vulnerability. Particularly the natural gas vulnerability index is increasing with increased demand in the winter months.

As a general evaluation concerning the EU and Turkey examined in this study, it can be understood from the model that the energy supply security risk increases in certain periods as an indicator of the openness of both Turkey and the European Union. The relatively higher openness of Turkey compared to the European Union enabled the energy vulnerability indexes to produce clearer results for Turkey according to the model. In this regard, it was observed that the indexes created for Turkey provided clearer results in the face of numerous cyclical effects.

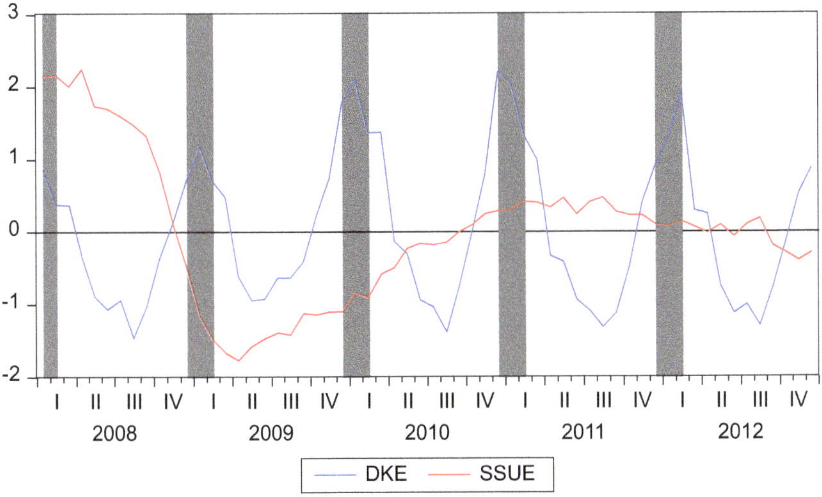

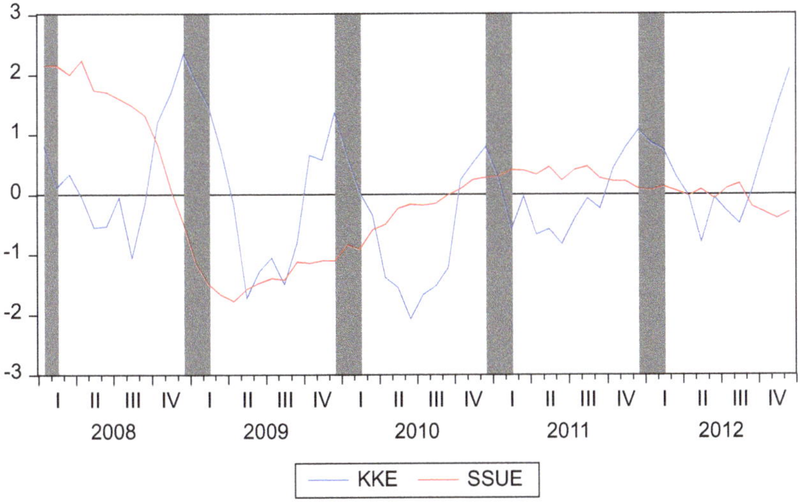

Chart 5 and 6: NVI-IPI Comparison of the EU and CVI-IPI Comparison of the EU

As is clear from the indexes created for both the European Union and Turkey, energy policies should be revised in order to ensure and/or increase the energy supply security. One of the most fundamental solutions to ensure energy supply security is to reduce foreign dependency on energy. Among the measurements to reduce foreign dependency are providing energy efficiency (density) and increasing the share of domestic resources in energy production. In addition, it is obvious that, in order to increase energy supply security, various other measures should be taken rapidly such as pipeline projects, diversification of the energy supply market and increasing the share of renewable energy.

References

Badea, C. A. (2010), Energy Security Indicators, Joint Research Center (JRC), European Commission, http://www.drustvo-termicara.com/resources/files/7fa5460.pdf, Date of Access: 12.12.2012"

Christos, V. R., Flamos, A., Psarras, J. (2009), Measurement of EU27 Oil Vulnerability, International Journal of Energy Sector Management, 3(2), 203–218

Delgado, M. B. (2011), Energy Security Indices in Europe, Economic Challenges for Energy Workshop, February, Madrid

Gnansounou, E. (2008), Assessing the Energy Vulnerability: Case of Industrialised Countries, Energy Policy, 36, 3734–3744

Gupta, E. (2008), Oil Vulnerability Index of Oil-Importing Countries, Energy Policy, 36, 1195–1211

Holland, S. M. (2008), Principal Component Analysis (PCA), Department of Geology, University of Georgia, Athens, GA 30602-2501, May

Jansen, J., Arkel, W., Ve ve Boots, M. (2004), Designing Indicators of Long-Term Energy Supply Security, https://publicaties.ecn.nl/PdfFetch.aspx?nr=ECN-C--04-007, Date of Access: 13.05.2013

Jolliffe, I. T. (2002), Principal Component Analysis, Springer Series in Statistics, Second Edition, Springer Nature: Switzerland

Löschel, A., Moslener, U., Rübbelke, D. (2010), Indicators of Energy Security in Industrialised Countries, Energy Policy, 38, 1665–1671

Öztürkler, H., Türkmen, G., (2013), Türkiye İçin Finansal Baskı Endeksi Oluşturulması, Türkiye Ekonomi Politikaları Araştırma Vakfı Politika Notu, Nisan, https://www.tepav.org.tr/upload/files/1378380018-2.Turkiye_icin_Finansal_Baski_Endeksi_Olusturulmasi.pdf, Date of Access: 18.05.2013

Sevinç, O. (2012), Enflasyon Ana Eğiliminin Temel Bileşenler Analiziyle İncelenmesi, TCMB Ekonomi Notları, Sayı 2012–08, 02 Mart

Murat Belke & Emrah Özel

Threshold Effect in the Inflation-Growth Nexus: Evidence from Developing Countries

1 Introduction

Today, the main target of macroeconomic policies is to provide a low level of inflation to ensure sustainable economic growth. Therefore, the primary goal of modern central banks is price stability. The price stability refers to a moderate, low inflation rate consistent with macroeconomic indicators that don't affect the decisions of economic units. Policymakers want to determine the inflation level around this rate. This inflation rate supports sustainable economic growth. The appropriate inflation rates of the national economies supporting sustainable growth differ according to the structure of their economies and the soundness and applicability of macroeconomics policies. Therefore, it is commonly accepted that there may be a unique threshold point for each country; when it is crossed, inflation will affect growth negatively. In this context, the main purpose of this study is to determine whether there is really a threshold inflation rate in terms of the inflation-growth nexus in the selected developing countries and what this rate is if there is a nonlinear relationship. This study pooled available data of 41 developing countries over the period 1965–2019. In this paper, evidence for the existence of an inflation threshold rate 19 % was found with using the panel threshold model developed by Hansen (1999). The findings also show that an increase in inflation in high-inflation regimes significantly reduced the level of economic growth.

The rest of the paper is organized as follows: Section 2 discusses the relevant theoretical and empirical literature review. Section 3 presents the dataset and econometric methodology. Section 4 includes the empirical results. Paper is concluded with policy recommendations.

2 Theoretical and Empirical Literature

The classical theory doesn't explicitly mention about the inflation-growth nexus. However, according to this theory the high wage costs of firms will lead to a decrease in profit levels, which may indicate that the relationship between the two variables is negative (Pentecost, 2000; Epaphra, 2016). According to Mundell (1963), who deals with the subject within the framework of the neo-classical growth theory, the nominal interest rate increases less than the inflation rate and causes the real interest rate to decrease. Thus, increasing investments cause an increase in capital accumulation and positively affect economic growth. Tobin (1965), who sees money as a store of value, argues that high inflation will cause individuals to substitute assets that generate more interest than money. As a result, capital density increases in the long run and promotes economic growth (Gokal and Hanif, 2004). This situation, which is known as the Mundell-Tobin effect in the literature, shows that the high inflation rate permanently increases the production levels.

In Keynesian theory, it is possible to explain the inflation-growth nexus through the interest channel. Accordingly, the increment in the money supply affects inflation level through the change in interest rate. Since money is a close substitution of bonds in the financial market, the expansion in the money supply brings out an excessive supply of money in the money market. As a result of excessive money supply, financial asset prices increase and interest rates decrease. In short run, enhancing investments as a result of the decrease in interest rates may increase the total demand and thereby proliferates the inflation rate. However, increasing inflation in the long run may cause production to shrink and money demand to decrease. Decreasing money demand may lead to an increase in the nominal interest rate in the long run (Epaphra, 2016). In summary, this view suggests that the inflation-growth nexus is positive in the short run.

According to the new Keynesian view, fluctuations in employment and production are largely due to fluctuations in nominal aggregate demand. Nominal shocks are important because nominal wages and prices are not completely flexible (Ball et al., 1988). Relative prices become more volatile as inflation increases with monetary growth. Therefore, the real wages of the employees change more during the contract period. Volatility in real wages triggers employment fluctuations. Decreasing returns to labor leads to a reduction in the marginal product of capital and thus production. As a result, there is a negative long run relationship between inflation and output growth (Vaona, 2012). There should be low and stable inflation for accelerating economic growth and fair income distribution (Ambler, 2007).

The empirical literature shows that current research produces mixed results. For this reason, the empirical literature is analyzed by classifying into four groups in terms of the presence and direction of the effect. Inflation has no effect on growth for studies in the first group (Sidrauski, 1967). Sidrauski (1967) confirmed the super neutrality of money by employing real money balances in the utility function. He claimed that inflation has no real effect on economic growth in the long-run. Studies in the second group suggest that inflation has a positive effect on economic performance (Tobin, 1965; Mundell, 1965; Dornbusch and Fischer, 1993; Shi, 1999; Mallik and Chowdhury, 2001). Tobin (1965) argued that high stable inflation can lead to high stable capital stock by addressing portfolio substitution for real capital, other than money that can accompany high inflation.

Despite these views, the studies in the third group suggest that inflation negatively affects growth (Friedman, 1976; Fischer and Modigliani, 1978; Stockman, 1981; Barro, 1995; De Gregorio, 1992; Roubini and Sala-i Martin, 1991; Andres and Hernando, 1997). On the other hand, studies in the fourth group claim that the relationship is not linear. It also shows that there are one or more threshold levels that determine the relationship between two variables. According to this approach, inflation below the optimal threshold level affects economic growth positively or there is no statistically significant relationship between the two variables. On the other hand, above the threshold level, the increase in the inflation rate slows down the economic growth (Fisher, 1993; Sarel, 1996; Malla, 1997; Bruno and Easterly, 1998; Khan and Senhadji, 2001; Faria and Carneiro, 2001; Drukker et al., 2005; Mubarik, 2005, Michael, 2008; Espinoza et al., 2010; Kremer et al., 2013).

Studies have suggested different inflation rate threshold levels for different countries, country groups (advanced countries, developing countries), regions (Latin America, MENA, EU, OECD, SADC etc.) and different analysis periods. Fisher (1993) claims that very high inflation rates are not consistent with sustainable growth, while Malla (1997) found a negative and significant relationship for OECD countries. Bruno and Easterly (1998) found that the relationship is not linear, like Fisher (1993), and that the effect differs in the bandwidth '15 %', '15–40 %' and '40 %'. Khan and Senhadji (2001), using the TAR model developed by Hansen (2000), estimated the inflation threshold level as 1–3 % for advanced countries and 11–12 % for developing countries. These results show that developing countries may be more resistant to higher inflation levels when compared to developed countries. A similar situation can be seen in the study by Kremer et al. (2013). The threshold level has been found for advanced and developing countries are quite different. According to Kremer et al. (2013), developed countries can determine their target inflation in the range of 1.94–2.76 % (around 2 %). Unlike developed countries, the target inflation range of developing countries may be in the wider range which is 12.85–19.11 % (around 17 %). Details on empirical studies are given in Table 1.

Table 1. Studies Investigating Threshold Level in Inflation-Growth Nexus

Authors	Countries & Period	Method	Findings/Optimal Threshold Value
Khan and Senhadji (2001)	140 advanced and developing countries (1960–98)	NNLS	The optimal inflation threshold level is 1–3 % for advanced countries; 7–11 % for developing countries.
Drukker et al. (2005)	138 advanced and developing countries (1950–2000)	PTR	The optimal inflation threshold level is 19.16 % for developing countries; the two inflation threshold levels for advanced countries are 2.57 % and 12.61 % respectively; the threshold level for all sample is 19.16 %
Espinoza et al. (2010)	165 advanced and developing countries (1967–2007)	PSTR	The optimal inflation threshold level is 10 % for developing countries.
Bick (2010)	40 developing countries (1960–2004)	Modified PTR	The optimal inflation threshold level is 12.03 % when regime barriers allowed;.19.16 % when not allowed.
López-Villavicencio and Mignon (2011)	44 OECD and emerging market countries (1961–2007)	PSTR	The optimal inflation threshold level is 2.7 % for advanced countries and 17.5 % for developing countries.
Vinayagathasan (2013)	32 Asian countries (1980–2009)	DPTR	The optimal inflation threshold level is 5.43 %.
Kremer et al. (2013)	124 advanced and developing countries (1950–2004)	DPTR	The optimal inflation threshold level is 2 % for advanced countries and 17 % for developing countries.
Eggoh and Khan (2014)	102 advanced and developing countries (1960–2009)	PSTR	The optimal inflation threshold level is 12.4 %.
Baglan and Yoldas (2014)	92 developing countries (1975–2004)	Flexible semiparametric panel data model	The optimal inflation threshold level is 12 %.
Das and Loxley (2015)	54 developing countries (1971–2010)	Quadratic model	The optimal inflation threshold level is 23.5 % for Latin America; 11 % for Asia, 23.6 % for Sub-Saharan Africa.

Table 1. Continued

Authors	Countries & Period	Method	Findings/Optimal Threshold Value
Aydın et al. (2016)	24 emerging market countries (1980–2013)	DPTR	The optimal inflation threshold level is 13.68 %.
Ibarra and Trupkin (2016)	138 advanced and developing countries (1950–2009)	PSTR	The optimal inflation threshold level is 4.5 % for advanced countries and 19.1 % for developing countries.

Note: NNLS (Non-linear least squares), PTR (Panel threshold regression by Hansen (1999)), PSTR (Panel smooth transition regression by Gonzalez et al. (2005)), DPTR (Dynamic panel threshold regression by Kremer et al. (2013)).

3 Data and Methodology

3.1 Data and Variables

This study, which examines the relationship between inflation and economic growth, uses a balanced panel data set of 41 developing countries. The country sample was selected according to the availability of the data.[1] The study uses five-year average data for the period between 1965 and 2019. In the empirical model, dependent variable economic growth is represented by the annual growth rate of real GDP per capita in constant 2010 prices. The threshold variable inflation rate was calculated as the annual percentage change of the consumer price index. Since the inflation rate variable contains negative values, it was subjected to semi-logarithmic transformation following Khan & Senhadji (2001). The semi-logarithmic transformation is implemented as follows.

$$\tilde{\pi}_{it} = \left\{ \begin{array}{ll} \pi_{it} - 1, & if\ \pi_{it} \leq 1\% \\ \ln(\pi_{it}), & if\ \pi_{it} > 1\% \end{array} \right\}$$

In the model, control variables that may affect economic growth are also employed. The set of control variables are; initial real income per capita level, population growth rate, the share of investments in GDP, trade openness measured by the share of exports plus imports in GDP, the share of public expenditures

1 The list of countries is given in annex.

Table 2. List of Variables

Variables	Symbol	Definition
Panel A: Dependent Variable		
Economic growth	grgdppc	Five-year average of the annual growth rate of real GDP per capita in constant 2010 prices
Panel B: Threshold Variable		
Inflation rate (π)	inf	Five-year average of the annual percentage change of the consumer price index
Panel C: Control Variables		
Initial income	initial	Five-year average of previous period's real GDP per capita in constant 2010 prices, in natural log
Population growth	gpop	Five-year average of the annual growth rate of population
Investment	inv	Five-year average of the annual percentage of gross capital formation as a share of GDP, in natural log
Openness	open	Five-year average of the annual percentage of export plus import as a share of GDP, in natural log
Government expenditure	gov	Five-year average of the annual percentage of general government final consumption expenditure as a share of GDP, in natural log
Life expectancy	life	Five-year average of total years of life expectancy at birth, in natural log.

in GDP and life expectancy. The symbols and definitions for the variables are shown in Table 2. All data used in the analysis were obtained from the World Bank World Development Indicators database.

Descriptive statistics and correlation matrix for all variables used in the study are given in Tables 3 and 4 in detail. As seen in Table 3, the economic growth rate is 1.78 % and the inflation rate is 25 % on average in the countries included in the analysis. The difference between the maximum value and the minimum value for the inflation rate is much larger than the economic growth rate. Therefore, it shows that the effects of different inflation rate levels on economic growth may differ. The panel threshold model used in the study is a suitable model. When we look at the correlation matrix in Table 4, there is a statistically significant and negative correlation between economic growth and the threshold variable inflation rate. According to this result, the economic growth decreases as the inflation rate increases.

Table 3. Descriptive Statistics

Variable	Mean	Median	Standart Deviation	Minimum	Maximum	N
grgdppc	1.776724	1.932756	2.933166	-12.3037	22.73479	410
initial	3882.502	2655.556	4365.883	218.3344	36437.37	410
inf	25.04452	8.049499	150.4095	-3.01611	2414.346	410
inv	22.38534	21.6468	7.245783	4.936859	52.43445	410
gpop	2.162759	2.25671	0.932464	-4.07274	6.135613	410
open	61.12676	54.74677	30.2989	8.570352	205.5394	410
gov	13.47026	12.7948	4.151063	3.626695	33.26386	410
life	63.02833	64.306	9.644567	28.6524	79.844	410

Table 4. Correlations Matrix

	grgdppc	inf	initial	gpop	inv	open	gov	life
grgdppc	1.00							
inf	-0.11*	1.00						
initial	0.02	0.01	1.00					
gpop	-0.14*	-0.06	-0.29*	1.00				
inv	0.30*	-0.12*	0.38*	-0.07	1.00			
open	0.13*	-0.32*	0.32*	-0.07	0.36*	1.00		
gov	-0.15*	-0.30*	0.11*	0.15*	0.11*	0.25*	1.00	
life	0.22*	0.07	0.63*	-0.42*	0.43*	0.27*	-0.06	1.00

Note: * indicates $p<0.05$.

3.2 Empirical Methodology

In empirical analysis, it is examined whether the threshold of inflation plays an important role in the relationship between economic growth and inflation. The panel threshold regression (PTR) method with a country-specific fixed effect developed by Hansen (1999) is used in this study. The main advantage of the method is that the threshold level can be determined endogenously rather than imposed by an external predetermined constraint. The structural equation for the panel threshold model developed by Hansen (1999) is as follows:

$$y_{it} = \mu_i + \beta'_1 x_{it}\, I(q_{it} \leq \gamma) + \beta'_2 x_{it}\, I(q_{it} > \gamma) + \varepsilon_{it} \quad (1)$$

In equation (1) y_{it} represents the dependent variable, and μ_i represents the unobserved individual fixed effects. Error term ε_{it} is assumed to be independent and identically distributed with an average of 0 and finite variance (σ^2). I (.), q_{it}, and γ characterize indicator function, regime-dependent variable and threshold level respectively. x_{it} is the vector of explanatory variables in the k-dimensional, and subscripts i and t represent units and time respectively. The equation (1) can alternatively be written as follows:

$$y_{it} = \begin{Bmatrix} \mu_i + \beta'_1 x_{it} + \varepsilon_{it}, & if\ q_{it} \leq \gamma \\ \mu_i + \beta'_2 x_{it} + \varepsilon_{it}, & if\ q_{it} > \gamma \end{Bmatrix}$$

When rewritten in general form:

$$y_{it} = \mu_i + \beta' x_{it}\ (\gamma) + \varepsilon_{it} \tag{2}$$

where $x_{it}\ (\gamma) = \binom{x_{it} I(q_{it} \leq \gamma)}{x_{it} I(q_{it} > \gamma)}$, and $\beta' = (\beta'_1 \beta'_2)$.

Observations are divided into two regimes according to whether threshold variable q_{it} is smaller or greater than threshold level γ. The regimes differ according to different estimation values of regression slope coefficients (β'_1, β'_2). In order to obtain β'_1 and β'_2, the elements in the x_{it} vector should not consist of time-invariant variables. Furthermore, Hansen (1999) assumes that the regime-dependent variable is not time-invariant. The estimates of slope coefficients β'_1 and β'_2 depend on the endogenously determined threshold level (γ) value. Hansen (1999) proposes the selection of grid search that minimizes the sum of residual squares $(S_1(\gamma))$ obtained from the least squares estimate of equation (1) to determine the threshold value (γ).

$$\hat{\gamma} = argmin_{\gamma} S_1\ (\gamma) \tag{3}$$

Once threshold prediction $(\hat{\gamma})$ is obtained, the slope coefficients ($\hat{\beta} = \hat{\beta}\ (\hat{\gamma})$ can be estimated accordingly.

4 Empirical Results

In order to determine the presence and level of the inflation threshold in the relationship between economic growth and inflation, the model expressed in equation (4) is estimated.

$$grgdppc_{it} = \mu_i + \beta'_1 x_{it}\, I\,(inf_{it} \leq \gamma) + \beta'_2 x_{it}\, I\,(inf_{it} > \gamma) + \varepsilon_{it} \quad (4)$$

The first stage of panel threshold regression analysis is determining whether the threshold effect is statistically significant or not. For this reason, the linear model has been tested against the nonlinear model. While the null hypothesis of the LR (likelihood ratio) test suggests that there is no threshold, the alternative hypothesis points to the presence of a single threshold.

According to the LR linearity test results reported in Table 5, the null hypothesis is rejected at a significance level of 10 %. Findings show that the appropriate model is a non-linear model with at least one threshold level. Therefore, it is not appropriate to use linear models in modeling the effect of inflation on economic growth. In the second stage, the test was repeated to determine the number of regimes. The results report that a single threshold level is significant and the two-regime model is appropriate.

Table 5. Linearity Test

Threshold	**Fstat.**	**Prob.**	**Bootstrapped Critical Values**		
			%90	**%90**	**%90**
Single	12.61*	0.0867	12.15	14.21	19.67
Double	9.26	0.19	12.71	19.96	51.25
Triple	10.18	0.27	15.07	18.98	25.53

Note: * indicates p<0.10.

The relationship between economic growth and inflation is estimated by the panel threshold regression model. In the model, inflation is both a threshold variable and a regime-dependent variable. Regression results are presented in Table 6. The estimated optimal inflation level is 19.01 %. In developing countries, the lower bound of the optimal threshold level at 95 % confidence level is 13.29 %, and the upper bound is 19.16 %.

The regime-dependent coefficients of inflation are negative both in the low-inflation regime ($\hat{\beta}_1$) and in the high-inflation regime ($\hat{\beta}_2$). However, the effect in the high-inflation regime (-0.692) was statistically significant, while the effect in the low-inflation regime (-0.247) was not significant. In addition, the adverse effect of inflation on economic growth in the high-inflation regime is greater than in the low-inflation regime. The results show that in developing countries, economic growth significantly decreased above the threshold level of inflation.

The findings are consistent with the results of many studies analyzing developing countries in the current literature. The estimated optimal threshold values

Table 6. Panel Threshold Regression Results

Dependent variable	**grgdppc**
Estimated Threshold Value	
$\hat{\gamma}$	19.01 %
95 % Confidence Interval	[13.29, 19.16]
Effect of Inflation	
$\hat{\beta}_1$ (Marginal effect, Low-inflation regime)	-0.247 (0.191)
$\hat{\beta}_2$ (Marginal effect, high-inflation regime)	-0.692*** (0.148)
Effect of Control Variables	
initial	-3.152*** (0.491)
gpop	-.162 (0.206)
inv	2.227*** (0.644)
open	1.612*** (0.602)
gov	-2.615*** (0.662)
life	2.532 (1.554)
constant	10.007 (6.163)
N	410
R^2	0.25

Note: * indicates p<0.10, ** indicates p<0.05, and *** indicates p<0.01.

obtained in these studies are as follows: Drukker et al. (2005) – 19.16 %; Pollin and Zhu (2006) about 15–18 %; Bick (2010) – 19.16 %; López -Villavicencio & Mignon (2011) – 17.5 %; Kremer et al. (2013) – 17 %; Ibarra and Trupkin (2016) 19.1 %.

The effects of control variables are consistent with theoretical expectations. The effect of the initial income level is negative and statistically significant. This shows that the convergence hypothesis envisaged in the neo-classical growth model is valid. Investments and trade openness affect economic growth positively and public spending negatively. The negative effect of the population growth on economic growth and the positive effect of life expectancy are not statistically significant.

5 Conclusion

One of the main targets of macroeconomic policies is to provide a low level of inflation to ensure sustainable economic growth. Inflation can reduce the economic growth rate by disrupting macroeconomic stability after a certain threshold level. How low the inflation rate targeted by policymakers will depend on which threshold level negatively affects growth. Therefore, accurate estimation of the threshold level of inflation is vital for policymakers to establish a sound macroeconomic policy.

Our evidence on the relationship between inflation and economic growth is directly related to the planning and implementation of monetary policy and the inflation targeting regime. There is a nonlinear relationship between inflation and economic growth. This shows that the monetary policy may have different effects on economic growth depending on the inflation level. The results are expected to guide monetary policy authorities, particularly those implementing the inflation-targeting regime. Central banks should establish policies to keep the inflation rate below the estimated threshold value. In developing countries that target a low level of inflation when implementing these policies, it may be necessary to strike a balance between macroeconomic stability and economic development. Therefore, poverty reduction and job creation can be identified as priority issues in developing countries instead of following a restrictive low inflation policy. In addition, the government's support with policies that encourage capital formation and reduce trade barriers will contribute positively to economic growth.

References

Ambler, S. (2007). The costs of inflation in New Keynesian models. Bank of Canada Review, 2007(Winter), 7–16.

Andres, J., & Hernando, I. (1997). Inflation and economic growth: Some evidence for the OECD countries. In Monetary Policy and the Inflation Process-BIS Conference Papers (Vol. 4, pp. 364–383).

Aydın, C., Akıncı, M., & Yılmaz, Ö. (2017). Ekonomik Büyüme Dinamizmini Enflasyon Ne Zaman Engeller? Yükselen Ekonomiler Üzerine Bir Dinamik Panel Eşik Modeli. Gazi Üniversitesi İktisadi ve İdari Bilimler Fakültesi Dergisi, 18(3), 748–761.

Baglan, D., & Yoldas, E. (2014). Non-linearity in the inflation–growth relationship in developing economies: Evidence from a semiparametric panel model. Economics Letters, 125(1), 93–96.

Ball, L., Mankiw,N. G., Romer, D., Akerlof, G. A., Rose, A., Yellen, J., & Sims, C. A. (1988). The new Keynesian economics and the output-inflation trade-off. Brookings Papers on Economic Activity, 1988(1), 1–82.

Barro, R. J. (1995). Inflation and Economic Growth. NBER, Working Paper, No. 5326.

Bick, A. (2010). Threshold effects of inflation on economic growth in developing countries. Economics Letters, 108, 126–129.

Bruno, M., & Easterly, W. (1998). Inflation crises and long-run growth. Journal of Monetary Economics, 41(1), 3–26.

Das, A., & Loxley, J. (2015). Non-linear relationship between inflation and growth in developing countries. Economic & Political Weekly, 50(37), 59–64.

De Gregorio, J. (1992). The effects of inflation on economic growth: Lessons from Latin America. European Economic Review, 36(2–3), 417–425.

Dornbusch, R., & Fischer, S. (1993). Moderate inflation. The World Bank Economic Review, 7(1), 1–44.

Drukker, D., Gomis-Porqueras, P., & Hernandez-Erme, P. (2005). Threshold effects in the relationship between inflation and growth: A new panel data approach (MPRA Paper No. 38225).

Eggoh, J. C., & Muhammad, K. (2014). On the nonlinear relationship between inflation and economic growth. Research in Economics, 68(2), 133–143.

Epaphra, M. (2016). Nonlinearities in inflation and growth nexus: The case of Tanzania. Journal of Economics and Political Economy, 3(3), 471–512.

Espinoza, R., Leon, H., & Ananthakrishnan, P. (2010). Estimating the inflation-growth nexus-a smooth transition model (IMF Working Paper, WP/10/76).

Faria, J. R., & Carneiro, F. G. (2001). Does high inflation affect growth in the long and short run?. Journal of Applied Economics, 4(1), 89–105.

Fischer, S., & Modigliani, F. (1978). Towards an understanding of the real effects and costs of inflation. Review of World Economics, 114(4), 810–833.

Fisher, S. (1993). The role of macroeconomic factors in growth. Journal of Monetary Economics, 32(3), 485–512.

Friedman, M. (1976). Inflation and unemployment. Nobel Memorial Lecture, the University of Chicago, Illinois, USA.

Gokal, V., & Hanif, S. (2004). Relationship between inflation and growth. Economics Department, Reserve Bank of Fiji, Working Paper, 4, 1–24.

Gonzalez, A., Terasvirta, T., & van Dijk, D. (2005). Panel Smooth Transition Regression Model and an Application to Investment under Credit Constraint. Working Paper in Economics and Finance, Stockholm School of Economics, 64.

Hansen, B. (1999). Threshold effects in non-dynamic panels: Estimation, testing and inference. Journal of Econometrics, 93(2), 345–368.

Hansen, B. (2000). Sample splitting and threshold estimation. Econometrica, 68(3), 575–603.

Ibarra, R., & Trupkin, D. (2016). Reexamining the relationship between inflation and growth: Do institutions matter in developing countries? Economic Modelling, 52, 332–351.

Khan, M. S., & Senhadji, A. S. (2001). Threshold effects in the relationship between inflation and growth. IMF Staff Papers, 48(1), 1–21.

Kremer, S., Bick, A., & Nautz, D. (2013). Inflation and growth: New evidence from a dynamic panel threshold analysis. Empirical Economics, 44(2), 861–878.

López -Villavicencio, A., & Mignon, V. (2011). On the impact of inflation on output growth: Does the level of inflation matter?. Journal of Macroeconomics, 33(3), 455–464.Malla, S. (1997). Inflation and economic growth: Evidence from a growth equation. Department of Economics, University of Hawaiâ™ I at Monoa, Honoulu, USA.

Mallik, G., & Chowdhury, A. (2001). Inflation and economic growth: Evidence from four south Asian countries. Asia-Pacific Development Journal, 8(1), 123–135.

Michael, Y. (2008). The relationship between inflation and unemployment in Ethiopia. M.A. Dissertation. Sudan: Department of Economics, Addis Ababa University.

Mubarik, Y. A., & Riazuddin, R. (2005). Inflation and growth: An estimate of the threshold level of inflation in Pakistan. Karachi: State Bank of Pakistan.

Mundell, R. A. (1963). Inflation and real interest. The Journal of Political Economy, 71(3), 280–283.

Mundell, R. A. (1965). Growth, stability and inflationary finance. The Journal of Political Economy, 73(2), 97–109.

Pentecost, E. J. (2000). Macroeconomics: An open economy approach (1st ed.). Macmillan Press Ltd., New York.

Roubini, N., & Sala-i-Martin, X. (1991). Financial development, the trade regime, and economic growth (No. 646). Center discussion paper.

Sarel, M. (1996). Nonlinear effects of inflation on economic growth. IMF Paper Series, 43(1), 199–215.

Shi, S. (1999). Search, inflation and capital accumulation. Journal of Monetary Economics, 44(1), 81–103.

Sidrauski, M. (1967). Rational choice and patterns of growth in a monetary economy. The American Economic Review, 57(2), 534–544.

Stockman, A. C. (1981). Anticipated inflation and the capital stock in a cash-in-advance economy. Journal of Monetary Economics, 8, 387–393.

Tobin, J. (1965). Money and economic growth. Econometrica, 33(4), 671–684.

Vaona, A. (2012). Inflation and growth in the long run: A new Keynesian theory and further semiparametric evidence. Macroeconomic Dynamics, 16(1), 94–132.

Vinayagathasan, T. (2013). Inflation and economic growth: A dynamic panel threshold analysis for Asian economies. Journal of Asian Economics, 26, 31–41.

APPENDIX

List of Countries

Algeria	Dominican Republic	Indonesia	Pakistan	Sri Lanka
Bolivia	Ecuador	Iran, Islamic Rep.	Panama	Thailand
Burkina Faso	Egypt, Arab Rep.	Jamaica	Paraguay	Togo
Burundi	El Salvador	Kenya	Peru	Turkey
Cameroon	Eswatini	Madagascar	Philippines	Uruguay
Chile	Gabon	Malaysia	Rwanda	
Colombia	Ghana	Mexico	Saudi Arabia	
Costa Rica	Guatemala	Morocco	Senegal	
Cote d'Ivoire	India	Niger	South Africa	

İbrahim Ethem Güney

The Impact of Geopolitical Risks on Stock Market Dynamics: Evidence from Turkey

1 Introduction

Stock markets are crucial for all countries since they provide signals about the current status of economies. In this respect, policymakers and industry professionals follow stock market dynamics very closely to examine economic activity and the growth of different industries and companies. On the other hand, investors also focus on stock markets for their portfolio management decisions. Hence, understanding the main drivers of stock market returns and volatility is of vital importance in finance literature. Various papers in the extant literature tried to analyze stock market returns and volatility with different types of linear, non-linear and non-parametric models. Aye et al. (2017) and Bekiros et al. (2016a, 2016b) provide detailed literature reviews on the predictability of stock market dynamics with several macroeconomic and financial predictors and differing uncertainties in economies.

However, the impact of geopolitical risks on financial markets and economies has been frequently emphasized by the reports of central banks and international organizations in recent years. Increasing geopolitical tensions associated with terrorist attacks, wars, and conflicts between countries negatively affect investors' sentiment, which may imply huge losses in share values of companies due to panic selling. Hence, it is essential to measure the effect of such risks on financial markets. In this regard, several papers investigated the impact of geopolitical risks on stock returns and/or volatility for different countries. Kollias et al. (2010, 2011a, 2011b, 2013) examined different terrorist attacks, wars and armed conflicts and their effect on stock market dynamics. They showed that the abovementioned problems increase stock market volatility and negatively affect stock returns. The impact on volatility was shown to be dominant. Balcilar et al. (2016b) utilized the non-parametric causality-in-quantiles test introduced by Balcilar et al. (2016a) to investigate the impact of geopolitical risks (GPRs) on stock markets of G7 countries. They found that geopolitical risks negatively affect stock returns for all countries except France and Japan. In addition, the causal impact on stock market volatility was only shown to be valid for Japan and the UK. Bouri et al. (2018) also applied the non-parametric causality-in-quantiles test to explore the impact of GPRs on Islamic equity and bond markets. Geopolitical risks were seen to affect bond market returns and volatility. However, they did not observe any impact on volatility for equity markets. In a concurrent study, Balcilar et al. (2018) worked with BRICS countries' data and revealed that geopolitical tensions negatively affect stock market volatilities, especially the ones at quantiles below the conditional median of returns (bad volatility). In another work, Apergis et al. (2017) utilized a non-parametric causality test to analyze the impact of GPRs on 24 global defense companies and showed that global geopolitical incidents mostly influence the future risk profile rather than the current performance of defense firms. Finally, Bouras et al. (2018), employed a panel GARCH model to investigate the role of country-specific and global GPRs on 18 emerging stock market dynamics. They found evidence about the impact of global GPRs but not country-specific ones on stock returns and volatility.

Most of the papers in the aforementioned literature utilized the monthly news-based GPR index constructed by Caldara and Iacoviello (2018)[1] to measure geopolitical risks. They developed a monthly index starting from 1985 that incorporates different geopolitical tensions such as military threats, regional tensions, and war risks. This gives authors the opportunity to capture the risks associated with geopolitical tensions and their impact on financial markets throughout recent history.

In line with the literature, in this chapter, my objective is to analyze the impact of geopolitical risks on Turkish stock market dynamics for the period 1988–2019 by using GPR indices proposed by Caldara and Iacoviello (2018). As an open economy, Turkey has exposure to different geopolitical risks due to its position at the crossroads between east and west and increasing instabilities in its neighborhood. This led the Turkish stock market to be oversensitive to geopolitical tensions. However, the existing literature on the impacts of geopolitical risks on the Turkish economy is very limited. Mansour-Ichrakieh and Zeaiter (2019) used the threshold vector autoregressive (VAR) method to analyze the impact of geopolitical risks associated with Saudi Arabia (regional) and Russia (global) on financial stress in Turkey. They concluded that although geopolitical risks stemming from Saudi Arabia were seen to negatively affect Turkish financial conditions, it was not the case for Russia. In a descriptive study, Terzi (2020) provided time-series graphs to show the correlation between geopolitical risks and Turkish money and financial market indicators.

1 The geopolitical risk indices were firstly introduced in the earlier version of this paper in 2016.

This chapter contributes to the extant literature by a twofold; firstly, to the best of my knowledge, there does not exist a paper in the literature that empirically analyzes the impact of geopolitical tensions on the Turkish stock market. Secondly, this chapter will be the first study in this literature that utilizes the time-varying Granger Causality approach developed by Rossi and Wang (2019). This method yields the continuous observation of Granger causality from geopolitical risks to stock market dynamics through the sample period. Hence, one can capture the time periods during which Granger-causality either arises, diminishes or disappears in the data. The empirical analysis shows that global geopolitical risks do not have an important impact on Turkish stock returns except rare events such as the 9/11 terrorist attacks to the World Trade Center in the United States. However, the effect on volatility is significant after 2000, especially during the 9/11 and Iraq invasion episodes. On the other hand, Turkey-specific geopolitical risks seem to have an important effect, especially on Turkish stock market volatility through our sample period. The impact on stock returns appears significantly during episodes such as the Iraq invasion and financial crisis periods.

2 Data

I use geopolitical risk (GPR) indices proposed by Caldara and Iacoviello (2019) to measure geopolitical risks in the empirical analysis. They developed these indices by searching expressions related to geopolitical events and risks from 11 well-known newspapers: The Boston Globe, the Chicago Tribune, The Daily Telegraph, the Financial Times, The Globe and Mail, The Guardian, the Los Angeles Times, The New York Times, The Times, The Wall Street Journal, and The Washington Post. The monthly index value is calculated by taking the ratio of the number of articles discussing rising geopolitical risks to the total number of published articles. The index dates back to 1985 and it is normalized to the average value of 100 for the period 2000–2009. The search words are classified into six groups; namely, geopolitical threats, nuclear threats, war threats, terrorist threats, war acts, and terrorist acts. The first four groups capture the words related to geopolitical threats and tensions. However, groups 5 and 6 cover actual acts of geopolitical risk. Caldara and Iacoviello constructed also country-specific GPR indices for 19 countries[2]. I utilize both global GPR and Turkey's GPR

2 Country-specific GPR indices were constructed for Turkey, Mexico, South Korea, Russia, India, Brazil, China, Indonesia, Saudi Arabia, South Africa, Argentina, Colombia, Venezuela, Thailand, Ukraine, Israel, Malaysia, Phillippines, and Hong Kong. See https://www.matteoiacoviello.com//gpr.htm for details.

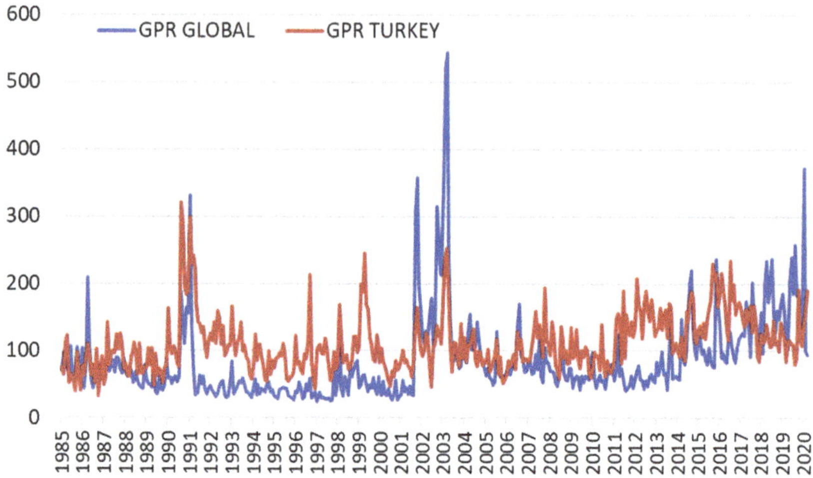

Figure 1: Global and Turkey Geopolitical Risk Indices for the Period 1985–2020

indices in my empirical analysis. Figure 1 illustrates these two indices. The first observation from Figure 1 is that global and Turkey specific GPR indices follow similar trends. However, Turkey related geopolitical risks dominate in some subsequent episodes. The peaks of global GPR are observed during different periods such as the terrorist escalation that led to the U.S. bombing of Libya (1986), the invasion of Kuwait by Iraq and the subsequent Gulf War (1990), 9/11 (2001), Iraq invasion (2003), major terrorist events in Europe, the Russian annexation of the Crimea peninsula (2013), the escalation of ISIS military operations in Iraq and Syria (2014), Paris attacks (2015) and finally coronavirus pandemic (2020) (see Caldaro and Iacoviello (2019) for details). GPR for Turkey increased during those periods as well. We also observe additional spikes in Turkey's GPR index in different episodes such as post-modern coup (1997), the capture of Ocalan (1999), conflicts with Russia starting with Turkey's shot down of Russian jet (2015), Ankara bombings (2015), and the failed coup attempt (2016).

To represent stock market dynamics, I include the monthly returns and realized volatility of the BIST 100 index to my sample. First, daily returns are calculated as percentage first differences of logged prices. Then, I compute realized volatility as the monthly sum of squared daily stock returns (i.e. the first-difference of the natural logarithm of the BIST 100 index times 100). Figures 2 and 3 illustrate the monthly returns and realized volatility, respectively. The key observation from these figures is that during the periods of higher global or

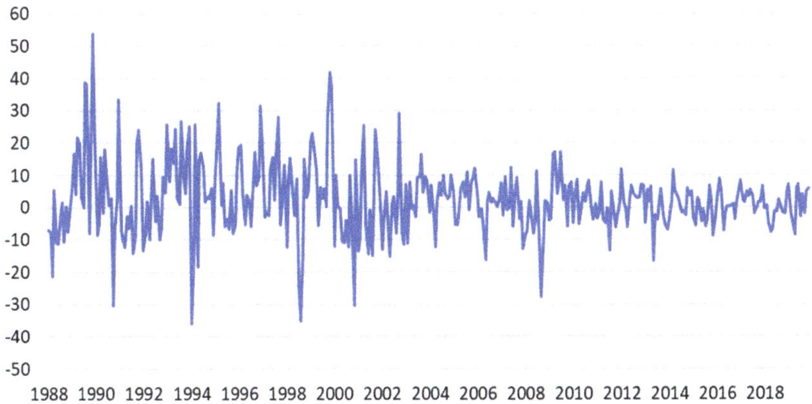

Figure 2: Monthly Stock Returns of BIST 100 Index for the Period 1988 – 2019
Source: Bloomberg

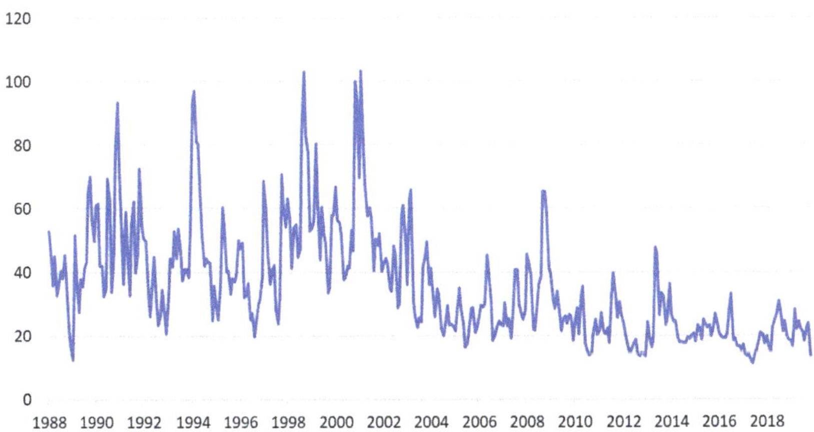

Figure 3: Monthly Realized Volatility of BIST 100 Index for the Period 1988 – 2019
Source: Bloomberg

Turkey-specific geopolitical tensions (such as the invasion of Kuwait by Iraq, post-modern coup in Turkey, 9/11, Iraq invasion, etc.) stock returns decreased dramatically and the volatility of BIST 100 index increased sharply. Turkish stock market didn't perform well during the Turkish banking crises in 1994 and 2001 and the global financial crisis in 2007–2009 neither.

I also incorporate macroeconomic variables to capture the role of them in stock market dynamics[3]. Monthly industrial production (IP) is chosen as an indicator of economic activity since real GDP growth data is quarterly available and IP is a successful indicator by having a very high correlation with GDP growth in Turkey. I use short term deposit rates (with maturity up to 1 month) to represent monetary policy stance which is available at the electronic data delivery system (EVDS) of CBRT since 2002 and IMF international financial statistics database for the period 1987–2002[4]. Monthly consumer price inflation (CPI) is also incorporated into our sample to capture the effect of price stability. Data are downloaded from Bloomberg terminal, EVDS of CBRT, and IMF database.

3 Methodology

In the empirical analysis, I employ the multivariate time-varying Granger causality test developed by Rossi and Wang (2019), which is robust to instabilities. By following the theoretical framework in Rossi and Wang (2019), a reduced-form Vector Autoregressive (VAR) model with time-varying parameters is utilized as follows:

$$C_t(L)\,x_t = v_t \tag{1}$$

$$C_t(L) = I - C_{1,t}L - C_{2,t}L^2 - \ldots - C_{k,t}L^k \tag{2}$$

$$v_t \overset{iid}{\sim} (0, \Sigma) \tag{3}$$

where $C_{i,t}$, $i = 1, .., k$ represent (nxn) time-varying coefficient matrix and $x_t = [x_{1,t},\ x_{2,t}, \ldots, x_{n,t}]'$ is $(nx1)$ vector of endogenous variables, whereas v_t stands for error terms[5]. Error terms can comply with idiosyncratic shocks which are assumed to be heteroscedastic and serially correlated. Iteration of equation (2) and projection of x_t onto the linear space created by $(x_{t-1}, x_{t-2}, \ldots, x_{t-k})'$ derives the following equation:

$$x_t = \beta_{1,t}x_{t-1} + \beta_{2,t}x_{t-2} + \ldots + \beta_{k,t}x_{t-k} + \varepsilon_t \tag{4}$$

---

3 See Engle and Rangel (2008), Engle and Ghysels (2013) for details.

4 Visit https://data.imf.org/?sk=4C514D48-B6BA-49ED-8AB9-52B0C1A0179B&sId=1390030341854 for details.

5 The lag length is chosen as 1 according to the Schwarz Information Criterion (SIC).

where $\beta_{i,t}, i = 1, \ldots k$ is a function of time-varying coefficients,
$[x_t, x_{t-1}, \ldots, x_{t-k}]'$ represent the variables in the model, and
ε_t is the heteroskedastic and serially correlated error term.

Finally, taking γ_t as an appropriate subset of the vector including $(\beta_{1,t}, \beta_{2,t}, \ldots, \beta_{k,t})$, robust Granger causality test figure out the validity of the null hypothesis in equation (5):

$$H_0 : \gamma_t = 0, \qquad \textit{for all } t = 1, \ \ldots, T \tag{5}$$

The null hypothesis is checked by using four test statistics as given in Rossi (2005), namely, the optimal exponential Wald test statistic (ExpW), optimal mean Wald test statistic (MeanW), Nyblom test statistic (Nyblom), and Quandt likelihood test statistic (SupLR). ExpW and MeanW were introduced in Andrews and Ploberger (1994). Nyblom test was proposed by Nyblom (1989) and SupLR test statistic depends on Sup-LR test developed by Andrews (1993).

I analyze the time-varying causality between geopolitical risks and stock market returns/volatility by using the following vectors of endogenous variables:

$$x_t = [GLOBALGPR_t, \ RET_t, IP_t \ , \ CPI_t \ , DEP_t \ ]' \tag{6}$$

$$x_t = [GLOBALGPR_t, \ VOL_t, IP_t \ , \ CPI_t \ , DEP_t \ ]' \tag{7}$$

$$x_t = [TURKEYGPR_t, \ RET_t, IP_t \ , \ CPI_t \ , DEP_t \ ]' \tag{8}$$

$$x_t = [TURKEYGPR_t, \ VOL_t, IP_t \ , \ CPI_t \ , DEP_t \ ]' \tag{9}$$

where $GLOBALGPR_t$ denotes global geopolitical risk index, $TURKEYGPR_t$ represents Turkey specific geopolitical risks, RET_t and VOL_t denotes the monthly return and realized volatility of BIST 100 index, $IP_t$is the monthly industrial production, CPI_tshows the monthly consumer price inflation, and DEP_t represents short term deposits.

4 Empirical Results

I first carry out reduced-form VAR-based robust Granger causality tests to analyze the impact of global or Turkey specific geopolitical risks on stock market parameters. Empirical results are summarized in Table 1. The test results show that that there exists a statistically significant Granger causality from both global

Table 1: Time-Varying Parameter Granger Causality Test Results (VAR Model)

Direction of Causality	Test Type	Test Statistic	p-value
$GLOBALGPR_t \rightarrow RET_t$	ExpW	16.51	0.00
	MeanW	5.59	0.21
	Nyblom	129.08	0.00
	SupLR	43.54	0.00
$GLOBALGPR_t \rightarrow VOL_t$	ExpW	171.99	0.00
	MeanW	40.22	0.00
	Nyblom	35.91	0.00
	SupLR	355.44	0.00
$TURKEYGPR_t \rightarrow RET_t$	ExpW	20.53	0.00
	MeanW	9.96	0.02
	Nyblom	187.37	0.00
	SupLR	52.39	0.00
$TURKEYGPR_t \rightarrow VOL_t$	ExpW	211.15	0.00
	MeanW	51.63	0.00
	Nyblom	438.91	0.00
	SupLR	433.74	0.00

and Turkey GPR indices to stock market return and volatility in Turkey, since all test statistics, except MeanW for causality from global GPR to stock returns, conclude the rejection of the null hypothesis.

Second, I display the tracks of Wald statistics over the sample period to analyze the episodes during which the impact of geopolitical risks on Turkish stock market dynamics strengthens/weakens. Figures 4–5 display the effect of global geopolitical risks on Turkish stock returns and volatility. The first observation is that Granger causality from the global GPR index to stock returns appeared rarely during our sample period. 9/11 terrorist attacks to the World Trade Center in the U.S. seem to have an important effect on BIST 100 stock returns since the wald statistic increased dramatically. On the other hand, global geopolitical tensions affected Turkish stock market volatility especially after 2000. 9/11, Iraq invasion, Syrian war, and the escalation of ISIS military operations in Iraq and Syria appear to be key events that mostly impacted BIST 100 volatility.

When we look at the effects of Turkey-specific geopolitical risks on the stock market, Granger causality is relatively stronger as seen in Figures 6–7. The impact on stock returns was very high during the Iraq invasion, which was an important geopolitical tension in the Turkish neighborhood. Another observation from

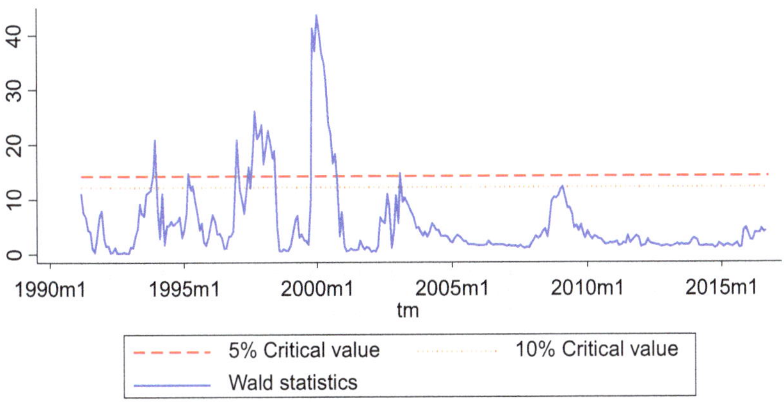

Figure 4: Time-Varying Wald Statistics (Testing GLOBALGPR Granger Causes RET)

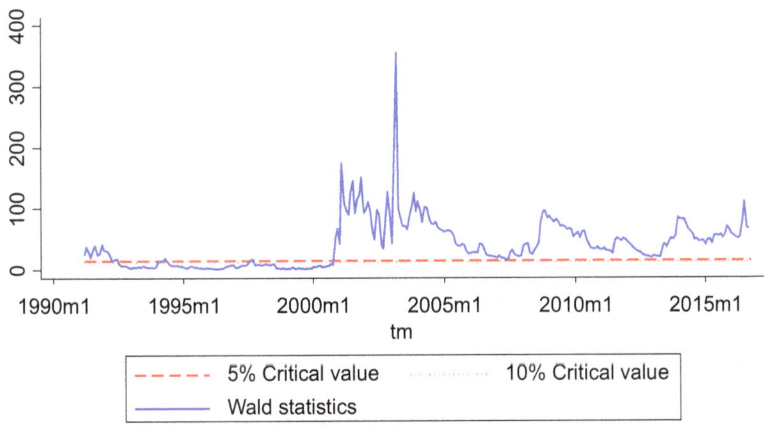

Figure 5: Time-Varying Wald Statistics (Testing GLOBALGPR Granger Causes VOL)

Figure 6 is that Granger causality increases during domestic banking (2000–2001) and global financial (2007–2009) crises. Hence, the influence of geopolitical tensions on Turkish stock returns seems to be amplified during financial crises. Finally, Figure 7 shows that there exists a significant impact of Turkey GPR on stock market volatility through our sample period. Causality strengthened

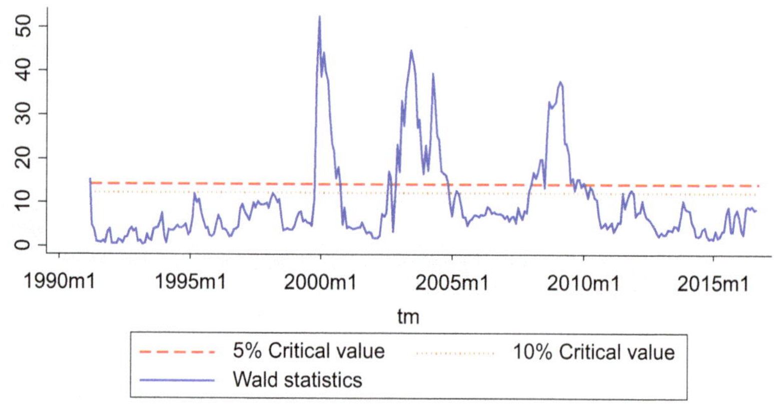

Figure 6: Time-Varying Wald Statistics (Testing TURKEYGPR Granger Causes RET)

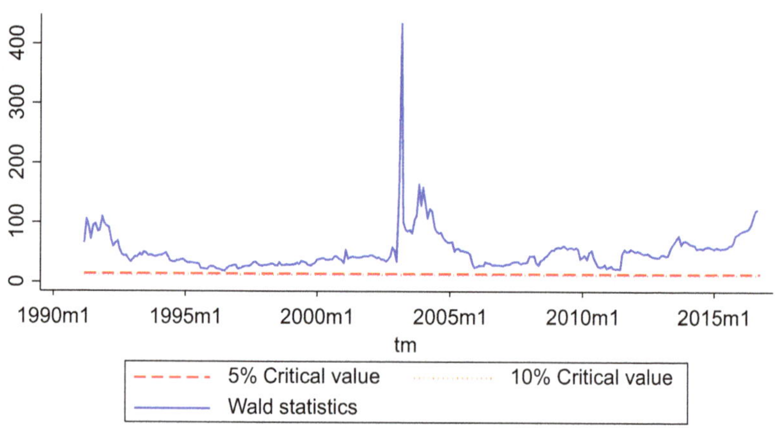

Figure 7: Time-Varying Wald Statistics (Testing TURKEYGPR Granger Causes VOL)

especially during the Iraq invasion, and with the escalated geopolitical tensions in Syria region.

5 Conclusion

In this chapter, I try to analyze the impact of geopolitical risks on Turkish stock market dynamics for the period 1988–2019. To this end, I use the multivariate time-varying Granger causality framework developed by Rossi and Wang (2019), which yields continuous observation of causality from geopolitical risks to stock returns and volatility through our sample period. In the empirical analysis, geopolitical risks associated with global tensions or Turkey-specific events are measured by using GPR indices proposed by Caldara and Iacoviello (2018). Stock market dynamics are represented by the monthly return and volatility of the BIST 100 index. I also control for the macroeconomic variables (industrial production, consumer price inflation, short term deposit rates) that may affect stock market behavior. Empirical evidence shows that both global and Turkey-specific geopolitical risks have an impact on Turkish stock market volatility. 9/11 terrorist attacks to the World Trade Center in the U.S., Iraq invasion, global financial crisis, Syrian war, and the escalation of ISIS military operations in Iraq and Syria are crucial events that drastically affected BIST 100 volatility. However, the impact of geopolitical risks on Turkish stock returns is relatively weaker. Geopolitical tensions associated with the Iraq invasion seem to be the key event that affects BIST 100 stock returns. Besides, the impact of geopolitical risks on stock returns is found to be high during the Turkish domestic banking crisis in 2001 and the global financial crisis of 2007–2009. This result reveals the amplifier role of financial instabilities when examining the relationship between geopolitical risks and stock market dynamics. To sum up, given the role of geopolitical risks on stock market dynamics, it would be useful for policymakers and finance professionals to consider such risks in their decision models.

References

Andrews, D. W. (1993). Tests for Parameter Instability and Structural Change with Unknown Change Point. Econometrica: Journal of the Econometric Society, 61(4), 821–856.

Andrews, D. W., and Ploberger, W. (1994). Optimal Tests When a Nuisance Parameter Is Present Only under the Alternative. Econometrica: Journal of the Econometric Society, 62(6), 1383–1414.

Apergis, N., Bonato, M., Gupta, R., and Kyei, C. (2017). Does Geopolitical Risks Predict Stock Returns and Volatility of Leading Defense Companies? Evidence from a Nonparametric Approach. Defence and Peace Economics, 29(6), 684–696.

Aye, G. C., Balcilar, M., and Gupta, R. (2017). International Stock Return Predictability: Is the Role of US Time-Varying?. Empirica, 44, 121–146.

Balcilar, M., Bekiros, S., and Gupta, R. (2016a). The Role of News-Based Uncertainty Indices in Predicting Oil Markets: A Hybrid Nonparametric

Quantile Causality Method. Empirical Economics, DOI: 10.1007/s00181-016-1150-0.

Balcilar, M., Bonato, M., Demirer, R., and Gupta, R. (2018). Geopolitical Risks and Stock Market Dynamics of the BRICS. Economic Systems, 42(2), 295–306.

Balcilar, M., Gupta, R., Pierdzioch, C., and Wohar, M.E. (2016b). Terror Attacks and Stock-Market Fluctuations: Evidence Based on a Nonparametric Causality-in-Quantiles Test for the G7 Countries. European Journal of Finance, 24(4), 333–346.

Bekiros, S., Gupta, R., and Kyei, C. (2016a). On Economic Uncertainty, Stock Market Predictability and Nonlinear Spillover Effects. North American Journal of Economics and Finance, 36, 184–191.

Bekiros, S., Gupta, R., and Majumdar, A. (2016b). Incorporating Economic Policy Uncertainty in US Equity Premium Models: A Nonlinear Predictability Analysis. Finance Research Letters, 18, 291–296.

Bouras, C., Christou, C., Gupta, R., and Suleman, T. (2018). Geopolitical Risks, Returns, and Volatility in Emerging Stock Markets: Evidence from a Panel GARCH Model. Emerging Markets Finance and Trade, 55(8), 1841–1856.

Bouri, E., Demirer, R., Gupta, R., and Marfatia, H.A. (2018). Geopolitical Risks and Movements in Islamic Bond and Equity Markets: A Note. Defence and Peace Economics, 30(3), 367–379.

Caldara, D. and Iacoviello M. (2018). Measuring Geopolitical Risk. International Finance Discussion Papers, 1222.

Engle, R.F., and Rangel, J.G. (2008). The Spline-GARCH Model for Low-Frequency Volatility and Its Global Macroeconomic Causes. Review of Financial Studies 21(3), 1187–1222.

Engle, R.F., Ghysels, E., and Sohn, B. (2013). Stock Market Volatility and Macroeconomic Fundamentals. The Review of Economics and Statistics, 95(3), 776–797.

Kollias, C., Papadamou, S., and Stagiannis, A. (2010). Armed Conflicts and Capital Markets: The Case of the Israeli Military Offensive in the Gaza Strip. Defence and Peace Economics, 21(4), 357–365.

Kollias, C., Papadamou, S., and Stagiannis, A. (2011a). Terrorism and Capital Markets: The Effects of the Madrid and London Bomb Attacks. International Review of Economics and Finance, 20(4), 532–541.

Kollias, C., Papadamou, S., and Stagiannis, A. (2011b). Stock Markets and Terrorist Attacks: Comparative Evidence from a Large and a Small Capitalization Market. European Journal of Political Economy, 27(S1), 64–77.

Kollias, C. S. Papadamou, S., and Arvanitis, V. (2013). Does Terrorism Affect the Stock-Bond Covariance? Evidence from European Countries. Southern Economic Journal, 79(4), 832–548.

Mansour-Ichrakieh, L., and Zeaiter, H. (2019). The Role of Geopolitical Risks on the Turkish Economy Opportunity or Threat. North American Journal of Economics and Finance, 50, 1–15.

Nyblom, J. (1989). Testing for the Constancy of Parameters over Time. Journal of the American Statistical Association, 84(405), 223–230.

Rossi, B. (2005). Optimal Tests for Nested Model Selection with Underlying Parameter Instability. Econometric Theory, 21(5), 962–990.

Rossi, B., and Wang, Y. (2019). Vector Autoregressive-Based Granger Causality Test in the Presence of Instabilities. The Stata Journal: Promoting Communications on Statistics and Stata, 19(4), 883–899.

Terzi, N. (2020). Potential Effects of Geopolitical Risks on Financial Markets in Turkey, European Congress on Economic Issues II, 96–105.

Özlem Topçuoğlu & Betül Buladi Çubukcu

Examining the Governmental Incentive Policies for Tourism in Turkey by the Provinces

1 Introduction

Tourism is accepted as an important solution especially for insufficient savings, limited export opportunities, rapid increase in foreign debts, and sustainability problem in underdeveloped and developing countries due to the global crisis in today's world, which has a high level of international competition. The tourism industry plays an important role in development since it accelerates the social and economic advancement by increasing the employment rates, ensuring the foreign capital's participation in economy, and increasing the foreign currency inflow. Thus, the United Nations World Tourism Organization (UNWTO) announced the year 2017 as "the Year of Sustainable Tourism for Development" and emphasized the importance of tourism for ensuring the economic, social, and cultural sustainability in the national and international areas. Sustainable tourism refers to meeting the necessities of current tourists and local people hosting these tourists by protecting the environmental and cultural heritage to be handed down to the next generations.

Given the contribution that this industry, which directly or indirectly affects the other industries, makes as an invisible export item, it is an undeniable fact that it should have an important share from the governmental incentives. Supporting and protecting the tourism industry requires legal regulation that should be made by the state, which is the largest shareholder. In balance with the other industries, the state supports the tourism industry within the limits of its capacity. The main function of an incentive system is the allocation of production factors, which are limited in any economy, to the economic activities determined before and, thus, increasing the investment, production, employment, and export.

Within this scope, the present study discusses the incentives given to the tourism industry within the scope of promotion law and examines the efficiency of incentives granted in Turkey by the provinces. The importance of tourism industry in the economy was emphasized and, by discussing the development of promotion law in the course of time, the supports and incentives of state for the tourism industry were explained. Moreover, a general efficiency assessment was made for the governmental incentives granted to the tourism industry. As a result of the efficiency assessment, although 262 inventive certificates were issued in total, it was determined that only 4 of 61 provinces receiving incentive reached the perfect efficiency level for both of CCR, which uses the assumption of variable return to scale, and BCC, which uses the assumption of constant return to scale, models.

2 Role and Importance of Tourism Industry in the Economy

The tourism refers to the whole of tourists activities aiming to meet their needs such as eating-drinking, accommodation, transportation, and guidage by leaving the place, where they live, and going to different destinations for different purposes such as recreational, commercial, educational, and cultural ones. Tourism industry has several distinctive characteristics. It is a service industry, is labor-intensive, requires high amounts of investment, has variable supply, and the demand in the tourism industry is affected by many variables (Kozak and Kozak, 2015). Tourism industry is very important for both the global economy and Turkey's economy. First, since it is a labor incentive industry, it has a positive effect on the employment. For the developing countries, it has significant positive contributions to the balance of payments by playing as an industry bringing foreign currency inflow. Moreover, it contributes to the economy by purchasing inputs from other sectors such as agriculture and manufacture. Finally, the tourism industry is also an industry that protects the investor sources but might also damage these sources (Olalı and Korzay, 1993).

Examining the tourism sector at the global level, according to World Tourism Barometer January 2020 published by the United Nations World Tourism Organization, the number of tourists in the world increased by 4 % in year 2019 and reached 1.5 billion. In year 2019, the number of tourists increased in all the regions. The rates of increase were 8 % in the Middle East, 5 % in Asia-Pacific, 4 % in Europe and Africa, and 1 % in America. In terms of the number of tourists, the country receiving the highest number of tourists in year 2019 was France with 89 million tourists. Turkey was ranked 6th in this list. The international tourism revenue in year 2018 was reported to be 1,462 billion USD. Examining the countries by the revenue from the tourism industry, the USA is ranked 1st with 214 billion USD, followed by Spain with 82 billion USD and France with 66 billion USD. Turkey is ranked 15th in this list (UNWTO, 2020).

Tourism industry has an important place in Turkey. With its contribution to both employment and foreign currency inflow, it is an industry that has a high potential for the Turkish economy. According to a research on tourism industry's size, structure, and contribution to economy by the Union of Mediterranean Tourism and Operators, 1 unit increase in demand in tourism industry creates 2 units increase in economy. Tourism directly stimulates 54 industries in the economy (AKTOB, 2014). With 12.2 % increasen in comparison to previous year, Turkey hosted 45.1 million foreign visitors in year 2019. When compared to the previous year, tourism revenues increased by 16.9 % in year 2019 and reached 34.5 billion USD (Turkish Republic Ministry of Culture and Tourism, 2019). It is also very interesting that Turkey having a good place in terms of the number of visitors is not ranked a good place in terms of tourism revenues.

3 Governmental Incentive Practices for Turkish Tourism Industry

The concept "incentive" can be defined as the financial and non-financial supports and encouragements given by the state in different forms in order to ensure the development of specific economic activities more and faster than the others (Çiloğlu, 1997). The incentives are important instruments, which the state uses in areas that it wants to support, in an economy. Moreover, the incentives are also important for directing the investments to the desired area.

When considering the incentive system utilized in Turkey in general, the incentive system put into force on 06.15.2012 with the Cabinet Decree Nr. 2012/3305 consists of 4 different practices. These are the general incentives, regional incentives, encouragement of priority investments, and incentives for strategic investments. Within the scope of these incentives, all or some of incentive instruments such as VAT exemption, customs duty exemption, tax reduction, support for employer's national insurance contribution, income tax withholding support, insurance premium support, coupon tax support, investment place allocation, and VAT refund are provided depending on the type of incentive (Turkish Republic, Ministry of Industry and Technology, Investment Incentive System).

Tourism industry is a sector having a high potential. However, investments in tourism are risky since they require high amount of investment at the beginning and they are sensitive to natural, economic, and politic events due to the human factor. For this reason, the governmental incentives are needed for the investments in tourism industry and the development of current industry. Nowadays, within the investment incentive system for tourism investors, general incentives, regional incentives, and incentives for the strategic investments are utilized. Within this scope, depending on the type of incentive, the VAT exemption, customs duty exemption, tax reduction, support for employer's national

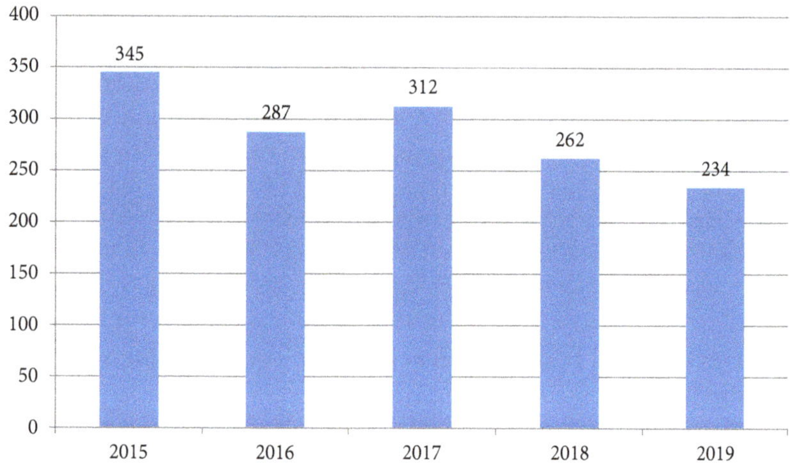

Figure 1. Number of Incentive Certificates

insurance contribution, income tax withholding support, insurance premium support, coupon tax support, and investment place allocation are applied.

Given the use of incentive system in the tourism industry, it can be seen that 234 investment incentive certificates were issued for tourism industry in year 2019. In Figure 1, the numbers of investment incentive certificates issued for tourism industry between 2015 and 2019 are presented. By the classes of incentive, 61 priority investment incentive certificates, 182 general incentive certificates, and 1207 regional incentive certificate were issued. Fifty-five of these certificates were issued for foreign capital companies and 1385 certificates for national capital investments (Turkish Republic, Ministry of Industry and Technology, Interactive Investment Incentive Certificate Statistics Report, 2019).

The amount of fixed investments in tourism industry for year 2019 was 6.67 billion TL. In Figure 2, the amounts of fixed investments in tourism industry between years 2015 and 2019 are shown. By the classes of incentive, the amounts of incentives were 2.47 billion TL for fixed investment priority investment incentives, 3.73 billion TL fixed investment general incentives, and 20.51 billion TL fixed investment regional incentives. By the type of capital, 7.95 % of investments were made by foreign capital and 92.05 % were made by the national capital (Turkish Republic, Ministry of Industry and Technology, Interactive Investment Incentive Certificate Statistics Report, 2019).

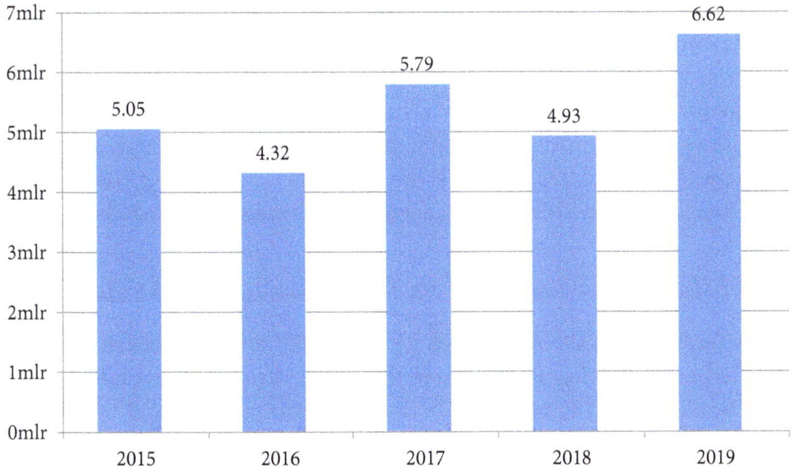

Figure 2. Fixed Investment Amounts

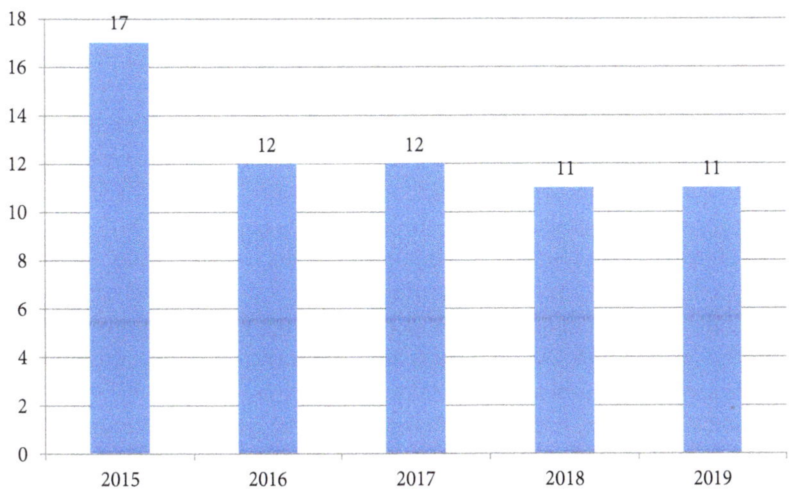

Figure 3. Employment Numbers of Enterprises with Incentive Certificates

Examining the employment, the number of employees in tourism companies having incentive certificate was 11,000 in year 2019. In Figure 3, the numbers of employees in tourism companies having incentive certificate between 2015 and 2019 are presented. By the class of incentives, 7,000 employees were employed within the scope of priority investment incentives and 50,000 employees within the scope of regional incentives (Turkish Republic, Ministry of Industry and Technology, Interactive Investment Incentive Certificate Statistics Report, 2019).

4 An Efficiency Assessment on Incentives in Tourism Industry

The performance measurements are an important criterion needed in almost any field and accepted as a guideline in today's rapidly changing conditions. The performance measurements can be performed in various areas and by using different methods. Since it is very useful in terms of measurement, the concept of "efficiency" is widely used in many practices.

The efficiency, which can be defined as the closeness of observed values to the ideal values, refers to how good the sources are used in production. The efficiency is divided into technical efficiency, scale efficiency, and total efficiency (Oum, YU and FU, 2003).

In literature, there are many methods used in the calculation of efficiency and the most widely used one among these methods is the Data Envelopment Analysis (DEA). DEA is a non-parametric method that is based on linear programming, producing the same type of outputs by using the same type of inputs and measuring the relative efficiencies of Decision-Making Units (DMUs) in having the same purpose. In DEA, the relative efficiency of a DMU is defined as the ratio of total outputs to total inputs, which are weighted using inputs and outputs obtained by linear programming. As a result of the analysis, the distinctive power problem arises between efficient and inefficient units when the number of efficient DMUs is extremely high. In order to overcome this problem, it is recommended in literature to take minimum (m+s+1) or 3(m+s) DMUs (m: number of inputs, s: number of outputs) for the reliability of research. This is named "golden rule" (Charnes et al., 1978). In DEA aiming to measure how good a DMU uses the sources in creating a set of output, the efficiency score of DMU showing the highest performance is 1, whereas the scores of other DMUs vary between 0 and 1.

The most widely preferred DEA models are CCR and BCC models. CCR model was developed by Charnes, Cooper, and Rhodes in 1978. CCR value aims to reveal a result by gathering technical efficiency, pure technical efficiency, and scale efficiency of DMU with the assumption of constant returns to scale. In

CCR model, the efficiency of a DMU is calculated by maximizing the ratio of weighted outputs to weighted inputs (Sowlati and Paradi, 2004). Developed by Banker, Charnes, and Cooper, BCC model is a model measuring the technical efficiency by using the variable return to scale (Kutlar and Babacan, 2008). The scale efficiency (SE) is calculated in order to determine the state of inefficiency. The value representing the relationship between the technical efficiency value (TE) in CCR model and the pure technical efficiency (PTE) in BCC model is named scale efficiency (SE). This efficiency is calculated as SE=CCR/BCC.

In DEA models, it should be determined which one of two approaches (input-oriented or output-oriented) will be chosen for measuring the technical efficiency. In the input-oriented approach, the minimum amount of input to be used in producing a specific amount of output (input minimization) is taken as base, whereas the amount of output to be produced by using a specific amount of input (output maximization) is taken as base in output-oriented approach (Benli, 2012).

The efficiency ranking of efficient DMUs can be determined. The super-efficiency model is used for this purpose. Developed and introduced by Andersen and Petersen (1993), the super-efficiency model is based on alternately removing each efficient DMU from the efficient production line and measuring the distance of removed DMU to the determined efficiency line. The DMU with the highest super efficiency score is the most efficient unit. By sorting efficient DMUs from the highest super efficiency score to the lowest one, the superiority ranking is obtained (Özden, 2008).

The input variables used in the efficiency analysis, which was performed in order to better understand the incentive policies implemented in the Turkish tourism industry that is the subject of this study, were the number of facilities with tourism operation license, the number of rooms, the number of certificates granted to the tourism industry, the promoted employment, and the promoted fixed investments in the tourism industry. The output variables were the total number of tourists and the total number of overnights.

The efficiency ranking and the efficiency and SE values calculated using input-oriented CCR and BCC models of year 2018, which is the most recent year of accessing all the input and output variables, are presented in Table 1.

The data obtained as a result of analyzes showed that, for year 2018, Afyonkarahisar (1 incentive certificate), Antalya (39 incentive certificates, one of the highest numbers of certificates), Aydın (3 incentive certificates), and Karaman (1 incentive certificate) achieved the perfect efficiency in both BCC and CCR. Among the provinces having no incentive certification, no provinces except for Eskişehir, Hakkâri, and Siirt achieved the perfect efficiency level.

Table 1. 2018 Input-Oriented CCR, BCC, SE Values and Efficiency Ranking

DMU	CCR	BCC	SE	Rank	DMU	CCR	BCC	SE	Rank	DMU	CCR	BCC	SE	Rank
Adana	0.585	0.880	0.664	0.585	Edirne	0.369	0.391	0.944	0.369	Malatya	0.398	0.401	0.994	0.398
Adıyaman	0.539	0.544	0.991	0.539	Elazığ	0.303	0.303	**1.000**	0.303	Manisa	0.337	0.358	0.943	0.337
Afyonkarahisar	**1.000**	**1.000**	**1.000**	1.190(4)	Erzincan	0.425	0.425	**1.000**	0.425	Mardin	0.325	0.329	0.987	0.325
Ağrı	0.110	0.133	0.825	0.110	Erzurum	0.772	0.775	0.996	0.772	Mersin	0.357	0.627	0.570	0.357
Aksaray	0.581	0.594	0.978	0.581	Eskişehir	**1.000**	**1.000**	**1.000**	1.111(6)	Muğla	0.451	0.513	0.879	0.451
Amasya	0.482	0.505	0.954	0.482	Gaziantep	0.728	0.873	0.834	0.728	Muş	0.487	0.496	0.982	0.487
Ankara	0.853	1.000	0.853	0.853	Giresun	0.218	0.238	0.920	0.218	Nevşehir	0.576	0.981	0.587	0.576
Antalya	**1.000**	**1.000**	**1.000**	1.949(2)	Gümüşhane	0.423	0.428	0.987	0.423	Niğde	0.644	0.678	0.949	0.644
Ardahan	0.611	0.629	0.971	0.611	Hakkâri	**1.000**	**1.000**	**1.000**	1.445(3)	Ordu	0.277	0.284	0.973	0.277
Artvin	0.196	0.236	0.832	0.196	Hatay	0.656	0.720	0.911	0.656	Osmaniye	0.267	0.504	0.530	0.267
Aydın	**1.000**	**1.000**	**1.000**	1.027(7)	Iğdır	0.214	0.451	0.475	0.214	Rize	0.146	0.189	0.773	0.146
Balıkesir	0.434	0.558	0.778	0.434	Isparta	0.645	0.669	0.964	0.645	Sakarya	0.377	0.387	0.976	0.377
Bartın	0.230	0.306	0.751	0.230	İstanbul	0.719	**1.000**	0.719	0.719	Samsun	0.316	0.445	0.710	0.316
Batman	0.358	0.407	0.881	0.358	İzmir	0.592	0.767	0.771	0.592	Şanlıurfa	0.519	0.626	0.828	0.519
Bayburt	0.465	0.575	0.809	0.465	Kahramanmaraş	0.129	0.135	0.953	0.129	Siirt	**1.000**	**1.000**	**1.000**	1.138(5)
Bilecik	0.628	0.630	0.996	0.628	Karabük	0.335	0.355	0.943	0.335	Sinop	0.238	0.327	0.726	0.238
Bingöl	0.804	0.887	0.906	0.804	Karaman	**1.000**	**1.000**	**1.000**	2.789(1)	Şırnak	0.535	0.636	0.841	0.535
Bitlis	0.461	0.470	0.981	0.461	Kars	0.313	0.320	0.977	0.313	Sivas	0.285	0.291	0.982	0.285
Bolu	0.353	0.354	0.995	0.353	Kastamonu	0.412	0.440	0.936	0.412	Tekirdağ	0.552	0.552	0.999	0.552
Burdur	0.249	0.258	0.964	0.249	Kayseri	0.964	**1.000**	0.964	0.964	Tokat	0.135	0.159	0.848	0.135
Bursa	0.489	0.869	0.563	0.489	Kilis	0.947	**1.000**	0.947	0.947	Trabzon	0.233	0.431	0.540	0.233
Çanakkale	0.442	0.631	0.701	0.442	Kırıkkale	0.766	0.844	0.907	0.766	Tunceli	0.323	0.568	0.569	0.323
Çankırı	0.247	0.345	0.717	0.247	Kırklareli	0.227	0.311	0.731	0.227	Uşak	0.428	0.429	0.997	0.428
Çorum	0.542	0.545	0.995	0.542	Kırşehir	0.631	0.634	0.995	0.631	Van	0.284	0.298	0.953	0.284
Denizli	0.812	**1.000**	0.812	0.812	Kocaeli	0.517	0.529	0.976	0.517	Yalova	0.309	0.339	0.912	0.309
Diyarbakır	0.668	0.680	0.982	0.668	Konya	0.636	0.823	0.772	0.636	Yozgat	0.416	0.418	0.995	0.416
Düzce	0.209	0.239	0.875	0.209	Kütahya	0.219	0.253	0.867	0.219	Zonguldak	0.313	0.319	0.981	0.313

Denizli, İstanbul, Kayseri, and Kilis achieved the perfect efficiency level in terms of BCC.

Moreover, it was also found as a result of the analysis that Mersin having 7 incentive certificates, Samsun having 7 incentive certificates, Trabzon having 15 incentive certificates, and Van having 7 incentive certificates couldn't achieve the sectorial efficiency although they have a higher number of companies, which have incentive certificate, when compared to the average of Turkey.

As a result of the super efficiency calculation, it was determined that Karaman was ranked 1st, Antalya 2nd, Afyonkarahisar 4th, and Aydın 7th among the provinces having incentive certificate and achieving the perfect efficiency.

5 Conclusion

Different countries utilize the incentive mechanism in different ways. In order to be able to cope with global events, to maintain its competitive power, to compete with its rivals, and to resolve the problem of unemployment (the most important problem), Turkey should support all of the industries needing incentive. Among them, the tourism industry that is considered the most competitive industry and having a dynamic structure and rapid development is accepted as an industry that is important for economic development. From this aspect, supporting the tourism industry would play an important role in increasing the investments in this area, creating new employment domains, increasing the number of employment, and increasing the national and per-capita income.

In the tourism promotion system, efficient auditing in any field from issuing the incentive certificates to the steps after the realization of investments is a must because ensuring the sufficient level of efficiency auditing after the incentives would be the driving force for the industry to achieve the expected objectives. Preventing the abuse of public sources is also important for following the incentives granted. However, the objective of audits is not to discourage the investors but to support them achieving the desired level of efficiency.

It is important for the incentives granted to be suitable for the dynamism of industry and to involve supportive components. By learning lessons from the preventive practices during the implementation of previous promotion laws, the new regulations should support the development of industry and increase the efficiency in the sector.

References

Akdeniz Turistik Otelciler ve İşletmeciler Birliği (AKTOB). (2014). Turizm Sektörünün Yapısı, Büyüklüğü ve Ekonomiye Katkısı. http://www.tuyed.

org.tr/wp-content/uploads/2014/02/AKTOB-arastirmasi.pdf. Access: Mart 31, 2020.

Andersen, P., and Petersen, P. C. (1993). A Procedure for Ranking Efficient Units in Data Envelopmen Analysis. *Management Science*, 39(10), 1261–124.

Benli, Y. K. (2012). Data Envelopment Analysis (DEA) and Malmquist Total Factor Productivity (TFP): An Empirical Evidence in Accomodation Businesses. *Ege Akademik Bakis*, 12(3), 369.

Charnes, A., Cooper, W. W., and Rhodes, E. (1978). Measuring the Efficiency of Decision Making Units. *European Journal of Operational Research*, 2(6), 429–444.

Çiloğlu, İ. (1997). Teşvik Sisteminin Değerlendirilmesi. *Hazine Dergisi*, 8(10).

Kozak, N. A., and Kozak, M. (2015). Genel Turizm, İlkeler-Kavramlar, Detay Yayıncılık.

Kutlar, A., & Babacan, A. (2008). Türkiye'deki Kamu Üniversitelerinde CCR Etkinliği-Ölçek Etkinliği Analizi: DEA Tekniği Uygulaması. *Kocaeli Üniversitesi Sosyal Bilimler Dergisi*, (15), 148–172.

Olalı, H., and Korzay, M. (1993). Otel İşletmeciliği. İstanbul: Beta Basım Yayım.

Oum, T. H., Yu, C., and Fu, X. (2003). A Comparative Analysis of Productivity Performance of The World's Major Airports: Summary of the Atrs Global Airport Benchmarking Research Report-2002. Journal of Air Transport Management, 9(5), 285–297.

Özden, Ü. H. (2008). Veri Zarflama Analizi (VZA) İle Türkiye'deki Vakıf Üniversitelerinin Etkinliğinin Ölçülmesi. *İstanbul Üniversitesi İşletme Fakültesi Dergisi*, 37(2), 167–185.

Sowlati, T., and Paradi, J. C. (2004). Establishing the "Practical Frontier" in Data Envelopment Analysis. Omega, 32(4), 261–272.

UNWTO. (2017). World Tourism Barometer.

UNWTO. (2020). World Tourism Barometer.

Edip Durmaz

Tekirdağ Industry in the Early Years of the Republic

1 Introduction

At the beginning of the 1800s, in the Ottoman Empire, there was an advanced industry ahead of its time that was producing in small workshops and organized as artisan organizations (guilds). This domestic and national industry both met the country's own needs and exported the product (surplus) to the abroad, especially in the field of textile. This relatively developed industrial infrastructure in the Ottoman Empire collapsed in the Tanzimat Period after 1839. The most important reason for this was that the Ottoman Local Industry, working with manpower, could not compete with the modern industry of the era that emerged in Europe and based on machine production (Sarc, 1940, p. 433)[1].

Despite all the attempts and efforts, both the capitulations given to the European states and the trade agreement with the USA, as well as the socio-economic conditions of the empire, did not allow Ottoman Empire to establish a modern industry (Kayapınar, 2017)[2]. As from 1850s, this situation prompted the Ottoman Empire to meet almost all of the products it needed by importing from abroad.

Republic of Turkey's industrial enterprises, that were inherited from the Ottoman Empire and were active and modern to a certain extent, were clustered in two large groups. In the first group; there were state owned factories such as Feshane (Önsoy,1988, p. 50)[3], Hereke Carpet and Silk Weaving Factory, Zeytinburnu Weaving Factory (Kurt, Kuzucu, Çakır & Demir, 2016)[4],

1 Ömer Celal Sarc, *Tanzimat ve Sanayimiz, Tanzimat I*, Milli Eğitim Yayını, Maarif Matbaası, İstanbul, 1940, s. 433.

2 Selda Kayapınar, "Osmanlı ABD Ticaret Antlaşması öncesi Amerika'nın Diplomasi Girişimleri", *Dumlupınar Üniversitesi Sosyal Bilimler Dergisi*, Sayı 51, Ocak 2017, s. 55.

3 Rifat Önsoy, *Tanzimat Dönemi Osmanlı Sanayii ve Sanayileşme Politikası*, Türkiye İş Bankası Kültür Yayınları, Ankara, 1988, s.50.

4 Mustafa Kurt, Kemalettin Kuzucu, Baki Çakır; Kemal Demir, "19. Yüzyılda Osmanlı Sanayileşmesi Sürecinde Kurulan Devlet Fabrikaları: Bir Envanter Çalışması", *Ankara Üniversitesi Osmanlı Tarihi Araştırma ve Uygulama Merkezi Dergisi* 40/Güz 2016, s. 256–258 (245–277).

Zeytinburnu Acid and Ether Factory (Özdemir, 2011, p.317)[5], etc. State owned factories were officially qualified institutions that mainly produced some products needed for the military of the country, and tried to meet some civilian needs in less variety and quantity. In the second group, there were factories belonging to private capital. The majority shares of the multi-partnered factories and the majority of the one-man businesses of these private capital factories, belonged to non-national elements, namely foreigners. The factories belonging to this private capital were generally concentrated in some fields such as textile, olive oil and cement production (Yaşa, 1980, p. 13).[6]

During the Tanzimat Period, the Ottoman Empire, whose domestic industry weakened rapidly and could not cope with Europe, had to take on an import substitute character that relied heavily on imports in the economy. In the Constitutional Period, the economy of the empire was largely based on imports from abroad. The state elites, who were not satisfied with this situation, wanted to make the Ottoman Empire economy again strong, self-sufficient, based on production, and free from import dependence, like the pre-Tanzimat period. In the last years of the Ottoman Empire, a number of attempts were made by governments to transform the country's economy dependent on imports from Europe into a productive structure again. The most important of such attempts by political elites to develop and strengthen the industrial infrastructure of the country is the "The Industrial Promotion Law" enacted in 1913 under the rule of "İttihat ve Terakki Partisi (Party of Union and Progress)" (Eldem, 1994, pp. 77–78)[7]. This law enacted in the last years of the Ottoman Empire in order to develop and strengthen the country's industry was revised, and updated in the Republican Period in 1927 (Tayanç, 1973, pp. 58–59)[8] and the Republic of Turkey's existing industry infrastructure was tried to be strengthened as far as possible in the circumstances of the day[9].

---

5 Mustafa ÖZDEMİR, *Osmanlı'dan Cumhuriyet'e Endüstriyel Mirasımız*, İTO Yayınları, İstanbul, 2011, s. 317.

6 Memduh Yaşa, *Cumhuriyet Dönemi Türkiye Ekonomisi*, Akbank Kültür Yayını, Apa Ofset Basımevi, İstanbul, 1980, s.13.

7 Vedat ELDEM, *Harp ve Mütareke Yıllarında Osmanlı imparatorluğu'nun Ekonomisi*, Türk Tarih Kurumu Yayınları Ankara, 1994, s. 77–78.

8 Tunç Tayanç, *Sanayileşme Sürecinde 50 Yıl*, Milliyet Yayınları, İstanbul, 1973, s. 58–59.

9 Only the investors whose at least 25 % of their capital is domestic could benefit from the 'Iindustrial Promotion Law' adopted in 1927. The government guaranteed some privileges for transport, land without charge, exemptions in some taxes and duties, and paying10 % premium on production figures to the industrial organizations benefiting

Despite the goal of industrializing development of the existing governments in power in the country between 1923 and 1929, serious changes could not be made in both the numerical and qualitative terms in the industrial infrastructure taken over from the Ottoman Empire, and a meaningful and satisfying industrial move could not be achieved (Boratav, 1998, p.40)[10]. Governments' attempts to create a strong industry were taking place in a time when the socio-economic conjuncture of the country was not convenient. The important problem that negatively affected the industrial infrastructure of the country in those years was the serious decrease in the urban population of the country that started with the Balkan Wars and ended with the Population Exchange (between 1912 and 1927). This decrease reached its highest point with 44 % in the West of Adapazarı–Muğla line which also included Tekirdağ province (Tezel, 2002, p. 100)[11].

In particular, the wars between 1911 and 1922 led to a decrease in the general population and urban population living across the country and a change in the existing ethnic structure. All that's happened affected Turkey's economy negatively (Tezel, 2002, p. 101)[12]. As Turkey was being affected negatively by all that's happened, it can be said that Tekirdağ was affected still further negatively. Because the population of Edirne province, where Tekirdağ was a sanjak, rose to 1.106.005 people, which was the peak point before 1912, but decreased to 627.500 people in 1914. Tekirdağ, a sanjak of Edirne province before the Republican era, also could not be exempted from these population movements in Edirne. It can be estimated that the population of Tekirdağ sanjak reached 177.000 people, which was the peak point in 1912 before the Balkan Wars (1319 Edirne Vilayeti Celilesi Salnamesi, 1903, pp. 237–238)[13]. Then, with the effect of the above-mentioned

---

from this law. The state also obliged public institutions and municipalities to use domestic goods, and to work with industrial organizations benefiting from this law.

10 Korkut BORATAV, *Türkiye İktisat Tarihi (1908–1985)*, Gerçek Yayınevi, İstanbul, 1998, s. 40.

11 Yahya Sezai TEZEL, *Cumhuriyet Döneminin İktisadi Tarihi (1923–1950)*, Tarih Vakfı Yurt Yayınları, İstanbul, 2002, s. 100.

12 Tezel, ibid, s. 101.

13 Calculated from *1319 Edirne Vilayeti Celilesi Salnamesi* (defa 28, 1319 sene-i maliye), (Edirne Vilayet Matbaası, 1903, pp. 1902–1123). The total population of Tekirdağ province was determined as 167,000, and the population of the old Saray sub-district (later became a district during the Republican period) was estimated as 9,000 based on the number of houses in the sub-district center and the number of villages connected to the sub-district; world population growth rate between 1920 and 1940 is given as 12.8 % for developing countries according to Türkiye İstatistiği Cep Yıllığı 1990 (DİE (Devlet İstatistik Enstitüsü), DİE Matbaası, Ankara, 1991, s. 292), so in order

developments, it can be said that the population of Tekirdağ province declined to 131,446 in 1927. Also a significant amount of population loss occurred during the mentioned period in the central district of Tekirdağ. The population, which was around 45.000 in 1912 before the Republican era, declined to 33.747 in 1927 (28 Teşrinievel 1927 Umumî Nüfus Tahriri, 1929, p. XI)[14].

The negative effects of death or migration of approximately 25 % of the population living in the Tekirdağ province center, and about 26 % of the entire Tekirdağ province population on Tekirdağ industry are inevitable. Not only that but also more devastating conditions, which involved Edirne that Tekirdağ was affiliated to until 1923 (T.C. Tekirdağ Valiliği, 2020)[15], hit a big blow to Tekirdağ industry.

2 Tekirdağ Industry during the Years 1927–1935

According to the first industrial census organized by the Republic of Turkey in the autumn of 1927, the situation of Tekirdağ province in industry is summarized in Table 1 below:

As can be seen from Table 1, in the fall of 1927 across Tekirdağ province, there were 606 workplaces operating in the field of industry, they were all active at the time of the census, and a total of 1,613 workers were working in these workplaces. The prominent industry branch was "agricultural, livestock, fishing, game animals industry" which had half of all enterprises alone. In addition, this branch of industry contained more than half of the population working in the industry, approximately 61 %. Another important industry branch was "metallurgical and machinery industry". In this industry branch, 132 workplaces were operating and 273 people were employed. Another important industry branch

to calculate 10-year population between 1902 and 1912, population growth rate was accepted as 6 %, and the estimated population of Tekirdağ province was found to be 177.000 in 1912.

14 As stated in *28 Teşrinievel 1927 Umumî Nüfus Tahriri* footnote 13 (Türkiye Cumhuriyeti Başbakanlık İstatistik Umum Müdürlüğü, Hüsnütabiat Basımevi, İstanbul, 1929, s. XI) the population growth rate was roughly 6 % for ten years and about 0.6 % for each year for the 1900s. Therefore, if wars, migrations and occupations had not occurred since the peak point of the population between 1912 and 1927, the population of Tekirdağ should have been about 9 % more on both provincial and provincial center basis; therefore, it should be noted that the loss in the population of Tekirdağ province and Tekirdağ province center is respectively 32.6 % and 38.6 %.

15 T.C. Tekirdağ Valiliği. (2020, March 24). 2020 tarihinde http://www.tekirdag.gov.tr/tekirdag/tarihi- adresinden alındı.

Table 1: Industrial Enterprises and Number of Employees in Industry Across Tekirdağ Province

Branches of industry in 1927	**Across Tekirdağ province**	
	Number of enterprises	**Number of employees**
Agricultural,livestock, fishing, game animals industry	318	976
Textiles industry	34	90
Timber and herbal products industry	92	162
Paper and cardboard industry	1	8
Metallurgical and machinery industry	132	273
Construction industry	21	92
Chemical industry	7	10
Unspecified industry	1	2
Industry branches total	**606**	**1.613**

Source: Sanayi Sayımı 1927, (1969), p. 37.

was "timber and herbal products industry". The number of enterprises operating in this industry branch was 92, and the number of the employees was 162. Considering proportionally, employment in the top three industry branches of province was respectively, 60.51 % in "agricultural, livestock, fishing, game animals industry", 16.52 % in "metallurgical and machinery industry", and 10.04 % in "timber and herbal products industry".

While the general outlook of the industry in Tekirdağ province in 1927 was as mentioned above, when we go into a little more detail as province center and rural, we have a picture like this:

As seen in Table 2 above, considering the number of enterprises; the majority of the province's industry, 65.51 %, almost 2/3, was clustered in Tekirdağ rural. In Tekirdağ province center, it is seen that almost 1/3, 34.49 % of the industry was clustered. Considering the number of employees in industry; it turns out that 68.82 % of the employees worked in the rural areas of Tekirdağ and 31.18 % of the employees worked in the province center of Tekirdağ. The number of employees in industry branches in Tekirdağ rural was 1.110, and in Tekirdağ province center was 503. The total number of employees in the industry across Tekirdağ province was 1.613. In Tekirdağ province center, there were 2.40 employees per enterprise, while in Tekirdağ rural there were 2.79 employees. Across Tekirdağ province, 471 of industrial enterprises had maximum 4 employees, and 135 of industrial

Table 2: Industrial Enterprises and Number of Employees in 1927 in Tekirdağ Province Center, Tekirdağ Rural and Across Tekirdağ Province

Branches of industry in 1927	**Tekirdağ province center**		**Tekirdağ rural**		**Across Tekirdağ province**	
	Number of enterprises	**Number of employees**	**Number of enterprises**	**Number of employees**	**Number of enterprises**	**Number of employees**
Agricultural, livestock, fishing, game animals industry	100	315	218	661	318	976
Textiles industry	17	47	17	43	34	90
Timber and herbal products industry	27	55	65	107	92	162
Paper and cardboard industry	1	8	-	-	1	8
Metallurgical and machinery industry	52	111	80	162	132	273
Construction industry	4	7	17	85	21	92
Chemical industry	7	10	-	-	7	10
Unspecified industry	-	-	1	2	1	2
Industry branches total	**209**	**503**	**397**	**1.110**	**606**	**1.613**

Source: Sanayi Sayımı 1927, (1969), p. 37.

enterprises had more than 4 employees (Tökin, 1946, p. 39)[16]. It is observed that Tekirdağ province center stood out in chemical and textile industries among all the industry branches shown in Table 2, and Tekirdağ rural was in the forefront in all other industry branches.

By 1935, the general outlook of the industry remained the same in Tekirdağ province, however, the weights of the rural and province center within the provincial industry had changed considerably. As the most important change in Tekirdağ industrial employment over the past 8 years, the weight of those

16 İsmail Husrev Tökin, *İktisadi ve İçtimai Türkiye Rakamlarla*, Cilt III, T. C. İstatistik Genel Müdürlüğü Yayını, Ankara, 1946, s. 39.

employed in industry in rural areas increased to 79.70 % in 1935, while it was 68.82 % in 1927. Industrial employment in Tekirdağ province center also decreased from 31.18 % in 1927 to 20.30 % in 1935. In the past eight years, although industrial employment in Tekirdağ province center grew numerically (rising from 503 employees to 1.374), its weight in provincial industrial employment decreased to 20.30 %, approximately in proportion of 1/3. In addition, it is observed that Tekirdağ rural increased its weight in provincial industrial employment both numerically and proportionally, and that it dominated 4/5 of almost all provincial industrial employment alone. When we go into some more details about Tekirdağ industry, we have a photo like the one below:

As can be seen from Table 3, in the fall of 1935 across Tekirdağ province, a total of 6.768 employees were working in the workplaces operating in the field of industry and active at the time of the census. The prominent branches of industry across Tekirdağ province were "construction and furniture industry" and "woodworking industry". In these two branches of industry, 1,211 and 1,183 people were working respectively, and these two branches of industry employed approximately 35 % of the population working in the industry. Other important industry branches were the "metallurgical industry" in which 965 people were employed, "garment industry" which employed 898 people, "food, beverages and tobacco industry" which employed 807 people and "stone and soil industry" in which 520 people were employed across the province. Considering the proportion of industrial employment in industry branches across the province, employment in the top six industry branches of the province was; 17.89 % in "construction and furniture industry", 17.48 % in "woodworking industry", 14.26 % in "metallurgical industry", 13.23 % in the garment industry, 11.92 % in "food, beverages and tobacco industry", and 7.68 % in "stone and soil industry".

Approximately 82.5 % of the people working in Tekirdağ province industry were employed in the six industries mentioned above. While the general view of the industry across Tekirdağ province was like this in 1935, it's necessary to go into a little more detail as Tekirdağ province center and Tekirdağ rural.

As seen in Table 3, when the number of employees in all industry branches is analyzed; 79.70 % of the province industry, almost 8/10 of it, was clustered in Tekirdağ rural. It is seen that 21.3 % of the industry, about 2/10 of it, was clustered in Tekirdağ province center. The number of employees in industry branches in Tekirdağ rural was 5,394 and in Tekirdağ province center was 1,374. In all industry branches shown in Table 3, Tekirdağ rural took the lead, and only in "paper and printing industry" the number of employment in both Tekirdağ province center and Tekirdağ rural seemed to be equal. Regarding the "electricity, gas and water production and distribution industry" in which Tekirdağ province

Table 3: Industrial Enterprises and Number of Employees in Tekirdağ Province Center, Tekirdağ Rural and Across Tekirdağ Province in 1935

Branches of industry in 1935	**Number of employees**						
	Tekirdağ province center			**Tekirdağ rural**			**Across Tekirdağ province**
	Man	**Woman**	**Total**	**Man**	**Woman**	**Total**	**Total**
Extraction et exploitation industry	4	-	4	33	-	33	37
Stone and soil industry	19	-	19	498	3	501	520
Construction and furniture industry	81	-	81	1.130	-	1.130	1211
Woodworking industry	215	5	220	861	102	963	1183
Metallurgical industry	138	-	138	761	66	827	965
Machinery and tool manufacturing industry	31	-	31	55	-	55	86
Chemical industry	-	-	-			3	3
Textiles industry	12	12	24	22	81	103	127
Paper and printing industry	16	-	16	16	-	16	32
Leather rubber, bone, horn, amber goods industry	39	-	39	90	-	90	129
Food, beverages and tobacco industry	227	3	230	563	14	577	807
Garment industry	258	30	288	498	112	610	898
Electricity, gas and water production and distribution industry	11	-	11	10	-	10	21
Mixed an various industry	-	-	-	-	2	-	2
Unspecified industry workers (seasonal workers)	*204*	*55*	*259*	*329*	*144*	*473*	*732*
Technical and administrative staff in industry	14	-	14	1	-	1	15
Industry branches total	**1.269**	**105**	**1.374**	**4.872**	**522**	**5.394**	**6.768**
Industry branches total after removing seasonal workers	*1.065*	*50*	*1.115*	*4.543*	*378*	*4.921*	*6.036*

Source: Genel Nüfus Sayımı 20 Ekim 1935 Tekirdağ Vilâyeti, (1937), Tome:52, p. 21–25, 104–108.

center took the lead, it should be accepted that this industry branch, which was accepted as an industry branch for those dates, does not contain direct industrial production and it should be stated that this branch of industry should be considered as a service branch. In column 15 of Table 3, seasonal temporary workers whose branches are not identified, are specified in italics. The total number of such seasonal temporary industrial workers across the province was 732.

In the paragraph above, all the numbers and rates given about Table 3 are given without taking into account 732 seasonal industrial workers. It is likely that these workers work only in the peak season and as seasonal industrial workers in the industry branches in which they were employed. Although the time of the peak season and the total number of days worked varies for each industry branch, it is useful to remind that these seasonal industrial workers were employed for an average of 2–3 months in the peak season and were not employed in the rest of the year. Considering this situation, this temporary seasonal 732-person industrial employment can roughly be estimated to correspond to 154 permanent employment[17].

It is necessary to briefly mention the situation of large industrial enterprises operating within Tekirdağ province, benefiting from the Industrial Promotion Law and supported by the state. Because, it would be useful to take a look at the large industrial enterprises in order to make evaluations about the enterprises owned by Tekirdağ industry in terms of volume and size, and to better understand the size of the industrial enterprises across Tekirdağ province. The situation of the big industrial enterprises operating in Tekirdağ province between 1932 and 1935 is summarized in Table 4 below.

As can be understood from Table 4 above, the number of industrial enterprises, which are supported by the state and can be called as large industrial enterprises between 1932 and 1935, varies between 19 and 6. The number of employees employed in these large industrial enterprises ranged from 143 to 179. Since 1935, it has not been possible to determine the number of employees in the enterprises in the columns indicated by * in Table 4. The reason for this was to switch to a counting method based on the number of working days instead of the number of people employed in industrial enterprises. The number of large industrial enterprises receiving incentives from the state and using machines with at least 10 horsepower in Tekirdağ province decreased steadily. Despite this decrease

17 Assuming that temporary workers work only for one season, an average of 2.5 months a year, and considering that 2.5 months in a year corresponds to 21 % a year, 732 temporary seasonal workers can be estimated to correspond to 154 permanent employment.

Table 4: Large Industrial Enterprises in Tekirdağ Province and Number of Employees in These Enterprises (1932–1935)

Large Industrial Enterprises in Tekirdağ Province								
Branches of industry	**1932**		**1933**		**1934**		**1935**	
	Number of enterprises	**Number of employees**	**Number of enterprises**	**Number of employees**	**Number of enterprises**	**Number of employees**	**Number of enterprises**	**Number of employees**
Flour industry	16	81	11	62	9	52	2	*
Alcohol industry	1	58	2	79	2	99	1	*
Mixed flour and olive oil industry	-	-	1	10	1	14	1	*
Electric industry	2	14	2	13	2	14	2	*
Industry branches total	19	143	16	164	14	179	6	*

Sources: Sanayi İstatistikleri Teşviki Sanayi Kanunundan İstifade Eden Müesseselerin 1932 ve 1933 Seneleri Faaliyetleri, (1934), p. 62–197; Sanayi İstatistikleri Teşviki Sanayi Kanunundan İstifade Eden Müesseselerin 1932 ve 1937 Seneleri Faaliyeti, (1939), p. 104–322.

in the number of enterprises, it is remarkable that while 143 employees worked in 19 large industrial enterprises in 1932, the number of employees in 6 major industrial enterprises in 1934 rose to 179. However, Industrial Promotion Law is a law that stipulates to support industrial enterprises of a certain size for a certain period of time. Industrial enterprises lost support from the state when the specified period expired. Therefore, some large industrial enterprises do not appear in the Table above after 1933. But the reason for this not being seen in the Table above is not because of their closure, but because they lost their state support. It is quite remarkable that while there were approximately 7.5 employees per these large industrial enterprises operating in Tekirdağ province in 1932, this number increased by nearly three times, to 29.8, in 1934. It is understood from the statistics that a significant portion (2/3) of the large industrial enterprises operating in Tekirdağ province are clustered in "flour and alcoholic beverage industry". When we go into a little more detail, it is seen that a large part of the big industrial enterprises in Tekirdağ province was opened in 1927 and later (two in 1927 and nine after 1928) (Uslubaş, 2013, p. 38)[18]. Yet another remarkable point is that, Tekirdağ ranks second in terms of production power and added value in alcoholic beverages industry in Turkey between 1932 and 1933[19].

3 Conclusion

When the state of Tekirdağ province industry is evaluated between the years 1927–1935, it is useful to underline some of the issues roughly. In the last years of the Ottoman State, the population of Tekirdağ decreased significantly and while Tekirdağ was a sanjak of one of the few major provinces (Edirne) of the Ottoman State, it became a province center with the declaration of the republic. In the first years of the republic, Tekirdağ was at a disadvantage in some aspects required for the development of the industry due to reasons such as decrease in both central and rural population, shrinkage in the surrounding population, closeness to Çanakkale Wars and war exhaustion experienced by the Greek occupation during the War of Independence. However, with a decision taken

18 Tolga Uslubaş, *Kronolojik Türkiye Tarihi Geçmişten Günümüze Türkiye,* Melisa Matbaacılık, İstanbul, 2013, s. 38; The date of 28 May 1927 is important due to the adoption of the Industry Promotion Law on this date, the number of large industrial enterprises in Tekirdağ has increased rapidly after the law came out.

19 *Sanayi İstatistikleri Teşviki Sanayi Kanunundan İstifade Eden Müesseselerin 1932 ve 1933 Seneleri Faaliyetleri,* Başvekâlet İstatistik Umum Müdürlüğü, Devlet Matbaası, İstanbul, 1934, 66–75.

by the political will of the period, Tekirdağ was first turned into a provincial center, and new immigrants to Turkey were first settled in Thrace and Tekirdağ. After 1923, together with the establishment of the Republic of Turkey, the current unfavorable conditions for Tekirdağ changed in a positive direction, and Tekirdağ made a very strong jump in the industry. With this industrial boom, the number of people employed in the industry (with seasonal workers) increased from 1,613 in 1927 to 6768 in 1935. However, in the same year, industrial employment across Turkey experienced a growth rate of almost one-fold (119 %). In these years, Turkey's growth rate experienced in industrial employment was much lower than the industrial employment increase rate in Tekirdağ. However, this record-breaking employment boom in the field of industry across Tekirdağ province could not be caught in terms of women's participation in the industrial workforce. While the ratio of women in the total population employed in the industry was 19.66 % in 1935 in Turkey, this rate was 9.26 % in Tekirdağ (Nüfus Sayımları 1927–1950, 1953, p. 13). More specifically, Tekirdağ could not reach even half the level of female industrial employment rate in Turkey in this period.

References

Başbakanlık Devlet İstatistik Enstitüsü, Sanayi Sayımı 1927. (1969). Ankara: Devlet İstatistik Enstitüsü Matbaası.

Başvekâlet İstatistik Umum Müdürlüğü. (1934). Sanayi İstatistikleri Teşviki Sanayi Kanunundan İstifade Eden Müesseselerin 1932 ve 1933 Seneleri Faaliyetleri. İstanbul: Devlet Matbaası.

Başvekâlet İstatistik Umum Müdürlüğü. (1939). Sanayi İstatistikleri Teşviki Sanayi Kanunundan İstifade Eden Müesseselerin 1932 ve 1937 Seneleri Faaliyeti. İstanbul: Cumhuriyet Matbaası.

1319 Edirne Vilayeti Celilesi Salnamesi. (1903). (defa 28, 1319 sene-i maliye). Edirne: Edirne Vilayet Matbaası.

Boratav, K. (1998). Türkiye İktisat Tarihi (1908–1985). (1. baskı). İstanbul: Gerçek Yayınevi.

DİE (Devlet İstatistik Enstitüsü). (1991). Türkiye İstatistiği Cep Yıllığı 1990. Ankara: DİE Matbaası.

Eldem, V. (1994). Harp ve Mütareke Yıllarında Osmanlı İmparatorluğu'nun Ekonomisi. Ankara: Türk Tarih Kurumu Yayınları.

Karpat, K. H. (2003). Osmanlı Nüfusu (1830–1914). Bahar Tırnakçı (çev.). İstanbul: Tarih Vakfı Yurt Yayınları.

Kayapınar, S. (2017). Osmanlı ABD Ticaret Anlaşması Öncesi Amerika'nın Diplomasi Girişimleri. Dumlupınar Üniversitesi Sosyal Bilimler Dergisi, (51), 39–56.

Kurt, M., Kuzucu, K., Çakır, B. ve Demir, K. (2016). 19. Yüzyılda Osmanlı Sanayileşmesi Sürecinde Kurulan Devlet Fabrikaları: Bir Envanter Çalışması. Ankara Üniversitesi Osmanlı Tarihi Araştırma ve Uygulama Merkezi Dergisi, (40), 245–277.

Önsoy, R. (1988). Tanzimat Dönemi Osmanlı Sanayii ve Sanayileşme Politikası. Ankara: Türkiye İş Bankası Kültür Yayını.

Özdemir, M. (2011). Osmanlı'dan Cumhuriyet'e Endüstriyel Mirasımız. İstanbul: İstanbul Ticaret Odası Yayınları.

Sarc, Ö. C. (1940). "Tanzimat ve Sanayimiz", Tanzimat I. İstanbul: Maarif Matbaası.

Tayanç, T. (1973). Sanayileşme Sürecinde 50 Yıl. İstanbul: Milliyet Yayınları.

Tezel, Y. S. (2002). Cumhuriyet Döneminin İktisadi Tarihi (1923–1950). (5. Baskı). İstanbul: Tarih Vakfı Yurt Yayınları.

Tökin, İ. H. (1946). İktisadi ve İçtimai Türkiye Rakamlarla. (Vol. 3). Ankara: T. C. İstatistik Genel Müdürlüğü Yayını.

Türkiye Cumhuriyeti Başbakanlık İstatistik Genel Direktörlüğü. Genel Nüfus Sayımı 20 Ekim (İlk Teşrin) 1935 Edirne Vilâyeti. (Tome: 52). (1937). İstanbul: Hüsnütabiat Basımevi.

Türkiye Cumhuriyeti Başbakanlık İstatistik Umum Müdürlüğü. (1929). 28 Teşrinievel 1927 Umumî Nüfus Tahriri. İstanbul: Hüsnütabiat Basımevi.

Türkiye Cumhuriyeti Başvekâlet İstatistik Umum Müdürlüğü. (1953). Nüfus Sayımları 1927–1950. Ankara.

Yaşa, M. (1980). Cumhuriyet Dönemi Türkiye Ekonomisi 1923–1978. İstanbul: Apa Ofset Basımevi.

http://www.tekirdag.gov.tr/tekirdag/tarihi- 24 Mart 2020 tarihinde erişildi.

Hicran Kasa

The Relationship between Domestic Violence Against Women and Economic Development: A Comparative Analysis

1 Introduction

The concept of gender and the stereotyped thoughts that exist on the basis of it begin at an early age, appear in all areas of life and make individuals' behavior towards their gender clear. In this regard, we confront with cases of violence that occur in time when patterns are not followed, which may have physical and psychological consequences. "Domestic violence" that we frequently encounter today and appearing for many reasons, can be defined as all kinds of learned and internalized behaviors of the human rights violating individuals' human rights including gender-based threats, imposition and control, aiming to exert pressure and superiority over each other, which may also result in psychological, sexual, economic and physical harm. This concept has turned into a social problem, rather than a special problem of individuals, and has become a socio-cultural and economic problem in which states and institutions play a role. Especially in the late 20th century, it became a problem that attracted the attention of experts, public and politics.

The biological sex of individuals is seen as an indicator of power over each other and this difference places certain roles on individuals. However, the reason for these roles that we have acquired in cultural and social processes is not because of our biological and anatomical differences, but rather they are the roles created by many factors such as behavior patterns, work sharing, religion, ethnic structure, traditions that can vary from culture to culture. Within these roles, gender-based differences generally put men at the top of the hierarchical structure, while women are in the second place in many areas such as education and employment due to their biological differences. Therefore, this problem is reflected in the economic policies of the countries and especially creates new costs in terms of elimination and affects the distribution of transfer expenditures. In this context; efforts towards women's labor force participation rate, education level, investments in their social security, social perspective towards women, and efforts to change the negative perspective towards them show the level of development of countries. Nongovernmental organizations, politicians, local administrations, bar associations, leaders, wise people, religious officials, activists and scientists are needed to provide these changes and transformations.

The World Bank describes physical, sexual, psychological and economic violence as a global pandemic that affects one in every 3 women or girls throughout their lives. Domestic violence, which does not recognize economic and social boundaries, remains a social problem that needs to be addressed in both developed and developing countries. In addition to being a social problem, the issue of domestic violence is an issue that results in undeniable economic consequences. Violence creates a huge economic burden in terms of increasing the use of social services while also causing loss of efficiency to the societies. The scope of this article to discuss if there exists a relationship between countries' economic growth and the intensity of domestic violence. Therefore, macroeconomic indicators such as employment, education level and per capita income have been determined by taking into consideration the criteria that come to the forefront in the studies of institutions such as OECD and UN (See OECD, 2011; UNDP, 2001). In this way, it is aimed to establish a relationship between the prevalence of women who have high labor force participation rates and education levels and the welfare levels of the countries they live in.

2 Literature Review

The concept of "development" as it is accepted today tends to show the result of an interaction between social and economic indicators (Sakarya and İbisoglu, 2015). Development, with this understanding; embodies the progress of economic, social, political and cultural structures of the countries and constitutes a whole (Dincer and Özaslan, 2004). Whereas, socio-economic development expresses social and economic development and takes into account qualitative development as well as quantitative development in the economy. This concept includes changes in the socio-cultural structure as well as changes and developments in the economic structure such as per capita income, increase in production or increase in economic income and increase in productivity growth. In other words, socio-economic development includes numerical and structural alteration together (Ozdemir ve Altıparmak, 2005). Therefore, the variables for determining the relationship between domestic violence and economic development subject to the study were determined by taking into consideration the criteria that come to the forefront in the studies related to socio-economic development. Concordantly, in the study entitled "The Cost of Domestic Violence to the Australian Economy" (Access Economics, 2004). [1], it is aimed to raise awareness by drawing attention to the costs caused by domestic violence. The findings were showed that the total annual cost of domestic violence is approximately $8.1 billion between 2002 and 2003 years. The reason for spending $3.5 billion of the total cost are pain, suffering, and premature mortality. The largest part of the remaining $4.6 billion is consumption costs, of which the largest component is lost household economies of scale. The next largest categories are production and administration and other, at $484 million and $480 million respectively. Based on the results achieved, another goal is to help policy makers decide how to allocate resources in the government's intervention areas.

Domestic violence against women is a common and important social problem also in Turkey. Furthermore, it creates many economic problems as well as the social problems. And yet the intensity of violence against women domestically will also make it possible to measure the costs it creates. For this purpose, according to a 2014 study, 36 % of married women have experienced physical violence, 12 % have experienced sexual violence, 42 % of women married after the age of 18 have experienced psychological violence and 30 % have experienced economic violence (HUNEE-ASPB, 2015). According to the results of another study, of women in Turkey subjected to this study throughout 26 cities, it is determined that 94, 3 % of them have experienced domestic violence (KAMER, 2015: 24)[2].

Although violence appears in many different categories, besides the socio-cultural studies, the "gender" category is increasingly becoming prominent as well as in studies in the fields of economy, law and healthcare (Boatcă and Lamnek, 2003). In this category, "women" are seen as the weak side due to their low education level, living in crowded households, unable to benefit from job opportunities, working in heavy and low-paying jobs, and experiencing problems such as social exclusion and domestic violence frequently (Yusufoglu, 2017). Role assignments that are gendered by the community, especially by the family, often lead to inequalities towards women. In the socialization process, roles assigned to women and men are internalized over time, based on traditions, social and

1 A report prepared for the Australian Government's Office of the Status of Women by Access Economics Pty Ltd, funded by the Australian Government under Partnerships Against Domestic Violence.

2 The research conducted within the scope of the Women's Rights is Human Rights Project was carried out in 26 cities, 23 cities in the Southeastern and Eastern Anatolia Region and 3 cities in the Black Sea Region (Artvin, Rize, Trabzon). As part of the project, 24,723 women were interviewed face-to-face (KAMER, 2015).

cultural structure. Therefore, while men, who are seen as the representatives of the authority, are placed at the top of the hierarchy, women are pushed aside and they are exposed to discrimination in many fields such as education and employment (Yavuz, 2016). The studies of James Garbarino (1999) and James Gilligan (1996, 2001) contributed to this discussion. The studies informed by 25 years of working with violent men, Gilligan has theorized that the impacts of social and economic inequalities, especially related economic deficiency, are the primary reason of behavioral violence.

With a survey of 211 enterprises in Peru, it was aimed to calculate the costs incurred due to labor productivity loss as a result of violence against women. It has been determined that approximately one fourth of all full-time workers (23.24 %) have been exposed to some kind of violence by their spouses or ex-spouses on average four times in the last 12 months. This has been observed to be equivalent to a loss of 70 million working days per year, a minimum of $ 6,744 billion, or a 3.7 % gross domestic product (GDP) disvaluation (Horna, 2014). However, the perspective and practices towards women employment and social security vary according to the development levels of the countries. This perspective also expresses the importance given by the society of that country to people, acceptance of universal values and its maturity. In working life, along with the women employment, it is closely related with facilitating this procedure by giving them social security, recording, change of the sectorial understanding, legislative and executive power (Aydın, 2016).

Violence is committed without class, ethnicity, and socio-economic level differences. However, some factors increase the dosage, size and continuity of the committed violence. Poverty, unemployment, and imbalance in income distribution are the leading factors (Askın and Askın, 2017). The effect of global integration upon women's employment was investigated by Demirtas (2017) between 1995 and 2012 based on the data from 113 countries. Countries in question are examined in two different categories, OECD countries and developing countries. In the model created for OECD countries, it has been observed that all globalization variables have a positive effect on women's employment. Foreign direct investments, on the other hand, affect women's employment in a positive way both in OECD countries and in developing countries. While the rate of openness and imports negatively affect women's employment in developing countries, exports have no impact. Finally, index of economic and social globalization in developing countries do not have any impact on women employment (Demirtas, 2017).

Although there are many different views on research, implementation and policy recommendations on the issue of domestic violence, there is consensus on one point. This is that violence and abuse occur not only in the family but in all kinds of relationships (Gelles, 1997).

In recent years, studies aiming to reveal the cost of violence against women in the world have been carried out. The conducted analysis deals with the cost of violence against women in four categories. The first category is the "direct cost" consisting of the services provided to victims and their children (health services, shelter, emergency telephone lines cost, psychological, social, legal counseling, etc.) legal services for victims and violators (law enforcement, prosecutor, time and effort of the judge), the education costs of the relevant experts.

The second category is the "cost that cannot be measured by money" of violence against women; this cost consists of components such as increased social violence, murder and increase in suicide. The third category is the so-called "economic multiplier effect" that results from the inability of the women exposed to violence to work and the decrease in her efficiency in working life. The fourth and the last category, the "social multiplier effect", is also cannot be measured in monetary terms, due to the impact of violence on the victim (decrease in social capital, decline in participation in democratic processes, decrease in quality of life) and consists of (the forward-looking consequences resulting from the fact that the children who are victims of violence and witness of domestic violence' school success and social life are influenced negatively) (Directorate, AKSG, 2016).

3 Analysis

The lack of research towards the causes of domestic violence in Turkey, preventability, the effects of socio-economic and socio-cultural factors upon violence attract attention. Therefore, in the second part of the study, national and international literature has been reviewed on the subject in question, and unemployment, education and how per capita income can affect domestic violence. In this context, a comparative analysis on developed and developing countries has been made in the third section. In the relevant analysis; based on the statistics obtained from OECD, World Bank and Eurostat databases, the intensity of domestic violence of countries where employment and education levels are observed is examined and it is analyzed whether the violence varies according to socioeconomic factors. In this regard, Table 1 shows the intensity of domestic violence primarily in lower middle and upper middle income countries. Table 3 shows the intensity of domestic violence in high-income countries. The income groups of the countries in the relevant tables have been prepared according to GNI per capita data calculated by the World Bank using the Atlas method.

Table 1: Prevalence of Domestic Violence in Lower and Upper Middle Income Countries

Upper Middle Income Countries		Lower Middle Income Countries	
Mexico	0.14	Ukraine	0.13
Turkey	0.38	Vietnam	0.34
Brazil	0.33	Tunis	0.20
Bulgaria	0.23	Nigeria	0.16
Iran	0.66	Pakistan	0.85
Iraq	0.21	Philippines	0.17
Thailand	0.44	Myanmar	0.33
Russia	0.20	Moldavia	0.46
Jordan	0.24	Indonesia	0.18
Bosnia Herzegovina	0.13	India	0.26
Azerbaijan	0.14	Bangladesh	0.53
South Africa	0.21	Ghana	0.24

Source: Gender, Institutions and Development Database (GID-DB) 2019

According to the data figured in Table 1; among the upper middle income countries, respectively, Iran, Thailand, Turkey are the countries with the highest intensity of violence against women, while respectively, Bosnia and Herzegovina, Azerbaijan, Mexico are the countries with the lowest intensity. Among the lower middle income countries, respectively, Pakistan, Bangladesh and Moldova are the countries with the highest intensity of violence against women, while, respectively, Ukraine, Nigeria and Philippines are the countries with the lowest intensity. Solely, comparisons with selected high income countries have been found appropriate to make inferences about how development levels have an impact on the direction and intensity of violence.

As can be seen from Tables 1 and 2, domestic violence rates are similar in middle income and high income countries. Among the middle income countries, the countries where violence is most common are Iran, Pakistan, Bangladesh, while among high income countries these are America, Denmark, Latvia and Finland. Although the per capita income levels are high, domestic violence rates are on average 20 % in developed countries figured in Table 3.

Structural adjustment programs, consisting of neo-liberal economic policies in the globalizing world, have increased poverty, made it permanent and caused a global problem while increasing unemployment in developed and developing countries. Increasing poverty leads to an increase in violence against women in the family along with many economic, social and psychological problems. It is to

Table 2: Prevalence of Lifelong Domestic Violence in High Income Countries

High Income Countries			
Australia	0.17	Netherlands	0.25
Belgium	0.24	Luxembourg	0.22
France	0.26	Latvia	0.32
Germany	0.22	Czech	0.21
Greece	0.19	Denmark	0.32
Hungary	0.21	Italy	0.19
Iceland	0.22	Korea	0.17
New Zealand	0.35	Japan	0.15
Norway	0.27	Lithuania	0.24
England	0.29	Portugal	0.19
America	0.36	Slovakia	0.23
Sweden	0.28	Finland	0.30

Source: Gender, Institutions and Development Database (GID-DB) 2019

be discussed what the role of employment and education in preventing domestic violence is. In this context, firstly, the labor force participation rate (Figure 1), which is the main determinant of household income level, and then the unemployment rates and education data (Table 3) of the countries, will be examined to investigate whether these variables have any effect on the violence rates of developed countries and developing countries.

Table 3 shows the percentage value of university graduates in the total female and male population between the ages of 25 and 64. As seen here, in middle income countries such as Mexico, Hungary, Turkey, Slovakia, Colombia, Costa Rica, the number of university graduates compared to developed countries such as Australia, America, the United Kingdom, Finland is lower. In addition to this, in the countries figured on the table and mostly reflecting the OECD countries (excepting Turkey, Mexico, Korea, Germany and Austria), number of female university graduates is higher than the number of male graduates. A similar situation exists when looking at the OECD average. The labor force participation rates of university graduates are shown in Figure 1. Accordingly, with the lowest labor force participation rate of university graduates countries are Turkey, Greece, United States of America and Korea, while the highest ones are Iceland and Lithuania.

When the female labor force participation rates according to income groups are analyzed, it is seen that 53 % of the female population older than 15 years

Table 3: Higher Education, Female, Male 25–64 Years Old Population Percentage, 2017

Countries	Female	Male	Countries	Female	Male
Australia	50.13	40.43	Norway	47.93	38.7
Austria	31.87	32.92	Poland	35.3	24.47
Belgium	43.66	36.86	Portugal	28.47	19.2
Canada	62.99	50.37	Slovakia	26.45	19.76
Czech Republic	25.48	22.42	Spain	38.93	33.75
Denmark	44.71	33.8	Sweden	48.62	35.48
Finland	52.15	36.64	Switzerland	37.9	47.22
France	37.54	32.77	Turkey	18.72	21.17
Germany	25.73	31.38	United Kingdom	46.88	44.59
Greece	32.71	29.31	America	49.55	43.04
Hungary	27	21.01	Argentina	24.95	17.49
Israel	50.52	34.65	Colombia	24.28	20.59
Ireland	48.97	42.22	Estonia	49.22	29.88
Italy	21.47	15.81	Indonesia	11.99	11.72
Japan	52.15	50.74	Israel	55.33	46.32
Korea	44.41	50.97	Latvia	42.14	24.92
Luxembourg	41.44	39.25	Slovenia	39.38	28.42
Mexico	16.4	18.58	OECD Avg.	39.99	33.75
Netherlands	37.57	36.76	Lithuania	47.33	32.63
New Zealand	40.4	34.88	Costa Rica	24.19	21.78

Source: OECD Database (https://data.oecd.org/eduatt/adult-education-level.htm)

are economically active in upper middle income and high middle income countries. This rate is 34.27 % in lower middle income countries. In all three income groups, female labor force participation rate is lower than male labor force participation rate. When looked at regionally, the region with the lowest female labor force participation rate is Middle East with 17.86 %, whereas, the region with the highest rate is Sub Saharan Africa.

The coexistence of the low labor force participation rate and the low level of education increases the violence against women in the family. Faramarzi et al. (2005) found that domestic violence and low education level, low income and unemployment are directly related. However, when the countries are analyzed in terms of intensity of violence, it is seen that the intensity of violence is also higher in some countries with high socioeconomic development level. For instance, in

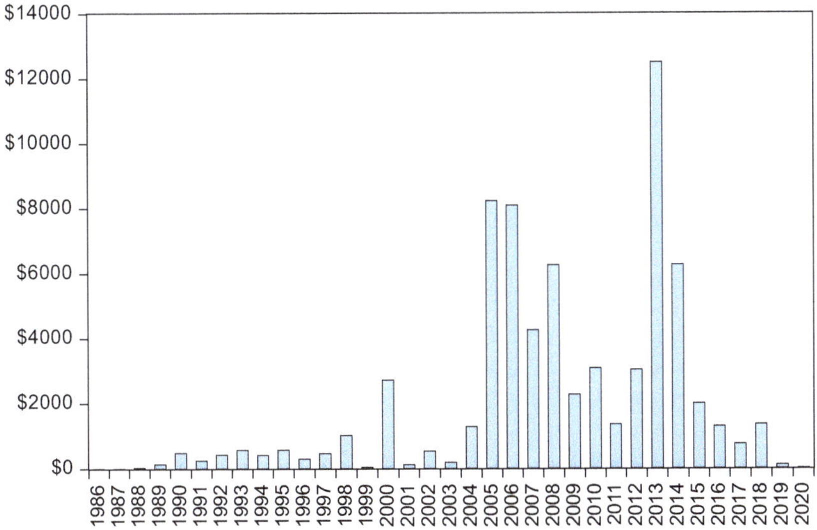

Figure 1: *Total Privatization Revenues in Turkey*

Source: *(ÖIB, 2020, Available at:* https: / / www.oib. gov. en / *Turkey-ozellestirme)*

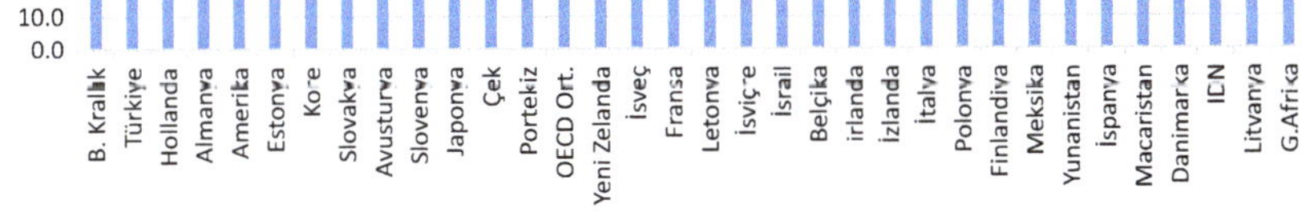

Graphic 1: Labor force participation rate (University graduates, 25–64 age group, 2017)

Source: OECD Database

Finland, which is taken as a model with the education model applied and is in the group of developed countries; the labor force participation rate of university graduates is 84.9 %, while female university graduates population rate is 52.15 %, and the prevalence of violence is 0.30 %.

Table 4: Labor Force Participation Rate, Female (%of Female Population Ages 15+)

İncome Groups	Female (%of female population ages 15+)	Male (%of male population ages 15+)
Upper middle income	53.872	74.490
Lower middle income	34.275	75.844
High income	53.153	68.388
East Asia & Pacific (excluding high income)	59.217	76.525
Europe & Central Asia (excluding high income)	48.727	69.705
Latin America & Caribbean (excluding high income)	52.052	76.967
Middle East & North Africa (excluding high income)	17.865	70.621
Sub-Saharan Africa (excluding high income)	61.431	72.505

Source: World Bank, 2019

4 Conclusion

Occurring within the family, gender based, aiming to put pressure and superiority on women; containing threat, imposition, control; resulting in psychological, sexual, economic and physical harm; any learned action that violates the human rights of women is called as domestic violence. In the last quarter of the 20th century, the issue of domestic violence has turned into an important problem that creates social and economic problems that attract the attention of experts, the public and politics, rather than being a special problem that is unheeded.

When the prevalence of violence against women is analyzed according to the welfare levels of the countries, it is observed that many countries in the high income group have a higher prevalence of violence compared to the countries in the lower income group. The said prevalence is a fact that is realized contrary to the expected in developed countries, where employment and education levels are relatively higher compared to middle income countries.

In Turkey, situated among the middle income countries, the employment rate of university graduate individuals is 75 %, high schools and their equivalents is 62.5 %, while secondary school and below graduates is 52.3 %.The labor force participation rate of the population aged 15- 65 in Turkey is 58 %. In this context, it is particularly similar to Mexico. However, when examined in terms of violence against women, this rate is 38 % in Turkey and 14 % in Mexico.

In sum, the intensity of violence against women is quite high even in countries where educated, high income individuals who have a certain status, is a job owner and even lives in high welfare level countries. Starting from this point of view, it has been observed that in addition to socio-economic factors, geographic characteristics such as region, population density or psychological characteristics such as behavior and thoughts, interests, motives, and life styles may be more effective in the occurrence of violence.

The intensity of domestic violence in countries such as Finland, Sweden and the USA, which draw attention with the effective education systems they implement today and whose per capita income levels are quite high, shows similarity to many middle income countries. Therefore, it can be said that despite all national and international developments, violence against women is a global problem that is widespread throughout the world and cultures regardless of geographical border, economic development and education level.

Thus, the expression that states violence is a learned behavior will be accepted regardless of economic concerns. The influence of the patriarchal ideology and acceptance of women as second-class citizens in countries with middle income and quite high density of domestic violence, such as Iran, Pakistan, Bangladesh, Turkey, Moldova, and Thailand is great. In addition, it is doubtful whether there is a sufficient institutional system for countries with low prevalence of violence against women and middle income (Ukraine, Iraq, Azerbaijan, etc.) in order for occurring or recording cases of violence by official authorities. Consequently, this change in consciousness will be possible in the long run through conscious government policies and education reforms. Likewise, in developing and developed countries, domestic violence is at so high levels that not only economic factors would be shown as the reason.

References

Access Economics. (2004). The Cost of Domestic Violence to the Australian Economy. Office of the Status of Women.

Aşkın, E. Ö., ve Aşkın, U. (2017). Kadına yönelik aile içi şiddet ve yoksulluk ilişkisi: aıle içi şiddet mağduru kadınlar üzerine bir araştırma. Kapadokya Akademik Bakış, 1(2), 16–37.

Aydın, S. (2016). Türkiye'de Kadının İstihdamı ve Kadına Dair Sosyal Güvenlik Uygulamaları. Çankırı Karatekin Üniversitesi Sosyal Bilimler Enstitüsü Dergisi, 7(1), 243–258.

Boatcă, M., Lamnek, S. (2003) Gegenwartsdiagnosen zu Gewalt im Geschlechterverhältnis. In S. Lamnek & M. Boatcă (Eds.), Geschlecht — Gewalt — Gesellschaft. Otto-von-Freising-Tagungen der Katholischen Universität Eichstätt-Ingolstadt. VS Verlag für Sozialwissenschaften, Wiesbaden.

Demirtaş, G., Yayla, N. (2017). Küresel Entegrasyonun Kadın İstihdamı Üzerine Etkisi: Ampirik Bir İnceleme. Journal of Yaşar University, 12(48), 339–349.

Dincer, B., Özaslan, M. (2004). İlçelerin Sosyo-Ekonomik Gelişmişlik Sıralaması Araştırması, DPT-BGYUGM, Ankara.

Dincer, B., Özaslan, M., Kavasoğlu, T. (2003). İllerin ve Bölgelerin Sosyo-Ekonomik Gelişmişlik Sıralaması Araştırması, DPTBGYUGM, Ankara.

Faramarzi, M., Esmailzadeh, S., Mosavi, S. (2005). A Comparison of Abused and Non Abused Women's Definitions of Domestic Violence and Attitudes to Acceptance of Male Dominance. European Journal of Obstetrics & Reproductive Biology, 122, 225–231.

Garbarino J. (1999), Lost Boys: Why Our Sons Turn Violent and How We Can Save Them. Free Press, New York.

Gelles, R. J. (1997). Intimate violence in families. Sage Publication, London.

Gilligan, J. (1996). Violence: Our Deadly Epidemic and It's Causes. G. P. Putnam's Sons, New York.

Gilligan, J. (2001). Preventing Violence. Thames & Hudson, London.

Horna, A. A. V. (2014). Gewalt gegen Frauen und die finanziellen Folgen Unternehmen in Peru. GIZ.

HÜNEE(Hacettepe Üniversitesi Nüfus Etüdleri Enstitüsü – ASPB (Aile ve Sosyal Politikalar Bakanlığı) (2015). Türkiye'de Kadına Yönelik Aile İçi Şiddet Araştırması 2014. Ankara: Elma Teknik Basım.

KAMER Kadın Merkezi. (2015). Kadın Hakları İnsan Haklarıdır Projesi

Müdürlüğü, A. K. S. G. (2016). Kadına Yönelik Şiddetle Mücadele Ulusal Eylem Planı 2016–2020.

OECD. (2011). A Composite Index for Monitoring Regional Development in OECD Regions, OECD Publishing, Paris.

Özdemir, A. İ., & Altıparmak, A. (2005). Sosyo-ekonomik göstergeler açısından illerin gelişmişlik düzeyinin karşılaştırmalı analizi. Erciyes Üniversitesi İktisadi ve İdari Bilimler Fakültesi Dergisi, 24(1), 97–110.

Sakarya, A., ve İbişoğlu, Ç. (2015). Türkiye'de illerin sosyo-ekonomik gelişmişlik endeksinin coğrafi ağırlıklı regresyon modeli ile analizi. Marmara Coğrafya Dergisi, (32), 211–238.

UNDP. 2001. Human Development Report 2001: Making New Technologies Work for Human Development. http://www.hdr.undp.org/en/content/human-development-report-2001.

Yavuz, R. A. (2016). Toplumsal cinsiyet eşitsizliği ekseninde kadın istihdamı ve ekonomik şiddet. Journal of Life Economics, 3(3), 77–100.

Yusufoğlu, Ö. Ş. (2017). Kadın yoksulluğu olgusuna sosyolojik bir yaklaşım: Elazığ örneği. Fırat Üniversitesi Uluslararası İktisadi ve İdari Bilimler Dergisi, 1(2), 99–126.

Adil Akinci

Privatization Revenues in Turkey in the Period of 1986–2020

1 Introduction

All of the economic thoughts that prevailed in the world economy until 1980 considered economic events as demand-side. Although Neo-Liberal economists put forward ideas that emphasize the supply side of the economy, their theoretical foundations remained weak. While the demand-based Keynesian economic approach depending on efficient fiscal policies was determinant of economic policies till 1970s after the Great Depression that was experienced in 1929, the inefficieny of Keynesian economic policies against the crises seen at the supply front and economic troubles which emerged as a result of increasing inflation and economic recession revealed the importance of supply in 1970s. "Supply-side economics", which emerged as a reaction to Keynesian economic policies, is an important economic approach that gives priority to the aggregate supply. The supply-side economics was called as *"Reaganomics" in the United States,* "Thatcherism" *in the United Kingdom, and* "Özalism" *in Turkey*, depending on country practices.

The supply-side economic approach envisaged reduction of state intervention in the economy, reduction of the public share in the economy and implementation of incentive policies to increase supply in order to maintain the competitive structure of the economy and to allow more resources to be left to the use of private sector. In order to reduce the public role in the economy within the framework of these policy proposals of the supply-side economic approach, privatization policies gained importance in the world and in Turkey after 1980.

The aim of this study is to examine the implementation of privatization policies in Turkey after 1980 within the framework of supply-side economic approach and the revenues gained from the privatization policies.

2 Evaluation of Privatization Policies

Along with the developments seen in the economy, changes occurred in the economic role of the state. The fundamental change in the economic role of state after 1980 was adoption of the thought by decision makers that it would be more suitable to transfer, by means of privatization, the state institutions and organizations to the market, due to the problems related to meeting of the financing need required for more effective, economical and efficient operation of the related institutions and organizations, and technology renewal as well as new investments (Susam, 2016. 210). The ownership, management and control of state owned enterprises (SOEs) owned by the state are generally transferred to the private sector via privatization (Özcan et al., 2019: 489). OECD (2009:5) described privatisation as "privatisation may be considered any material transaction by which the state's ultimate ownership of corporate entities is reduced" in its "Report on good practice" that it issued regarding privatization. The following factors are prominent among the reasons of appearance of SOEs (Mahmoud, 1992: 34):

- Promoting industry in non-industrialised countries,
- Making production in strategically-important industries,
- Making production in the areas where the private sector cannot be engaged in production and where large capital investments need to be made,
- Expanding the public sector,
- Guaranteeing the sale of goods and services at reasonable prices for low- income groups,
- Social and political reasons.

In short, the reasons for establishment of SOEs are to ensure economic development, operate natural monopolies by the state, do the jobs that the private sector cannot achieve and cannot enter, and to guide the economy, lead the private sector and regulate the distribution of income (Öztürk, 2020: 207).

In general, privatization practices are based on two important assumptions. The first of these assumptions is the assumption that the productivity and production possibilities of privatized state enterprises will increase. The second assumption is that the sector where the state enterprise operating in the monopoly market through privatization exists is regulated and opened to competition (Pietrogiovanna, 2009:4).

- The following points stand out as the main reasons for privatization (Sarıkamış, 2005: 10).
- Using SOEs for political purposes,
- Making loss by marginalised SOEs that do not provide political benefits and interets,
- Failure to employ skilled and well-educated staff due to the prominence of political nepotism rather than merit system in selection of staff,
- Failure to liquidate the loss-making SOEs and compensation of the damages from the public budget,
- The ability of the private sector to provide funding from financial markets more easily and under more appropriate conditions than the state.

Table 1: *Objectives of Privatization by General Impact Areas*

In terms of development and effectiveness of economy;	Creating a market economy Promoting private entrepreneurship and expanding the private sector's share in the economy, Increasing macro-economic or sectoral efficiency and promoting competition, Opening monopoly areas to competition, Developing effective capital market by mobilizing savings, Ensuring integration of the country's economy with the world economy, Creating employment.
In terms of income distribution;	Ensuring spread of capital throughout the base, Supporting provision of justice in income distribution, Ensuring spread of welfare throughout society, Attracting foreign capital investments, Strengthening the middle class, Promoting entrepreneurship.
In terms of financial aspects;	Reducing the burden of public debt, Reducing the financial burden of state enterprises on the Treasury, Ensuring contribution of the private sector to realization of large-scale investments, Creating new resources to boost tax revenues, Reducing budget pressures arising from public business.
In terms of political aspects;	Reducing the public share within the economy, Redefining the areas in which the public will operate by enabling the state to withdraw from production and concentrate on its essential functions, Creating the necessary environment for developing and supporting private sector activities, Preventing the immoderate use of public assets by public administration, Reducing the impact of decisions made or not made by political anxiety on the economy.

Source: (ÖIB, 2019: 46)

In general, the objectives of privatization vary according to the existing economic conditions of countries and the characteristics of the economic sectors that countries have, and their impact areas are generally presented in Table 1 (ÖIB, 2019: 46).

There are also some approaches against privatization practices.

The most important approach of those opposed to privatization practices is that unemployment will increase after privatization and that income and wealth distribution will be adversely affected by the sale of SOEs to individuals or organizations with high income levels (Tandırcioğlu, 2002: 200)

The acquisition of the private sector, which took over the state enterprise through privatization, due to the securities and real estate owned by the public enterprise (Orkunoğlu, 2010: 4),

The transfer of a monopoly SOEs to the private sector through privatization may cause the private sector to abuse its monopoly status as it targets the principle of maximum profit. In this case, the well-being and living standards of consumers will reduce as a result of privatization (Güngör, 2012: 132).

3 Privatization Methods

The literature shows that privatization methods are quite numerous. Among privatization methods, complete privatization, privatization of operations, contracting out, franchising and open competition methods will be addressed.

3.1. Complete Privatization

Complete privatization is a method of privatization in which both ownership and management are transferred to the private sector through the sale of state assets entirely to the private sector (Özcan et al., 2009: 490; Dayar, 2002: 4). According to the Commission on Government Forecasting and Accountability (CGFA), this method is implemented in three ways. The first practice is to privatize state-managed SOEs through the sale of stocks on various exchanges. The second practice is to privatize SOEs by selling it to only one person or group. The third practice is voucher privatization in which ownership of SOEs is sold to all citizens or SOEs employees free of charge or at a very low price (CGFA, 2006:1–2).

3.2. Privatization of Operations

Privatization of operations is the transfer of management of all functions of SOEs to the private sector through privatization, reserving ownership. With this privatization method, responsibility of operations is transferred to the private sector while the state continues its supervisory role (Brooks, 2004:471).

3.3. Contracting Out

Contracting out is a method of privatization that allows a designated service to be produced by the private sector rather than SOEs under contract. The cost of services produced by the private sector under contract is paid by the state. The costs arising under the contract due to service production are financed by income collected by the state as a tax or service usage fee (Johnston & Seidenstat, 2007: 234–235).

3.4. Franchising

Franchising is a method of privatization in which the state grants exclusive rights to a private sector business to serve in a particular geographical area (Brooks, 2004: 472). Franchising is a means of privatization that aims to grant or allow use of the rights of production or distribution of goods or services within the economies where natural monopolies are strong or under market conditions where there is no competition (Özcan et al., 2009: 491). Franchising method provides economy of scale and organizational advantages to the company that is the only manufacturer or service provider in the market (Fiedler & Wight, 2003: 181).

3.5. Open Competition

Open competition is a method of privatization in which many private sector firms are empowered to compete for customers within the public authority. This method is not efficient in the sectors where economies of scale do not exist (Brooks, 2004: 472).

4 Privatization Revenues in Turkey

With the Economic Stability Measures of 24 January 1980, the export-based industrial strategies that were outward-oriented were put into practice, and the policies and practices aiming at privatization of SOEs were put into effect by abandoning import-substitution industrialization strategies and statist practices in Turkey. In 1990s, reforming of SOEs was one of the most important issues, and in 1994, the Privatization Administration (ÖIB) and the High Council for Privatization (HCP) were established and the privatization practices were accelerated (Öztürk, 2020: 220). As of the end of 2020, there are 16 SOEs subject to the Decree Law No. 233 on State Economic Enterprises. There are five organizations that are not covered by Decree Law No.233 (HMB, 2020).

The revenues gained from privatization activities between 1986 and 2020 are presented in Table 2 by privatization methods. As it can be seen in Table 2, the share sale income and plant-operation sale/transfer income have a significant

Table 2: *Amounts Related to Privatization Transactions in the period of 1986–2020 (Dollar -$)*

Years	Sale of Shares	Plant-Operation Sale/Transfer	Hotel/Social Facility Sale	Real Estate Sale/ Transfer	Other Asset Sale/Transfer	Transfer to State Institutions	TOTAL
1986	710,394	-	-	244,501	-	-	954,895
1987	527,286	-	-	305,556	-	-	832,842
1988	26,501,676	-	-	355,311	-	-	26,856,987
1989	130,418,523	708,755	-	72,682	-	-	131,199,960
1990	485,946,739	-	-	42,428	-	-	485,989,167
1991	223,534,099	-	-	20,307,521	-	-	243,841,620
1992	422,881,905	-	-	0	-	-	422,881,905
1993	539,124,954	15,382,956	-	13,030,810	-	-	567,538,720
1994	407,141,008	4,613,346	-	385	-	-	411,754,739
1995	391,084,738	70,097,879	22,875,474	46,914,568	21,028,449	20,455,382	572,456,490
1996	219,978,800	50,949,596	3,807,656	4,052,095	10,856,000	2,354,760	291,998,907
1997	251,150,000	204,334,179	6,150,000	1,810,488	-	2,073,297	465,517,964
1998	939,828,905	48,564,275	-	17,899,991	4,385,985	9,035,988	1,019,715,144
1999	7,137,821	975.000	3,100,000	7,636,137	-	19,479,693	38,328,651
2000	2,594,192,776	11,451,000	760,000	49,276,179	-	60,855,896	2,716,535,851
2001	500,000	54,900,000	-	1,241,547	-	63,159,549	119,801,096
2002	406,082,441	-	-	7,961,615	126,000	122,305,486	536,475,542
2003	57,106,015	102,335,079	-	18,612,060	289,616	8,744,721	187,087,491
2004	1,069,574,083	109,193,000	-	29,126,799	5,850,000	69,098,247	1,282,842,129
2005	7,844,098,036	31,491,500	291,007,000	14,324,630	11,305,593	30,013,471	8,222,240,230
2006	7,391,001,890	157,800,000	305,410,001	157,677,272	126,559	84,149,738	8,096,165,461
2007	1,841,866,802	755,000,000	38,900,000	863,859,019	635,000,000	124,003,838	4,258,629,659
2008	3,932,631,209	2,230,000,000	-	6,345,290	305,000	89,923,688	6,259,205,187

2009	2,265,000,000	-	-	5,242,153	486,743	4,256,263	2,274,985,158
2010	2,582,532,746	384,767,797	-	90,000,991	20,501,739	3,887,907	3,081,691,179
2011	575,000,000	639,784,000	-	137,176,629	-	6,457,498	1,358,418,127
2012	2,706,136,050	-	-	312,305,159	-	2,251,038	3,020,692,247
2013	8,631,560,806	3,427,020,000	-	407,789,255	-	19,178,261	12,485,548,323
2014	2	4,828,450,000	-	1,053,340,726	-	384,101,474	6,265,892,203
2015	4,217,121	1,749,500,000	1,677,596	185,833,698	-	54,811,675	1,996,040,089
2016	-	1,087,806,339	-	198,470,763	-	6,255,345	1,292,532,447
2017	147,864,423	414,731,823	-	93,243,960	-	95,024,830	750,865,036
2018	4,533,748	1,114,495,932	-	95,577,317	-	143,962,029	1,358,569,026
2019	785	33,203,365	-	82,284,217	-	477.363	115,965,730
2020	-	-	-	8,827,828	-	3,230	8,831,058
Total	46,099,865,783	17,527,555,321	673,687,727	3,931,189,579	710,261,683	1,426,320,668	70,368,881,261

Source: (ÖIB, 2020, Available at: https: / / www.oib. gov. en / Turkey-ozellestirme)

share within total revenues. While the share of share sales income in total privatization revenues is approximately 65 %, the share of plant-operation sale/transfer income in total privatization revenues is 24 %. It is observed that the complete privatization method was heavily used in Turkey between 1986 and 2020.

According to Table 2, the highest share of total privatization income, after share sale income and plant-operation sale/transfer income, is obtained from real estate sale/transfer income with 0.5 %, transfer to state institutions with 0.2 %, and other asset sale/transfer income and hotel/social facility sale with 0.1 %. It is seen that hotel/social facility sale revenues and other asset sale/transfer revenues were obtained especially after 1995 and remained constant for certain years. According to Table 2, the privatization revenues in Turkey began in 1986 primarily through share sales and real estate sale/transfer.

In Figure 1, the total revenues gained from privatization in Turkey between 1986 and 2020 are presented.

As it can be seen in Figure 1, privatization practices that started in 1980s in the world experienced their real momentum in Turkey after 2003. Due to the failure of coalition governments in 1990s to demonstrate the political commitment required for privatization, lack of legal and institutional framework and lack of financing opportunities, the privatization practices failed to produce the expected results (Üçer, 2018: 558). The main problems of the Turkish economy in 1990s include some macroeconomic problems such as high budget deficits, chronic inflation, insufficiency of savings and unstable growth. High inflation and devaluation followed one another and the inability of sustaining macroeconomic imbalances in the public sector became the leading reason of November-2000 and February-2001 crises. On April 14, 2001, the "Transition to Strong Economy Programme (TSEP)" was put into practice in order to strengthen and sustain Turkey's financial and fiscal structure (Güler, 2019: 81). With the TSEP, it was aimed to control the discipline and inspection in the public finance and ensure transparency and accountability in the funding process and in this context, the role of the state in the economy was envisaged to be reduced. As a natural result of these objectives, the privatization of SOEs was accelerated (Öztürk, 2020: 223). Reserving the date of negotiations for accession to the European Union (EU) in 2004 increased the interest of foreign capital in Turkey, and there was intense foreign demand, especially for the service sectors with high profit rates on the domestic market. The privatization revenue amounting to around $ 27 billion was generated between 2004 and 2009 (Inam et al., 2016: 256). Although the global crisis in 2009 reduced privatisation revenues, the highest privatisation revenue after 2003, which was the fastest period of privatisation, was gained in 2013 with approximately $ 12.5 billion.

5 Conclusion

The main objectives of the privatization of SOEs are to reduce the role of the public in the economy, to cover high budget deficits and to increase the competitive structure of the sectors by increasing the functioning of the market economy. The success of privatization practices and their results depends on the countries' economic infrastructures and levels of development. Considering the privatization practices in Turkey, until 2000s, due to gaps in legal and institutional infrastructure as well as deficiencies in the economic development level, the desired success was not achieved in privatization practices. After 2000, the developments in legal and institutional infrastructure as well as achievements in the economic field by ensuring political stability and diplomatic breakthroughs, especially developments in the EU process, affected the success of privatization practices and other macroeconomic variables.

The main reasons for the privatisation of SOEs are the problems of inefficient operation of SOEs and their burdens on the public budget due to their duty losses. Considering the reasons for appearance of SOEs and the contribution of these institutions to the development of the economy as well as their ability to ensure more effective use of resources by investing in the areas where it is not possible to invest by private sector, we are faced with the need to consider how else SOEs can be operated in line with the economic growth and development goals. Political myopia issues such as the practice to recruit more than enough personnel to win votes, and the unavailability of qualified labour force due to political appointments to the boards of directors of SOEs during political unstability are also required to be considered within the scope of privatization.

In line with the economic resources and opportunities that the country has, the re-thinking of the place of SOEs in the economy, and the monitoring and inspection of the performance of SOEs taken over by the private sector within the scope of privatization are presented as policy proposals.

References

Brooks, R.C. (2004), "Privatization of Government Services: An Overview and Review of the Literature", Journal of Public Budgeting, Accounting & Financial Management, 16(4), pp.467–491.

CGFA. (2006), "Government Privatization History, Examples, and Issues", Available at: http://cgfa.ilga.gov/Upload/2006Gov_Privatization_Rprt.pdf, (20.04.2020).

Dayar, H. (2002), "Türkiye de Belediye Hizmetlerinin Özelleştirilmesi ve Etkileri Kütahya Belediyesi Örneği", Dumlupınar Üniversitesi Sosyal Bilimler Dergisi, (7), pp.313–326.

Fiedler, J.L. and Wight, J.B. (2003), "Privatization and the Allure of franchising: A Zambian Feasibility Study", International Journal of Health Planning and Management, 18, pp.179–204.

Güler, H. (2019), "Türkiye'de Mali Kriz Sonrası Kurallı Maliye Politikasının Bir Aracı Olarak Özelleştirme Politikaları", Siyaset, Ekonomi ve Yönetim Araştırmaları Dergisi, 7(1), pp.77–92.

Güngör, G. (2012), "Tarihi Açıdan Türkiye'de Özelleştirme Uygulamalarının Değerlendirilmesi", Sakarya İktisat Dergisi, (2), pp.125–151.

HMB. (2020), Kamu İşletmeleri Listesi, Available at: https://ms.hmb.gov.tr/uploads/2020/01/Kamu-Isletmeleri-Listesi_22.01.2020.pdf, (27.04.2020).

İnam, B., Giray, F. and Tüzüntürk, S. (2016), "Liberalleşme Sürecinde Özelleştirme, Doğrudan Yabancı Yatırımlar ve Ticaret Serbestliği: Bazı AB Ülkeleri ile Türkiye Karşılaştırması", Ömer Halisdemir Üniversitesi İktisadi ve İdari Bilimler Fakültesi Dergisi, 9(4), pp.251–270.

Johnston, V.R. and Seidenstat, P. (2007) "Contracting Out Government Services: Privatization at the Millenium", International Journal of Public Administration, 30(3), 231–247, DOI: 10.1080/01900690601117713.

Mahmoud, M.F. (1992), "Privatization: A Solution to Problems of Public Enterprises", Journal of KAU: Econ&Adm., (5), pp.33–49.

OECD. (2009), "Privatisation in the 21st Century: Recent Experiences of OECD Countries Report on Good Practices", Available at: https://www.oecd.org/corporate/ca/ corporategovernanceof stateownedenterprises/48476423.pdf, (12.04.2020).

ÖİB. (2019), Faaliyet Raporu 2019, Available at: https://www.oib.gov.tr/faaliyet-raporlar%C4%B1, (19.04.2020).

Orkunoğlu, I.F. (2010), "Özelleştirme ve Alternatifleri", Akademik Bakış Dergisi, (22), pp.1–22.

Özcan, S.E., Odabaşı, Y. ve Özçelik, Ö. (2019), "Devlet Girişimlerinin Özelleştirilmesi, Dünya'da ve Türkiye'de Özelleştirme Uygulamaları", Ed. Odabaşı, Y., Yılmaz, Z., *Seçilmiş Göstergelerle Türkiye Ekonomisi Geçmişten Günümüze*, Ekin Yayınevi, Bursa.

Öztürk, N. (2020), Kamu Maliyesi, Ekin Yayınevi, 5.Edition, Bursa.

Pietrogiovanna, R.G. (2009), "The Benefits of Privatization? The Mexican Experience in the Telecommunications Industry Paper to be Presented at the Emerging Research on Political Economy and Public Policy Conference the London School of Economics and Political Science", Available at: https://

pdfs.semanticscholar.org/be04/6ca643e8d63 bb53b709665bbaf3f4c578c2b. pdf?_ga=2.23950845.691596210.1586639202-786683560,1585783055, (12.04.2020).

Sarıkamış, C. (2005), "Türkiye'de Özelleştirme Çalışmaları", Muhasebe ve Finansman Dergisi, (28), pp.9–12.

Susam, N. (2016), *Kamu Maliyesi Temel Kavram ve Esaslar*, Beta Yayınevi, 2. Baskı, İstanbul

Tandırcıoğlu, H. (2002), "Geçiş Ekonomilerinde Özelleştirme", Dokuz Eylül Üniversitesi Sosyal Bilimler Enstitüsü Dergisi, 4(3), pp.198–226.

Üçer, S.E. (2018), "Türkiye'de Özelleştirmenin Üç Dönemi: 1980'ler, 1990'lar ve 2001 Sonrası", 1. Uluslararası İKSAD Sosyal Bilimler Kongresi, Mardin, Türkiye, 9 - 11 Mart 2018, ss.554–563.

İkrabin Aytekin

Tax Amnesties and the Applications in Turkey

1 Introduction

It is probable to assess tax amnesties as a call to taxpayers who show weakness in voluntary compliance for several reasons. Taxpayers are called to pay their tax debts, which they did not pay, with the guarantee of getting rid of monetary or penal prosecutions associated with these debts in whole or in part. In several cases, amnesties are often employed because they constitute an increase in tax revenues in the short term and sometimes for administrative and political purposes. Particularly in developing countries where amnesty is frequently applied, amnesties are not ordinarily implemented along with comprehensive tax reform, so even if an increase in incomes is obtained in the short run, the adverse effects are more prevailing in the long run.

The concept of amnesty in tax law is more obscure than the concept of amnesty under criminal law in terms of the theoretical framework. Notwithstanding, the amnesty mechanism is applied more commonly in tax applications. Amnesty appears as a mechanism that has a great place not only in developing countries but also in developed countries. For instance, tax amnesties were employed at the provincial level (in approximately forty states since the 1980s) in OECD countries like Austria, Australia, Belgium, Finland, France, Greece, Ireland, Italy, Portugal, and Switzerland, and in the United States. However, in countries such as Chile, Argentina, Bolivia, Brazil, India, Mexico, and Turkey, amnesties have a broad practice area for various reasons, and it is observed that amnesties become routine in a sense. (Alm, 2005, pp. 98–6)

Tax (and insurance premium) amnesties also have been a mechanism frequently applied in Turkey. The law numbered 7143 frames the ultimate example of amnesties (tax and insurance premium) practiced almost every year since 1960.

In the second part of the study, a theoretical and qualitative evaluation of tax amnesties will be performed first. In the second part, specific tax amnesties in Turkey will be discussed. In the third and last part, the study will be concluded with an evaluation in the scope of the conclusion.

2 Tax Amnesties: A Theoretical and Qualıtatıve Evaluatıon

The application of tax amnesties in various countries is an implication of the presence of financial, economic, political, and social reasons that make amnesties' inevitable'. The features of taxpayers who benefit from tax amnesties are the essential issue to be highlighted in order to exhibit the amnesty cycle because of some features separating taxpayers who benefit from tax amnesties from other taxpayers. A relationship can be built between the almost routine amnesty mechanism in the appearance of a taxpayer type that has a habit of laundering with amnesty and does not accomplish his tax obligations due to the expectation of amnesty. If such taxpayers hold a notable share in the total, this situation should be analyzed in terms of weakness in tax applications. On the other hand, the presence of a taxpayer that 'takes advantage of' amnesty also makes the objectives of amnesty debatable. The most crucial reason why amnesties are frequently employed in developing countries in practice (in addition to the political necessity) is to achieve the much-required immediate income. Still, if it can be discussed that the tax collection momentarily growing because of tax amnesty is truly associated with delayed payments thanks to the expectation of amnesty, the collection rise that is the most notable issue of amnesty defense also does not have a basis because the rise in the collection in the short term consists of intentionally delayed tax debts. It is possible that amnesty causes a decrease in tax revenues in the long run and transforms honest taxpayers into the taxpayers who 'watch for an amnesty.

In this part, the sorts of tax amnesties and the factors requiring amnesties will be discussed first. Later, the standard features of taxpayers benefiting from amnesty will be emphasized, and an answer will be inquired to the question, "Are there any features that separate the taxpayers benefiting from amnesty from other taxpayers?". Potential effects of amnesties in the short and long term will be the last heading of this part.

1.1 Types of Amnesties

Amnesties may vary in terms of participation, the scope of amnesty, motif, and duration. Taxpayers, whose status is excluded from the knowledge of the tax administration, are commonly involved in the scope of amnesty, although they have tax obligations that they have not accomplished for any reason. Taxpayers, who are recognized not to accomplish their tax obligations, sometimes cannot engage in the amnesty. Tax amnesties may change in terms of scope. Instead of all tax types, only income tax, corporation tax, or capital kept in abroad can be covered in the scope of amnesty. Hence, it is reasonable to mention partial and general tax amnesties. (BIRD, 2003, p. 21). Tax amnesty is to give up some of the tax and tax-related receivables (interest and penalties) in addition to the investigation and prosecution. Still, according to the purpose, the calculation method of receivables within the scope of amnesty varies. Substantially, interest rates on applied debt can be reduced, or it is wholly given up. The duration of the amnesty can also be retained differently. Although amnesty is usually assigned based on a period, it sometimes involves a perpetual amnesty mechanism within tax systems. For instance, in the U.S. tax system, the amnesty mechanism for income tax was in effect between 1919 and 1952. (Alm, 2005, pp. 2–3).

1.2 Cost-Benefit Analysis of Tax Amnesty

The benefits and costs of amnesty can be listed as such (Alm, 2005, p. 4):

(1) The benefits of amnesty:

- A sudden rise in tax revenues
- A decrease in administration costs and judicial burden
- A potential rise in voluntary tax compliance with reinforced tax practices after amnesty
- Providing a soft transition to the new system if reinforced tax practices become part of comprehensive tax reform, including a reasonable penalty system and more favorable tax administration.

(2) Costs of tax amnesty:

- A small (and exaggerated) rise in tax income only in the short term and drop in the long term
- A decrease in voluntary compliance after the application of tax amnesty. This potential decrease is the result of factors like the expectation of new amnesty, the sense of injustice caused by amnesty in honest taxpayers, and the fact that amnesty drives to the perception that administration is ineffective in tax practices.
- Another of the shortcomings of tax amnesties is the rest in the emphasis on "crime" of tax evasion. (Kellner, 2005, p. 346)

The points summarized in the articles will be reviewed explicitly both in the following subtitles of this section and in the third section.

1.3 Features of Taxpayers Benefitted from Amnesties

The proposition that "all beneficiaries of tax amnesties are problematical individuals for various reasons and with differing degrees of tax compliance" will not be overemphasized. For this purpose, it will be informative to begin analyzing the behavior of tax-evading taxpayers while examining the tax amnesty. The goal of tax-evading taxpayers is to maximize their anticipated benefits, depending on the (perceived) chance of being caught, the extent of the penalty, and their approach to risk. The taxpayers who seek to assure their net income increase because of unpaid tax also undertake the risk of paying the penalty as well as their tax obligations when they are caught. (Fisher et al., 1989, p. 16)

Taxpayers are generally sought to be persuaded to revise these factors via tax amnesties. It is propagated that the chance of having an audit increases, the penalties will be strictly implemented, and the public's view of tax evaders will be more harmful. The belief that the probability of audit increases may have a definite influence on those who do not accomplish some of their obligations. Still, post-amnesty propaganda may not hold the same impact on individuals who do not report their entire income and are not even taxpayers because the marginal benefit achieved by tax evasion for these taxpayers may be much higher than the marginal cost. Thus, despite the increased marginal cost because of the reinforced tax practice, the marginal benefit may remain high. (Fisher et al., 1989, p. 16)Empirically, taxpayers with very high tax debt and taxpayers with very low tax debt have been determined to engage less in amnesties (Marchese & Privileggi, 2001, p. 24).

A static tax amnesty model valid for a certain period cannot be adequate to define the features of those who are tax-free. Because the potential taxpayer who can benefit from tax amnesty is separate from a typical taxpayer. He is a taxpayer who resorted to tax evasion in the past, may plan tax evasion in the future, and therefore considers the possible influence on future tax evasion when deciding whether to benefit from the amnesty. If the variables of this reckoning are assessed more obviously, the possible outcomes of participation in amnesty can be listed as such (Dönmez, 1992, p. 64):

(i) Fines follow the determination of unpaid tax debt in the form of monetary, penal, or social pressure. Participation in tax amnesty is sought to be supported with the amnesty of fines. Still, fines could not be emerged at all if tax obligations were accomplished on time. Hence, what the amnesty offers is not enough for the taxpayer who earlier saw the tax evasion optimal and hence becomes a tax evader. The amnesty applied to the crime only makes sense for the taxpayer, who considers that the chance of getting captured is now high. Likewise, it may be significant to get rid of the penalty for the taxpayer who has repented of tax evasion he practiced in the past and decided not to evade tax anymore.

(ii) Getting rid of guilt may be particularly significant for the taxpayer, who feels more guilty than anticipated after the tax evasion. In other words, the individual who has decided to tax evasion and then regretted can find an opportunity to get rid of guilt through the amnesty mechanism.

(iii) The taxpayer may perceive the high chance of past tax evasion actions happening after the amnesty or the chance of discovering tax evasion actions in the following periods. In order to benefit from the amnesty, it will be more challenging for the individual, for instance, who expresses that the income tax declaration was not entirely declared in the past, to practice the same kind of action in the future. Nevertheless, for this purpose, the individual who intends tax evasion in the future will not seek any amnesty. Furthermore, besides the debts included by a tax amnesty, the individual may also have some obligations outside the scope. In the case of demanding to benefit from tax amnesty, the taxpayer may not consider the advantage of tax amnesty worrying that his liabilities, which are outside the scope, will emerge. (Fisher et al., 1989, p. 16)

Briefly, both the taxpayers who benefit from tax amnesties and the taxpayers who do not participate even though they have tax noncompliance reconsider their cost-benefit analysis during the period when they do not accomplish their obligations. Perceptions that the chance of getting caught, mentioned above, rises with amnesty and that the punishment will be harshly practiced when caught influences participation in the amnesty. Besides these factors, more subjective characteristics like age, education, and marital status (Ritsema et al., 2003, p. 4) may also be decisive in the determination to participate in the amnesty. Consequently, it is decided that among the taxpayers who benefit from tax amnesties, those in their forties, married people, and the people receiving undergraduate education (even if they have not graduated) are prevalent.

1.4 The Influence of Amnesty on the Taxpayer's Behavior

Amnesty is possible to influence the taxpayers' view of tax. For honest taxpayers, tax amnesties can be regarded as a privilege that the system awards to tax evaders. On the other side, the spread of the idea that tax amnesties are not applied for once, and that new amnesties are inevitable is another cause for the long-term adverse effects of tax amnesties.

One of the central concerns debated in discussions on tax amnesty is how the tax amnesty will influence the taxpayers' voluntary tax compliance over time. Of course, because of benefiting from tax amnesty, an improvement in tax revenues is seen in the short term. Nevertheless, the answer to the question of what kind of change happens in the long term in terms of tax compliance is an essential point in the tax amnesty analysis. The next theoretical framework can be modeled on the relationship between amnesty and tax compliance: (Alm, 2005, pp. 25–26)

(1) Tax compliance will reduce after the amnesty.

- Honest taxpayers are expected to be adversely affected by amnesty. Because amnesty can be regarded as a mechanism of unlawful laundering of dishonest taxpayers (in various cases).
- Another cause for this hypothesis is the expectation of a new tax amnesty. Particularly in developing countries, amnesties are often applied to influence the requirement of an increase in tax revenues and voter behavior. Tax amnesty has become a rule in the countries belonging to this group. For instance, in a period covering thirty-five years, tax amnesty was practiced seven times in India and 21 times in Argentina (BIRD, 2003, p. 22). Also, in Turkey, the amnesty mechanism is often applied both in taxes and in social insurance premiums. Therefore, each amnesty causes new amnesty expectations.

(2) The expectation of amnesty will reduce over time. The statement that a new amnesty is never considered and that the amnesty is applied for once may direct to a decrease in expectation depending on the state's previous amnesty report and the credibility of the current administration.
(3) Giving weight on reinforced tax practice with amnesty may prevent a potential decrease in voluntary tax compliance after amnesty. In other words, if amnesty is backed by efficient control, it may display the anticipated effect. As addressed in the following pages, there are findings suggesting that compliance with reinforced tax practice can be accomplished at the same level without applying to amnesty.
(4) If the amnesty is followed by an effective audit mechanism, taxpayers may raise their tax compliance by assuming that those who do "free-riding" by not paying taxes will be caught.

The findings (Alm, 2005, pp. 23–25) achieved by testing the above theoretical framework with the experimental analysis method show that there is a close relationship between tax amnesty and tax compliance. Besides showing that tax compliance has reduced after the tax amnesty, the experimental analysis also puts forward that a well-designed amnesty can also prevent this decline. The necessary condition for this situation is to assure effectiveness in tax auditing after tax amnesty. The reason for the reduction in tax compliance is the expectation of new tax amnesty. The announcement that the new tax amnesty is clearly not considered does not present full progress in preventing. Because those who have a high level of tax compliance before amnesty are not negatively affected by the amnesty, and even if they maintain the same compliance levels, a decline in the tax compliance of the taxpayers who follow the lower compliance rates. It is a finding suggesting that tax amnesties may adversely affect some taxpayers' perception of tax. Still, it has been discovered that the tendency deriving from taxpayers whose compliance level is relatively low and from new amnesty expectations can be prevented with a more reinforced tax application. Hence, the rise in the audit rate regarded by the taxpayer along with the tax amnesty and revealing that the penalties will be practiced strictly will extend the enhancing effect of the amnesty. This situation was repeated in Torgler and Schaltegger (2005). Still, contrary to the conclusion that Alm et al. reached concerning the effect of reinforced tax application on increasing compliance after tax amnesty, Torgler and Schaltegger (2005) discovered that the reinforced tax application after amnesty did not affect increasing voluntary compliance. Subsequently, maintaining the pre-amnesty tax application in the same way after the amnesty, and strengthening this situation did not make any difference in terms of voluntary compliance (Torgler & Schaltegger 2005, p. 427).

With tax amnesty, taxpayers are provided the opportunity to accomplish the tax obligations that they have not before fulfilled within a specified period. Here it is probable to presume that there is a relationship between the characteristics of taxpayers benefiting from tax amnesties and increasing tax compliance in the short term after the tax amnesties. In general, taxpayers who have not accomplished their obligations with tax amnesties are encouraged to "start with a clean slate." This encouragement is also proposed to be supported by more established control and harsh penalties to increase tax compliance. Possibly especially the increase in tax revenues and the increase in tax compliance in the long term should be compared with tax amnesty and the potential difference between stricter audit and only strict audit policy. (Fisher et al., 1989, p. 15)

Tax amnesties lead to an increase in tax revenues in the short term at a lower cost. The reasons for this increase are (i) the self-exposure of those who are not taxpayers and (ii) those who do not accomplish some of their obligations despite being taxpayers to benefit from the amnesty, and (iii) the quick collection by getting rid of the judicial processes of the determined incompatibilities. By tax amnesties, the tax administration can distinguish non-taxpayers and taxpayers who fail to accomplish their obligations partially or entirely, without incurring the cost of inspection and auditing. Taxpayers, who cannot be determined unless without tax amnesty, stand out with the motivation to benefit from tax amnesties. These new findings extend the chance of increasing tax revenues in the post-amnesty period. On the other side, it is probable to create an adverse approach to tax revenues amnesty through taxpayers who do not benefit from tax amnesties. Consequently, honest taxpayers can wait instead of accomplishing their obligations with the idea of benefiting from future tax amnesties. Because some of the taxpayers will obtain new information on the extent of tax evasion through the amnesty mechanism and will have the realistic opportunity to evaluate their predictions of the possibility to be caught when they evade tax and then prefer to tax evasion (in a more equipped way). (Fisher et al., 1989, pp. 15–16)

2 Result

The application of tax amnesties in various countries is an implication of the presence of financial, economic, political, and social reasons that make amnesties 'inevitable'. Still, the difference in the behaviors and tax perceptions of honest taxpayers who do not benefit from tax amnesties requires the argument that amnesty may harm tax compliance in the long run. It is probable that a taxpayer type, which has a habit of laundering with the amnesty and does not accomplish its tax obligations in expectation of amnesty, is widespread in the country, and it will create a vicious cycle of decline in the compliance and new amnesty. Tax amnesty can profoundly influence the understanding that tax evasion is a crime, and the opinion that tax evasion is viewed as a crime is popular. All these improvements may extend the already existing defects in tax applications, principally in less developed countries. Repeated application of amnesties in developing countries causes an increase in tax revenues in the short term. Still, if it can be argued that the rising tax collection is due to delayed payments motivated by the expectation of amnesty, the collection rise is the most prominent issue in the amnesty defense also needs a basis.

Accordingly, the amnesty in Turkey must be assessed from this long-term perspective. The taxpayers' benefiting from the last amnesty law is regarded as the success of Turkey, but on the other hand, it is taken as an indication of why the amnesties are inevitable in Turkey. It also sets light to the relationship between amnesty, voter behavior, and political gain. Shortly, it is probable to build an analogy between the classic 'a chicken-egg' situation and amnesty. Another critical point is that amnesties are accepted as part of tax reform and do not turn into a routine. Otherwise, it is deduced from our history of amnesty in which both the administration and taxpayers would have to plan for new amnesties while also waiting for the tax collection provided by amnesty.

References

Akdoğan, Abdurrahman, Kamu Mâliyesi, Ankara: Gazi Kitabevi, Onuncu Baskı, 2005.

Alm, James, "Tax Policy Analysis: The Introduction of a Russian Tax Amnesty", Internatinal Studies Program, WorkingPaper 98-6, Georgia State Andrew School of Policy Studies, 1998, SSRN: http://ssrn.com/abstract=471321 [1 October 2005].

Alm, James, Michael McKee and William Beck, "Amazing Grace: Tax Amnesties and Compliance", National Tax Journal, v. 43, no 1, 1990, pp. 23–37.

Asutay, Mehmet, "Searching for Opportunistic Political Business Cycles in Turkey", the Annual Conference of the European Public Choice Society, April 15–18, 2004, www.diw.de/english/produkte/veranstaltungen/epcs/papers/ [Access Date: 2 September 2005].

Berksoy, Turgay ve İbrahim DEMİR, "Politik Vergi Çevrimleri: Türkiye'de Vergi Yükü Üzerinde Politik Etkiler", 19. Türkiye Maliye Sempozyumu, Uludağ Üniversitesi İİBF Maliye Bölümü, Belek-Antalya, 2004, pp. 513–532.

Bırd, Richard, "Administrative Dimensions of Tax Reform", International Tax Program Paper 0302, 2003. www.rotman.utoronto.ca/iib/ITP0302.pdf [Access Date: 10 October 2005].

Bülbül, Duran ve Karadeniz Hülya, "Vergi ve Sigorta Prim Atlarının Kayıt Dışı Ekonomi Üzerine Etkisi", 19. Türkiye Maliye Sempozyumu, Uludağ Üniversitesi İİBF Maliye Bölümü, Belek-Antalya, 2004, pp. 801–812.

Can, İsmail, "Ekonomik Krizlere Karşı Uygulanması Gereken Vergi Politikası", Maliye Dergisi, no. 142 (January-April), 2003, pp. 69–107.

Doğrusöz, Bumin, 21-03-2002, "Vergi Reformu ve Vergi Afları", Dünya Gazetesi, http://www.turmob.org.tr/turmob/basin/21.03.2002(2) [Access Date: 30 October 2005]

Dönmez, Recai, Teoride ve Uygulamada Vergi Afları, Anadolu Üniversitesi, Eskişehir, 1992.

Erdem, Metin, Doğan Şenyüz ve İsmail Tatlıoğlu, Kamu Maliyesi, Bursa: Ekin Yayınevi, İkinci Baskı, 1998.

Fısher, Ronald C., John H. Goddeerıs and James C. Young, "Participation in Tax Amnesties: The Individual Income Tax", National Tax Journal, v. 42, no 1, 1989, pp. 15–27.

Gelir İdaresi Başkanlığı, Vergi İstatistikleri, http://www.gelirler.gov.tr/gelir2.nsf [Erişim: 3 Kasım 2005]. KIZILOT, Şükrü "IMF yüzde 380'cik yanıldı", Hürriyet, 7/7/2004 MARCHESE, Carla and Fabio PRIVILEGGI, "Who participates in tax amnesties? Self-selection of risk-averse taxpayers", http://econpapers.repec.org/paper/ucaucapdv [Access Date: 1 September 2005].

Kellner, Martin. "Tax Amnesty 2004/2005- an Appropriate Revenue Tool?", German Law Journal, v. 5, no 4, 2004, pp. 339–346.

Nordhaus, William D. "The Political Business Cycles", Review of Economic Studies, vol. 42, no. 2, 1975, pp. 1–69.

Resmi Gazete, 4811 Sayılı Vergi Barışı Kanunu, no 25033, Tarih: 27/2/2003.

Rıtsema, Christina M., "Economic and Behavioral Determinants of Tax Compliance: Evidence from the 1997 Arkansas Tax Penalty Amnesty Program", the 2003 IRS Research Program, June 2003. www.economia.unitus.it/mare/IRSArkansasamnestv.pdf [Access Date: 2 Eylül 2005].

Saban, Nihal, "Vergi Suçlarında Affı Anayasa ile Sorunsallaştırmak", pp. 451–475, www.anayasa.gov.tr/anyarg18/saban.pdf [Erişim: 15 Ekim 2005].

Şener, Orhan, Teori ve Uygulamada Kamu Ekonomisi, Beta, 7. Baskı, 2001.

TBMM, "16.1.2003 Tarihli ve 4792 Sayılı Vergi Barışı Kanunu ve Anayasanın 89 uncu Maddesi Gereğince Cumhurbaşkanınca Bir Daha Görüşülmek Üzere Geri Gönderme Tezkeresi", http://www.tbmm.gov.tr/sirasayi/donem22/yil01/ss53m.htm

Torgler, Benno, Tax Morale: Theory and Empirical Analysis of Tax Compliance, 2003, University of Basel.

Torgler, Benno and Christoph A. Schaltegger, "Tax Amnesties and Political Participation", Public Finance Review, v. 33, no 3, 2005, pp. 403–431.

Unakıtan, Kemal, "2004 Yılı Bütçe Sunuş Konuşması", Maliye Dergisi, no 144 (May-December), 2003, pp. 5–37.

Unakıtan, Kemal, "2005 Yılı Bütçe Sunuş Konuşması", Maliye Dergisi, no 146 (May-December), 2004, pp. 5–41.

Vatan, "Vergi Barışı'ndan 4,7 Katrilyon Geldi" http://www.vatanim.com.tr [Access Date: 28.10.2004].

World Bank, Amnesties, http://www1.worldbank.org/publicsector/pe/tax/amnesties.htm [Access Date: 10 Ekim 2005]

Selim Tüzüntürk

The Applications of Two-Sample Hotelling's T^2 Test and One-Way Multivariate Analysis of Variance (MANOVA) Test

1 Univariate Analyzes

Statistical hypothesis testing is one of the methods of *statistical inference*[1]. Parametric and non-parametric hypothesis testing[2] are the two main approaches of statistical hypothesis testing (Tüzüntürk, 2015: 272). The main distinction point between these two approaches is the distribution shape of the population data whether it is normally distributed or not. Because, a parametric hypothesis testing is such an approach in which the shape of the population data is either assumed to be completely or approximately normally distributed and on the other hand a nonparametric hypothesis testing is such an approach in which the shape of the population data is not assumed to be a specific distribution shape (Tüzüntürk, 2018a: 53). Some commonly used univariate parametric tests are shown in Table 1 below[3].

The below hypothesis tests are used for drawing inferences about unknown population mean (or means)[4]. For instance, One Sample t Test determines whether populations mean is significantly different from some hypothesized value. Two Sample t Test is used to test the difference between two population means. The One-Way ANOVA Test is used to determine whether there any statistically significant differences between the means of three or more populations. A *univariate outlier analysis*[5] should be performed for each one of these cases at the beginning

1 Statistical inference is making inference about the population parameters by using sample data. Point estimation, interval estimation and hypothesis testing are the three forms of statistical inference. While, in the point estimation an unknown population parameter is calculated from the sample data with a single number, in the interval estimation it is calculated with interval values (with lower and upper bounds).

2 See Aytaç (1991, 2004) and Aytaç and Arlı (2018) for theoretical details of these main approaches.

3 In this table, ANOVA is the abbreviation of *Analysis of Variance*.

4 Proportion tests are also available for one sample and two samples. However, these are not included here.

5 Univariate outlier analysis can be performed by using a Box-Whiskers diagram or Histogram.

Tab. 1: Some Basic Univariate Parametric Tests

Number of Sample	Test Name
One Sample Tests	(i) One Sample Z Test (n≥30) (ii) One Sample t Test (n<30)
Two Sample Tests	(i) Independent samples test: Two Sample t Test (ii) Dependent samples test: Paired t Test
k Sample Tests (k>2)	(i) Independent samples tests: One-Way ANOVA Test Two-Way ANOVA Test Interaction Effect in Two-Way ANOVA Test (ii) Dependent samples tests: One-Way Repeated Measures ANOVA Test Two-Way Repeated Measures ANOVA Test

of the analysis. Because, if there is an outlier (or outliers) in the sampled data, normality tests with outlier(s) lead to incorrect results. If any outliers are detected in the outlier analysis, then they should be removed from the sample data.

Parametric tests require that the assumption of normality is met. After ensuring that there is no outlier in the sampled data, normality assumption can be safely checked. There are various methods such as interval method, graphical methods (histogram, box plot and etc.), skewness and kurtosis measures and quartiles and hypothesis tests (Tüzüntürk, 2018a). Common *univariate normality tests* are as follows: Kolmogorov-Smirnov test, Anderson-Darling test, Ryan-Joiner test and Shapiro-Wilk test. The null and alternative hypothesis are: "*H_0: The population is normally distributed, H_1: The population is not normally distributed*". If the null hypothesis is rejected, then non-parametric counterparts[6] of the parametric tests are used, if not, then parametric tests are used.

After ensuring that the normality assumption is satisfied, *homogeneity of variance assumption* which is essential for two sample and k sample tests should be checked[7].

6 See Tüzüntürk (2018a) for counterparts.

7 There are other assumptions that are assumed in performing these tests. However, we particularly focused on these two main assumptions up on the mainstream of this book chapter's subject matter.

Tab. 2: Hypothetical Data Structure for Two Sample t Test

Monthly Spending on food (Currency of Turkish Lira)	**Generation Type (1= Generation X, 2=Generation Y)**
800	1
950	2
.	.
.	.
.	.
820	1
875	2

The assumption of homogeneity of variance means that the variance within each of the populations is equal. Common *homogeneity of variance tests* are as follows: *Levene's (1960) Test, Hartleys's (1950) Test* (*or Hartley's* F_{max}) and *Bartlett's (1937) Test*. The null and alternative hypothesis are: "*H_0: The variances of the populations are equal (Homogeneity, H_1: The variances of the populations are not equal (Heterogeneity)*" and "*H_0: The variances of the populations are equal (Homogeneity, H_1: At least one population variance is different (Heterogeneity)*". If the assumption of homogeneity of variance is violated, then *robust tests*[8] that were developed by Welch (1947; 1951) and Brown and Forsythe (1974(a); 1974(b)) can be used in parametric testing of the sampled data[9]. These tests are Welch's t test, Welch's F test and Brown-Forsythe test which are the counterparts of the two sample t test and One-Way ANOVA.

Particularly, the above types of analysis are called *univariate analysis*[10]. *Uni* means *one*. In the univariate analysis, each variable (attributes) is explored separately (one by one). For instance, while performing Two Sample t Test (or Independent Samples t Test) the sampled data structure should be in such form that is shown in Table 2 above. In this example, one variable (attribute) that is monthly spending on food is explored for two categories (generation types[11]).

8 These tests are called robust because they can be used as a parametric test in case of the violation of the assumption of homogeneity of variance.

9 See Tüzüntürk (2018a) for computer applications.

10 Univariate analysis can be descriptive or inferential.

11 Western cultural generation types and birth years are as follows: Traditionalists (1900–1945), Baby Boomers (1946–1964), Generation X (1965–1980), Generation Y (1981–2000), Generation Z (2001–2012) and Generation Alpha (2013–2023).

Tab. 3: Hypothetical Data Structure for One-Way ANOVA Test[a]

Monthly Spending on food (Currency of Turkish Lira)	Generation Type (1= Generation X, 2=Generation Y, 3=Generation Z)
800	1
950	2
750	3
.	.
.	.
.	.
820	1
875	2
770	3

[a] When one categorical variable (for instance gender) is included, then this data structure turns into *Two-Way ANOVA Test*.

Whether the population means of the two type of consumers' monthly spending are equal or not is tested by calculation of the *t statistic*[12]. The hypotheses that are going to be tested are as follows: "H_0: $\mu_1 = \mu_2$ (Population means are equal), H_1: $\mu_1 \neq \mu_2$ (Population means are not equal)".

On the other hand, while performing One-Way ANOVA the sampled data structure should be in such form that is shown in Table 3 above. In this example, only one variable (attribute) that is monthly spending on food is explored for three categories. Whether the population means of the three type of consumers' monthly spending are equal or not is tested by calculation of the *F statistic*[13]. The hypotheses that are going to be tested are as follows: "H_0: $\mu_1 = \mu_2 = \mu_3$ (All population means are equal), H_1: $\mu_1 \neq \mu_2 \neq \mu_3$ (Not all of the population means are the same (at least one population mean is different))".

At the end, if there is a statistically significant difference between population means, then which means differ should be determined. To do so, sample means are compared for Two Sample t Test and on the other hand Post-hoc Tests are used for One-Way ANOVA Test[14].

12 Formula can be found in any text books of statistics.
13 Formula can be found in any text books of statistics.
14 See Tüzüntürk (2018a) for Post-Hoc Test computer applications.

2 Multivariate Analyzes

Multivariate analysis is a statistical analysis of data that was collected on *more than one dependent variable* (*outcome or response variable*). Variables are explored all together in the multivariate analyzes. *Hotelling's T^2 Test (One Sample Hotelling's T^2 Test and Two Sample Hotelling's T^2 Test)* and *MANOVA Test (One-Way MANOVA and Two-Way MANOVA)* are the common parametric hypothesis tests that are used for the multivariate data.

Two Sample Hotelling's T^2 Test is the multivariate extension of Two Sample t Test for difference means. Two Sample Hotelling's T^2 Test determines whether the two group means for all response variables are equal or not. *One-Way Multivariate Analysis of Variance* (One-Way MANOVA) *Test* is an extension of the One-Way Univariate Analysis of Variance (One-Way ANOVA) Test. One-Way MANOVA Test determines whether the three or more group means for all response variables are equal or not.

In multivariate analyzes, *univariate outlier analysis* and *multivariate outlier analysis*[15] should be performed at first as is in the univariate analysis. Hotelling's T^2 and MANOVA tests are parametric hypothesis tests that require multivariate normally distributed data[16]. Similar to univariate case, normality and homogeneity assumptions should be checked for them. Mardia (1970), Henze and Zirkler (1990), Doornik and Hansen (2008), Royston (1983), Mudholkar, Srivastava and Lin (1995) and Srivastava and Hui (1987) are some of the scientists that developed multivariate normality tests[17] that are used to check the data for the purpose of checking multivariate normality assumption (Tüzüntürk, 2018b: 246). The hypotheses of multivariate normality test that are going to be tested are as follows: "*H_0: The variables come from a multivariate normal distribution, H_1: The variables do not come from a multivariate normal distribution*".

In addition to the multivariate normality check, *multivariate homogeneity of variance test* should be performed[18]. In this situation, *Box's (1949) M Test*

15 Bivariate outlier analysis can be performed by using scatter plots for two dimensional spaces. Multivariate outlier analysis can be performed by using Mahalanobis Distance (MD) and Cook's D.

16 In this situation, performing univariate normality tests are not adequate. *Multivariate normality* of the data should be checked by using multivariate normality tests.

17 The names of the tests are called with the identical names of the scientists: Mardia Test, Henze-Zirkler Test, Doornik-Hansen Test, Royston Test and so on.

18 In this situation, performing univariate homogeneity test (Levene's (1960) test) is not adequate. Multivariate normality of the data should be checked. Multivariate homogeneity of variance test should be checked.

Tab. 4: Hypothetical Data Structure for Hotelling's T^2 Test

Monthly Spending on food (Currency of Turkish Lira)	**Monthly Spending on clothing (Currency of Turkish Lira)**	**Generation Type (1= Generation X, 2=Generation Y)**
800	600	1
950	650	2
.	.	.
820	620	1
875	675	2

or *Box's M Test of Equality of Covariance Matrices* is performed. The hypotheses of multivariate homogeneity of variance test that are going to be tested are as follows: "*H_0: The observed covariance matrices for the dependent variables are equal across groups, H_1: The observed covariance matrices for the dependent variables are not equal across groups*".

In performing Two Sample Hotelling's T^2 Test, the sampled data structure should be in such form that is shown in Table 4 above[19]. In this example, two variables (attributes) that are monthly spending on food and monthly spending on clothing are explored together for two categories (generation types). Whether the population means of these two groups for all response variables are equal or not is tested by calculation of the *T^2 statistic (or Hotelling's T^2 statistic)*[20]. The hypotheses that are going to be tested are as follows: "H_0: $\boldsymbol{\mu}_1 = \boldsymbol{\mu}_2$, H_1: $\boldsymbol{\mu}_1 \neq \boldsymbol{\mu}_2$". Here, $\boldsymbol{\mu}_i$'s are px1 vectors:

$$H_0 : \begin{bmatrix} \mu_{11} \\ \mu_{21} \end{bmatrix} = \begin{bmatrix} \mu_{12} \\ \mu_{22} \end{bmatrix} \quad and \quad H_1 : \begin{bmatrix} \mu_{11} \\ \mu_{21} \end{bmatrix} \neq \begin{bmatrix} \mu_{12} \\ \mu_{22} \end{bmatrix}$$

19 In this example, monthly expenses of households are explored whether they are different on the average or not in terms of two generation types. As is mentioned, multivariate analysis is conducted with more than one outcome variable. Here, there are two outcome variables: monthly spending on food and monthly spending on clothing. Simultaneously, more outcome variables such as monthly spending on entertainment, medical, housing, transportation and son on can be added to the analysis. And there is one categorical variable with two categories.

20 See Tatlıdil, (2002: 118) and Alpar (2011: 199) for the formula of this statistic.

Tab. 5: Hypothetical Data Structure for One-Way MANOVA Test

Monthly Spending on food (Currency of Turkish Lira)	**Monthly Spending on clothing (Currency of Turkish Lira)**	**Generation Type (1= Generation X, 2=Generation Y, 3=Generation Z)**
800	600	1
950	650	2
750	550	3
.	.	.
820	620	1
875	675	2
775	575	3

On the other hand, while performing One-Way MANOVA Test, the sampled data structure should be in such form that is shown in Table 5 above[21].

In this example[22], two variables (attributes) that are monthly spending on food and monthly spending on clothing are explored together for three categories (generation types). Whether the population means of these three groups for all response variables are equal or not is tested by calculation of the common statistics such as *Wilk's Lambda, Pillai's Trace, Hotelling's Trace and Roy's Largest Root*[23]. The hypotheses that are going to be tested are as follows: "H_0: $\mu_1 = \mu_2 = \mu_3$, H_1: $\mu_1 \neq \mu_2 \neq \mu_3$". Here, μ_i's are px1 vectors:

$$H_0 : \begin{bmatrix}\mu_{11}\\ \mu_{21}\end{bmatrix} = \begin{bmatrix}\mu_{12}\\ \mu_{22}\end{bmatrix} = \begin{bmatrix}\mu_{13}\\ \mu_{23}\end{bmatrix} \quad and \quad H_1 : \begin{bmatrix}\mu_{11}\\ \mu_{21}\end{bmatrix} \neq \begin{bmatrix}\mu_{12}\\ \mu_{22}\end{bmatrix} \neq \begin{bmatrix}\mu_{13}\\ \mu_{23}\end{bmatrix}$$

21 In this example, monthly expenses of households are explored whether they are different on the average or not in terms of three generation types. As is mentioned, multivariate analysis is conducted with more than one outcome variable. Here, there are two outcome variables: monthly spending on food and monthly spending on clothing. Simultaneously, more outcome variables such as monthly spending on entertainment, medical, housing, transportation and son on can be added to the analysis. And there is one categorical variable with three categories. More categories such as traditionalists, baby boomers and generation alpha can be added to the analysis as well. In such situation, categorical variable with six categories is involved to be explored.

22 When one categorical variable such as gender variable is included into this data structure, then this data structure turns into *Two-Way MANOVA (Two-Way MANOVA) Test.*

23 See Alpar (2011: 206–208) for the formula of these statistic.

These hypothesis can be generalized for *k groups*: "*H_0: The multivariate means of all groups are equal, H_1: The multivariate means of all groups are not equal*".

3 Research Design and Methodology

The target population of this study is the Generation X, Generation Y and Generation Z population who live in Bursa, Turkey, and who go to a name-brand coffee shop which is Starbucks every week and drink coffee. *Web-based survey method* was used in the collection of data. Fifty individuals were surveyed and analyzes were performed through that gathered survey information. Song, Wang and Han's (2019) survey questions[24] of Brand image (six items), brand satisfaction (six items), brand trust (five items), brand love (five items), brand respect (four items) and brand loyalty (nine items) was used which was particularly prepared for a name-brand coffee shops. Besides, demographic data gathered such as gender, home city, age, and education.

Two Sample Hotelling's T^2 Test and One-Way MANOVA Test used (*brand image, brand satisfaction, brand trust, brand love, brand respect and brand loyalty*), which were computed by averaging the scores of items as the dependent variables. Genders (female and male) and home cities (five big city[25] and other cities) of the respondents were used as independent variables for Two Sample Hotelling's T^2 Tests. Generation type (Generation X, Generation Y and Generation Z) of the respondents was used as independent variable for One-Way MANOVA Test. This research aimed to find out the answers of the following research questions:

RQ1: Is there is a significant difference between females and males (gender) when considered jointly on the variables brand image, brand satisfaction, brand trust, brand love, brand respect and brand loyalty for Starbucks coffee shop?

RQ2: Is there is a significant difference between five big city and other cities (home city) when considered jointly on the variables brand image, brand satisfaction, brand trust, brand love, brand respect and brand loyalty for Starbucks coffee shop?

---

24 Five point Likert scale from "Extremely disagree" (1) to "Extremely agree" (5) answered by the respondents.

25 Five big cities are the most populated cities of Turkey: İstanbul, Ankara, İzmir, Bursa and Antalya.

RQ3: Is there is a significant difference between Generation X, Generation Y and Generation Z (three generation) when considered jointly on the variables brand image, brand satisfaction, brand trust, brand love, brand respect and brand loyalty for Starbucks coffee shop?

4 Research Findings

Some descriptive statistics are as follows: Out of fifty respondents, twenty of them are female (40 %) and thirty of them are male (60 %). Twenty three respondents' home city is five big cities (46 %) and twenty seven respondents' home city is other cities (54 %). Out of fifty respondents, nine of them are Generation X type (18 %), twenty four of them are Generation Y type (48 %) and seventeen of them are Generation Z type (34 %). All the respondents are well educated individuals who graduated from universities.

4.1 Normality Assumption Check

After the data entry, data cleaning was performed for detecting missing data, incorrect entry and outlier(s) in order to work with qualified data. Then, univariate, bivariate and multivariate normality assumptions was explored by using STATA package. Normality test results are shown in the following Tables 6, 7 and 8.

In the below three tables, it is seen that all the p-values are greater than alpha (p-values $\geq \alpha = 0.05$) which show that the null hypothesis can't be rejected for each of these cases. This indicates that six dependent variables come from univariate normal, bivariate normal and also multivariate normal distributions.

Tab. 6: Test for Univariate Normality

Variable	p-value for Skewness	p-value for Kurtosis	Joint p-value
Brand image	0.3317	0.9000	0.6078
Brand satisfaction	0.3745	0.6299	0.5878
Brand trust	0.1687	0.9044	0.3663
Brand love	0.4301	0.7026	0.6720
Brand respect	0.9908	0.8759	0.9878
Brand loyalty	0.7748	0.7547	0.9141

Tab. 7: Doornik-Hansen Test for Bivariate Normality

Pair of variables		Chi-Square	df	p-value
Brand image	Brand satisfaction	8.11	4	0.0877
	Brand trust	6.37	4	0.1732
	Brand love	6.50	4	0.1649
	Brand respect	1.95	4	0.7448
	Brand loyalty	4.53	4	0.3394
Brand satisfaction	Brand trust Brand love	1.14	4	0.8871
	Brand respect	2.66	4	0.6171
	Brand loyalty	2.07	4	0.7229
		2.56	4	0.6336
Brand trust	Brand love	4.80	4	0.3089
	Brand respect	3.69	4	0.4500
	Brand loyalty	5.23	4	0.2640
Brand love	Brand respect	1.88	4	0.7570
	Brand loyalty	1.90	4	0.7534
Brand respect	Brand loyalty	1.67	4	0.7955

Tab. 8: Test for Multivariate Normality

Test Name	Chi-Square	p-value
Mardia mSkewness	68.664	0.1193
Mardia mKurtosis	0.003	0.9545
Henze-Zirkler	0.396	0.5293
Doornik-Hansen	8.895	0.7119

Now, multivariate homogeneity of variance tests can be performed and then Two Sample Hotelling's T^2 Tests and One-Way MANOVA Test can be tested for the three RQs[26].

4.2 Two Sample Hotelling's T^2 Test for Gender Difference Jointly on Six Dependent Variables

The observed covariance matrices for the dependent variables are found to be equal across two gender groups, Box M = 14.404, F = 0.578, p-value = 0.930.

26 These analyses were performed by using SPSS package.

There was a significant difference between females and males when considered jointly on the variables brand satisfaction, brand trust, brand love, brand respect and brand loyalty, Wilk's $\Lambda = 0.747$, $F (6, 43) = 2.427$, p-value = 0.041, partial $\eta^2 = 0.253$.

A separate ANOVA was conducted for each dependent variable, with each ANOVA evaluated at an alpha level of 0.025. There was a significant difference between females and males on *brand satisfaction*, $F (1, 48) = 9.343$, p-value = 0.004, partial $\eta^2 = 0.163$, with females (mean = 3.675) scoring higher than males (mean = 3.089). There was a significant difference between females and males on *brand trust*, $F (1, 48) = 8.910$, p-value = 0.004, partial $\eta^2 = 0.157$, with females (mean = 4.080) scoring higher than males (mean = 3.453). There was not a significant difference between females and males on any one of the other dependent variables (brand image, brand love, brand respect and brand loyalty).

4.3 Two Sample Hotelling's T^2 Test for Home City Difference Jointly on Six Dependent Variables

The observed covariance matrices for the dependent variables are found to be equal across two home city groups, Box M = 29.814, F = 1.226, p-value = 0.217.

There was a significant difference between five big cities and other cities when considered jointly on the variables brand satisfaction, brand trust, brand love, brand respect and brand loyalty, Wilk's $\Lambda = 0.609$, $F (6, 43) = 4.606$, p-value = 0.001, partial $\eta^2 = 0.391$.

A separate ANOVA was conducted for each dependent variable, with each ANOVA evaluated at an alpha level of 0.025. There was a significant difference between five big cities and other cities on *brand image*, $F (1, 48) = 5.650$, p-value = 0.021, partial $\eta^2 = 0.105$, with five big cities (mean = 3.8551) scoring higher than other cities (mean = 3.4074). There was a significant difference between five big cities and other cities on *brand satisfaction*, $F (1, 48) = 10.683$, p-value = 0.002, partial $\eta^2 = 0.182$, with five big cities (mean = 3.6522) scoring higher than other cities (mean = 3.0432). There was a significant difference between five big cities and other cities on *brand trust*, $F (1, 48) = 11.194$, p-value = 0.002, partial $\eta^2 = 0.189$, with five big cities (mean = 4.0696) scoring higher than other cities (mean = 3.3926). There was not a significant difference between five big cities and other cities on any one of the other dependent variables (brand love, brand respect and brand loyalty).

4.4 One-Way MANOVA Test for Generation Type Difference on Six Dependent Variables

The observed covariance matrices for the dependent variables are found to be equal across three generation groups, Box M = 62.830, F = 1.134, p-value = 0.257.

In Table 9, p-values which are so close to zero indicate that there was a significant difference between Generation X, Generation Y and Generation Z when considered jointly on the variables brand satisfaction, brand trust, brand love, brand respect and brand loyalty:

Tab. 9: Multivariate Tests

Test Name	Value	F	df.	p-value	partial η^2
Pillai's Trace	0.538	2.635	12	0.005	0.269
Wilk's Λ	0.514	2.760	12	0.003	0.283
Hotelling's Trace	0.843	2.880	12	0.002	0.296
Roy's Largest Root	0.698	5.001	6	0.001	0.411

A separate ANOVA was conducted for each dependent variable, with each ANOVA evaluated at an alpha level of 0.025. There was a significant difference between Generation X, Generation Y and Generation Z on *brand satisfaction*, F (2, 47) = 6.321, p-value = 0.004, partial $\eta^2 = 0.212$, with Generation Z (mean = 3.7549) scoring higher than Generation X (mean = 3.3148) and Generation Y (mean = 3.0208). There was a significant difference between Generation X, Generation Y and Generation Z on *brand trust*, F (2, 47) = 6.429, p-value = 0.003, partial $\eta^2 = 0.215$, with Generation Z (mean = 4.1294) scoring higher than Generation X (mean = 3.8667) and Generation Y (mean = 3.3417). There was not a significant difference between Generation X, Generation Y and Generation Z on any one of the other dependent variables (brand image, brand love, brand respect and brand loyalty).

References

Alpar, R. (2011). *Uygulamalı Çok Değişkenli İstatistiksel Yöntemler*, Ankara: Detay Yayıncılık.

Aytaç, M. (1991). *Uygulamalı Parametrik Olmayan İstatistik Testleri*, Bursa: Uludağ Üniversitesi Basımevi.

Aytaç, M. (2004). *Matematiksel İstatistik*, Bursa: Ezgi Kitabevi.

Aytaç, M. & Arlı, N. B. (2018). *Sosyal Bilimlerde Parametrik Olmayan İstatistiksel Yöntemler*, Bursa: Ezgi Kitabevi.

Bartlett, M. S. (1937). Properties of Sufficiency and Statistical Tests. *Proceedings of the Royal Statistical Society. Series A*, 160, 268–282.

Box, G. E. P. (1949). A General Distribution Theory for a Class of Likelihood Criteria. *Biometrika*. 36(3–4), 317–346.

Brown, M. B. & Forsythe, A. B. (1974a). The Small Sample Behavior of Some Statistics Which Test the Equality of Several Means. *Technometrics*. 16, 129–132.

Brown, M. B. & Forsythe, A. B. (1974b). Robust Tests for the Equality of Variances. *Journal of the American Statistical Association*. 69, 364–367.

Doornik, J. A. & Hansen, H. (2008). An Omnibus Test for Univariate and Multivariate Normality. *Oxford Bulletin of Economics and Statistics*. 70, 927–939.

Hartley, H. O. (1950). The Maximum F-Ratio as a Short Cut Test for Homogeneity of Variance. *Biometrika*. 37, 308–312.

Henze, N. & Zirkler, B. (1990). A Class of Invariant Consistent Tests for Multivariate Normality. *Communications in Statistics- Theory and Methods*. 19(10), 3595–3617.

Levene, H. (1960). Robust tests for equality of variances. In Ingram Olkin, Harold Hotelling and et al. (Eds.), *Contributions to Probability and Statistics: Essays in Honor of Harold Hotelling*. Stanford, California, USA: Stanford University Press, pp. 278–292.

Mardia, K. V. (1970). Measures of Multivariate Skewness and Kurtosis with Applications. *Biometrika*. 57, 519–530.

Mudholkar, G., Srivastava, D. & Lin, C. (1995). Some p-Variate Adaptations pf Shapiro-Wilk Test of Normality. *Communication in Statistics- Theory and Methods*. 24(4), 953–985.

Royston, J. P. (1983). Some Techniques for Assessing Multivariate Normality Based on the Shapiro-Wilk W. *Applied Statistics*. 32(2), 121–133.

Song, H., Wang, J. H. & Han, H. (2019). Effect of Image, Satisfaction, Trust, Love, and Respects on Loyalty Formation for Name-Brand Coffee Shops. *International Journal of Hospitality Management*. 79, 50–59.

Srivastava, M. S. & Hui, T. K. (1987). On Assessing Multivariate Normality Based on Shapiro-Wilk W Statistic. *Statistics & Probability Letters*. 2, 263–267.

Tatlıdil, H. (2002). *Uygulamalı Çok Değişkenli İstatistiksel Analiz*. Ankara: Ziraat Matbaacılık.

Tüzüntürk, S. (2015). Performing Parametric and Nonparametric Statistical Methods Using Higher Education Service Quality Data. *Paradoks Economics, Sociology and Policy Journal*. 11(1), 265–293.

Tüzüntürk, S. (2018a). *Sosyal Bilimlerde İstatistiksel Araştırmanın Temelleri*, Bursa: Aktüel 16.

Tüzüntürk, S. (2018b). Çok Değişkenli Normallik Varsayımının LISREL ve STATA Paket Programları ile Test Edilmesi. In Kenan Terzioğlu and Süreyya Dal (Eds.), *Ekonometride Güncel Konular*, Ankara: Gazi Kitabevi, 243–260.

Welch, B. L. (1947). The Generalization of Student's Problem When Several Different Population Variances Are Involved. *Biometrika*, 34, 28–35.

Welch, B. L. (1951). On the Comparison of Several Mean Values: An Alternative Approach. *Biometrika*, 38, 330–336.

Yavuz Selim Hacıhasanoğlu

Climate Change and Financial Risks

1 Introduction

Rise in energy usage because of economic growth stimulates carbon dioxide (CO_2) emission which constitutes the primary sources of greenhouse effects and climate change. A higher volume of CO_2 in the atmosphere has a potential risk on the environment such as rising sea level, increasing temperature, more frequent and intensive extreme weather events, and diminishing agricultural productivity. Hence, the cost of economic growth is pollution in the form of air, water, and land.

In recent years, climate change and its effect have been started to discuss extensively. Policies related to reducing climate change can be summarized under two headings in terms of their objectives:

1. generating energy from renewable sources (e.g., solar or wind energy instead of fossil fuels),
2. increasing energy efficiency (for example, heating and cooling systems to operate with less energy).

Significant reductions in investment costs have been achieved through R&D activities in both areas. Hence, renewable energy or energy-saving investments are now profitable alternatives. This strengthens the expectations that the trend towards investments in those areas in the coming period will accelerate.

To reduce greenhouse gas emissions, many countries signed the Kyoto Protocol in 2005 which is followed by the Paris Agreement in which 189 nations had a consensus in 2015 to combat global warming and climate change by limiting the global average temperature increase.[1] Moreover, the effect of climate change on the financial system is on the agenda of many central banks and international organizations. For instance, the 2019 Global Financial Stability Report of IMF has for the first time put the issue of climate change and financial risks under the heading of "sustainable finance".

1 See Chenet et al. (2017), Ducret and Scolan (2017), and Chenet (2019) for more details.

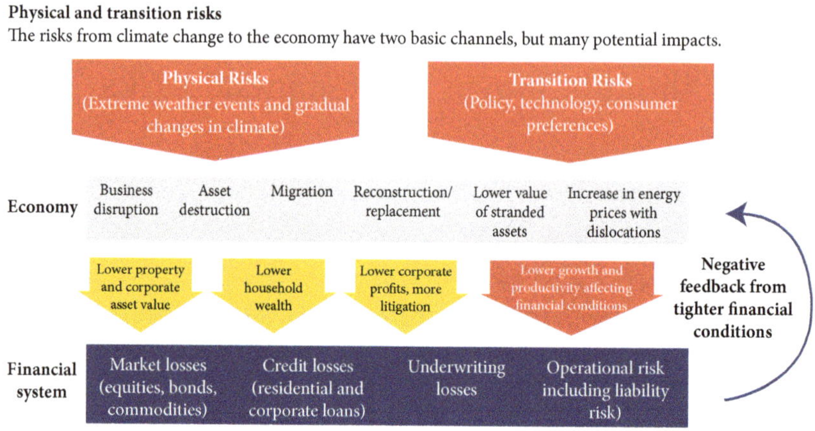

Figure 1: Climate Change and Risks

Source: IMF (2019), Global Financial Stability Report

Implementation of policies to reach the Paris Agreement goal may cause a sudden fall in carbon-intensive firms' asset prices, the default of those firms and even the default of countries extensively using carbon-intensive production technologies.

The main purpose of this chapter is to explain the financial risks related to climate change. The second section explains channels of climate change risks and the third section defines the concept of stranded assets. The fourth section gives details of financial risk. Finally, section five concludes.

2 Channels of Climate Change Risks

The IMF Global Financial Stability Report (2019) explains two potential channels of climate change risks to the economy (Figure 1): physical risk and transition risk.

2.1 Physical Risks

This channel is considered as a direct channel and consists of physical damage in infrastructure, production facilities and private and public properties as well as disruption in economic activity because of more frequently seen extreme weather events that occur with human-induced climate change (e.g., heavy rains, and storms). Figure 2 clearly shows that both catastrophe losses (green line at the left panel) and the number of events (blue line at the right panel) because of

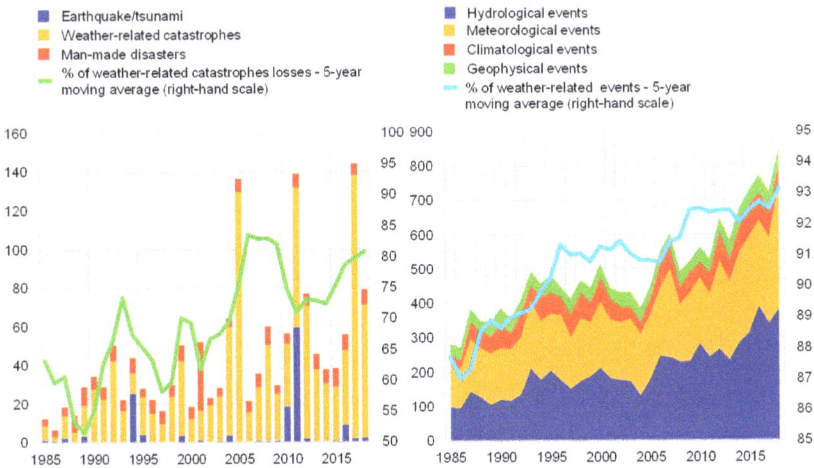

Figure 2: Catastrophe Losses and Number of Loss Events

Source: Swiss Re Institute, Munich Re NatCatService and ECB Financial Stability Review (2019)

climate change have been increased from 1985 to 2018 which means a value of losses for financial institutions.

2.2 Transition Risks

Relative to physical risk from climate change, transition risk is a new concept. Economies are in a position to move to a low-carbon economy with greener and less polluting technologies. Carbone-intensive sectors will be negatively affected by this transition. The negative impact of asset prices and business environment as a result of the trend towards creating a sustainable ecosystem compatible with environmental factors through changes in production technology, climate policy, and consumer sentiment is called as transition risk (e.g., policies discouraging brown energy sources and encouraging the widespread use of renewable energy). In this regard carbon-intensive industries, financial institutions that have exposure to those industries, and individuals who depend on these industries are exposed to transition risk.

3 Stranded Assets

Ratification of the Paris Agreement by 189 countries requires a dramatical reduction in carbon emission to restrict global warming (Millar et al., 2018). This implies a revolution in the energy generation of economies (Peake and Ekins, 2017). There are two different ways to transform economies to reduce carbon emissions. The first way is to invest in energy efficiency and significantly save energy consumption while the second way is to revert from brown energy technologies and use more green energy. In the transition to a low-carbon economy, asset prices such as energy-inefficient houses and power plants unanticipatedly decrease which is called asset stranding in the literature. These unanticipated changes in asset prices deteriorate financial stability in the medium and long-run.

Assets which have the potential to devaluate because of a transformation to renewable energy sources and the usage of energy-efficient technologies can be summarized in four groups:

1. Old buildings with low energy efficiency: this group consists of houses without heat insulation and consuming high energy.
2. Electricity production infrastructure using fossil fuels: Energy production and storage facilities with high greenhouse gas emissions (e.g. power plants using coal, diesel or natural gas).
3. Industrial production facilities with high use of fossil fuels: Plants using fossil fuels in production (e.g. steel industry).
4. Vehicles working with fossil fuels: Cars with high fossil fuel usage rate, vehicles, and machinery used in transportation.

According to the International Energy Agency (IEA) data, approximately 31 % of global energy consumption is realized by buildings and 60 % by transportation and industrial organizations with equal shares (IEA, 2019). Hence, the struggles to reduce greenhouse gas emissions are primarily to use renewable resources in electricity generation and to increase energy efficiency. In this way, significant reductions can be achieved in greenhouse gas emissions, particularly from industry and buildings. In the later stages, the electrical energy produced from renewable sources and energy-efficient technologies will gradually replace fossil fuels at every stage of people's lives (e.g., non-energy industry and transportation).

4 Financial Risks

In this section we concentrate on the 3 effects of climate change-related to financial stability:

1. the effect on financial institution because of stranded assets
2. the effect on government because of stranded assets
3. the spillover effect through affected parties in economies

4.1 Financial Institutions

Reaching climate change objectives not only necessitates a transformation to green energy technologies but also significant progress in the energy efficiency of production systems and buildings. Investing in energy efficiency is particularly important in countries with extreme weather events such as the Gulf Region countries. Moving to better energy efficiency standards significantly reduce energy bills (Zancanella et al., 2018) and decrease carbon emissions globally.

Since current physical assets (energy generation infrastructure, industrial factories, vehicles, and buildings) in the world mainly use fossil fuels, the transformation of them has significant financial stability risks. In addition, the values of current physical assets may diminish because of extreme weather events such as the risk of losing values in mortgage portfolios due to rising sea levels. Hence, exposure of the financial system to stranded assets comes out as an important risk for financial stability. Because drop within the market values will successively lead to a major reduction or fluctuation within the price of various financial properties as these properties are backed by brown assets using fossil fuels. Examples of such financial assets are mortgage-backed housing credits, firm credits backed by physical capital, stock and bonds backed by the energy generating firms' physical capital, and insurance agreements based on these financial instruments.

The fluctuation or sudden fall in asset prices affects the financial system, especially through the collateral channel. Studies have been increasing in recent years by many central banks and related international institutions such as BIS, the European Central Bank (Financial Stability Report, 2019), and OECD (Röttgers et al., 2018) to closely monitor climate change and related financial risks. For example, the Bank of England tries to include risks associated with climate change in stress test scenarios. While the Fed follows the financial risks associated with climate change, it prefers not to take policy action. On the other hand, it can be said that the private sector in the USA has made serious progress in this regard. In the recently published BIS study (Fender et al., 2019), risks related to the issue and policy recommendations to central banks are summarized.

In addition to the studies carried out by central banks and related institutions, it is seen that the governor of central banks also contributes to public awareness and awareness of the society through press releases. For example, the new ECB president Lagarde said in his priority statements that she added that the assets exposed to climate change risks in the banks of the euro area need to be reduced.[2] Former Bank of England governor Mark Carney (2015) emphasized that assets can suffer serious depreciations from climate change and this will have serious consequences for the financial system.[3]

To overcome financial risks because of climate change, financial institutions should measure these risks using stress testing tools and decrease their balance sheet exposures to assets that will be negatively affected in the energy transition process.

4.2 Government

As governments' tax revenues depend mainly on sectors using brown energy, they should also decarbonize their budgets for similar assets. After the global financial crises, many central banks have enlarged their balance sheets and it is not clear what percentage of their budgets are subject to energy transition risks because of climate change.

4.3 Spillover Effect

Another important aspect of financial stability risks is the potential spillovers from affected parties (financial institutions or governments) to parties that are not subject to climate change risks. This feedback effect in the financial system could be a result of both the physical and transition risks.

Correct pricing of climate change risks by the financial markets eliminates sudden value losses of financial assets in the transition process. On the other hand, based on the above-mentioned risks, while the need for financial markets to adjust for climate change is necessary, it is not possible to say that financial markets adequately price risk related to climate change.[4]

5 Conclusion

Energy transition and extreme weather-related losses contain significant financial stability risks. In the transition to a low-carbon economy, asset prices such as energy-inefficient houses and power plants unanticipatedly reduce and these unanticipated changes in asset prices deteriorate financial stability in the medium and long-run.

---

2 See https://www.ft.com/content/61ef385a-1129-11ea-a225-db2f231cfeae

3 See https://www.bankofengland.co.uk/speech/2015/breaking-the-tragedy-of-the-horizon-climate-change-and-financial-stability

4 See Chenet (2019) for more details of the inefficient pricing of the market.

Current physical assets (energy generation infrastructure, industrial factories, vehicles, and buildings) in the world mainly use fossil fuels and exposure of the financial system to brown assets comes out as an important risk on financial stability. In addition, incorrect pricing of climate change risks by the financial markets is increasing this risk. Hence, the measurement of financial exposures of governments and financial institutions to climate change risks is important to take necessary policy actions.

References

Carney, M. (2015). "Breaking the Tragedy of the Horizon—Climate Change and Financial Stability." Speech delivered at Lloyd's of London, September 29. https://www.bankofengland.co.uk/speech/2015/breaking-the-tragedy-of-the-horizon-climate-change-and-financial-stability

Chenet, H. (2019). "Climate Change and Financial Risk", SSRN Working Paper.

Chenet, H., Hilke, A. and Duan, W. (2017). Finance Sector Alignment with International Climate Goals – Reviewing Options and Obstacles, Green-Win Project. 2° Investing Initiative.

Ducret, M. and Scolan, M. (2017). Climate — The Financial Challenge. Les Petits.

ECB. (2019). "Climate Change and Financial Stability" Financial Stability Review, European Central Bank.

Fender, I., McMorrow, M., Sahakyan, V., & Zulaica, O. (2019). Green bonds: the reserve management perspective. BIS Quarterly Review, September.IEA (2019) "World Energy Outlook 2019", IEA, Paris https://www.iea.org/reports/world-energy-outlook-2019

IMF. (2019). "Sustainable Finance" Global Financial Stability Review, International Monetary Fund, October.Millar, R. J., Hepburn, C., Beddington, J. and Allen, M. R. (2018). "Principles to guide investment towards a stable climate", Nature Climate Change, 8(1), pp. 1–3. doi: 10.1038/s41558-017-0042-4.

Peake, S. and Ekins, P. (2017). "Exploring the financial and investment implications of the Paris Agreement", Climate Policy, 17(7), pp. 832–852. doi: 10.1080/14693062.2016.1258633.

Röttgers, D., Tandon, A. and Kaminker, C. (2018). "OECD Progress Update on Approaches to Mobilising Institutional Investment for Sustainable Infrastructure", OECD Environment Working Papers, No. 138.

Zancanella, P., Bertoldi, P. and Boza-Kiss, B. (2018) "Energy efficiency, the value of buildings and the payment default risk" Publications Office of the European Union, ISBN 978-92-79-97751-0.

Pelin Çelik

Analyzing Financial Performance of Paper Products, Printing and Publishing Companies Traded at BIST via Fuzzy TOPSIS Methodology

1 Introduction

The paper production in Turkey is started in 1936, in İzmit. Until 1960s industrial and cultural paper products were manufactured by Turkish Pulp and Paper Plants Operation (SEKA). After 1980s, private industry investments started (Çabuk et al. 2014: 67; Üçüncü et al. 2018: 93). Besides the annual capacity was around 10 thousand tons, it reached to 1 million thousand tons in 2001 (TMMOB, 2003). Trade data of the paper and paper products in Turkey obtained from ISO (Istanbul Chamber of Industry) are given in Table 1. As seen from the table, both import and export rates are increasing among the years.

Today, national and international competition among companies is becoming increasingly important. Therefore, it will be a great advantage for firms to know their position among the other companies of the sector in order to monitor their financial situation and keep their companies alive. Financial analysis helps companies to make decisions about their future and provides important information about financial decisions to companies. Financial ratios are often used to determine financial performance. Financial ratios are commonly used to assess a firm's performance and financial position. A firm's performance assessment helps investors make investment decisions and gain insight into the firm.

In the literature there are few studies about financial performance evaluation using Fuzzy TOPSIS method. Wang (2008), evaluated financial performance of airline companies operating in Taiwan. Grey Relational Analysis (GRA) was applied to cluster financial ratios and Fuzzy TOPSIS was used for selecting the best performing airline company. Wang (2014), analyzed financial performance of Taiwan container shipping companies by Fuzzy Multi Criteria decision making methods. GRA was applied for clustering the financial ratios. Then financial performances of container shipping companies are ranked by Fuzzy TOPSIS method. Keshavarz et al. (2014), aimed of maximising the financial and non financial performance of coil manufacture industry in Iran. For this purpose they used Fuzzy Analytic Hierarchy Process (FAHP) and Fuzzy TOPSIS. The

Table 1. Trade of the Paper Industry (Million $)

	2010	2011	2012	2013	2014	2015	2016	2017	2018/7
Export	1.217	1.427	1.669	1.937	1.738	1.613	1.760	1.977	1.272
Import	2.820	3.110	2.961	3.169	3.266	2.776	2.816	2.912	1.797
Export/ Import Coverage Rate	0.43	0.45	0.56	0.61	0.53	0.58	0.62	0.67	0.70

results showed that process technology is more important than product technology and management in the coil industry in Iran.

Shaverdi et al. (2016), developed a financial performance evaluation framework to rank the petrochemical companies in Iran, based on FAHP and Fuzzy TOPSIS. The companies are ranked by using the methods comparatively. The results showed that both methods gave the same results. Eyüboğlu and Çelik (2016), evaluated the financial performance of 13 Turkish Energy companies traded at BIST for the periods of 2008–2013. They used FAHP to determine the weights of the financial ratios and Fuzzy TOPSIS to rank the alternatives.

Aytekin and Karamaşa (2017), analyzed financial performance of six insurance companies traded at BIST. FAHP was used for weighting the criteria (financial ratios) and Fuzzy TOPSIS was used for the ranking of the companies. Perçin and Aldalou (2018), proposed a financial performance evaluation model for Turkish airline companies, based on financial ratios, utilizing the integrated FAHP and Fuzzy TOPSIS. FAHP was used for weighting the ratios and Fuzzy TOPSIS was used for ranking the alternatives.

Financial performance measurement is mostly made through financial ratios. From this point, it is aimed to evaluate the financial performance of paper products, printing and publishing companies which are traded at BIST. In the light of the financial information obtained from Public Disclosure Platform, 10 financial ratios were obtained by using 2013–2018 data. These financial ratios were analyzed by using Fuzzy TOPSIS method and the best and the worst performing firms are determined.

Following the introduction section, Fuzzy TOPSIS Method is summarized. In the last part of the study, the application is explained. In the conclusion part of the study, a general evaluation was made within the scope of the information obtained as a result of the application and suggestions were made for future studies.

2 Methodology

2.1 Fuzzy TOPSIS Method

TOPSIS, which is developed by Hwang and Yoon, 1981 (Aliakbari Nouri et al. 2015: 374), is a technique that mostly used by researchers in performance evaluation studies. The most important feature of TOPSIS method is choosing the alternative, which has the shortest distance from the positive ideal solution and the farthest from the negative ideal solution (Perçin and Aldalou, 2018: 590). Briefly, the positive ideal solution comprises of all best values obtainable of criteria, whereas the negative ideal solution constituted of all worst values obtainable of criteria (Wang and Lee, 2007: 1763). In TOPSIS method the ratings of alternatives are precise numbers, however due to vagueness of the decision data, precise numbers are ineligible to model real life decision problems (Lee et al., 2012: 41).

The usefulness of using fuzzy approach is to appoint the relative importance of attributes analyzing fuzzy numbers instead of crisp numbers (Mohaghar, 2012: 69). The steps of Fuzzy TOPSIS are as follows (Kuo et al., 2007; Çakır and Perçin: 2013; Eyüboğlu and Çelik, 2016)

Step 1. Creating the data matrix

Firstly, ratings are calculated by using Equation (1):

$$\tilde{X}_{ij} = \frac{1}{s}\left[\tilde{x}_{ij}^{1} \oplus \tilde{x}_{ij}^{2} \oplus \ldots \tilde{x}_{ij}^{s}\right] \qquad (1)$$

Where $\tilde{x}_{ij}^{s}$ is the performance rating value obtained from s-th decision maker. The fuzzy evaluation matrix is created using Equation (2):

$$D = \begin{bmatrix} \tilde{x}_{11} & \cdots & \tilde{x}_{1j} & \cdots \tilde{x}_{1n} \\ \vdots & & \vdots & \vdots \\ \tilde{x}_{i1} & \cdots & \tilde{x}_{ij} & \cdots \tilde{x}_{in} \\ \vdots & & \vdots & \vdots \\ \tilde{x}_{m1} & \cdots & \tilde{x}_{mj} & \cdots \tilde{x}_{mn} \end{bmatrix} \qquad (2)$$

where $\tilde{x}_{ij} = (a_{ij}, b_{ij}, c_{ij})$.

Step 2. Normalizing the evaluation matrix

The normalized fuzzy matrix is $\tilde{R} = \left[\tilde{r}_{ij}\right]_{mxn}$. B represents benefit criteria and C presents cost criteria.

$$\begin{aligned} r_{ij} &= \left(\frac{a_{ij}}{c_j^*}, \frac{b_{ij}}{c_j^*}, \frac{c_{ij}}{c_j^*}\right), \quad j \in B \\ r_{ij} &= \left(\frac{a_j^-}{c_{ij}}, \frac{a_j^-}{b_{ij}}, \frac{a_j^-}{a_{ij}}\right), \quad j \in C \\ c_j^* &= \max_i c_{ij}, \quad \mathit{if}\, j \in B \\ a_j^- &= \min_i a_{ij}, \quad \mathit{if}\, j \in C \end{aligned} \tag{3}$$

After normalization, the fuzzy elements take the values between [0,1].

Step 3. Calculating the weighted normalized fuzzy decision matrix

The weighted normalized decision matrix is $\tilde{V} = \left[\tilde{v}_{ij}\right]_{mxn}$;

$$\tilde{v}_{ij} = \tilde{r}_{ij} \otimes w_j, \tag{4}$$

$i = 1,2,\ldots,m$, and $j = 1,2,\ldots,n$

Step 4. Calculating the positive and negative ideal solutions

Fuzzy Positive Ideal Solution (FPIS) and Fuzzy Negative Ideal Solution (FNIS) can be given as:

$$\begin{aligned} A^* &= (\tilde{v}_1^*, \tilde{v}_2^*, \ldots, \tilde{v}_n^*) \\ A^- &= \left(\tilde{v}_1^-, \tilde{v}_2^-, \ldots, \tilde{v}_n^-\right) \end{aligned} \tag{5}$$

where $v_j^* = (1,\ 1,\ 1)\,,\ v_j^- = (0,\ 0,\ 0)$ *and* $j = 1,\ 2, \ldots, n$

Step 5. Calculating the distances from FPIS and FNIS

Using Equation (6) and (7), the distances from FPIS and FNIS are calculated.

$$d_i^* = \sum_{j=1}^{n} d\left(\tilde{v}_{ij}, \tilde{v}_j^*\right), i = 1, 2, \ldots, m \tag{6}$$

$$d_i^- = \sum_{j=1}^{n} d\left(\tilde{v}_{ij}, \tilde{v}_j^-\right), i = 1, 2, \ldots, m \tag{7}$$

The distance between two triangular fuzzy numbers $\tilde{a} = (a_1, a_2, a_3)$ and $\tilde{b} = (b_1, b_2, b_3)$ is calculated by Equation (8):

$$d\left(\tilde{a}, \tilde{b}\right) = \sqrt{\frac{1}{3}\left[(a_1 - b_1)^2 + (a_2 - b_2)^2 + (a_3 - b_3)^2\right]} \tag{8}$$

Step 6. Computing the closeness coefficients

Closeness coefficients of each alternative computed by Equation (9):

Table 2. Companies in the Paper Products, Printing and Publishing Sector

Company Code	Company Name
ALKA	Alkim Paper Industry and Trade Co.
BAKAB	Bak Packaging Industry and Trade Co.
DOBUR	Doğan Burda Journal, Publishing and Marketing Co.
DURDO	Duran Doğan Publishing and Packaging Co.
HURGZ	Hürriyet Journalism and Printing Co.
IHGZT	Ihlas Journalism Co.
KAPLM	Kaplamin Packaging Industry and Trade Co.
KARTN	Kartonsan Cardboard Industry and Trade Co.
OLMIP	Olmuksan International Paper Packaging Industry and Trade Co.
PRZMA	Prizma Press, Printing, Publishing Industry and Trade Co.
SAMAT	Saray Printing, Paper, Paperwork Trade and Industry Co.
TIRE	Mondi Tire Kutsan Paper and Packaging Industry Co.
VKING	Viking Pulp and Paper Mill. Co.

$$CC_i = \frac{d_i^-}{d_i^* + d_i^-}, \quad i = 1, 2, \ldots, m \tag{9}$$

If CC_i value of the alternative is close to 1, then the alternative is the best choice.

3 Results

The aim of the study is to evaluate the financial performances of Turkish paper product, printing and publishing companies during the period of 2013–2018. All financial statements are taken from Public Disclosure Platform.

The firms that traded at BIST are given in Table 2.

In the study, four group of ratios are selected as liquidity, financial structure, activity and profitability. Financial performances of firms are found by 10 financial ratios. The ratios are as follows;

To reach the values of the six periods, the representative indicator of company i on indicator j presented with the triangular fuzzy number $(g_{ij}^l, g_{ij}^m, g_{ij}^r)$ is defined as:

$$g_{ij}^l = \min\left\{b_{ij} | e = 2013,\ 2014, ..., 2018\right\}, \tag{10}$$

Table 3. Financial Ratios

Group of Ratio	Financial Ratios	Code
Liquidity	Current Assets/Current Liabilities	L1
Financial Structure	Total Liabilities/Total Assets	F1
	Equity Capital/Total Assets	F2
	Equity Capital/Total Liabilities	F3
	Current Assets/Total Liabilities	F4
	Fixed Assets/Equity Capital	F5
Activity	Net Sales/Total Assets	A1
	Net Sales/Equity Capital	A2
Profitability	Net Profit/Equity Capital	P1
	Net Profit/Total Assets	P2

$$g_{ij}^{m} = \frac{1}{6} \sum_{e=2013}^{2018} b_{ij}(e) \tag{11}$$

and,

$$g_{ij}^{r} = \max \left\{ b_{ij}(e) \middle| e = 2013,\ 2014, \ldots,\ 2018 \right\} \tag{12}$$

Reaching the triangular fuzzy numbers, the fuzzy numbers of financial ratios are shown in Table 4.

Then applying Equation (3) normalized fuzzy matrix is found as in Table 5.

After applying the Equations (6–9) of Fuzzy TOPSIS method, the ranking of the firm is found as in Table 6.

As seen in Table 3, PRZMA, KARTN and ALKA have the highest scores while HURGZ and VKING has the lowest scores for the period of 2013–2018.

4 Conclusions

The performance evaluation of the paper products, printing and publishing firms is an important issue especially in competitive business environment both for investors and also for the firms that are in the same sector as it demonstrates firm's position in the sector. Besides comparing a firm with others can identify the competitive strength and weakness. From this point of view the results of the study provides important information to the companies for looking over their goals and strategies.

Table 4. Triangular fuzzy numbers of financial ratios (Decision Matrix)

	L1			F1			F2			F3			F4		
ALKA	2,394	3,085	3,575	0,233	0,293	0,334	0,666	0,707	0,767	1,995	2,475	3,301	1,955	2,588	3,018
BAKAB	1,106	1,380	1,571	0,461	0,567	0,630	0,370	0,433	0,539	0,588	0,787	1,169	0,859	0,972	1,129
DOBUR	2,223	2,818	3,595	0,385	0,472	0,548	0,452	0,528	0,615	0,823	1,153	1,599	1,605	1,970	2,406
DURDO	0,793	0,987	1,133	0,718	0,809	0,881	0,119	0,191	0,282	0,135	0,244	0,393	0,513	0,571	0,651
HURGZ	0,873	1,317	2,417	0,268	0,511	0,606	0,394	0,489	0,732	0,650	1,121	2,736	0,554	0,766	1,618
IHGZT	4,305	4,621	5,000	0,142	0,171	0,195	0,805	0,829	0,858	4,134	4,904	6,036	1,580	2,079	2,477
KAPLM	0,788	0,885	1,038	0,638	0,720	0,812	0,188	0,280	0,362	0,232	0,400	0,566	0,752	0,809	0,914
KARTN	1,307	2,923	5,138	0,116	0,179	0,216	0,784	0,821	0,884	3,622	4,857	7,597	1,239	2,534	4,453
OLMIP	1,289	1,831	2,601	0,284	0,455	0,678	0,322	0,545	0,716	0,475	1,440	2,525	1,249	1,639	2,208
PRZMA	4,801	14,559	43,863	0,024	0,072	0,125	0,875	0,928	0,976	6,986	18,504	40,446	3,955	9,633	20,127
SAMAT	1,110	1,293	1,610	0,690	0,732	0,762	0,238	0,268	0,310	0,312	0,368	0,450	0,861	0,889	0,909
TIRE	0,910	1,051	1,264	0,521	0,624	0,706	0,294	0,376	0,479	0,416	0,626	0,919	0,858	0,983	1,148
VKING	0,439	0,538	0,625	0,848	0,909	0,998	0,002	0,091	0,152	0,002	0,103	0,179	0,264	0,307	0,339

	F5			A1			A2			P1			P2		
ALKA	0,207	0,356	0,528	0,759	1,143	1,603	1,134	1,617	2,337	-0,078	0,134	0,313	-0,060	0,094	0,215
BAKAB	0,890	1,068	1,232	0,833	0,958	1,043	1,667	2,258	2,549	0,023	0,107	0,221	0,010	0,044	0,084
DOBUR	0,120	0,169	0,265	1,535	1,603	1,661	2,495	3,076	3,478	-0,150	0,040	0,189	-0,073	0,026	0,116
DURDO	1,933	3,155	4,300	0,762	0,867	0,983	3,301	5,023	6,989	-0,611	-0,127	0,267	-0,084	-0,008	0,075
HURGZ	0,774	1,391	1,578	0,483	0,633	0,770	0,659	1,379	1,776	-0,897	-0,234	0,419	-0,354	-0,078	0,307
IHGZT	0,741	0,782	0,876	0,271	0,327	0,431	0,328	0,395	0,528	-0,024	0,023	0,177	-0,019	0,019	0,143
KAPLM	1,179	1,577	2,064	1,074	1,370	1,547	3,269	5,336	7,966	-0,472	-0,060	0,189	-0,092	-0,008	0,062
KARTN	0,535	0,719	0,934	0,602	0,940	1,306	0,768	1,141	1,563	0,010	0,118	0,279	0,008	0,098	0,233
OLMIP	0,454	0,560	0,626	1,143	1,296	1,439	1,885	2,547	3,551	-0,056	0,032	0,071	-0,030	0,019	0,051
PRZMA	0,499	0,551	0,632	0,211	0,333	0,431	0,236	0,359	0,457	0,002	0,021	0,057	0,002	0,020	0,056
SAMAT	1,204	1,306	1,374	0,684	0,980	1,298	2,607	3,737	5,455	-0,111	-0,004	0,113	-0,033	-0,001	0,030
TIRE	0,839	1,075	1,282	1,032	1,217	1,379	2,837	3,325	4,226	0,009	0,083	0,285	0,004	0,027	0,085
VKING	4,710	69,778	384,179	0,698	0,785	0,899	5,174	89,325	500,001	-48,855	-8,938	-0,449	-0,185	-0,097	-0,043

Table 5. Normalized Fuzzy Matrix

	L1			F1			F2			F3			F4		
ALKA	0,055	0,070	0,082	0,233	0,293	0,334	0,683	0,725	0,786	0,049	0,061	0,082	0,097	0,129	0,150
BAKAB	0,025	0,031	0,036	0,462	0,568	0,631	0,379	0,443	0,552	0,015	0,019	0,029	0,043	0,048	0,056
DOBUR	0,051	0,064	0,082	0,385	0,473	0,549	0,463	0,541	0,630	0,020	0,029	0,040	0,080	0,098	0,120
DURDO	0,018	0,022	0,026	0,719	0,810	0,883	0,122	0,196	0,289	0,003	0,006	0,010	0,025	0,028	0,032
HURGZ	0,020	0,030	0,055	0,268	0,511	0,607	0,404	0,502	0,750	0,016	0,028	0,068	0,028	0,038	0,080
IHGZT	0,098	0,105	0,114	0,142	0,172	0,195	0,825	0,849	0,879	0,102	0,121	0,149	0,079	0,103	0,123
KAPLM	0,018	0,020	0,024	0,640	0,721	0,813	0,193	0,287	0,370	0,006	0,010	0,014	0,037	0,040	0,045
KARTN	0,030	0,067	0,117	0,117	0,179	0,217	0,803	0,842	0,906	0,090	0,120	0,188	0,062	0,126	0,221
OLMIP	0,029	0,042	0,059	0,284	0,456	0,679	0,330	0,559	0,734	0,012	0,036	0,062	0,062	0,081	0,110
PRZMA	0,109	0,332	1,000	0,024	0,072	0,125	0,896	0,951	1,000	0,173	0,458	1,000	0,197	0,479	1,000
SAMAT	0,025	0,029	0,037	0,691	0,733	0,763	0,244	0,275	0,318	0,008	0,009	0,011	0,043	0,044	0,045
TIRE	0,021	0,024	0,029	0,522	0,625	0,707	0,301	0,386	0,491	0,010	0,015	0,023	0,043	0,049	0,057
VKING	0,010	0,012	0,014	0,850	0,910	1,000	0,002	0,093	0,155	0,000	0,003	0,004	0,013	0,015	0,017
	F5			A1			A2			P1			P2		
ALKA	0,001	0,001	0,001	0,457	0,688	0,965	0,002	0,003	0,005	-0,186	0,321	0,747	-0,195	0,305	0,700
BAKAB	0,002	0,003	0,003	0,501	0,577	0,628	0,003	0,005	0,005	0,055	0,255	0,526	0,031	0,142	0,272
DOBUR	0,000	0,000	0,001	0,924	0,965	1,000	0,005	0,006	0,007	-0,357	0,094	0,449	-0,239	0,084	0,378
DURDO	0,005	0,008	0,011	0,459	0,522	0,592	0,007	0,010	0,014	-1,458	-0,303	0,636	-0,275	-0,027	0,245
HURGZ	0,002	0,004	0,004	0,291	0,381	0,463	0,001	0,003	0,004	-2,139	-0,558	1,000	-1,151	-0,253	1,000
IHGZT	0,002	0,002	0,002	0,163	0,197	0,259	0,001	0,001	0,001	-0,056	0,055	0,423	-0,063	0,060	0,465
KAPLM	0,003	0,004	0,005	0,646	0,825	0,931	0,007	0,011	0,016	-1,125	-0,144	0,451	-0,298	-0,026	0,202
KARTN	0,001	0,002	0,002	0,362	0,566	0,786	0,002	0,002	0,003	0,024	0,281	0,664	0,027	0,320	0,758
OLMIP	0,001	0,001	0,002	0,688	0,780	0,866	0,004	0,005	0,007	-0,134	0,075	0,169	-0,099	0,061	0,165
PRZMA	0,001	0,001	0,002	0,127	0,201	0,260	0,000	0,001	0,001	0,006	0,051	0,136	0,007	0,066	0,182
SAMAT	0,003	0,003	0,004	0,412	0,590	0,781	0,005	0,007	0,011	-0,264	-0,009	0,270	-0,106	-0,004	0,096
TIRE	0,002	0,003	0,003	0,622	0,733	0,830	0,006	0,007	0,008	0,022	0,197	0,680	0,012	0,088	0,278
VKING	0,012	0,182	1,000	0,420	0,473	0,542	0,010	0,179	1,000	-116,477	-21,308	-1,071	-0,603	-0,315	-0,141

Table 6. Scores of the Firms

	D_i^*	D_i^-	CC_i	Rank
ALKA	7,705854	120,0912	0,939702	3
BAKAB	7,928397	119,5857	0,937823	6
DOBUR	7,796573	119,8053	0,938899	4
DURDO	9,071418	118,7062	0,929006	11
HURGZ	9,987551	118,6748	0,922374	12
IHGZT	8,199982	119,3422	0,935708	8
KAPLM	8,638104	119,0791	0,932365	10
KARTN	7,533899	120,18	0,94101	2
OLMIP	8,03725	119,5659	0,937014	7
PRZMA	7,419252	120,7664	0,942121	1
VKING	76,41131	89,72015	0,540055	13

Financial ratios of 13 companies in the paper product, printing and publishing, calculated from the data of 2013–2018, analyzed by Fuzzy TOPSIS, which is a popular method for Multi Criteria Decision Making problems. As a result of Fuzzy TOPSIS, the best company is selected as PRZMA, while the worst is VKING.

This study can be diversified by using different financial ratios. Also it can be extended by calculating the same ratios for different sectors.

In this study, Fuzzy TOPSIS method is chosen for evaluating the financial performance of the firms. In future studies, various methods like Grey Relational Analyses, Fuzzy ELECTRE and Fuzzy PROMETHEE can be used.

References

Aliakbari Nouri, F., Khalili Esbouei, S. and Antucheviciene, J. (2015). A Hybrid MCDM Approach Based on Fuzzy ANP and Fuzzy TOPSIS for Technology Selection. INFORMATICA, 26(3), 369–388.

Aytekin, A. and Karamaşa, Ç. (2017). Analyzing Financial Performance of Insurance Companies Traded in BIST via Fuzzy Shannon's Entropy Based Fuzzy TOPSIS Methodology. Alphanumeric Journal, The Journal of Operations Research, Statistics, Econometrics and Management Information Systems, 5(1), 71–84.

Çabuk, Y., Karayılmazlar, S., Aytekin, A., Onat, S. M. and Kurt. R. (2014). The Turkish Paper and Paperboard Industry: a Study of the Statistical Assessment, Analysis and Forecast. Journal of the Faculty of Forestry Istanbul University, 64(1), 67–79.

Çakır, S. and Perçin, S. (2013). R&D Performance Measurement in EU Countries Using Combined Entropy Weight-TOPSIS Method. Uludağ Journal of Economy and Society, 1, 77–95.

Eyüboğlu, K. and Çelik, P. (2016). Financial Performance Evaluation of Turkish Energy Companies with Fuzzy AHP and Fuzzy TOPSIS Methods. Business and Economics Research Journal, 7, 21–37.

Keshavarz, E., Heydari, T., Rohani, A. and Bagheri, S. M. (2014). Using Fuzzy AHP and Fuzzy TOPSIS Methods for Prioritisation of Technological Competencies to Maximise the Financial and Non-Financial Performance. International Journal of Business Information Systems, 16(3), 297–320.

Kuo, M.-S., Tzeng, G.-H. and Huang, W.-C. (2007). Group Decision-Making Based on Concepts of Ideal and Anti-ideal Points in a Fuzzy Environment. Mathematical and Computer Modelling, 45(3–4), 324–339.

Lee, C., Chiang, C., & Chen, C.(2012). An Evaluation Model of e-Service Quality by Applying Hierarchical Fuzzy TOPSIS Method. International Journal of Electronic Business Management, 10, 38–49.Mohaghar, A., Fathi, M. R., Faghih, A. and Turkayesh, M. M. (2012). An Integrated Approach of Fuzzy ANP and Fuzzy TOPSIS for R&D Project Selection: A Case Study. Australian Journal of Basic and Applied Sciences, 6(2), 66–75.

Perçin, S. and Aldalou, E. (2018). Financial Performance Evaluation of Turkish Airline Companies Using Integrated Fuzzy AHP and Fuzzy TOPSIS Model, Uluslararası İktisadi ve İdari İncelemeler Dergisi, 18. Eyi Özel Sayısı, 583–598.

Shaverdi, M., Ramezani, I., Tahmasebi, R. and Rostamy, A. A. A. (2016). Combining Fuzzy AHP and Fuzzy TOPSIS with Financial Ratios to Design a Novel Performance Evaluation Model. International Journal of Fuzzy Systems, 18(2), 248–262.

Üçüncü, T., Akyüz, K. C., Akyüz, İ., Bayram, B. Ç. and Ersen, N. (2018). Evaluation of Financial Performance of Paper Companies Traded at BIST with TOPSIS Method, Kastamonu Univ. Journal of Forestry Faculty, 18(1), 92–98.

Viswanadham, N. and Samvedi, A. (2013). Supplier Selection Based on Supply Chain Ecosystem, Performance and Risk Criteria. International Journal of Production Research, 51, 6484–6498.

Wang, Y. J. (2008). Applying FMCDM to Evaluate Financial Performance of Domestic Airlines in Taiwan. Expert Systems with Applications, 34, 1837–1845.

Wang, Y. J. (2014). The Evaluation of Financial Performance for Taiwan Container Shipping Companies by Fuzzy TOPSIS. Applied Soft Computing, 22, 28–35.

Wang, Y.-J. and Lee, H.-S. (2007). Generalizing TOPSIS for Fuzzy Multiple-criteria Group Decision-making. Computers & Mathematics with Applications, 53(11), 1762–1772.

Yunus Düger

An Analysis on the Effects of COVID-19 (Coronavirus) on Human Rights

1. Introduction

Having broken out in Wuhan, the capital of China's Hubei province in late 2019, COVID-19 (Coronavirus) pandemic is going to cause major transformations in social, financial, commercial and employment structures and policies of many countries at national and international scale, notably in healthcare. Causing a much severe effect than other epidemics in recent history, COVID-19 adversely affects all human beings regardless of their economic, social or cultural discrimination across almost the entire globe. Measures taken or cannot be taken by governments to fight the pandemic have a direct or indirect impact on many fundamental rights and liberties from the perspective of human rights. As a part of the measures, the risk to impose arbitrary detention rules, the pressure of the public authority on freedom of expression and respective criminal sanctions tend to be disproportionate. In addition, this causes cases incompatible with human dignity in terms of precarious employment, total failure to meet healthcare requirements or particularly exercising the rights to health such as no access to medical device and equipment for all, as well as other socio-economic rights and liberties. COVID-19 pandemic is set to bring up problems that have been around in many countries for a long time now such as income inequality, insufficient healthcare, public health and housing conditions, politics and governance based on market economy dominated by competitive and capitalist interests in particular, and "the human being understanding " shaped by them.

Such current or potential problems reiterate the essentiality of two main elements to succeed in fight against COVID-19 (Coronavirus) pandemic that threatens fundamental human rights such as the right to health and life for all the people across the globe. The first one is the understanding of governance based on human rights upholding the provision and improvement of human potentialities such as healthcare purely on grounds of being a human as the value of human beings and knowledge of human dignity play a central role. The other one is the rapid increase in the number of well-informed citizens who acknowledge or attach importance to aspects in which human dignity or value is at risk, and thus avoid putting the rights of other people to health and life at risk through their own actions.

However, two aforementioned elements seem to be problematic in both developed and underdeveloped countries. COVID-19 pandemic in particular entails revising the sense of governance where the principles individualism and utilitarianism, competitive market economy and downsizing state play a central role and governments establish and run organizations and public institutions based on the aforementioned principles.

2. Concept of Human Rights

The idea of human rights is based on the fact that every human being is dignified and valuable, and thus the violation of a fundamental right by any member of mankind stands for harming "the human dignity" and "value". From this point of view, the answer to why human rights need to be safeguarded is disguised in the words of human dignity or human value (Tepe, 2007: 146).

Kuçuradi shows the correlation between human dignity and human rights through its conceptualization based on the concept of human value (Kuçuradi, 2007a: 70). Kuçuradi explains what human value means as follows:

> By human value, I refer to the particular role of a human being among other creatures. What grants this particular role to human beings is the entirety of their qualities and potentialities that differ them from other creatures. These potentialities are considered to be human-specific activities and products. These qualities, on the other hand, are in addition to the qualities that are common with other creatures. These qualities or potentialities constitute human value or dignity (Kuçuradi, 2009: 73).

Human rights cover the entirety of rights that all human beings have without any discrimination on the sole basis of being human as a requirement of human value. What is meant by human rights is the recognition and acknowledgment of the value of human beings solely based on being human no matter what their states and circumstances are (Soysal, 1997: 126).

People must be treated in a certain way just because they are human beings. This is because people fail to develop some of their human potentialities once they are not treated as human (Kuçuradi, 2007b:30). For instance, human potentialities such as the fundamental rights to life and nutrition cannot be expected to be provided and improved when people are not provided with sufficient housing, employment and healthcare conditions, and their demands for such fundamental rights are not met.

To predicate human rights, a need arises for a version of anthropology that acknowledges people just because they are human beings, and takes into account the conditions to achieve what is humane, and be freed from theological and normative concepts (Höffe, 2004: 138–141). In other words, governments and people need to be free of some human designs. Formed based on religious and ethical norms, value judgments, racial, gender-based, cultural, ideological or economic and similar causes, and having an influence on government policies and actions taken in various aspects, human designs can impede human potentialities and their improvement just because people are human beings. This could eliminate the capability to equally provide all citizens with fundamental human potentialities such as healthcare in a sufficient way without causing any discrimination.

3. Some Problems Caused by COVID-19 (Coronavirus) in Terms of Human Rights

COVID-19 pandemic causes many problems in terms of human rights from a variety of perspectives such as limited access to healthcare services, arbitrary and disproportionate imposition of emergency measures, limitations on freedom of expression and thought, and actions taken against people, arbitrary detention and readily-imposed arrests, and problems of occupational health and safety.

In addition, COVID-19 pandemic brings about effects that promote views and actions of stigmatization and discrimination of citizens and ethnic groups by some countries and of racism and xenophobia (COVID-19 guidance, 2020).

3.1. Discrimination and Xenophobia-Racism

An epidemic is a key element that could potentially cause fear over people, racism and xenophobia. Coronavirus (COVID-19) pandemic currently leads to social and political fractures in societies, and stimulates reactions of discrimination and racism on grounds of fear (Abubakar, Bhopal, Devakumar, Shannon, 2020). From this point of view, Coronavirus pandemic has adversely affected liberties of people in many aspects, and led to unacceptable behaviors such as xenophobia, discrimination or racist attacks against foreign nationals (Baker & Park, 2020).

Communicable diseases have been historically associated with the concept of marginalization. Actions of discrimination against Chinese people have boomed since COVID-19 broke out and spread in Wuhan, China. This has caused actions of individual "*microaggression*" or violence for the collective restriction of workplaces of Chinese people. Additionally, political leaders seem to exploit the COVID-19 crisis in an effort to consolidate racist discrimination, impose stricter border policies and associate public health restrictions with anti-immigration discourses. For instance, Matteo Salvini, the former Prime Minister of Italy, linked COVID-19 to African refugees and pointed to border shutdowns. In the same vein, Donald Trump associated the pandemic with foreign policies and trade talks through his reference to coronavirus, which comes with acute respiratory distress, as "Chinese virus" (Abubakar et al., 2020). The statements made by some heads of governments such as Donald Trump, the President of the United States, to call COVID-19 pandemic a "Chinese virus" in a way to target a certain country and people promote xenophobia, and cause the persistence of anti-Asian sentiments, especially against China. That is why this causes harassment of people of Asian origin in the United States. Park argues that what lies behind the word "Chinese virus", which is uttered on purpose as a part of American discourse, is the idea of a racist attack as a consequence of the reiteration that white people are superior to Asian people (Baker and Park, 2020). In the same vein, the racist statements of doctors in France about how the vaccine to fight coronavirus should be tested out on African people first are unacceptable in terms of human rights.

As noted by the UN Special Rapporteur on Racism, "political statements and reactions that stigmatize and marginalize certain populations and make them vulnerable to violence in the midst of COVID-19 pandemic are unacceptable, unforgivable and incompatible with the obligations of governments about the human rights law" (Eviatar, 2020).

3.2. Problems of Healthcare Rights for People in Detention and Prisons

After COVID-19 was declared a global pandemic and rapidly spread, a need has arisen to specifically focus on certain places at risk such as prisons where people are deprived of liberty, detention centers, settlements where migrants are held, and addiction rehabilitation centers (IASC, 2020:2). In many countries, the aforementioned places are inadequate from the healthcare standpoint for detainees, prisoners, convicted people and their staff members. The World Health Organization has listed basic protective measures to take to right the COVID-19. They cover two main components: The first one is to wash hands on a frequent basis, and keep a safe distance from other people. The other one is to seek early medical aid in case of fever, cough or respiratory distress, and to be well-informed. While it is easy for many people to take such basic and protective measures, the exercise of these rights to health is highly limited in detention and prisons, and a need arises for numerous public authorities to make sure that the aforementioned rights can be exercised to a sufficient extent (Penal

Reform International Briefing, 2020:4). The fundamental right to life in physical and mental well-being shall remain in force for people in prisons and detention. In addition, they have the right to equal access to healthcare services as the rest of the society (Coyle, 2002:49). According to the International Covenant on Economic, Social and Cultural Rights[1], "The States Parties to the covenant recognize the right of everyone to the enjoyment of the highest attainable standard of physical and mental health". This imposes an obligation on states to provide detainees and prisoners with fundamental rights such as the right to health provided to all other people.

Even though physical and mental well-being of prisoners is cited as a fundamental right in many domestic and international norms, healthcare services to the most of the prisoners in many countries are provided in line with a lower standard than that of other people in society, and some of them never receive treatment. In addition, access to water can be limited based on security concerns or lack of infrastructure in cells or wards. Some hygienic supplies such as hand disinfectants are not available in sufficient quantity in most of the prisons, and they are usually banned as they contain alcohol (Penal Reform International Briefing, 2020:5). However, one must remember that detainees or prisoners are first and foremost human beings no matter how terrible their alleged or committed crime is. It is imperative to make sure that medical resources and healthcare services provided for them are equal to that of other members of the society. The obligation of states to provide people in prisons with decent healthcare services and resources constitutes an important aspect of the international human rights law.

In suspicious or confirmed COVID-19 cases, people in prisons must be provided with easy access to public and private healthcare services without facing some challenges. Authorities of prisons must be in cooperation and coordination with public health services and other healthcare service providers. This is of importance for the purpose of safeguarding the equality in care as set out in the UN's Nelson Mandela Rules. Given the particular risks concerning COVID-19, early release practices must be adopted for the elderly and the sick in prisons (Penal Reform International Briefing, 2020:5).

---

1 The International Covenant on Economic, Social and Cultural Rights was adopted and submitted for ratification, approval and accession in accordance with the UN General Assembly's Resolution No. 2200 A (XXI) of December 16, 1966. Entry Into Force: 3rd of January, 1976

3.3. Dilemma between the Right to Health and Concerns of Economic Stability

The global spread of COVID-19 is a consequence of reluctance shown by many governments to take steps that should have been taken much earlier as they did not want to unsettle financial markets further. In fact, COVID-19 pandemic exacerbates crises of inequality in social, economic and medical aspects caused by neo-liberal economic superiority or the system in place for decades. The concept of neo-liberalism, which began to come to fruition nearly twenty-five years ago, is a dominant factor in limiting healthcare expenses in many countries, and making global decisions that manifest themselves in the form of liberalization, privatization and commoditization of healthcare services just like it is the case for other social sectors. In addition, there has been a dilemma between the requirement to strengthen universal healthcare systems in particular and the sufficiency of actions taken to promote some poor segments of the society. From this point of view, many healthcare and human rights advocates have criticized that the universal healthcare policy is at risk as it is under the influence of a mighty neo-liberal mindset rather than elimination of inequalities in healthcare with direct focus on the right to health. Such tensions have evidently risen to the surface during COVID-19 pandemic that has disrupted economies, and exposed the insufficiency of healthcare services and social security, and adverse aspects of precarious employment (Forman, 2020).

3.4. Limitations on Freedom of Thought and Civil Liberties, and Arbitrary Detention

COVID-19 pandemic brings about adverse effects on the rights to health, and limitations on freedom of expression and other civil liberties, censorship on true information or arbitrary detention and some other adverse developments concerning fundamental rights. In his capacity as the Regional Director of Amnesty International, **Nicholas Bequelin argues that** there is no room for censorship, discrimination, arbitrary detention and violations of human rights to fight the coronavirus pandemic. Violations of human rights do not make things easier but difficult and reduce the effectiveness of response in any emergency "that concerns public health" (Bequelin, 2020).

Additionally, quarantines that limit the right to movement can be justified only when they are imposed in line with the principles of proportionality, temporality, legitimate purposes, absolute necessity, voluntariness and non-discrimination. Quarantines must be imposed with respect to human dignity. The rights of people in quarantine must be respected, and they must be provided with access to healthcare services, food and other needs (Bequelin, 2020). The response to the public health emergency caused by COVID-19 pandemic may require emergency measures. However, an emergency cannot lead to the disregard of obligations for human rights. Emergency measures that governments need to take as a part of the right against the pandemic must be based on necessity and proportionality. The imposition of emergency measures must be just and humane. In some cases, some reforms introduced as a part of legislation to fight the pandemic might serve as a legitimate basis for some oppressive legal reforms to be made permanent even after the pandemic and the state of emergency is over. In addition, some limitations and sanctions on freedom of press and thought and the way people are treated are alarming in terms of human rights (Bachelet, 2020:1) This is because the freedom of thought stands for not being subject to torture or inhumane treatment, arbitrary detention or restriction to other rights such as right to assembly, communication, education and employment on grounds of views that oppose dominant ones. However, some healthcare professionals in some countries have been fired for finding the response of their public authorities to COVID-19 pandemic unsuccessful and insufficient or criticizing those authorities for they are at risk. In some countries, healthcare professionals avoid expressing such criticism for their fear of losing their job or being sanctioned by administrative and legal means. However, the interference with or harm to the right of healthcare professionals, which improves human potentialities such as the right to employment, on grounds of criticism that should be considered part of freedom of thought is the violation of a human right.

In this sense, journalists in some countries are being punished for their report on shortages of masks as some actions are ambiguously conceptualized as a part of response to baseless news or incorrect information about COVID-19. In addition, regular people seem to be readily arrested on grounds of their social media posts (Bachelet, 2020:1). Some actions are taken in a way to harm fundamental human rights as no balance is struck between the freedom of thought for some critical views that would not constitute a crime and statements that put public security or peace at risk.

5. Conclusion

COVID-19 (Coronavirus) pandemic has reiterated how unprepared governments and international organizations and agencies are about safeguarding and improving fundamental rights such as the right to health and life. In another aspect, the alliances such as the European Union, where countries join forces for certain economic and political interests and powers, are not that humane and truthful given their attitudes and actions against the pandemic that threatens mankind at individual and societal scales.

COVID-19 pandemic can offer an opportunity for governments to revise their healthcare systems at national and international level based on human and fundamental rights in years to come. In addition, it could be noted that the success of response to COVID-19 pandemic that puts public health at risk depends on respect to and limitation on fundamental rights and liberties, economic, social and other rights in accordance with human value and dignity.

Governments have to make tough decisions to fight the COVID-19. In addition, international law allows for immediate actions against major threats. However, measures must be imposed in line with necessity and non-discrimination and in proportion to the risk in question. Governments must adopt their healthcare strategies in consideration of not only medical aspects of the pandemic but also consequences of measures, which are taken as a part of response, on human rights with specific focus on some differences such as gender, age and ethnicity (COVID-19 guidance, 2020).

References

Abubakar, I., Devakumar, D., Shannon, G., Bhopal Sunil, S. (2020). "Racism and Discrimination in COVID-19 Responses", https://www.thelancet.com/journals/lancet/article, (05.04.2020).

Bachelet, Michelle (2020). "COVID-19 Pandemic" – Informal Briefing to the Human Rights Council Statement by Michelle Bachelet, UN High Commissioner for Human Rights, https://www.ohchr.org, (12.04.2020).

Baker, Brandon& Park, Josephine (2020). Discusses the History of Asian-American Racism in The U.S. and How It Connects to Today's Use of 'Chinese Virus' to Describe COVID-19, penntoday.upenn.edu: https://penntoday.upenn.edu/news/why-asian-american-racism rampant-during-coronavirus, (05.04.2020).

Bequelin, Nicholas (2020). "Censorship, Discrimination, Arbitrary Detention and Human Rights Violations Have No Place in the Fight Against the Coronavirus Epidemic", https://www.amnesty.org, (08.04.2020).

Covıd-19 Guidance, United Nations Human Rıghts Office of the High Commissioner, https://www.ohchr.org, (13.04.2020).

Coyle, Andrew (2002). "A Human Rights Approach to Prison Management", Handbook for Prison Staff. Thırd Edıtıon, Institute for Criminal Policy Research at Birkbeck, University of London, London: International Centre for Prison Studies, https://www.prisonstudies.org, (07.04.2020).

Eviatar, Daphne (2020). "Human Rights Guidelines for the Fight Against COVID-19", https://www.justsecurity.org, (07.04.2020).

Forman, Lisa (2020). "The Evolution of the Right to Health in the Shadow of COVID-19", https://www.hhrjournal.org/2020/04/the-evolution-of-the-right-to-health-in-the-shadow-of covid-19, (08.04.2020).

Höffe, Otfried (2004). "Human Rights in Intercultural Debate", Human Rights in Turkey and World in the Light of Fifty-Year Experience, Ed. by. İoanna Kuçuradi ve Bülent Peker. Ankara: Turkey Philosophical Society Publications, 126–155.

IASC Inter-Agency Standing Committee (IASC) secretariat (Circulated on: 27 March 2020), "Interim Guidance COVID-19: Focus on Persons Deprived of Their Liberty", interagencystandingcommittee.org, (10.03.2020).

Kuçuradi, İoanna (2007a). Human Rights Concepts and Problems. Ankara: Turkey Philosophical Society Publications.

Kuçuradi, İoanna (2007b). "Human Rights: Concept and Types". Human Rights (Conferences, Panels and Symposiums). Ankara: Ankara Bar Association Human Rights Center Publications, 2nd Edition. 27–45.

Kuçuradi, İoanna (2009). "Philosophy and Human Rights", Philosophical Bases of Human Rights. Ankara: Turkey Philosophical Society Publications, 2nd Edition, 73–80.

Penal Reform International BriefingNote (2020). "Coronavirus: Healthcare and Human Rights of People in Prison", https://www.penalreform.org/resource/coronavirus-healthcare-and-human-rights-of-people-in, (07.04.2020).

Soysal, Mümtaz (1997). The Meaning of the Constitution in 100 Questions. İstanbul: Real Publishing House.

Tepe, Harun (2007). "Anthropological Foundations of Human Rights", Human Rights (Conferences, Panels and Symposiums). Ankara: Ankara Bar Association Human Rights Center Publications, 2nd Edition. 141–167.

Ali Kestane

The Role of Internal Control System in Strengthening Corporate Management in Banks: Provincial Case of Kilis

1 Introduction

The form of competition required for businesses to survive in the international markets has changed due to the ever-developing technology; and, the use of information technologies has tended to increase. The emergence of e-commerce applications in order to meet the demands and expectations of the customers in the markets in which the enterprises operate, has made it difficult to record and control the activities carried out by these enterprises, and required their management approaches to be reorganized. The banking sector has taken its share from the emerging changes and developments, and the digitalization movement has started for taking the operations related to their services under control and managing them. Trust, which is an indispensable value for the stakeholders of banks, requires that the efficiency and productivity of the systems used should be restructured starting from controlling the operations performed and managing them. Particularly the fact that cyber security applications have been more influential in the recent years has raised curiosity about the role of internal control systems for making corporate governance practices of the banks effective. Hence, the key to the fact of trust, which needs to be ensured by the banks within themselves and to their stakeholders, is the effective use of internal control systems; and, it is a known fact that trust is the key tool of corporate governance. In the light of this view, how the effectiveness of the internal control systems used by the banks in their branches operating in border provinces apart from their general directorates shaped the corporate governance approaches has been a topic of discussion. Therefore, in this study, it was aimed to determine the role of internal control systems in making corporate governance in the banking sector more effective. Based on the purpose of the research, the studies conducted on the concepts of corporate governance and internal control in the literature are presented hereby below.

2 Studies on Corporate Governance and Internal Control Systems in the Literature

In line with the changes in the competitive structures of enterprises with the increased use of technology, a new era has begun in the context of recording and controlling the activities carried out as well as managing them. Therefore, there have been discussions on the relationship between internal control systems and corporate governance and various studies have been carried out. In this part of the study, studies on internal control systems and corporate governance are presented.

As a result of the study that was theoretically investigated and carried out by Sarı (2013) about the importance of internal control system in corporate governance in enterprises, it was emphasized that an efficient and productive internal control system was required in order to establish effective corporate governance. Çiğdem (2018) investigated the impact of the internal control system on corporate governance approach in 38 companies within the scope of the BIST Corporate Governance Index; it was concluded that there was a positive significant relationship between the Control Environment, which was one of the components of the Internal Control System, and the Corporate Governance. Yaş (2019) investigated the relationship between internal control systems and corporate governance through the survey method on companies traded on the stock exchange; he concluded that with the establishment of an effective internal control system in enterprises, corporate governance approach could be created and it could make a significant contribution to achieving the objectives of corporate governance. Black et al (2019) investigated the importance of corporate governance in developing countries (Brazil, India, Korea and Turkey) and as a result of the study, they found that corporate governance disclosures and board structures (mainly structural independence) had a positive value in all countries. This indicated that regulators and investors have done a good job by focusing on disclosure and board structure when evaluating governance and responding to the investor pressure for better management of corporate administrators. Wood et al. (2019) investigated the corporate governance and company performance in emerging markets by presenting evidence from Turkey; they concluded that corporate governance approach could be weak due to the fact that a significant amount of companies in Turkey were family businesses emphasized that this was common in various markets. Bhaumik et al. (2019) investigated corporate governance strategies within the selected developing countries and stated that, since the foreign investments of the companies in developing economies led them to increase their governance capacities, they defended national policy reforms which forced local companies to develop similar skills; they concluded with an approach that supported the development of corporate governance both at the national and enterprise level. Lobo et al. (2020) investigated the relationship between the financial weakness in internal controls, which was described in Part 302 of the 2002 Sarbanes-Oxley Act (SOX), and the risk of future stock price collapse; they concluded that companies with weak internal control had lower financial reporting sensitivity, and therefore, their administrators could hide negative information about the business and create differences in the opinions of investors about the valuation of the company. In their study, in which they developed a framework for the use of structured data in cyber security and internal control, Canelon et al. (2020) demonstrated that the types of analyzes that needed to be performed on data types structured with job descriptions could determine the obtained results by combining potential connections between cyber security and internal controls. In their study on the relationship between the variables at national level and corporate governance at the level of enterprises, Almaskati et al. (2020) found that there was a positive relationship between the business profits and value at the level of enterprise for businesses that required high amount of funding and operated in financially developed countries by taking the effects of financial development state of a country as well as the external funding requirements of a company based on a sampling volume of 3301 businesses from 43 countries.

3 Application

In this part of the study, it was aimed to determine the views of the administrators of the bank branches operating in Kilis, Turkey in 2019 about the role of internal control on strengthening corporate governance. Explanations were made regarding the purpose and importance of the study; the scope of the study was determined and information was presented about its content.

3.1 The Purpose and Importance of the Study

In this study, it was aimed to determine the views of the administrators of the bank branches operating in Kilis, Turkey in 2019 about the role of internal control on strengthening corporate governance.

Determining the views of the administrators of the bank branches operating in Kilis, Turkey in 2019 about the role of internal control on strengthening corporate governance, identifying the current situation of the application related to the internal control systems used in corporate governance practices, and presenting suggestions for the steps that should be taken in the future through determining the perception levels of administrators indicate the importance of this study. In addition, exploration of how the corporate governance approach to banking activities at the border are carried out and the importance of the internal control system at the border indicate the difference of the study from other studies.

3.2 Scope and Limitations of the Study

The scope of the study includes the employees of the bank branches operating in Kilis, Turkey in 2019. The administrators of the bank branches constituted the sampling of the study with the aim of making sound interpretations in order to determine the role of internal control systems in strengthening corporate governance and providing information users with more reliable and consistent information.

3.3 Acquisition and Analysis of Data

Data of the study were collected through face to face surveys, which were administered between **01/09/2019 and 31/12/2019** to the administrators of the bank branch operating in Kilis. When creating the content of the survey administered, a ***validated*** study (**Acındı, 2007**) was made use of, and adaptations were made by adding new dimensions within the scope of the theme of the study. The survey created was composed of 31 questions in 3 groups. In the first group of questions, there were 26 items for determining the opinions of bank branch administrators on the role of internal control in strengthening corporate governance; in the second group, there was one item on raising awareness about compliance with corporate governance principles; and, there were 4 statements in the third group of questions on the demographic (age, gender, education and title) characteristics of administrators. Each item was coded from 1 to 5 and degrees of agreement were formed as **"Strongly Disagree", "Disagree", "Neutral", "Agree" and "Strongly Agree"**. The information and data obtained through the survey were organized, reviewed and coded in line with the purpose of the study. For application **68** survey forms were distributed and out of the **64** survey forms obtained, **50** were found to be suitable for evaluation. The obtained data were encoded on "Microsoft Excel 2016" and transferred to "SPSS (Statistical Package for the Social Sciences) 25.0"; appropriate analyzes ***(descriptive statistics, frequency distribution, nonparametric variance analysis; Kruskal Wallis H test and Mann-Whitney U test)*** were made, and, the results were edited and evaluated.

The application of statistical tests appears in various studies to depend on the provision of certain assumptions; the most important of the assumptions mentioned above is agreed to be the fitness of the analyzed distribution to normal distribution. In practice, in many cases, it is assumed that the data come from a population with a normal distribution, and it is observed that the reason for that is the effort to adapt the nature and human behaviors to the normal distribution in general (Özdamar, 2013: 103). In this context, in terms of applying parametric tests, non-parametric tests can be used if there is a data set that is not normally distributed as a result of validity tests or if the normal distribution assumption is not desired to be used (Baş, 2019: 96). In terms of the application of the non-parametric tests, it is considered sufficient to obtain the data independently and randomly, measure the data with an ordinal or classifying scale, and not demonstrate normal distribution (Karagöz, 2010: 19). In this study where the data were chosen randomly, whether the data had normal distribution was tested and non-parametric T-test (*Mann-Whitney U)* was used in comparing the two groups due to the fact that the data did not have normal distribution, and non-parametric variance analysis (*Kruskal Wallis H test)* was performed for the comparison of multiple groups. (Eymen, 2007: 117).

Kruskal Wallis H test is a non-parametric one-way variance analysis method. It is used to test whether the distribution of X scores of K independent sample are the random samples of communities with similar median values. K-W test is the non-parametric alternative of parametric one-way analysis of variance (Baş, Kurnaz and Kestane, 2019; 253–254). For example; testing whether there is a difference between the job satisfaction scores of the faculty members from three different universities.

Mann-Whitney U test is used to compare whether the two populations have similar distribution. It is widely used as an alternative to the t-test, which is one of the parametric tests, in non-parametric tests (Bayram, 2017; 116). For example, determining whether the stress scores of female and male students are different from each other.

3 Findings and Evaluation

In this part of the research, (i) the information obtained about the demographic characteristics of the participants; (ii) results about the mean (standard deviation) values regarding their statements on the role of internal control in strengthening corporate governance; (iii) frequency analysis results, (iv) *Kruskal Wallis H* test and (V) *Mann-Whitney U test results* are summarized and interpreted.

Table 1: Demographic Characteristics of the Administrators

Description		Number	Percentage (%)	Description		Number	Percentage (%)
Position	Manager	6	12		Aged between 18–25	3	6
	Authorized Administrator	12	24		Aged between 26–30	17	34
	Authorized Executive Assistant	3	6	Age	Aged between 31–36	25	50
	Customer Relations Manager	23	46		Aged between 37–42	3	6
	Portfolio Manager	6	12		43 Years Old and Over	2	4
	Total	50	100		Total	50	100
	Associate Degree	4	8	Gender	Female	19	38
Education	Undergraduate Degree	44	88		Male	31	62
	Postgraduate Degree	2	4		Total	50	100
	Total	50	100				

Looking at Table 1, it is seen that the positions of the bank administrators participating in the study are from varied positions in the banks. The ages of the administrators are mostly in the range of 31–36 years (50 %). Among the participants of the study, 19 (38.0 %) are female and 31 (62.0 %) are male. The educational statuses of bank administrators are 4 (8.0 %) associate degrees, 44 (88.0 %) undergraduate degrees and 2 (4.0 %) postgraduate degrees.

When the responses of the bank administrators to the first 26-item survey questions are examined in Table 2, it is seen that the majority of them gave close answers to the "I agree" and "I strongly agree" option. It is seen that they preferred more negative options only in Questions 7, 9 and 22 when compared to other questions. In addition, it is understood that 45 (90 %) administrators mentioned that the principles of the corporate governance are followed and 5 (10 %) people responded to this question negatively.

Table 2: The Role of Internal Control Systems in Strengthening Corporate Governance in Banks

	Descriptions and Questions	Number	Percentage	Number	Percentage
		1		**5**	
Question 1 (A1)	Administration supports the effective functioning of the internal control system and ensures that this approach is adopted by the employees of the company.	2	4 %	11	22 %
Question 2 (A2)	The internal control system business policies and objectives are coherent.	2	4 %	14	28 %
Question 3 (A3)	There is an effective coordination between the units in order to achieve the objectives of internal control.	2	4 %	11	22 %
Question 4 (A4)	The audit committee allocates sufficient resources and time to monitor business risks that may affect the internal control system continuously.	1	2 %	15	30 %
Question 5 (A5)	The duties, powers and responsibilities of the employees are determined clearly and they are constantly updated.	3	6 %	9	18 %
Question 6 (B1)	Risk assessment is made on the basis of departments within the enterprise.	-	-	12	24 %
Question 7 (B2)	There is a sufficient and constantly updated action plan to manage risk and mitigate its effects.	4	8 %	10	20 %
Question 8 (B3)	Administration and employees have fully understood the risks that are acceptable by the management.	2	4 %	9	18 %

(continued on next page)

Table 2: Continued

	Descriptions and Questions	Number	Percentage	Number	Percentage
Question 9 (B4)	Process and controls are constantly updated in accordance with changing risks.	4	8 %	9	18 %
Question 10 (C1)	There are written standards set for each process and unit based on the analysis of business processes.	2	4 %	10	20 %
Question 11 (C2)	There are controls that limit the loss of records and assets as well as preventing fraud. (Such as physical controls and separation of duties. . .)	1	2 %	14	28 %
Question 12 (C3)	There are procedures to complete the accounting of transactions accurately.	2	4 %	20	40 %
Question 13 (C4)	The transactions are recorded and separately approved by the performer and the controller.	2	4 %	20	40 %
Question 14 (C5)	The controls defined in the policy and procedure guidelines are also practiced as intended.	2	4 %	14	28 %
Question 15 (C6)	Changes in legal regulations are transferred to the internal control system by the administration on time and in full.	3	6 %	17	34 %
Question 16 (D1)	There is a common language structure of internal control, which is understood and supported by all employees.	2	4 %	15	30 %
Question 17 (D2)	Procedures have been established to guarantee the accuracy of the information that forms the basis of financial reporting.	2	4 %	11	22 %

Table 2: Continued

	Descriptions and Questions	Number	Percentage	Number	Percentage
Question 18 (D3)	There are check procedures concerning the data flowing between independent systems is transferred accurately.	-	-	16	32 %
Question 19 (D4)	There is an emergency action plan, which is created against an important disruption in the IT infrastructure and is constantly updated.	1	2 %	11	22 %
Question 20 (E1)	The effectiveness of the internal control system is constantly evaluated and monitored by the administration.	1	2 %	17	34 %
Question 21 (E2)	The unit that supervises the internal control system is prohibited from taking operational responsibilities that may conflict with the observer role.	2	4 %	13	26 %
Question 22 (E3)	Performance criteria created in the light of the goals and plans of the organization are used.	4	8 %	10	20 %
Question 23 (F)	Activities in the enterprise are carried out in accordance with laws and regulations.	2	4 %	19	38 %
Question 24 (G)	The activities are carried out in a way to secure the interests of all stakeholders and administrators.	2	4 %	17	34 %
Question 25 (H)	Sufficient and necessary information regarding business activities is shared with relevant parties (shareholders, administrators, public institutions and organizations etc.) in a timely and effective manner.	1	2 %	22	44 %

(continued on next page)

Table 2: Continued

	Descriptions and Questions	Number	Percentage	Number	Percentage
Question 26 (I)	In maintaining the business activities, the interests of the stakeholders are secured, the duties and responsibilities of the administration are explained and the objectivity of the decisions taken is monitored by the board of directors.	3	6 %	18	36 %
Question 27: *Compliance with Corporate Governance Principles: Yes, 45 (90.0); No, 5 (0.10)*					

In the study, the results of the non-parametric Mann-Whitney U (t Test), which was performed due to the fact that the compliance with corporate governance principles and genders included two groups, (t Test) and the non-parametric Kruskal Wallis H (variance analysis), which was performed due to the fact that the title, age and education status included more than two groups, (variance analysis) are presented below, and the results of the variables that have significant relationship among each other are presented in tables.

Looking at Table 3, the level of significance *was interpreted according to 0.05–0.10 %* It was identified that the attitudes of the bank administrators towards the role of internal control system in strengthening corporate governance demonstrated statistically significant differences within the context of questions A5 *(Sig. 0.067),* B2 *(Sig. 0.054)* C5 *(Sig. 0.067)* C6 *(Sig. 0.076)* D1*(Sig. 0.029)* E3 *(Sig. 0.029).* According to the responses of the administrators (frequency distribution), *the attitudes towards the questions A5, B2, C5, C6, D1, E3* differed according to the manager, the authorized manager or other position holders and this indicated that the position had a statistically significant effect on the internal control system. On the other hand, it was understood that the views of the bank administrators statistically differed in terms of corporate governance approach within the context of questions "G and I". (Sig., 092). This means that the attitudes of administrators towards questions G. and I. differed according to the authorized manager or other position holders, and this indicated that the position had a statistically significant effect on corporate governance understanding.

Looking at Table 4, it is identified that the attitudes of bank administrators towards the role of the internal control system in strengthening corporate governance has statistically significant differences within the context of questions

Table 3: Results of the Kruskal Wallis H (Variance Analysis) According to the Positions of Bank Administrators in the Context of Internal Control and Corporate Governance

Results of the Kruskal Wallis H (Variance Analysis) According to the Positions of Bank Administrators in the Context of Internal Control							
Description	**Kruskal-Wallis H**	**df**	**Asymp. Sig.**	**Description**	**Kruskal-Wallis H**	**df**	**Asymp. Sig.**
A1	6.552	4	0.162	C5	8.788	4	0.067
A2	6.889	4	0.142	C6	8.461	4	0.076
A3	4.689	4	0.321	D1	10.756	4	0.029
A4	3.873	4	0.423	D2	4.176	4	0.383
A5	8.784	4	0.067	D3	0.344	4	0.987
B1	5.558	4	0.235	D4	5.594	4	0.232
B2	9.287	4	0.054	E1	4	4	0.406
B3	0.793	4	0.939	E2	4.324	4	0.364
B4	6.59	4	0.159	E3	9.396	4	0.052
C1	2.757	4	0.599	**Results of the Kruskal Wallis H (Variance Analysis) According to the Positions of Bank Administrators in the Context of Corporate Governance**			
C2	3.229	4	0.52	F	3.386	4	0.495
C3	1.199	4	0.878	G	7.992	4	0.092
C4	6.357	4	0.174	H	7.59	4	0.108
				I	7.975	4	0.092

A1 (Sig. 0.084), C2 (Sig. 0.041), D2 (Sig. 0.097) E2 (Sig. 0.029). According to the responses (frequency distribution) of the administrators, their attitudes towards A1, C2, D2, E2 questions differ according to their associate, undergraduate and postgraduate degrees; and it shows that the educational status of administrators has a statistically significant effect on the internal control system.

On the other hand, it is seen that the views of the bank administrators statistically differed in terms of corporate governance approach within the context of questions "F (Sig.,055). and I (Sig.,060)". This means that the attitudes of the administrators towards questions F. and I. differed according to their associate, undergraduate and postgraduate status; and it shows that the educational status of the administrators has a statistically significant effect on their understanding of corporate governance.

According to Table 5, there is a statistically significant difference in the attitudes of bank administrators in the context of corporate governance within the scope

Table 4: Results of Kruskal Wallis H (Variance Analysis) According to the Educational Status of Managers in the Context of Internal Control and Corporate Governance

Kruskal Wallis H According to Educational Status (Variance Analysis) Results							
Description	**Kruskal-Wallis H**	**df**	**Asymp. Sig.**	**Description**	**Kruskal-Wallis H**	**df**	**Asymp. Sig.**
A1	4.962	2	0.084	C5	0.522	2	0.77
A2	2.949	2	0.229	C6	2.03	2	0.362
A3	0.198	2	0.906	D1	0.132	2	0.936
A4	0.053	2	0.974	D2	4.661	2	0.097
A5	0.16	2	0.923	D3	0.993	2	0.609
B1	0.011	2	0.994	D4	2.944	2	0.23
B2	0.862	2	0.65	E1	1.395	2	0.498
B3	0.249	2	0.883	E2	7.167	2	0.028
B4	2.029	2	0.363	E3	3.518	2	0.172
C1	0.403	2	0.817	**Results of Variance Analysis (Kruskal Wallis H) According to the Educational Status of Bank Administrators in the Context of Corporate Governance**			
C2	6.411	2	0.041	F	5.804	2	0.055
C3	0.985	2	0.611	G	0.319	2	0.853
C4	0.43	2	0.806	H	0.422	2	0.81
				I	5.624	2	0.06

Table 5: Results of Variance Analysis (Kruskal Wallis H) According to Ages of Bank Administrators in the Context of Internal Control and Corporate Governance

Results of Variance Analysis (Kruskal Wallis H) According to Ages of Bank Administrators in the Context of Internal Control				**Results of Variance Analysis (Kruskal Wallis H) According to Ages of Bank Administrators in the Context of Corporate Governance**			
Description	Kruskal-Wallis H	df	Asymp. Sig.	F	9.312	4	0.054
"No statistically significant results were found."				G	2.717	4	0.606
				H	1.485	4	0.829
				I	0.855	4	0.931

Table 6: Mann-Whitney U (t-test) Results in Terms of Compliance with Corporate Governance Principles in the Context of Internal Control and Corporate Governance

Mann-Whitney U (t Test) Results in terms of Compliance with Corporate Governance Principles in the Context of Internal Control							
Description	**Mann-Whitney U**	**Wilcoxon W**	**Asymp. Sig. (2-tailed)**	**Description**	**Mann-Whitney U**	**Wilcoxon W**	**Asymp. Sig. (2-tailed)**
A1	51.5	66.5	0.03	C5	97	112	0.598
A2	40.5	55.5	0.015	C6	67.5	82.5	0.124
A3	86	101	0.355	D1	57.5	72.5	0.061
A4	87	1122	0.388	D2	86.5	101.5	0.351
A5	94	109	0.526	D3	106	1141	0.822
B1	112	1147	0.986	D4	89	1124	0.408
B2	63	78	0.096	E1	100	115	0.665
B3	112.5	127.5	1	E2	76	91	0.205
B4	97	1132	0.602	E3	77	92	0.223
C1	79	94	0.249	**Mann-Whitney U (t Test) Results in terms of Compliance with Corporate Governance Principles in the Context of Corporate Governance**			
C2	57.5	72.5	0.061	F	69.5	84.5	0,128
C3	96.5	111.5	0.579	G	69	84	0.132
C4	79.5	94.5	0.25	H	58	73	0.057
				I	60	75	0.066

of the question "F (Sig., 0.054). This means that the attitudes of administrators towards question F differed according to their age intervals, and this shows that ages of the administrators have a statistically significant effect on their understanding of corporate governance. On the other hand, it is understood from the table that age did not have a significant effect on the internal control system.

As displayed in Table 6, compliance with corporate governance principles are evaluated with respect to the role of the internal control system in strengthening corporate governance in terms of revealing the gap in the perceptions of the bank administrators between the real case and the case they reported; and, a statistically significant difference is found in questions A1 *(Sig. 0.030)*, A2 *(Sig. 0.015)* B2 *(Sig. 0.096)* C2 *(Sig. 0.061)* D1 *(Sig. 0.061)*. According to the responses of the administrators (frequency distribution), the attitudes obtained from the questions *A1, A2, B2, C2, D1* show that there is a relationship between internal control system and corporate governance principles in strengthening corporate governance; and it has a statistically significant effect on the internal control and corporate governance system. On the other hand, it is seen that the views of the bank administrators statistically differed in terms of corporate governance approach within the context of questions "H (Sig.,057). and I (Sig.,066)". This shows that the attitudes of the administrators towards questions H. and I. differed significantly in compliance with corporate governance principles and had a statistically significant effect on their understanding of corporate governance.

Looking at Table 7, the attitudes of bank administrators towards the role of the internal control system in strengthening corporate governance are identified to have statistically significant differences within the context of questions A1 (Sig. 0.019), A3 (Sig. 0.027) C2 (Sig. 0.011), D2 (Sig. 0.028). This means that the attitudes of the administrators towards questions A1, A3, C2, D2 differed according to their genders; and this shows that the gender status of the administrators has a statistically significant effect on the internal control system on strengthening corporate management. However, it is understood from Table 7 that it has no effect on corporate governance approaches.

4 Conclusion and Recommendations

The emergence of e-applications in business operations based on the common use of technology that has attracted attention in recent years has changed the form and direction of competition and created great reactions within the international economy. Particularly, due to the fact that finance institutions operate in mainly in the service sector, the content and size of e-applications evolved in a different way, orientation to automation from people-oriented service practices gained great importance. The banking sector, which is accepted as the locomotive player of the system together with the international financial institutions, has taken its share from this case and the form of banking applications has eroded. Shifting the activities carried out in this context from manual operation to digital applications has also deeply affected the recording and control of these activities. The applications such as Bigdata, Industry 4.0, ACL, and ERP (Enterprise Research Planning) created a different perspective on the recording of banking activities and also had significant effects on security applications. The fact that the constraint of the sector is money and trust necessitated the reshaping of the internal control systems of the banks; and it is very important that the e-applications shall be developed accordingly. Due to the changes and developments, corporate governance approaches of the banks have also changed with the introduction of modern technology products and there was a requirement for rehabilitation. From this point of view, the reliability of the financial

Table 7: Results of the T Test (Mann-Whitney U) in Terms of the Genders of Bank Administrators in the Context of Internal Control

Results of Variance Analysis (Kruskal Wallis H) According to Ages of Bank in Terms of the Genders of Bank Administrators in the Context of Internal Control

Description	Mann-Whitney U	Wilcoxon W	Asymp. Sig. (2-tailed)	Description	Mann-Whitney U	Wilcoxon W	Asymp. Sig. (2-tailed)
A1	188	684	0.019	C5	247	743	0.319
A2	219.5	715.5	0.116	C6	278.5	774.5	0.735
A3	192	688	0.027	D1	278.5	468.5	0.737
A4	285	781	0.842	D2	214	710	0.074
A5	230	726	0.171	D3	242.5	738.5	0.267
B1	253	749	0.374	D4	290	786	0.922
B2	259	449	0.461	E1	260	450	0.46
B3	259.5	755.5	0.468	E2	291	787	0.94
B4	217	713	0.107	E3	218.5	714.5	0.107
C1	278	774	0.726	**Results of Variance Analysis (Kruskal Wallis H) According to Ages of Bank**			
C2	174	670	0.011	**in Terms of the Genders of Bank Administrators**			
C3	281.5	471.5	0.781	**in the Context of Corporate Governance**			
C4	248	744	0.317	"No statistically significant results were found."			

information provided to the information users regarding the records, control, risk management and corporate governance along with the activities carried out for both internal and external stakeholders of the banks has been an important concern. It has become an inevitable necessity for information users to determine how these problems occurred in the banking sector as well as how and through which methods they are treated.

In this study, it was aimed to determine the views of the administrators of the bank branches operating in Kilis, Turkey in 2019 about the role of internal control on strengthening corporate governance. Determining the opinions of the administrators of bank branches operating in Kilis as of 2019 regarding the role of internal control in strengthening corporate governance;

- Identifying the current situation in practice and the perceived reality related to the internal control systems used within the corporate governance applications,

- Presenting suggestions for future steps to be taken by identifying the gaps in the practice through determining the perception levels of the administrators about the subject, demonstrate the importance of the study.

Moreover, revealing the challenges and benefits in practice with the introduction of automation-based applications in internal control systems based on the corporate governance approach with respect to the banking activities in the borderline, demonstrates the difference of the study from other studies. The scope of the research was constituted by the employees of the bank branches operating in Kilis in Turkey in 2019. However, the sampling of the research was limited with the administrators of the banks in order to determine the internal control and corporate governance understanding of the information users accurately and to present more realistic, consistent and reliable information. In the study, with the aim of determining the views of bank branch administrators about the role of internal control systems in strengthening corporate governance, data obtained through the survey were analyzed using the SPSS 25.0 program *(descriptive statistics, frequency distribution, nonparametric variance analysis; Kruskal Wallis H test and Mann-Whitney U test)*, and the following key conclusions have been reached:
In terms of Demographic Characteristics of the Administrators, it was concluded that;

- Most of the administrators (46.0 %; 23 people) worked as customer relations managers,
- Their average age was 28,
- A majority of them were male (62.0 %; 31 people),
- They mostly had (88.0 %; 44 people) graduate degrees.

In terms of Responses to Survey Questions, it was concluded that;

- The majority of the administrators responded as "I agree" and "I strongly agree",
- They preferred more negative options only in questions 7, 9 and 22 when compared to other questions,
- Among all, 45 (90 %) administrators mentioned that the principles of the corporate governance were followed and 5 (10 %) of them responded to this question negatively.

Kruskal Wallis H Test in the Context of Internal Control concluded that;

- The attitudes obtained regarding the questions *A5, B2, C5, C6, D1, E3* indicated that the attitudes towards the questions varied according to the manager,

the authorized manager or other position holders, and the position had a statistically significant effect on the internal control system,
- The attitudes obtained regarding the questions A1, C2, D2, E2 differed according to the undergraduate, graduate and postgraduate status of the administrators, and their educational status had a statistically significant effect on the internal control system,
- Ages of administrators did not have a significant effect on the internal control system.

Kruskal Wallis H Test in the Context of Corporate Governance concluded that;

- The attitudes obtained regarding the questions G. and I. differed according to the authorized manager or other position holders, and this indicated that position had a statistically significant effect on corporate governance approach,
- Attitudes of the administrators obtained towards questions F. and I. differed according to their associate, undergraduate and postgraduate degrees; and it indicated that the educational status of the administrators had a statistically significant effect on their understanding of corporate governance.
- The attitudes of administrators obtained regarding question F differed according to their ages; and this indicated that ages of the administrators had a statistically significant effect on their understanding of corporate governance.

T Test in Context of Internal Control (Mann-Whitney U) concluded that;

- The attitudes of the administrators obtained through questions A1, A3, C2, D2 differed according to their genders; and this indicated that the gender status of the administrators had a statistically significant effect on the internal control system for strengthening corporate management.

T Test in the Context of Corporate Governance (Mann-Whitney U) concluded that;

- The attitudes obtained from the questions *A1, A2, B2, C2, D1* indicated that there was a relationship between internal control system and corporate governance principles in terms of strengthening corporate governance and that compliance with corporate governance principles had a statistically significant effect on the internal control and corporate management system,
- The attitudes of the administrators obtained from questions H. and I. differed significantly in compliance with corporate governance principles and had a statistically significant effect on their understanding of corporate governance.

Based on the key results mentioned above, it is understood that the education, gender, age and positions of administrators working in bank branches in Kilis in 2019 were effective on their understanding regarding the role of internal control system on their corporate governance approaches. Moreover, within the scope of the theme of this study, in terms of filling the gap between the perception and information gap between the compliance with the corporate governance principals in the bank branches and the attitude expressed by the administrators, it was understood that the corporate governance principles were respected and this respect was shaped according to many variables ranging from gender to position based on the internal control system. At this point, when the internal control system is considered as a control center in ensuring effective corporate governance, the importance of social demographic characteristics of administrators has been demonstrated, which reveals the difference of the study. On the other hand, the results have demonstrated that the education levels of the administrators should be improved. Training constraint indicates that in order to ensure that the administrators make more accurate decisions in the future, internal control can be evaluated in multiple ways from the control environment to the risk assessment activities, from the control activities to the information, communication and monitoring activities; and an important step may be taken for corporatization in the banking sector. In future studies on strengthening the corporate governance approach in the banking sector, performing richer analysis of social values with more data would create economic added value in practice.

References

Acındı, A. (2007), İşletmeler İç Kontrol Sistemlerinin Etkinliğinin Ölçülmesi, Yüksek Lisans Tezi, İstanbul Teknik Üniversitesi Fen Bilimleri Enstitüsü, İstanbul.

Baş, M. (2019), Bağlantılı K Örneklem İle Parametrik Olmayan Cochran Q Testi: Bist 100 Uygulaması. *Uluslararası Afro-Avrasya Araştırmaları Dergisi*, 4(8), 94–107.

Baş, M., Kurnaz, N. ve Kestane, A. (2019), *Statistical Analysis of Corporate Sustainability in the TRNC Banking Sector After the Crisis.* Studies on Interdisciplinary Economics and Business Volume II. Germany: Perter Lang.

Bayram, N. (2017), *Sosyal Bilimlerde SPSS İle İleri Veri Analizi. (6. Bs.).* Isparta: Ezgi Kitabevi.

Black, B., Carvalho, A. G. D., Kim, W. and Yurtoglu, B. (2019), Which Aspects of Corporate Governance Do and Do Not Matter in Emerging Markets, *ECGI Working Paper Series in Finance*, 1–50.

Bhaumik, S., Driffield, N., Gaur, A., Mizkievicz, T. and Vaaler, P. (2019), Corporate Governance and MNE Strategies in Emerging Economies. *Journal of World Business*, 54(4), 234–243.

Canelon, J., Huerta, E., Leal, N. and Ryan, T. (2020), Unstructured Data for Cybersecurity and Internal Control, *Proceedings of the 53rd Hawaii International Conference on System Sciences*, 5411–5420.

Çiğdem, C. F. (2018), *İç Kontrol Sisteminin Kurumsal Yönetim Üzerindeki Etkileri: BIST Kurumsal Yönetim Endeksi Kapsamındaki Şirketlerde Uygulama*, Doktora Tezi, İnönü Üniversitesi Sosyal Bilimler Enstitüsü, Malatya.

Eymen, U. E. (2007), *SPSS 15.0 Veri Analiz Yöntemleri*. www.istatistikmerkezi.com (25.02.2020).

Karagöz, Y. (2010), Nonparametrik Tekniklerin Güç ve Etkinlikleri. *Elektronik Sosyal Bilimler Dergisi*, 9(33), 18–40.

Lobo, G., Wang,C., Yu, X. and Zhao, Y. (2020), Material Weakness in Internal Controls and Stock Price Crash Risk. *Journal of Accounting, Auditing & Finance*, 35(1), 106–138.

Özdamar, K. (2013), *Paket Programlar ile İstatistiksel Veri Analizi I, (9. Bs.)*. Eskişehir: Nisan Kitabevi.

Sarı, A. (2013), *İşletmelerde Kurumsal Yönetim Açısından İç Kontrol ve İç Denetimin Önemi*, Yüksek Lisans Tezi, İstanbul Ticaret Üniversitesi Sosyal Bilimler Enstitüsü, İstanbul.

Wood, G., Ciftci, İ., Tatoglu, E., Demirbag, M. and Zaim, S. (2019), Corporate Governance and Firm Performance in Emerging Markets: Evidence from Turkey. *International Business Review*, 28(1), 90–103.

Yaş, C. (2019), *İç Kontrol Sistemlerinin Kurumsal Yönetim İle İlişkisi*, Yüksek Lisans Tezi, Okan Üniversitesi Sosyal Bilimler Enstitüsü, İstanbul.

Ali Özbek & Ali Altinbay

The Effects of Organizational and Professional Commitment on the Behaviors of Auditors Working in Independent Audit Firms

1 Introduction

In today's business world, the need for reliable information on financial statements is increasing day by day. The attitudes and behaviors of independent auditors play a key role in providing this need for reliable information. Auditors working in independent audit firms faced with great criticism and troubles as a result of the Enron-Arthur Andersen case, which can be considered as a milestone especially for audit firms. The exhibition of fraudulent and undesirable auditor behaviors, that appeared with the Enron scandal, caused that the professional commitment as well as organizational commitment of auditors working in audit firms began to be suspected and questioned. Furthermore, the questioning dysfunctional auditor behaviors, that are an important part of the quality of audit, was also of great importance. In this study, various suggestions on what kinds of effects organizational and professional commitment may have on the behaviors of auditors working in independent audit firms, and on preventing or reducing dysfunctional auditor behaviors were also presented.

2 The Concept of Organizational Commitment

Undoubtfully, the employees who are loyal to their business and have a high organizational commitment help their business to survive and to maintain its success by gaining competitive advantage (Özcan et al., 2016: 287). High levels of organizational commitment of employees also play a very important role in the growth and development of businesses with their establishment.

In our rapidly globalizing world, organizations pay attention to the individual performances of employees. Organizations always need employees whose efficiency and performance are at the desired level. Moreover, the attitudes and behaviors that affect the individual performance of employees also gain great importance. In this respect, organizational commitment constitutes one of the concepts that affect the attitudes of employees. The concept of organizational commitment mostly refers to the establishment of a psychological bond between the employee and the organization (Aydın and Basım, 2017: 774). In other words, it can also be expressed as the degree or indication of an employee's commitment to his/her organization.

In their study which is one of the most commonly used sources in the literature studies regarding the concept of organizational commitment, Allen and Meyer reduced the organizational commitment to sub-dimensions and described it as emotional, normative and continuance commitment. While emotional commitment focuses on employees' emotional dependence on their organizations, normative commitment focuses on employees' obligations to stay in their organizations, and continuance commitment focuses on the ability of employees to continue their existence with respect to staying at their organization (Allen and Meyer, 1990).

Organizations make huge investments in human resources to achieve their goals in accordance with their organizations. The basis of these investments is to ensure that the employees stay in the organization by increasing their performance. The employees who have established bond with their organization will be able to work more enthusiastically and efficiently in their workplaces, so they will also be useful in increasing profitability, which is one of the main objectives of organizations. Otherwise, employees who cannot establish or decrease this bond will face consequences such as absenteeism, a decrease in performance and leaving the organization (Aksoy and Özkan, 2015: 4). In this respect, it is also possible to express the concept of organizational commitment as the degree of commitment individuals feel towards the organizations where they work. Furthermore, the fact that the employees adopt and develop their loyalty and thus increase their effort and performance within the organization will play an important role in achieving organizational success.

3 The Concept of Professional Commitment

In our daily life, commitment may appear in various forms. An individual may have various forms of commitment such as commitment to another individual, group, team, culture, faith, or community. Commitment may also cause an individual to feel himself/herself important in his/her group or organization (Duru, 2015: 37).

The basic building block of organizational commitment is based on professional commitment. Professional commitment, as well as organizational commitment, is also crucial for organizational plans that businesses will create for the future. It is unlikely to talk about organizational commitment in a place where there is no professional commitment (Uysal, 2013: 94).

The concept of professional commitment was first expressed by Greenhouse by stating that career commitment in Morrow's model should be given importance. This concept, which is also expressed as a career commitment, was explained in the way that people should care about their own jobs or their careers throughout their lives (Morrow, 1983: 487). When the concept of professional commitment is considered conceptually, it can also be expressed as an individual's attitude towards his/her job (Blau, 2002: 279). In other words, it can also be explained as an individual's loyalty to his/her job or the level of importance he/she attaches to his/her job.

One of the conditions for the employees to be successful, effective and efficient in their job is that they love their job. The fact that working conditions are ensured at the desired level and the employees love their job, in a sense, they are committed to their job will positively affect their perspective on life as well as their professional career. Because the majority of people spend most of their life at work (Büyükyılmaz et al., 2018, s.68).

Professional commitment improves employees' belief in their profession and helps them to accept the values of the profession. With such a commitment, it is usual for employees to desire to stay in their profession and to show the necessary care for their profession (Aranya et al., 1981: 271). Moreover, employees with high professional commitment may have a strong tendency to continue their membership in their organizations for a long term or to show the care and effort that are important for their profession (Singh and Gupta, 2015: 1195).

4 Dysfunctional Auditor Behaviors

The events that occurred in the firms such as Enron, Worldcom, Tyco International, and Parmalat, which have significant effects on the audit sector, came to the fore with fraud and counterfeiting. In the cases filed and the relevant processes, dysfunctional behavior patterns of the auditors working in independent audit firms were questioned and their failures were mostly received strong criticism. Because the evaluations that the auditors have reached by their job concern a large part of the society, that needs information on financial statements, and directly affect their decisions.

Dysfunctional auditor behaviors have been discussed by many researchers since they have the possibility of affecting or reducing the quality of audit related to the audit studies. Because a significant decrease in the quality of the audit may cause substantial damages to the society and the economic system in addition to the relevant financial statement users.

Dysfunctional auditor behaviors are is usually associated with the decrease in the quality of audit. The situations such as the completion of audit work earlier than planned, collecting inadequate audit evidence, accepting poor statements of customers, superficial view on audit evidence, and inadequate audit reports indicate dysfunctional auditor behaviors (Paino et al., 2012a: 37–38). However, under any circumstances, auditors should be able to be independent against all users who need information about financial statements and should be able to prepare fair audit reports (Yuen et al., 2013: 221–222).

The auditors working in independent audit firms may be under time budget pressure to finish the audit work within a specified period of time, which may lead to their inefficiency and poor quality of audit (Martin et al., 2016: 23–24). Moreover, the concept of time budget pressure can also be expressed as the natural conflict between the collection of sufficient and competent audit evidence by auditors. Behaviors such as early completion of the audit work and failure to allocate enough time for auditing may result from this type of pressure (Azad, 1994: 17–24). Furthermore, early completion of the audit works may usually cause auditors to take poor decisions about audit conclusions (Andreas, 2016: 92).

In case of accepting poor statements of customers during the audit works occurs when auditors take their customers' poor statements into consideration although they have the opportunity to obtain evidence on the audit work (Kasigwa et al., 2013: 25–26). Nevertheless, the fact that the auditors review the information and documents superficially during the audit works and ignore the issues that can be considered important is considered among the dysfunctional auditor behavior.

5 Effects of Organizational and Professional Commitment on Dysfunctional Auditor Behaviors

Most of the empirical studies on the behaviors of auditors working in independent audit firms are carried out by developed countries such as the USA, the UK and France. There are very few studies on auditor behaviors in the less developed countries and in the developing countries in which Turkey is also included. For this purpose, it is great importance to carry out studies on auditor behaviors either in developing countries or in underdeveloped countries.

Auditor behaviors have attracted the attention along with the recent scandals occurring in the field of audit and the increasing number of lawsuits filed against audit firms in relation to these scandals. The situations arising from reasons such as the fact that the necessary organizational and professional commitment of the auditors in independent audit firms are not at the desired level may cause audit firms to have troubles and may lead to dysfunctional auditor behaviors. As a natural consequence of this situation, it may also cause auditors to fail to detect financial fraud and corruption, that may be considered significant in the financial statements, and even to make wrong decisions. Literature studies on what kinds of effects organizational and professional commitment may have on dysfunctional auditor behaviors were carried out and their results are indicated below.

In the study carried out together by Sunyoto and Sulıstıyo in Indonesia, an attempt to analyze the effects of organizational commitment and professional commitment on dysfunctional auditor behaviors was made in a questionnaire study on 407 auditors. The sampling method was chosen in the analysis part of the study, and an attempt to test the multiple regression analyzes was made in the SPSS program. As a result of the study, it was determined that the auditors with high organizational commitment tended to avoid dysfunctional auditor behaviors, and that professional values could be preserved due to high professional commitment, and therefore, the reduction of professional values could be prevented (Sunyoto and Sulistiyo, 2019: p. 23).

In the study carried out by Paino et al., a questionnaire study was conducted on 225 auditors working in the audit firm in Malaysia, and what kinds of effects organizational and professional commitment may have on dysfunctional auditor behaviors was investigated. As a result of the study, it was determined that professional and organizational commitment had effects on shaping the behaviors of auditors working in the audit firm (Paino et al., 2012b: 1434).

In a different study carried out by Sulıstıyo and Ghozali, it was attempted to determine the effects of professional commitment along with religious beliefs on dysfunctional auditor behaviors. In the study, a questionnaire study was conducted on 397 auditors. The study was analyzed by establishing regression models in the SPSS program. As a result of the study, it was concluded that the religious beliefs and professional commitment of auditors had an effect on dysfunctional auditor behaviors and partially reduced the undesired behaviors (Sulistiyo and Ghozali, 2017: 1047).

In an empirical study carried out by Otley and Pierce, the questionnaire technique was applied to collect data on Irish independent auditors. In the analysis study, various regression models were established, and as a result of the study, it was determined that organizational commitment had significant effects on dysfunctional auditor behaviors of independent auditors. (Otley and Pierce, 1996: 65).

In the study carried out by Shafer et al., the questionnaire technique was applied on tax practitioners in China. Analysis results were achieved by using various regression analysis and structural equation modeling on the data obtained.

As a result of the study, it was indicated that employees with higher professional commitment may have more moral power against fraudulent events or unethical behaviors, which may cause employees not to bow to the pressure of their customers or their effects may be limited (Shafer et al., 2016: 125).

In the empirical study carried out by Sulıstıyo et al., the questionnaire technique was applied on 386 auditors by applying sampling method in data collection, and it was attempted to analyze them in the SPSS program by using the regression models established. As a result of the study, it was determined that professional commitment and auditor independence may be more likely to reduce dysfunctional auditor behaviors (Sulıstıyo et al., 2018: 93).

When the literature studies are reviewed, it is observed that organizational and professional commitment had significant effects on the behaviors of auditor in various studies. In particular, this situation is considered to be very important in that auditors are able to do their job willingly and to make their evaluations properly, and the employee turnover rates of audit firms would be low.

6 Conclusion

Auditors make significant contributions to the national economy since they decide on the financial statements prepared by businesses and try to reveal reliable information, accuracy and reality. However, auditors may engage in dysfunctional auditor behaviors while conducting audit works, which may lead to a decrease in the quality of audit. Thus, it is an expected situation that they will affect information users' decisions on financial statements positively or negatively. It is the responsibility of independent auditors to conduct independent audit activities at the desired quality level.

The fact that the auditors working in independent audit firms have professional commitment plays an important role in internalizing their profession and in staying in their job and continuing their job by becoming professional in their job (Selimoğlu and Yeşilçelebi, 2014: 27–29). Similarly, auditors will also increase the success of the audit firms as a result of the fact that they want to work continuously in independent auditing firms they work for and do not want to leave their job and they have established an organizational bond among themselves.

In conclusion, it is considered that the fact that professional and organizational commitment are at the desired level for the auditors working in independent audit firms will lead to an obstacle or a possible decrease in observing dysfunctional auditor behaviors. Therefore, it is considered that this situation will be positively reflected on the quality of independent audit.

In the study, it is possible to offer various suggestions to increase the commitment of auditors working in independent audit firms. For the auditors working in independent audit firms, various meetings, trainings and seminar programs should be organized on introducing and popularizing the job and providing career opportunities by the Public Oversight, Accounting and Auditing Standards Authority, which is the superior organization, together with the audit firms. The conditions that interfere with the professional and organizational commitment of auditors within the audit firms should be detected, and solution policies should be developed. In-service training programs and various activities can also be organized to increase commitment. In this regard, significant duties fall to the leaders in the audit firms. Leaders should be able to perform performance evaluations fairly to increase the commitment of the working auditors, and they should be able to produce various policies and strategies to ensure that they remain permanent in the audit firms. Leaders should be able to encourage employees by ensuring their participation while doing them, and they should be models to employees through their behaviors.

References

Aksoy, C., & Özkan, F. (2015). Analysıs of Relatıonship Among Reputatıon Management, Organizational Commitment and Organizational Performance: Comparıson of Public and Prıvate Banks, TURAN-CSR International Scientific Refereed Journal, 7(26), 3–14.

Allen, N. J., & Meyer, J. P. (1990). The Measurement and Antecedents of Affective, Continuance and Normative Commitment to the Organization, Journal of Occupational Psychology, 63(1), 1–18.

Andreas. (2016). İnteraction Between Time Budget Pressure and Professional Commitment Towards Underreporting of Time Behavior, Procedia Social and Behavioral Sciences, 219, 91–98.

Aranya, N., Pollock, J., & Amernic, J. (1981). An Examination of Professional Commitment in Public Accounting, Accounting, Organizations and Society Oxford, 6(4), 271.

Aydın, E., & Basım, N. (2017). The Role of Perceived Supervisor Support in the İnteraction between Work-Family Conflict and Organizational Commitment: An Empirical Study, Business and Economics Research Journal, 8(4), 773–784.

Azad, A. N. (1994). Time Budget Pressure and Filtering of Time Practices İn İnternal Auditing: A Survey, Managerial Auditing Journal, 9(6), 17–25.

Blau, G. J. (2002). The Measurement and Prediction of Career Commitment, Journal of Occupational Psychology, 58, 277–288.

Büyükyılmaz, O., Vargün, H., & Uygurtürk, H. (2018). The Effect of Occupatıonal Commitment on Job Satısfactıon: A Research on Professional Accountants, Kafkas University Economics and Administrative Sciences Faculty, 9(17), 53–71.

Duru, E. (2015). The Psychometric Properties of the General Belongingness Scale: A Study of Reliability and Validity, Turkish Psychological Counseling and Guidance Journal, 5(44), 37–47.

Kasigwa, G., Munene, J. C., Ntayi, J., & Nkote, I. (2013). Reduced Audit Quality Behavıor Among Auditors İn Uganda, African Journal of Accounting, Economics, Finance and Banking Research, 9(9), 25–37.

Martin, R., Stammerjohan, W., & Drake, A. (2016). The Effects Conflicting Messages on Audit Accuracy and Effıcıency, Academy of Accounting and Financial Studies Journal, 20(2), 23–43.

Morrow, P. C. (1983). Concept Redundancy in Organizational Research: The Case of Work Commitment, Academy of Management Review, 8(3), 486–500.

Otley, D. T., & Pierce, B. J. (1996). The Operation of Control Systems İn Large Audit Firms, American Accounting Association, 15(2), 65–84.

Özcan, M., Geçici, E., & Günlük, M. (2016). The Effect of Accountants' Emotional Intelligence Level on Their Organizational Commitment, Ege Academıc Revıew, 16(2), 287–302.

Paino, H., Smith, M., & İsmail, Z. (2012a). Auditor Acceptance of Dysfunctional Behaviour: An Explanatory Model Using İndividual Factors, Journal of Applied Accounting Research, 13(1), 37–55.

Paino, H., Thani, A., & SI, S. I. (2012b). Organizational and Professional Commitment on Dysfunctional Audit Behaviour, African Journal of Business Management, 6(4), 1434–1440.

Selimoğlu, S. K., & Yeşilçelebi, G. (2014). The Effect of Professional Commitment on Independent Audit Quality: A Research of Independent Auditors, The Journal of Accounting and Finance, (64), 27–52.

Shafer, W. E., Simmons, R. S., & Yip, R. W. (2016). Social Responsibility, Professional Commitment and Tax Fraud, Accounting, Auditing & Accountability Journal, 29(1), 111–134.

Singh, A., & Gupta, B. (2015). Job İnvolvement, Organizational Commitment, Professional Commitment and Team Commitment a study of Generational Diversity, Benchmarking an International Journal, 22(6), 1192–1211.

Sulistiyo, H., & Ghozali, I. (2017). The Role of Religious Control in Dysfunctional Audit Behavior: An Empirical Study of Auditors of Public Accounting Firm in Indonesia, Journal of Applied Business Research, 33(5), 1047–1058.

Sulistiyo, H., Darsono, D., & Subchan, S. (2018). An Empirical Study on the Role of Auditor Independence in Reducing Dysfunctional Audit Behavior of Public Accountants in Indonesia, Romanian Society for Quality Assurance, 19(167), 93–97.

Sunyoto, Y., & Sulıstıyo, H. (2019). Locus of Control, Dysfunctional Audit Behavior and the Mediating Role of Organizational Commitment, Romanian Society for Quality Assurance, 20(170), 19–24.

Uysal, H. (2013). Effect of Organizational Climate to Professional Commitment Development of Intern Workers, Business and Economics Research Journal, 4(3), 93–110.

Yuen, D. C., Law, P. K., Lu, C., & Guan, J. Q. (2013). Dysfunctional Auditing Behaviour: Empirical Evidence on Auditors' Behaviour in Macau, International Journal of Accounting and İnformation Management Emerald Group Publishing Limited, 21(3), 209–226.

Gülay Tamer

Communication in Health Organizations

1 The Concept of Health and Features of Health Services

World Health Organization (WHO) defines "health" as "not only the absence of illness and disability, but also the physical, mental and social well-being". (WHO, 1998). According to this definition, health is a multidimensional concept and therefore multiple factors will directly and indirectly affect health status. Combined with the evolving society, growth and awareness of providing the absence of illness is conceptualized as being good (Öngören, 2015, p.1). Health is an indispensable part of our social life. The patient can be identified as "a person assessed (examined) by a doctor or other therapy service member" (Landgraf et al. 2006: 11).

In today's patients; More information about diseases and treatments appears to be an increase in acquisition and decided to participate in medical decision-making process. These developments gradually increase the area of health, the mass media effectively with their health information is easier to be accessed. (Ergin, 2011) disease prevention and improving the community's health status is among the priority objectives of each country. Health care, diagnosis of diseases, treatment and prevention of diseases as well as rehabilitation, covers all improvement of the individual and community level health activities. The explanation of communication in health institutions; The concept of health and health services and features are important to know.

Environmental, behavioral (lifestyle), is the inheritance of four important factors affecting the health status and health services; besides population, cultural systems, natural resources and effective economic system. Health Service; are the social services. Services is continuous, intensive in terms of technology and supply based on the human factor is extremely expensive. Health Service; preventive health care, curative health care, rehabilitation and health promotion, including service are divided into four groups (Öztek et al., 2015).

a) The main purpose of preventive health services are services aimed at keeping the society away from disease factors and eliminating the disease factors. It is the whole of the services that include environmental interventions to prevent health problems caused by negativities, family planning, early diagnosis tests, providing healthy nutrition, providing health education, physical biological and social environment.

Preventive health services can be grouped into two groups as personal and environmental services of preventive health services for individuals;

- Early diagnosis and treatment,
- Prophylactic Treatment
- Immunization (vaccination)
- Sufficient and balanced nutrition provision
- Family planning
- Personal hygiene
- Health education

These group services are services carried out by healthcare personnel, especially within the health sector. Preventive services are always more economical, easy and effective services than treatment services (Öztek et al. 2015).

- provision of clean potable water
- disarming of waste
- the prevention of air pollution
- Vector combat
- Industrial health
- Food Control
- Noise and radiation prevention.

Environmental protective services are services that should be carried out multidisciplinary. The health sector provides consultancy, supervision and training services in this area.

b) therapeutic health services; is under the responsibility of a specialist physician; services carried out in cooperation with other healthcare team members. Therapeutic healthcare services also classified as in two ways: outpatient and inpatient services. Outpatient treatment services; This includes services related to diagnosis and treatments that do not require hospitalization to the inpatient treatment institution. Family health centers, practices, hospital polyclinics, emergency services, ambulatory surgery centers, home care institutions, workplace infirmary are examples of this group. Inpatient treatment services; This standard covers services related to diagnosis and treatments requiring hospitalization.
c) Hospitals are the best example for this group. Therapeutic services;
   1. Primary care services,
   2. Secondary care services

d) Secondary care services are divided into three groups. Therapeutic services are services carried out entirely by the health sector and by the health manpower. For these services to be both effective and economical and for the satisfaction of the service users and service providers, they must be staged in the steps described above and a referral chain must be provided between these steps. When the patients' health problems are solved at the appropriate level, there will be no unnecessary intensity and loss of workforce, so the patients will receive the most effective service. (Öztek et al., 2015)

e) Rehabilitation services; These are the services provided to regain mental and physical skills lost by people as a result of illness and accident. Rehabilitation services; medical or social rehabilitation services including two-way and multi-disciplinary approach to the daily lives of these individuals without giving a burden to their families and continue the buttons provided.
f) Health promotion services; are the services provided to increase the health status of healthy people. The basic responsibility for health promotion belongs to the individual; It is aimed to increase the physical and mental health, quality of life and life of the person. (Öztek et al, 2015)

2 Communication Concepts and Communication in Health Care Organizations

Human is a social entity. In order to sustain his life, he needs to constantly communicate with his environment and this is based on understanding and understanding. Especially understanding is the most desired situation. There are many definitions about communication. The fact that the communication process is not a stationary but a dynamic process is effective in this. "Communicare", which is the Latin equivalent of the word communication and used as "communication" in English, means doing something together, combining, sharing, participating or consulting and discussing (Arlt, 1998: 23).

Contact; It is the process of changing and transmitting emotions, thoughts, knowledge, attitudes and opinions, and the way of behavior through a relationship between the source and the recipient through meaningfully agreed symbols, using some channels from one person to another (Yüksel, 2010: 11). Communication is always and everywhere; It plays an important role in all stages of our life. Communication has three main features. These; communication activity requires people, communication requires sharing, and communication is symbolic. When the receiver and the sender give the same meaning to the message, exactly communication occurs, so the symbols, gestures, sounds and words used in communication are important. Looking at the basic communication process, it is seen that it consists of seven elements. These are respectively; sender (source), sender and receiver form of detection and evaluation (coding), message, channel (communication tool), receiver or target (the party to which the message is intended to be transmitted), feedback (noise), noise (any disruptive environment that prevents the message from being transmitted) factor) (Okay, 2012)

Three forms of communication are examined: verbal, nonverbal and written communication. If it is considered that, health professionals communicate with the staff and patient/patient families 24 hours a day, it is seen that contact has essential role in the provision of health services. If the anxieties and fears that patients face during the diagnosis and treatment process, communication management in these processes may become even more important (İlhan, 2017). Health communication is the form of communication that has taken place for the target groups of people and groups related to health. According to Hurrelmann, health communication is involved in the health care process and/or as a citizen related to health and illness and public/public health policy. This involves the communication and exchange of information, opinions and feelings between professional service providers or people who are patients (Weinig et al., 2004: 91). This communication can take place between the patient-physician, other health-related staff and the patient or healthcare professionals (Okay, 2012).

3 Healthcare Professionals and Patient Communication

Considering the interaction models between physician and patient; It is known that paternalistic (patriarchal) approach model, information model and sharing model are widely used (Özçakır, 2004: 411–415). In the patriarchal model, the doctor decided; the informative model; It is the type model that the physician gives the technical details to the patient. In the explanatory model, it is the model that the physician receives the consent of after giving information about the benefits, danger, and the like of possible intervention or treatment. Finally, the sharing model has defined the interaction models that the physician and the patient decide together (Özçakır et al. 2004). When we consider the concept of "there is no disease, there is a patient", it will be important to develop the type of relationship according to the patient instead of establishing the same relationship model for each patient (Atıcı, 2007)

People who have a complex structure; The behaviors it displays under different places, times and conditions also differ (Göksu, 2007: 199). Personal characteristics, behaviors, education level, values, beliefs, culturally adopted attitudes, uncertainties about the health, uncertainties and expectations affect the physician-patient relationship directly or indirectly. Also; The development of a sense of trust between the physician and the patient, communication, holistic approach to the patient, conditions arising from the physician, the patient, the disease and the system, and technological changes are other factors that affect this relationship (Atıcı, 2007).

Health employee; Being aware of the distinction of professional and social communication, one should know that communication for the purpose of aid is important, where the most important step is to be aware of the recognition and understanding of the patient. Communication skills that help the patient benefit are affected by the individual characteristics of the employee, the ability to use methods that facilitate communication, the problems encountered in the relationship with the patient, the way of starting, maintaining and terminating communication (İlhan, 2017).

Health worker and empathy; empathy is the key to successful communication. It is a person's understanding of his feelings and thoughts by putting himself in the place of the person he is communicating with. It is the important stages of empathy that the person replaces himself with the other person, perceives them correctly, feels and transmits them and replaces them.

In the stages of effective communication between the healthcare worker and the patient, it is very important to use attention and smiling face, effective listening, effective and consistent verbal and non-verbal communication, correct assessment of the patient's body language, and use a plain and understandable language. In order to create an environment where the patient can easily open himself; An empathic approach and feedback should be provided as to whether the information is properly understood. In the communication that the healthcare worker establishes with the patient, he has the responsibility of first knowing himself and then getting to know and understand the patient and his/her relatives (İlhan, 2017).

Steps in meeting with the patient; meeting, working with the patient, terminating the communication.

- **Meet;**
  Determining the patient's grievances
  Determining the reason for seeking medical help
  Accepting, reliable and open communication
  Managing the relationship together
  Exposing the patient's feelings, thoughts
  Determining the purpose of working with the patient

- **Working with Patients**
  Ensuring that the patient develops insight
  Exposing situations that cause tension in the patient
  Dealing with change/recovery behavior

Evaluate the maintenance process and achievement of goals

- **Ending Contact**

A solution is sought for the behaviors that arise as a result of emotions such as anger, grief and loss that may arise due to the end of communication.

Successful communication techniques that improve communication for the benefit of the patient;

(a) Trying to understand the patient, empathy/sympathy/influence
(b) Asking appropriate questions for appropriate techniques
(c) Listen-Think-Speak
(d) Touch
(e) Reflection
(f) Summarizing
(g) Putting the individual in the foreground and caring, not the transactions
(h) Evaluation and development of the responsibility of the health worker

(a) Trying to understand the individual, empathy/sympathy/influence: empathy requires the ability and reach the other person's emotional environment. When health professionals develop their knowledge and skills, empathy, compassion and interaction with patients will be more effective.
(b) Asking questions using the correct technique: when the health care worker arrives at the patient data; open-ended, the researcher and the questioner will be able to summarize the closed and coherent questions.
(c) Listen-Think-Speak: listening and talking is an integral interaction triad. It is important to be really willing to listen, to make it a habit to listen carefully, to leave assessment at the end of the speech, to offer encouraging reactions to listening.
(d) Touch: an effective way of interacting with patients. It can be helpful in building confidence, but the privacy of patients should not be ignored.
(e) Projection: feelings of individuals to direct their own thoughts and questions that reflect an individual's good thinking or understanding is allowing communication method.
(f) Summary: The discarding of irrelevant information is necessary for the consistency of the interaction. The summarization of the main points is toward the end of the meeting.
(g) Putting the individual in the foreground, not the procedures: Instead of putting the patient in the foreground, it is necessary to ensure the cooperation of the patients and their relatives during the treatment and care process.

(h) Assessment and development of the responsibility of the health worker: Communication messages established by the health worker are also important as one of the factors affecting the professional status of the society (İlhan, 2017).

Time management is the most stressful situation among healthcare professionals; a sense that everything in health services is urgent is common to both staff and their patients and families. The job is urgent for everyone. All, however, has an order of importance, and if the challenge of dealing with difficult people is applied to time management problems, communication success will be more difficult to achieve. According to experts, individuals who are defined as difficult people; people who think they are very good despite their knowledge and education level are insufficient, who do not accept their mistake with maturity, insist on misunderstanding, those who do not care about what they say, those who do not respect others, those who do not empathize, who always say that I am right, only think that their job is important and valuable, constantly around people and events control over creating and directing the employees. In communicating with difficult people; sufficient knowledge is required about the work done and effective communication skills should be applied successfully. In addition to communicating with difficult people, special approaches to communication are also needed in specific situations. The approaches of pediatric patients and their relatives, people with mental health problems, hearing impairment and end-stage patients differ from one another. Healthcare professionals should have the knowledge and skills to act in a specific situation (İlhan, 2017).

4 Communication with Patients with Special Conditions

4.1 Communicating with Angry Patient

Anger is a natural reaction of the organism to events in the face of a threat. Feeling threatened, self-esteem decreased, anxious mood that arises due to various reasons are anger and anger. The behavior of teaching and/or defending against the enraged person impairs communication. Anger can cause friction and misunderstanding among people, so the healthcare professional; It should recognize anger, understand it and develop an answer accordingly.

When communicating with patients who experience anger, the healthcare worker should pay attention to the following points: firstly, he should observe the body language and behavior of the patient correctly, control his own feelings calmly and calmly in his approach to the patient, allow the patient to express his feelings, and avoid discussing and fighting with him. If the patient is acting harmful to himself and his environment, he should be taken to a safer area. Judicial and condescending behaviors should be avoided (MEB, 2015).

4.2 Communicating with Anxious Patient

It is a mixture of panic, intense anxiety, anxiety, fear, and may occur unexpectedly. This seizure gives the person such a feeling of intense fear and restlessness that the feeling that something bad will be accompanied or even fear of death can be added. In case of panic seizure, when the person applying to the hospital is encountered; It is important to take it to a calm environment, to behave calmly and to provide an environment of trust. The person should be told that this attack will pass and if necessary, it should be supported with exercises (MEB, 2015).

4.3 Communication with the Patient with Impaired Mental Health

Unrealistic perceptions and thoughts may develop in individuals with severe mental health. All communication principles such as respect, empathy and acceptance apply to these patients. Apart from this, unrealistic perceptions and thoughts of the individual should not be supported, it is necessary not to take a hasty approach, and to resort to concrete explanations by avoiding abstract concepts as much as possible. While communicating with these patients, it should be prevented from harming the patient and the health team by paying attention to the safe distance (MEB, 2015).

4.4 Communication with the Patient with a History of Trauma

Trauma; It can be defined as events that occur suddenly and unexpectedly, disrupt the daily order, create anxiety, anxiety and panic, and disrupt the processes of interpretation of the person with their previous lives. Natural disasters such as earthquakes, floods, fire, exposure to physical, psychological and sexual violence, traffic accidents, domestic violence, rape are traumatic experiences.

To help these individuals; It is important to allow, listen, and support to explain and share, and should be guided to receive psychiatric support when necessary (MEB, 2015).

4.5 Communication with the Patient in the Terminal Period

Patients in the terminal period; periods of surprise, anger, denial, negotiation, depression and acceptance. It's a difficult time for the patient himself and his colleagues. The main purpose of engaging with the patient who has spent the last few days is to improve the quality of the patient's remaining life. During this time, it is important to share emotionally with the patient and help them make short-term plans that will make the patient happy for the remaining days (MEB, 2015).

4.6 Communication with the Elderly Patient

Depending on aging, physical and mental changes occur. There may be carelessness, decreased perception, slowing down thinking speed. The elderly individual may find it difficult to adapt to these changes. When communicating with elderly patients, it is important to consider the socio-cultural characteristics of the patient, to use plain and understandable language, to consider that the people in this period are more sensitive and fragile, to establish eye contact with the elderly person and to set the tone correctly in communication. Medical terms should be avoided in explanations regarding the disease and treatment of the elderly (MEB, 2015).

References

Arlt, H.J. (1998). Kommunikation, Öffentlichkeit, Öffentlichkeitsarbeit PR von Gestern für Morgen-Das Beispiel Gewerkschaft. Wiesbaden: Westdeuscher Verlag.

Atici, E. (2007a). Factors Affecting Patient-Physician Relationship. Uludag University Faculty of Medicine Journal, 33(2), 91–96.

Atici, E. (2007b). Patient-Physician Relationship Concept. Journal of Uludağ University Faculty of Medicine, 33(1), 45–50.

Ergin, A. (2011). Communication in Health Services. Ankara: Anı Publishing.

Göksu, T. (2007). Organizational Behavior. In Salih Güney (Ed.), Management and Organization (pp. 182–199). Ankara: Nobel Publishing.

İlhan, M. (2017). Communication of Healthcare Professionals Beta Basımevi İstanbul, 2017.

Landgraf et al. 2006: 11 (Landgraf R./Huber F./Bartl R. (2006). Patient als Partner Möglichkeiten und Einflussfaktoren der Patientintegration im Gesundheitswesen, Wiesbaden: Deutscher Universitaetsverlag.).

MEB. (2015). Health Services Communication in Health Ankara, 2015. http://www.megep.meb.gov.tr/mte_program_modul/moduller/Sa%C4%9Fl%C4%B1kta%20%C4%B0leti%C5%9Fim.pdf

Okay, A. (2012). Health Communication. Istanbul: Derin Publications.

Öngören, B. (2015). Sociologically Healthy Body Image. Journal of Social and Humanities Researches, 34, 25–45.

Özçakır, A. (2004). Physician-Patient Relationship: The Patient's Place in the Decision Making Process. Turkey Clinical Journal of Medical Sciences, 4(24), 411–415.

Özçakır, A., Dağdeviren, N. & Görpelioğlu, S. (2004). Course Notes for Family Doctors -1. Stage, February 18, 2012, http://aile.bsm.gov.tr/docs/AH_Kurs_Notlari.pdf.

Öztek, Z., Üner, S. & Eren, N. (2015). Health Services and Health Management. Public Health Fundamentals-3; Edt. Professor Dr. Cagatay Guler, Prof. Dr. Levent Akın, Hacettepe University Press, Ankara.

Weinig, O.,/Leissner, A.,/Wegener, W. &/Ballmann, R. (2004). Gesundheits kommunikation im Öffentlichen Gesundheitswesen Bewaeltigung von Risik that under Kristen that, in Norderstedt: Book on Demand GmbH.

WHO(1998). Health Promotion Glossary, WHO/HPR/HEP 98.1, http: // whqlibdoc.who.int/ hq/1998/WHO_HPR_98.1.pdf

Yüksel, A. H. (2011). Definition of Communication and Its Basic Components. In Uğur Demiray (Ed.), Effective Communication. Ankara: Pegem Publishing.

Yavuz Selim Düger

'Willful Blindness' as a Dark Side of Organizational Behavior: Can Effective Leadership Overcome This Challenge?

1 Introduction

In the past 20 years in the world, the technological and cultural change that has taken place has had a significant impact on people's behavior patterns. In today's business organizations, this change has led to a growing increase in disputes among employees and also the emergence of conflicts between employees and leaders. These conflicts have harmed the attitudes and behaviors of individuals towards work, organization, and colleagues. In order for businesses to exist in the future and compete, they must first achieve unity and harmony within themselves. Managers and employees are crucial factors in the managing of organizational processes effectively, and creating harmony between them is critical to achieving organizational success (Maqsood et al., 2013:139). Therefore, it is possible to state that employees' attitudes and behaviors play a decisive role in ensuring organizational harmony and achieving organizational success. For this reason, management attaches importance to the factors that shape the attitudes and behaviors of the employees and, focus on the development of these factors (Kanten and Ülker, 2014:17).

As a result of some researches in the literature, it was concluded that several significant factors such as leadership style (Purcarea, et al. 2009:401), human resources management (Inanlou and Ahn, 2017:87), organizational culture (Zeyada, 2018:419), and organizational climate (Farooqui, 2012:294) have a positive impact on employees' attitudes and behaviors. However, if these processes of factors could not be managed effectively, the impact on employees' attitudes and behavior is most likely to be negative. As a result of the attitudes and behaviors arising from different personality traits, the conscious/intentional actions of individuals to damage to work, colleagues or organization, and also to cause costs, are defined as the dark side of behavior in organizations. The dark behaviors within the organization have direct or indirect costs, both financial and non-financial; decrease in organizational efficiency, increase in costs, damaging the reputation and image, loss of customers, decrease in market share, decrease in organizational satisfaction, increase in labor turnover rate, etc. The way to deal with these dark behaviors will be possible by creating an ethical oriented organization culture, adopting a zero-tolerance policy, developing a fair reward system, ensuring the participation and support of the employees and adopting effective leadership behaviors (Binboğa et al., 2018:383; Kanten and Ülker, 2014:32).

Although willful blindness behavior seems less harmful than many negative organizational behaviors, its effects will likely be more destructive in the long-term. Willful blindness behavior appears as the behavior of being inactive, ignoring and eventually being silent, believing that nothing will change, similar to the learned helplessness behavior. It is thought that it will be very difficult to eliminate willful blindness, which is a psychological phenomenon of employees. However, it is thought that effective leadership behavior will contribute positively to overcoming willful blindness behavior, which is seen as a new dark face of organizational behavior since the leadership style will influence the behaviors of the employees towards work and organization (Özgür, 2011:215). To summarize, it is thought that the effect of negative attitudes and behaviors of employees could be decreased by adopting a management behavior that reduces the impact of anxiety and stress in the business environment, encourages employees to struggle difficulties, does not neglect employees, leads with wisdom and kindness, and have more positive feelings such as hope, resilience, and optimism. In this study, the positive impact of effective leadership on the elimination process of the behavior of willful blindness, which is considered as the dark side of organizational behavior, will be evaluated.

2 The Dark Side of Organizational Behavior

In the literature, it seems that researchers focus on commonly positive behaviors in organizations with an optimistic perspective. Most studies in the literature focused on the beneficial behaviors of employees such as work engagement, organizational identification, job embeddedness, job commitment, workplace friendship, professional vitality, prosocial organizational behavior, proactive behavior, ethical behavior, innovative behaviors and entrepreneurial behaviors (Kanter and Kanter, 2016:3–6).

Recently, efficiency and profitability for organizations have caused gain importance with emerging high competition and thereby new research has begun to eliminate the negative individual and organizational behaviors that are ignored, unheeded, paid no attention or suppressed. The dark behaviors in an organization are generally defined as the tendency of employees to systematically harm to coworkers or organization by exhibiting ethical and illegal acts to gain power, achieve high gains, maintaining the status, rising and revenge within the organization (Linstead et al., 2014:166–170). Counterproductive work behaviors, workplace incivility, social loafing behavior, cyberloafing behavior, deceive behavior, revenge behavior, gossip, and rumor, selfishness, and exclusion in the workplace are examples of unfavorable attitudes and behaviors of employees. Also, whistle-blowing, cynical attitudes, impression management, political behaviors, and organizational silence it can be given as problematic attitudes and behaviors that can have positive and negative consequences (Kanter and Kanter, 2016:3–6; Griffin and Lopez, 2005:990). Moreover, there are also worse behaviors, such as bullying, workplace violence, aggression, retaliation, discrimination, sexual harassment, mobbing, impression management, sharing confidential company information, careerism, that may occur to harm themselves, others and the organization (Cohen, 2018:4; Binboğa et al., 2018:383; Linstead et al., 2014:167; Griffin and O'Leary-Kelly, 2004:4–7).

According to Cohen (2018), all unethical behaviors that cause harm to the organization or employees are generally considered as counterproductive work behaviors. Also, all the unfavorable organizational behavior aforementioned, namely counterproductive work behaviors, represents the extra-role behavior shown to harm the organization or employees. According to Vardi and Wiener (1996), the motivation sources underlying unfavorable organizational behavior are gaining individual benefit, making a benefit or harm to the organization. Nevertheless, individuals' negative organizational behaviors could arise from personality traits, the dark side of personality (narcissist, machievallist, and psychopath), lack of conscience, emotional imbalance, lack of organizational justice, poor leadership or destructive leadership (Cohen, 2018:6–7).

Heffernan (2011) defined willful blindness behavior as the situation of ignoring business-facing setback by employees or leaders until everything comes out in the organization. This definition indicates that willful blindness behavior is a situation that employees or leaders intentionally unheeded or ignore the negative situations that occur within the organization. Willful blindness behavior will be considered as a dark side of organizational behavior, due to the intentional occurrence of harm to the organization similar to the dark side of organizational behavior.

3 Willful Blindness Behavior

Willful blindness is a concept that was first used in legal terminology and it is defined as "*a term used in law to describe a situation in which a person seeks to avoid civil or criminal liability for a wrongful act by intentionally keeping himself or herself unaware of facts that would render him or her liable or implicated"*. Willful blindness is also called deliberate ignorance (see https://en.wikipedia.org/wiki/Willful_blindness). Individuals choose to blind themselves to unpleasant information because they feel comfortable for a short time when they ignore risks and threats. However, this causes the problem to grow further. Individuals only realize their blindness when the problem becomes a crisis and question how it happened (Ong, 2012:22).

Heffernan (2011) stated that the willful blindness behavior does not always lead the person to disaster, it answers the purpose for the individual at the point of continuing social relations, to feel psychologically comfortable and to think positively. However, a person feels more comfortable psychologically when the person more ignores unpleasant situations, ultimately causes the problems to become even bigger and more complicated. Willful blindness is in a way deceiving one's self.

Heffernan (2011) deals with the concept of willful blindness from a psychological point of view and investigates it from daily life to working life. Heffernan (2011) also explored the patterns and causes of willful blindness behavior, which he described as the dark side of human behavior. Heffernan (2011) stated that willful blindness is a human phenomenon and it is a sense that extremely difficult to avoid. It is difficult to know where willful blindness arises from exactly however, it may arise from personality traits and some factors in working life. However, Burke (2016) argued that willful blindness could occur due to various factors such as "*cognitive limits, information overload, fatigue, working too hard, desire to please others and be liked by them*". Willful blindness is an emotion that swiftly penetrates and spreads among people after emerged. According to Tecer (2018), willful blindness is a virus that spreads secretly within the organization and this disease has a very serious cost to the enterprise. In today's business world where willful blind behavior is so common, businesses rapidly transform their organizational structures (Heffernan, 2011:1–5). Thus, businesses think that they can increase the decreased efficiency and profit.

Willful blindness is a situation that ignoring unfavorable behaviors by employees or managers and it arises with the desire of individuals to feel safe, prevent conflict, reduce anxiety, protect prestige, gain financial motivation, and retain power. This serious hazard faced by organizations is not an unknown and suddenly emerged problem, on the contrary, it is a problem that is almost known by everyone in the organization and ignored, and also individuals felt comfortable when hidden (Heffernan, 2011:1–5). When employees make mention of incorrect practices, poor management policies, and ineffective procedure within the organization, they think that nothing will be changed, their opinions will not be taken into account, they will be punished, and they cannot be promoted, therefore, they are silent and ignore all of any things. Managers do not want their employees to voice their mistakes and their weaknesses to appear, at this point, they chose to ignore the problems by exhibiting oppressive and autocratic management behavior (Tecer, 2018:2–3).

Hall (2019) suggests 9 items to overcome willful blindness and change employee silence within the organization:

(1) Working with people who think differently, (2) Getting rid of the hierarchical organizational structure, (3) Encouraging cooperation among employees, (4) Employing new people, (5) Revealing mistakes and learn from a mistake, (6) Getting feedback from employees, (7) Respecting employees' opinions, (8) Consider the employees in the decision-making process, (9) Diversifying the communication channels.

Tecer (2018) mentioned four steps to prevent willful blindness in organizations:

(1) Determining the main source of blindness, (2) Analyzing the situation, (3) Making systemic and managerial radical changes within the organization, (4) Creating a clear and transparent organizational culture.

Heffernan (2015) suggests five steps to reduce or eliminate the effects of willful blindness in organizations:

(1) **Creating a culture of discussion:** It is necessary to prepare a business environment where constructive discussions and different ideas are respected, open to critical thinking and encouraged. Thus, employees can produce effective solutions to problems by exhibiting more innovative behaviors.
(2) **Providing psychological safety:** Creating a work environment where employees will feel psychologically safe and good. An environment where employees can say their ideas without fear will motivate them more.
(3) **Creating a collaboration culture:** Instead of promoting competition among employees, encourage collaboration will increase the sharing of information within the organization. A collaborative working culture will increase synergy within the organization. However, employees are being in a struggle for contributing more to their organizations.
(4) **Aligning organizational culture:** The organization needs to constantly review its corporate values and goals and align employees' values and goals with organizations' values and goals. Uniting employees with a common purpose leads to the emergence of different ideas and opinions on how to achieve organizational goals.

(5) **Beneficial leadership behavior**: Leaders must demonstrate the culture of collaboration and organizational values. Leaders must declare that employees respect their opinions and are free to express those ideas. Leaders should state that they are open to constructive criticism and that any constructive criticism of employees will be taken into account. The attitudes and behaviors of the leader could be taken as a role model by employees. As a result, leaders create a constructive culture of cooperation and encourage this environment, thus they can minimize the impact of blindness in the organizations.

4 Effective Leadership versus Willful Blindness

Effective leaders guide their employees and increase their organizational commitment, encourage them to work as a team to achieve the organization's goals and objectives. The most important features of effective leaders are coaching employees, developing employees, determining the skills needed by the organization, managing change, inspiring employees, encouraging employees to innovate and leading the organizational culture (Wolper, 2016:67). Effective leaders focus on employee satisfaction and strive to increase employee productivity. The most important features that distinguish effective leaders from others are their high-level of tenacity and commitment, well communication and relational skills, motivation for success and having an incentive side such as coaching and mentoring (Hopkins et al., 2006:252). Besides, effective leaders are individuals with high emotional intelligence, self-awareness, understanding of others, and high levels of self-efficacy (Rupprecht et al., 2019:1). In this sense, it should be considered that an effective leader will be extremely successful in overcoming unfavorable organizational behavior.

In some researches, it was concluded that effective leadership has a positive influence on the individual, team and organizational outcomes (Avolio et al., 2009:422). Particularly, effective leadership has a positive effect on employees' performance and satisfaction, trust in the leader, empowerment and innovative climate (Muchiri et al., 2011:463). Effective leaders' these features will lead to an increased voice in the organization. Many researchers claim that transformational leadership, that affects the values and demands of employees and ensure considering organizational benefit rather than own benefit, is conceptualized as effective leadership (Muchiri et al., 2011:464). According to Avolio and Bass (2002), transformational leadership involves being role models, inspire, persuade, show understanding, develop employees, challenge assumptions and encourage problem-solving, support employees, coaching, and mentoring. Indeed, effective leadership also has all these behavioral features alike. Effective leadership, which focuses on employee satisfaction and performance, will have a critical role in the process of coping with the dark side of organizational behavior. Also, an effective leader will well implement a process that will eliminate blindness of employees in the organization thanks to having all these features.

Rupprecht et al. (2019) stated that mindfulness behavior is an effective leadership development tool. Mindfulness behavior positively affects leaders' decision-making processes, relationship quality, ability to change organizational structure and organizational culture. Besides, some studies have revealed that the mindfulness behavior of the leader is effective in improving unfavorable situations such as stress and burnout in the workplace environments and increases the wellbeing and performance of the employees (Rupprecht et al., 2019:1–2). Thanks to the mindfulness behavior of an effective leader, organizational silence and willful blindness will be eliminated. Also, if leaders fail to manage stress in the workplace, employees think that leader is harming the organization or demonstrating poor leadership. One of the most effective ways to manage stress is mindfulness. For leaders to have mindfulness behavior, they must observe all events one step behind, allow to be criticized, and have a strong sense of curiosity (Levin, 2018).

In fact, all this information about effective leadership characteristics and behavior demonstrates that effective leadership generally leads to the fact that the employees are happy and psychologically wellbeing, increase the level of satisfaction and loyalty, the increase of organizational support and the consideration of their feelings, thoughts, and ideas by their leaders. As a result of all this, it is inevitable for an employee who loves his job, organization, and leader to exhibit positive organizational behavior instead of dark behavior. Likewise, willful blindness behavior is expected to be minimized with effective leadership.

5 Conclusion

Employees' psychological wellbeing is critical for high efficiency and performance. However, employees are negatively affected psychologically by unpleasant situations (poor management, wrong practices, discrimination, injustice, etc.) occurring within the organization. In this case, employees ignore unfavorable situations, that is, they become blind to feel comfortable. The fact that the employees ignore the problems for a long time and remain silent causes the performance of the employees to decrease, the absenteeism rates and the turnover rates to increase.

Organizations seek to employ obedient employees to avoid weaknesses in management. This situation not only hidden the exposure of problems and false decisions within the organization but also causes the problems and risks to grow and become dangerous. To overcome this situation, the leadership must listen to and respect dissent opinions instead of suppressing dissenters within the organization. In other words, the leader should not be weakening others by using the power that has, but rather should be open to critical thinking and take advantage of other people's perspectives. Employees who adopted behaviors that whatever the leader says always is true, maybe get in the leader's good books, but lead the business to disaster.

All of this shows that the power that leaders have is the most important factor that triggers blindness. So much so that the leader may choose to live in an environment surrounded by blindness, with a desire to ignore the problems and the facts. But when everything arises or affairs get worse in the organization, willful blindness is not considered an excuse for leaders. Also, the dark personality of the leader (narcissist, machievallist, and psychopathy) intercepts them from seeing unfavorable situations in the organization and can lead to the disconnection between employees and the leader and the initiation of willful blindness behaviors in employees.

Leadership style/behaviors are both the source and solution of employees' negative organizational behavior. All of the behavior of leaders exhibited in the organization has an impact on the employees. Therefore, leaders should act in a way that causes minimum harm to employees and should consider employees' expectations, ideas, and well-being. In this context, an effective leadership style/behavior that values the employees, contributes to them, increases their morale and motivation, focuses on their satisfaction, and aims to increase the efficiency of employees and the organization, is seen as an important element for organizational success. Effective leadership who having superior behaviors is seen as a significant factor in the process of overcoming unfavorable organizational behaviors such as willful blindness at the same time. Indeed, effective leadership is also essential for the carries out and well management of the various practices (such as, creating a culture of discussion and cooperation, aligning the organizational culture with employee values, making changes in the organizational structure, taking into account employees in the decision-making process, etc.) proposed by Hall (2019), Tecer (2018) and Heffernan (2015) to struggle and overcome with willful blindness. Consequently, it is thought that with unfavorable organizational behavior and also willful blindness could be struggled by only an effective leadership style.

References

Avolio, B. J. & Bass, B. M. (2002). Developing Potential Across a Full Range of Leadership: Cases on Transactional and Transformational Leadership. New York: Psychology Press Taylor & Francis Group.

Avolio, B. J., Walumbwa, F. O. & Weber, T. J. (2009). Leadership: Current Theories, Research, and Future Directions. Annual Review of Psychology, 60(1), 421–49.

Binboğa, G., Eğin, E., & Gülova, A. (2018). Örgütsel Davranışın Karanlık Yüzü ve Türkçe Literatürün İncelenmesine Yönelik Bir Araştırma. Finans Ekonomi ve Sosyal Araştırmalar Dergisi, 3(1), 382–399.

Burke, R. J. (2016). The Healthy Organization: Reducing High-Risk Individual Behaviors and Organizational Toxicity. In R.J. Burke & C.L. Cooper (Eds.), The Fulfilling Workplace: The Organization's Role in Achieving Individual and Organizational Healthy. New York: Routledge.

Cohen, A. (2018). Counterproductive Work Behaviors: Understanding the Dark Side of Personalities in Organizational Life. London: Routledge Publishing.

Farooqui, M. R. (2012). Measuring Organizational Citizenship Behavior (OCB) as a Consequence of Organizational Climate (OC). Asian Journal of Business Management, 4(3), 294–302.

Griffin, R. W. & Lopez, Y. P. (2005). 'Bad behavior' in Organizations: A Review and Typology for Future Research. Journal of Management, 31, 988–1005.

Griffin, R. W. & O'Leary-Kelly, A. M. (2004). The Dark Side of Organizational Behaviour. San Francisco: Pfeiffer Publishing.

Hall, B. (2019). Willful Blindness: Addressing the Epidemic of Silence in Organizations. Available at: https://www.interact-intranet.com/blog/willful-blindness-addressing-the epidemic-of-silence-in-organizations/ (01.04.2020).

Heffernan, M. (2011). Willful Blindness: Why We Ignore the Obvious at Our Peril. London: Walker & Company/Bloomsbury Publishing.

Heffernan, M. (2015). How Organisations Can Counter Wilful Blindness. Available at: https://www.hcli.org/articles/how-organisations-can-counter-wilful-blindness (04.04.2020).

Hopkins, M. M., O'Neil, D. A. & Bilimoria, D. (2006). Effective Leadership and Successful Career Advancement: Perspectives from Women in Health Care. Equal Opportunities International, 25(4), 251 – 271.

Inanlou, Z. & Ahn J-Y. (2017). The Effect of Organizational Culture on Employee Commitment: A Mediating Role of Human Resource Development in Korean Firms. The Journal of Applied Business Research, 33(1), 87–94.

Kanten, P. & Ülker, F. (2014). Yönetim Tarzının Üretkenlik Karşıtı İş Davranışlarına Etkisinde İşe Yabancılaşmanın Aracılık Rolü. Muğla Üniversitesi Sosyal Bilimler Enstitüsü Dergisi, (32), 16–40.

Kanter, P. & Kanter S. (2016). Örgütlerde Davranışın Aydınlık ve Karanlık Yüzü, Ankara: Nobel Yayınevi.

Levin, M. (2018). Harvard Research Reveals How Mindful Leaders Develop Better Companies and Happier Employees. https://www.inc.com/marissa-levin/harvard-research-reveals-how-mindful-leaders-develop-better-companies-happier-employees.html (10.04.2020).

Linstead, S., Maréchal, G., & Griffin, R. W. (2014). Theorizing and Researching the Dark Side of Organization. Organization Studies, 35(2), 165–188.

Maqsood, S., Bilal, H., Nazir, S. & Baig, R. (2013). Manager's Leadership Styles and Employee's Job Satisfaction. Human and Social Science Research, 1(2), 139–144.

Muchiri, M. K., Cooksey, R. W., Di Milia, L. V. & Walumbwa, F. O. (2011). Gender and Managerial Level Differences in Perceptions of Effective Leadership. Leadership & Organization Development Journal, 32(5), 462 – 492.

Ong, G. (2012). Wilful Blindness in Healthcare. Available at: http://news.sma.org.sg/4405/Event2.pdf (03.04.2020).

Özgür, B. (2011). Yönetim Tarzları ve Etkileri. Maliye Dergisi, 161, 215–230.

Purcarea, A. A., Fleaca, E. & Dumitriu, D. (2009). The Influence of Leadership on Employees' Behavior. Bulletin UASVM Horticulture, 66(2), 401–406.

Rupprecht, S., Falke, P., Kohls, N., Tamdjidi, C., Wittmann, M., & Kersemaekers, W. (2019). Mindful Leader Development: How Leaders Experience the Effects of Mindfulness Training on Leader Capabilities. Frontiers in Psychology, 10:1081, 1–15.

Tecer, B. (2018). İş Hayatında İstemli Körlük (Willful Blindness). Available at: https://hbrturkiye.com/blog/is-hayatinda-istemli-korluk-willful-blindness (15.01.2020).

Vardi, Y. & Wiener, Y. (1996). Misbehavior in Organizations: A Motivational Framework. Organization Science, 7, 151–165.

Willful blindness, Available at: https://en.wikipedia.org/wiki/Willful_blindness (04.04.2020).

Wolper, J. (2016). Developing Effective Leaders. Available at: https://situational.com/ wordpress/wpcontent/uploads/2016/06/TD_Magazine_Developing_Effective_Leaders_May2016.pdf (25.01.2020).

Zeyada, M. (2018). Organizational Culture and Its Impact on Organizational Citizenship Behavior. International Journal of Academic Research in Business and Social Sciences, 8(3), 418–429.

Abdullah Tirgil & Yasin Acar

Mental Illness, Gender, and Labor Supply

1 Introduction

The relationship between health and labor supply has attracted economists' interests since empirical research has some evidence showing that health status is crucial in explaining a variety of economic phenomena, such as earning differentials (Chirikos & Nestel, 1985). In addition to this fact, mental health is also one of the crucial parts of the general health status of individuals. Mental health includes our emotional, psychological, and social well-being, which affects how we think, feel, and act and which also helps determine how we handle stress, relate to others and make choices. Mental health is important at every stage of life, from childhood and adolescence through adulthood. Mental health problems could occur by many factors, such as biological elements, life experiences, and mental health problems inherited from the history of the family.

The financing of mental health services necessitates a significant amount of resources all over the world. Evidence has shown that the consequences of mental health diseases such as absenteeism and early death increase the total cost. For example, 31.9 million days of absenteeism occurred in France in 2000 because of depression. Also, it is estimated that the decrease in working performance causes five times more loss than absenteeism (Ministry of Health, 2011). In terms of public finance, mental health services are financed from the outside of the health system differently from other healthcare areas. Loss of work, absenteeism, sick leave, inability to work, unemployment insurance, working with low performance, early retirement, care fees constitute 60–80 % of the cost of severe mental illnesses. According to the study of Mental Health Profile of Turkey, 18 % of the population is experiencing lifelong mental illness (Ministry of Health, 2011).

There are also economic costs of mental health problems. Firstly, patients due to mental health problems have to live dependent on their families. In some cases, either patient is out of the labor market or one member of his family is out of the labor force because the family member must look after the patient. When regular follow-up and treatments cannot be performed, the frequency and severity of exacerbation increases, and the frequency and duration of hospitalization extend. For this reason, the patient, who has not been able to produce economic value, increases the cost for the country (Ministry of Health, 2011).

WHO (2019) announced that mental disorders like depression and anxiety disorders cost the global economy $1 trillion each year in lost productivity. Furthermore, according to the WHO report, the cost of the increase in mental health disorders in every country in the world to the global economy will reach $16 trillion between 2010 and 2030 if no collective action is taken. Another risk factor for a mental health problem is considered to be unemployment. Workplaces with a negative environment may also cause mental health problems among workers that are likely to decrease economic productivity.

Ojeda, Frank, Mcguire, & Gilmer (2010) investigated the effects of mental health on work using the US National Survey on Drug Use and Health, and they found that mental illness reduces the rate of work for male employees who were born in the US rather than immigrants and females.

The previous study has demonstrated that most people experiencing serious mental disorders wish and able to work (Macias, DeCarlo, Wang, Frey, & Barreira, 2001). However, their employment rates remain relatively low. For instance, large-scale population surveys report that the unemployment rate of those with mental disorders is to be at least three times higher than that of their nondisabled counterparts. Sixty-one percent of working-age adults with mental health disabilities are outside of the labor force, compared with only 20 % of working-age adults in the general population (Cook et al., 2005). On the other hand, Mechanic, Bilder, & McAlpine (2002) showed that workers with mental illness are not discriminated in terms of employment opportunities such that half the population with mental disorders has jobs corresponding to an employment rate of about two-thirds that of the general population. They highlight that educational attainment plays a significant role in being employed in high-status positions for both the general population as well as persons with mental disorders.

The relationship between work and mental health can be examined in two different ways. First, work might be a source of mental health or illness. Evidence indicates that stressful jobs can affect mental health (Gabriel & Liimatainen, 2000; Siegrist, 1996). Work, at the same time, could be a kind of therapy thanks to the communication of employees in an office environment (Keough & Huebner, 2000). Second, mental health might be correlated to absenteeism, causing poor organizational behavior (Cox, Griffiths & Rial-Gonzalez, 2000). Taris (2002) also argue that people out of work for any reason might have a disadvantage due to mental illness in job interviews, and this reduces their probability of getting involved in the workforce again. In their pioneering piece Bartel & Taubman (1979) examined white male twins born between 1917 and 1927 by using clinical data and self-report for the population of them and determined that psychoses and neuroses have negatively associated with employment and hours worked.

Besides mental health, employment status might be influenced by other factors such as gender, age, having children, and marriage (Hunt, 1999). There is a large literature on the labor market status of females in terms of employment and wage discrimination. However, we do not mention them all here since our main focus is whether mental health affects employment status, although we include gender and age as control variables in our model. However, Livanos, Yalkin, & Imanol (2009) investigate the factors determining the employment status of females in Greece and the UK in order to explore the differences in the labor market status between males and females. Using the Labor Force Survey (LFS), they found strong evidence of gender differences in both countries. A study conducted in the USA showed that people with mental disorders have less chance to be employed (Benham & Benham, 1982). Extra hours of labor supply are also an indicator of increased work stress, which is associated with mental health (Golden & Wiens-Tuers, 2006). Another analysis examined the possible relationship between mental health status and employment controlling for respondents' sociodemographic and family characteristics. As a result, it is found that better health is associated with employment. The study also emphasizes that medical conditions negatively affect labor supply for men (Ettner, Frank, & Kessler, 1997). Alexandre & French (2001) aimed to examine the relationship between depression and employment, highlighting the fact that about 5 % of employees experience depression in the US. Their results obtained from probit models indicate that the likelihood of being employed falls due to depression. From all these findings, we understand that mental health problems are associated with employment. Therefore economic benefits might be revealed by providing a good treatment of depression among employees who cope with mental disorders.

Using data from the Turkey Health Surveys, this chapter seeks to construct a complete picture of the employment statuses of individuals with mental illness as well as socio-economic variables.

2 Methods

2.1 Data

We utilize data from the Turkey Health Surveys (THS) implemented in 2008, 2010, and 2012 by the Turkish Statistical Institute (TurkStat). The datasets are nationally representative surveys of noninstitutionalized Turkish citizens aged 15 years and older. The datasets provide information on a wide range of variables, including employment status, depressed feelings, gender, age, marital status, education level, number of kids, health status, alcohol consumption, and BMI for individuals. Our sample includes adults aged 15–64. In 2008, 14,655 individuals were surveyed to produce estimations for rural and urban areas. 14,447 and 28,055 individuals were surveyed in 2010 and 2012, respectively.

2.2 Dependent Variable

In this study, we examine the labor market outcome, whether the respondent is currently employed. The question asked to quantify the employment status is, "Have you worked for pay in the last week even if it is at least for one hour." The outcome variable is a discrete variable, taking the value of 1 if the individual responds to the question "Yes-Employed," and 0 if the individual responds "No-Unemployed." Employed individuals can include housemakers, students, retired individuals, self-employed, and unpaid family workers.

2.3 Independent Variables

The THS datasets provide a large variety of health measures. The main factor of interest in this study is mental health. We also control for the self-assessed overall health of individuals. To quantify mental health, individuals respond to the question "how frequently you felt depressed in the last four weeks," using a scale from 1 to 5, where 1 means 'every time', 2 means 'most of time', 3 means 'some times', 4 means 'rarely' and 5 means 'never.' We transform this variable into a discrete variable, where 0 indicates 'never/rare' and 1 indicates 'every time/ most of the time/sometimes" for our analysis. Our self-reported health status comes from the response to the question in the survey, "how is your overall health?" using a scale from 1 to 5, where 1 indicates 'very good' and 5 indicates 'very bad.' To ease interpretation, we transform this variable into a discrete variable where 1 means 'good/very good' health status, and 0 means 'very bad/bad/ moderate' health status.

In addition to the health indicators, we also control for individuals' other characteristics, which we hypothesize that they have an impact on the respondent's labor market outcome. These characteristics are four age groups dummies, including 25–34, 35–44, 45–54, 55–64 (15–24 being the reference group) age groups; respondent's gender; a marital status dummy whether the respondent is single or married; the number of kids in the household; a discrete variable (yes/ no) of alcohol consumption whether the respondent ever used alcohol; BMI of respondents; and 26 statistical area dummies to control for regional fixed effects.

2.4 Statistical Analysis

We first report the summary statistics of all variables that we exploit in the regression analysis by depression status. Then, we implement a linear probability model to explore the relationship between labor market outcome and depression for the whole sample, controlling for the other determinants of employment status. To see differential impacts of depression on the probability of employment for females and males, we run separate linear regressions as these groups show various dynamics on labor market outcomes. To study depression on the probability of employment, we utilize the following equation:

$$y_{it} = \partial_0 + AX_{it} + BR_i + T_t + e_{it}, \quad (1)$$

where y_{it} is the respondent's probability of employment, X_{it} denotes background characteristics of individuals, R_i are dummies for 26 statistical area dummies to account for regional fixed effects, T_t is for survey years, and e_{it} is the unobserved error term.

3 Empirical Results

Table 1 presents mean values by depression status for all covariates that we use in the regression analysis. Employed individuals comprise 41 % of the sample. It seems that depressed individuals are less likely to be employed than non-depressed individuals by 30 % and 42 %, respectively. It appears that depressed individuals are more likely to report being female than non-depressed individuals by 70 % and 53 %, respectively. Concerning alcohol consumption, there does not appear to exist any statistically significant difference between depressed and non-depressed individuals. Moreover, depressed individuals report having higher BMI than non-depressed individuals. Non-depressed people seem to be healthier than depressed people. Furthermore, there seems to exist statistically significant differences between depressed and non-depressed persons in terms of educational attainment, where non-depressed individuals have more middle school, high school, and university education in comparison to depressed persons.

Table 2 presents the multivariate analysis results of depression on the probability of employment, including other control variables. The results from the linear probability models report that depression significantly reduced the employment for the full sample and males by about 3 percentage points (pp) and 7 pp, respectively. However, for the female subsample, although the sign of the coefficient is negative, the estimation does not produce a statistically significant

Table 1. Descriptive statistics by depression status

	Non-depressed	**Depressed**	**Full sample**
Employed***	0.42 [0.49]	0.30 [0.46]	0.41 [0.49]
Female***	0.53 [0.50]	0.70 [0.46]	0.55 [0.50]
Married	0.70 [0.46]	0.69 [0.46]	0.70 [0.46]
Number of kids*	0.98 [1.20]	1.02 [1.27]	0.98 [1.21]
Ever consumed alcohol	0.22 [0.42]	0.22 [0.42]	0.22 [0.42]
BMI***	25.64 [4.84]	26.00 [5.33]	25.67 [4.88]
Good health***	0.73 [0.45]	0.44 [0.50]	0.70 [0.46]
Education level			
No school***	0.12 [0.33]	0.19 [0.39]	0.13 [0.33]
Primary***	0.37 [0.48]	0.45 [0.50]	0.37 [0.48]
Middle***	0.20 [0.40]	0.15 [0.36]	0.19 [0.40]
High school***	0.19 [0.39]	0.14 [0.35]	0.19 [0.39]
University+***	0.12 [0.33]	0.06 [0.24]	0.12 [0.32]
Age group			
15–24***	0.22 [0.41]	0.15 [0.36]	0.21 [0.41]
25–34	0.24 [0.42]	0.23 [0.42]	0.23 [0.42]
35–44***	0.22 [0.42]	0.25 [0.43]	0.22 [0.42]
45–54***	0.19 [0.39]	0.22 [0.41]	0.19 [0.40]
55–64**	0.13 [0.34]	0.15 [0.36]	0.13 [0.34]
N	45,597	4,374	49971

Notes: mean coefficients; standard deviatians in brackets. * $p < 0.05$, ** $p < 0.01$, *** $p < 0.001$

result. Females are less likely to be employed compared to males in Turkey by about 4 pp. As expected, age is a crucial variable in determining the probability of being employed. For most of the estimates, education increases the employment for both females and males. Interestingly, as the number of kids increases, female employment decline in part due to the cultural motives which encourage women with kids to stay home and take care of their kids. Having more kids, by contrast, is associated with increased employment for men. Another impressive result that came out of Table 2 is that while a rise in BMI reduces female employment, it increases male employment.

4 Discussion

This study used nationally representative datasets to investigate the relationship between mental health and employment. We implemented a linear probability

Table 2. Estimation results for employment

Dependent variable: Employment	All	Women	Men
Depressed	-0.034***	-0.007	-0.067***
	(0.009)	(0.009)	(0.016)
Female	-0.424***	-	-
	(0.005)		
Age group			
15–24	*Ref.*	*Ref.*	*Ref.*
25–34	0.240***	0.109***	0.336***
	(0.009)	(0.010)	(0.014)
35–44	0.268***	0.143***	0.315***
	(0.009)	(0.011)	(0.015)
45–54	0.138***	0.068***	0.119***
	(0.010)	(0.012)	(0.017)
55–64	-0.059***	-0.016	-0.182***
	(0.011)	(0.012)	(0.018)
Married	0.064***	-0.047***	0.197***
	(0.007)	(0.008)	(0.011)
Education level			
No school	*Ref.*	*Ref.*	*Ref.*
Primary	0.008	-0.009	0.050**
	(0.008)	(0.009)	(0.019)
Middle	0.010	-0.027***	0.035*
	(0.010)	(0.010)	(0.020)
High school	0.054***	0.030***	0.073***
	(0.010)	(0.011)	(0.020)
University+	0.239***	0.398***	0.135***
	(0.011)	(0.014)	(0.020)
Number of kids	-0.004*	-0.020***	0.006*
	(0.002)	(0.003)	(0.004)
Ever consumed alcohol	0.052***	0.047***	0.038***
	(0.006)	(0.011)	(0.007)
BMI	-0.001***	-0.004***	0.004***
	(0.001)	(0.001)	(0.001)
Good health	0.039***	-0.004	0.075***
	(0.006)	(0.007)	(0.009)
Constant	0.456***	0.328***	0.148***
	(0.026)	(0.029)	(0.036)

(continued on next page)

Table 2. Continued

Dependent variable: Employment	All	Women	Men
R-squared	0.339	0.160	0.269
N	45290	23808	21482

Notes: Robust standard errors in parentheses and clustered at the household level. * $p < .1$, ** $p < .05$, *** $p < .01$. Sample in all columns includes adults age 15–64. The dependent variable is an indicator variable equal to 1 if the individuals reports being employed. The key explanatory variable is an indicator variable equal to 1 if the person reports being depressed in the last four weeks. Individual demographic controls include a female dummy, four age groups dummies (see text), two marital status dummies, four education dummies, the number of kids, alcohol consumption, BMI, and good health.

model to isolate the impact of depression on the employment statuses for females and males separately. Our findings indicate that depression significantly reduced employment for males. However, for females, although the coefficient estimate is negative as expected, the estimate is not precise. Our findings are consistent with the literature, where studies argue the negative effects of mental illness on different types of labor market outcomes, including earnings, hours worked, and wages (Bartel & Taubman, 1986; Benham & Benham, 1982).

In light of these findings, we could firmly state that policymakers need to expand mental health services in Turkey. They can take advantage of some public health interventions as a means to improve individuals' life quality, which, in turn, can promote economic benefits in increasing work time and reducing sick leave.

This study is subject to certain limitations. The econometric approach we implement does not yield a causal association between mental illness and employment. The findings should be interpreted as associations rather than causal links. There could be some unobserved factors such as motivation or social network affecting both depression and employment or reversed causality between employment and depression.

Notwithstanding limitations, we find that as the number of kids increases, the probability of female employment declines. The reason for this could be that women may not earn enough money to support childcare, so they prefer leaving their job and raise their kids at home. On the contrary, with more kids, male employment tends to increase, which supports the role of men as the bread-winner in Turkey.

Another interesting outcome that emerges from our analysis is that as BMI increases, the likelihood of employment declines for females, while the contrary is true for men in Turkey. Other studies investigating the relationship between employment prospects and obesity find similar results (Caliendo & Lee, 2013; Greve, 2008). One possible explanation for this outcome could be that females might be working in the service sector where the presentation and good-looking is of utmost importance to the customer and employers while males are mostly working in heavy industries where having a masculine body does not cause any problem.

Further research should examine the impact of various measures of mental health on different measures of labor market outcomes, including wages, hours worked, and earnings, for different subregions of Turkey.

References

Alexandre, P. K., & French, M. T. (2001). Labor supply of poor residents in Metropolitan Miami, Florida: The role of depression. The Journal of Mental Health Policy and Economics, 4, 161–173.

Bartel, A., & Taubman, P. (1979). Health and labor market success: The role of various diseases. The Review of Economics and Statistics, 61(1), 1–8.

Bartel, A., & Taubman, P. (1986). Some economic and demographic consequences of mental illness. Journal of Labor Economics, 4(2), 243–256.

Benham, L., & Benham, A.(1982). Employment, earnings, and psychiatric diagnosis. In Victor R. F. (Ed.), Economic aspects of health (pp. 203–220). Chicago: University of Chicago Press.Caliendo, M., & Lee, W.-S. (2013). Fat chance! Obesity and the transition from unemployment to employment. Economics & Human Biology, 11(2), 121–133.

Chirikos, T. N., & Nestel, G. (1985). Further evidence on the economic effects of poor health. The Review of Economics and Statistics, 67(1), 61–69. Cook, J. A., Leff, H. S., Blyler,C. R., Gold, P. B., Goldberg, R. W., Mueser, K. T., . . . & Dudek, K. (2005). Results of a multisite randomized trial of supported employment interventions for individuals with severe mental illness. Archives of General Psychiatry, 62(5), 505–512.

Cox, T., Griffiths, A., & Rial-Gonzalez, E.(2000). Research on work-related stress. European Agency for health and safety at work. Luxembourg: Office for Official Publications of the European Communities. Ettner, S. L., Frank, R. G., & Kessler, R. C. (1997). The impact of psychiatric disorders on labor market outcomes. ILR Review, 51(1), 64–81.

Gabriel, P., & Liimatainen, M.-R. (2000). Mental Health in the Workplace Introduction Executive Summaries. Geneva: International Labour Office.

Golden, L., & Wiens-Tuers, B. (2006). To your happiness? Extra hours of labor supply and worker well-being. The Journal of Socio-Economics, 35(2), 382–397.

Greve, J. (2008). Obesity and labor market outcomes in Denmark. Economics & Human Biology, 6(3), 350–362.

Hunt, J.(1999). Determinants of Non-employment and Unemployment Durations in East Germany. NBER Working Paper Series No. 7128; Cambridge, MA. Keough, J., & Huebner, R. A. (2000). Treating dementia: The complementing team approach of occupational therapy and psychology. The Journal of Psychology, 134(4), 375–391.

Livanos, I., Yalkin, Ç., & Imanol, N. (2009). Gender employment discrimination: Greece and the United Kingdom. International Journal of Manpower, 30(8), 815–834.

Macias, C., DeCarlo, L. T., Wang, Q., Frey, J., & Barreira, P. (2001). Work interest as a predictor of competitive employment: Policy implications for psychiatric rehabilitation. Administration and Policy in Mental Health and Mental Health Services Research, 28(4), 279–297.

Mechanic, D., Bilder, S., & McAlpine, D. D. (2002). Employing persons with serious mental illness. Health Affairs, 21(5), 242–253.

Ministry of Health. (2011). Ulusal ruh sağlığı eylem planı (2011–2023). Ankara, TC Sağlık Bakanlığı.

Ojeda, V. D., Frank, R. G., McGuire, T. G., & Gilmer, T. P. (2010). Mental illness, nativity, gender and labor supply. Health Economics, 19(4), 396–421.

Siegrist, J. (1996). Adverse health effects of high-effort/low-reward conditions. Journal of occupational health psychology, 1(1), 27.

Taris, T. W. (2002). Unemployment and mental health: A longitudinal perspective. International Journal of Stress Management, 9(1), 43–57.

WHO.(2019). Mental Health in the workplace. Available at: https://www.who.int/mental_health/in_the_workplace/en/ Access date: 08.04.2020.

Yeşim Kaya Koçyiğit

Building and Maintaining a Competitive Advantage in the Age of Industry 4.0

1 Introduction

The industrial revolution began by means of the emergence of the mechanization such as steam engines and mass extraction of coal in the 18th century. Since new technological advancements allowed to be developed new type machines by stimulating having been found new sources of energy such as electricity, gas and oil, the second revolution underwent at the end of the 19th century. The third era of the industrial revolution focused on automation by means of the emergence of computers in the second half of the 20th century. Using the machines as an alternative to manpower became widespread in this era. These first three industrial revolutions have determined a framework for Industry 4.0, and it has brought together humans, robots and automation. As a result of the facilities of the collaboration of these factors in Industry 4.0, competition has become more and more severe for current enterprises. Thanks to the technological facilities in the age of Industry 4.0, competitors can offer high quality and differentiated products and services to the market in a very short time, and at the lowest cost. It is quite difficult to achieve a competitive advantage in such a competitive environment. Therefore, in this study, after explaining the Industry 4.0 and its features, the areas that enterprises should focus on was highlighted, and the steps to be taken in these areas was explained to achieve a competitive advantage in this period.

2 Building and Maintaining a Competitive Advantage in the Age of Industry 4.0

It is difficult to define Industry 4.0, as Industry 4.0 has become more complex than ancient three terms, and its meaning is more than smart manufacturing, which is explicitly included the transformation of the manufacturing, the cyber-physical systems which are keys to the establishment of smart factories, and the coordination of the endpoints such as storage, logistics, recycling, energy systems. It can be said that these endpoints support the manufacturing. By working together with intelligent networks, intelligent logistics and even intelligent buildings, cyber-physical systems provide establishing the smart factories (Farkas, 2018).

In Industry 4.0 is determined as «an umbrella term used to describe a group of connected technological advances that provide a foundation for increased digitization of the business environment». It bears a resemblance to the definition of Industry 4.0 made by McKinsey as "the next phase in the digitization of the manufacturing sector, driven by four disruptions: the astonishing rise in data volumes, computational power, and connectivity, especially new low-power wide-area networks; the emergence of analytics and business-intelligence capabilities; new forms of human-machine interaction such as touch interfaces and augmented-reality systems; and improvements in transferring digital instructions to the physical world, such as advanced robotics and 3-D printing" (Skobelev and Borovik, 2017). As can be understood from these identification efforts, Industry 4.0 does not have a single agreed definition, as Industry 4.0 refers to the transformation in a group of areas and human-machine interaction. Therefore, there is currently no uniform definition based on consensus.

The key to success for today's enterprises is the competitive advantage. "Competitive advantage is the ability that a firm can create more economic value than competitors firms. Economic value is the difference between the perceived benefits gained by customers and the full economic cost of products they purchase. Therefore, the size of a company's competitive advantage is the difference between economic value a company can create and the economic value its competitors can generate" (Barney and Hesterly, 2006). Competitive advantage is at the heart of a firm's performance in competitive markets (Klein, 2002). Ademik and Nowicki (2020) identified the key barriers and potential source that result in the failure of processes of creating competitive advantage of enterprises in the age of Industry 4.0., the so-called Black Points in their paper. According to them, contemporary organizations that want to create a competitive advantages in the age of Industry 4.0 should focus on three specific platforms: Human Resource Platform, Knowledge Platform, and Technological Platform. These platforms are related to each other. Human Resource Platform is the source of multiplying Black Points in the next two platforms. The barriers occurring in the Knowledge Platform also initiate new issues in the Technological Platform. If organizations are able to cope with Black Points in these platforms, they can have more opportunities to create competitiveness in the conditions of Industry 4.0. They can achieve a competitive advantage by employing knowledge and good practices in these platforms. So, things needed to be made in these platforms by organizations will be tried to explain.

All enterprises aim to gain a competitive advantage to make a profit and continue their lives. This happens during the interaction between the external environment and the enterprises. If the enterprises are able to use its valuable, unsubstituted and inimitable company resources to respond properly to environmental opportunities and threats, they can achieve and maintain a competitive advantage. Therefore, enterprises are required to review their actions on the three major platforms mentioned above and reorganize them to fit the Industry 4.0 era. Superiority achieved can't be mostly continued due to the counter-attacks of the competitors. Therefore, special efforts should be made to be sustainable in a competitive advantage.

2.1 Human Resource Platform

According to Koçyiğit and Akkaya (2020), because today's high technology and external environment highly change, current enterprises have to be more flexible and have the agile abilities. Not only having agile abilities is enough, but also they need to be able to use these abilities effectively. Therefore, they can be obliged to adjust to the external environment by changing the organizational climate, organizational structure.

There is a common opinion that being made the manufacturing process and other organizational tasks via technological facilities might result in the layoff. However, the reality isn't essentially so. Jobs that people have isn't routinely be lost, however, their jobs can go through certain transformations that must be accepted. New working positions will be able to demand more complex tasks as a result of automatization. (Trstenjak, 2018). Therefore, the changes in all processes of enterprises and manufacturing in the age of Industry 4.0 have required the qualified human resources. The existence of technology alone is not enough to compete for current enterprises. Enterprises that can use the organization, technology, human and innovation in interaction will be able to achieve to competitive advantage. That is, it can be said that human is more important than ever.

The purpose of human resources management-related all functions is to ensure the competitive advantage in the sector in which the entity operates and to ensure that its life can be maintained in a better position (Mondy and Martocchio, 2016). According to Shamim et al. (2016), HR practices like training, staffing, compensation, performance appraisal, job design should strategically drive organizations into learning and innovation. Managers have to enhance both individual learning and organizational learning by redesigning the human resources practices for the innovativeness, flexibility, knowledge management capacity, creativity. To provide knowledge and competence related to new technologies and processes of Industry 4.0 in companies, all functions of human resource management need to be integrated and operated as a whole. (Hecklau et al., 2016). Current enterprises should focus on strategic human resources management. As a strategic business partner, HR helps to identify and develop the employees who have the necessary competencies for excellent performance by building the recruitment systems, training programs, performance management, and structures compensation programs.

Hecklau et al. (2017) have identified the competencies needed in Industry 4.0 by examining the many studies. They categorize the competency into four such as personal, domain, social and methodological elements. *Personal competencies* include employees' motivations, attitudes, as well as social values. These competencies are purely personal, they are difficult to train. For this reason, job specifications should be determined according to the needs of new business processes. In recruitment, people who have different skills, are compatible with the culture and strategic goals of the organization, open to new experiences should be chosen. By means of this, not only performances will be increased, but also resistance to change will be declined. Resistance to change can create an obstacle for enterprises by invalidating the financial investments and slowing down or disrupting the transformation and development. According to Yukl (2013), even if people initially have enthusiasm and support for a dramatic change, these enthusiasm and supports might disappear as they have difficulty in the solution of problems. Because the solution of the problem means costs and sacrifices for them. For this reason, the change in organizations should be gradual and slow. The reasons for the change should be explained and some substantial evidence for the changes that will be able to bring success should be shown. Leaders need to support people to cope with stress, anxiety, and depression induced by change. Both having a reliable leader who has a loyalty to change and the existence of an attractive vision are considerably important to change.

Comprising the elements skills and knowledge, *domain competencies* are equal to technical competencies such as knowledge networks, understanding and writing codes, awareness of cybersecurity, deeper process understanding, thinking and acting. Not only financial compensations but also nonfinancial compensations should be offered to employees who have domain competencies in order to attract and retain them. According to Trstenjak (2018), know-how will be the key factor of success in the market. Having the know-how will stimulate new and innovative ideas, provide continuous improvement. Thus, enterprises will be able to create greater value than their competitors. For this reason, organizations should support both individual and organizational learning. They have to make a budget for education activities, also encourage their employees to attain education programs. Organizations in Industry 4.0 should set the training programs in harmony with the current needs of them. Existing staff should be trained and developed even for knowledge and skills beyond today's job requirements. These activities should also have continuous development cycles that use the learnings from past cases. Training programs are able to improve the skills and innovative capabilities of the employees. When enterprises have innovative and creative workforce, this understanding of the workforce can be reflected in processes and problem-solving. Thus, methodological competencies also will be able to be improved.

Methodological competencies include all abilities and skills for general problem-solving and decision-making. In addition to training and development programs, it should be provided for attending relevant subordinates on decisions in order to improve the methodological competencies. This has many benefits. The subordinates feel important themselves and they are motivated, because their ideas have been asked for. They are more willing to implement the decision by considering their contribution to the decisions taken. Over time, subordinates develop by learning how to make decisions under various conditions.

Social competencies include attitudes, abilities and skills to form social relationships easily and cooperate and communicate with others. These competencies enable a person to reach common goals at a fair level in social interactions. In the such term which the human-human, human-robot, and robot-human relationships are normally accepted due to automatization and robotization, humans must be given safety and be motivated (Trstenjak, 2018). They should be offered opportunities to maintain their status, to achieve self-actualization, to gain the acceptance of others by expressing themselves.

We can say in short that today's enterprises firstly need to determine their strategies to adapt to changes in environmental conditions, second they need to weight aforesaid competencies in harmony with these strategies. Afterward they should try to provide employees to gain these competencies via the functions of strategic human resources management. These are the competencies that will ensure sustainability in Industry 4.0.

2.2. Knowledge Platform

The question of how organizations will be managed has arisen due to technological innovation and customer demands for sophisticated technology and services. Powerful abilities for information sharing can ensure that organizations featly adapt to uncertain environmental conditions and improve the long-term value. Sharing information with both internal and external stakeholders is very important. Powerful abilities for information sharing means that gain the information, keep on the memory of the organization by providing the control of information, as well as share this information with regarding people and organizations.

Information sharing means that useful information is distributed to people who need this information when working. To increase the positive results of information sharing such as avoiding redundancy, minimizing sharing costs and being more responsive, organizations should answer four main questions (Sun and Yen, 2005): What to share? Whom to share with? How to share? When to share?

The information shared should include the information on demand of last customers, sales forecasting, features of product and services, order status, levels of inventory, the level of use of capacity, waiting time, and expected quality. These types of product-, process-, and project-related information can be obtained through different methods and systems. "In order to be able to react adequately to time-intensive factors such as production changes and disturbances, it is necessary to develop solutions and find ways to optimize production which requires lean and responsive processes. The required responsiveness can be achieved on the basis of information and transparency. Even today, verbal and paper-based information exchange is the most widely accepted form of communication. To support computer-related information transfer, information carrier technologies such as auto-ID systems are indispensable tools. At the shop floor area, information is transferred via verbal, written or computer-related communication. Production Data Acquisition (PDA), Machine Data Acquisition (MDA), Shop Floor Programming (SFP), NC programming systems and tool management systems are the most frequently used applications in the shop floor area. In order to support business processes, a multiple of task-specific IT-systems and cyber-physical-systems (CPS) are used nowadays. Cyber-Physical Systems as well as production-oriented IT-systems, such as Enterprise Resource Planning (ERP) and Manufacturing Executive Systems (MES), are a standard to enable horizontal and vertical networking. With ERP and MES, a good starting point for the implementation of I 4.0 technologies has already been created. However, the adjustments to the existing IT-system landscape require a high commitment of resources such as time, capital and labor. CPS and lean production apps offer an adequate solution in order to achieve a complete networking on both the horizontal and vertical level, to control the scope of investment as well as to maintain existing and proven IT systems" (Müller et al., 2017).

The use of these information and communication technologies for information sharing with both internal and external environment will enhance the acquisition of quality information. So enterprises can adapt to environmental changes by acting properly. It can be said that they can gain a competitive advantage by means of this. Because in literature, there are so many studies that have proven the impact of knowledge management and sharing on the competitive advantage. The studies of Lustri D. (2007), Ubud and Nanere (2010), Hadian et al. (2014) are a few of them.

2.3. Technological Platform

Technological advances have dramatically been undergone in the age of Industry 4.0, and organizations need the use of technologies to build and maintain a competitive advantage in the market by generating benefits.

Farkas (2018) states that Industry 4.0 will be able to provide the expected increase and improvement in manufacturing via 9 technological pillars:

1. "Autonomous robots – autonomous, cooperative robots, high-end sensors, intelligent operation, standardized interfaces
2. Additive manufacturing – 3D printing, especially for producing prototypes and individual components, decentralized options: less transportation and stock
3. Augmented reality – for maintenance, logistics, various standardized operation processes, display, with additional information for example by using special glasses
4. Simulation – simulation of value networks, optimization of real-time data originated from intelligent systems
5. Horizontal and vertical system integration – complete enterprise data-integration based on data transfer standards, preconditions for establishing a fully automated value chain (from the supplier to the customer, from management to the workshop)
6. The industrial Internet of things – the network of machines and products, multidirectional communication between the network members
7. Cloud-based systems – the management of a large amount of data in open systems, real-time communication between manufacturing systems
8. Cybersecurity – operation in networks and open systems, organizing intelligent machines, products and system into a network
9. Big Data and analytics – the full evaluation of available data (e.g. from ERP1, SCM2, MES3, CRM4 and from data of machines), the support of real-time decision making and optimization"

By means of these pillars, Industry 4.0 provides the design and implementation of competitive products and services. They also improve the processes of production, logistics and management. Today's enterprises should constitute the new business models to increase the customer value and gain a competitive advantage by combining these technologies.

In the current scientific literature, new business models in Industry 4.0 are expected to enable the production of personalized products and services, an increase in their values, integration of product and service processes, as well as innovative solutions (Iansiti and Lakhani 2014). Laudien and Daxbröck (2016) conducted a multi-case study and identified three archetypes business models in manufacturing companies in the context of Industry 4.0. Most firms only aimed to increase the value created in the processes. So they had updated their current business models. Three out of eleven companies joined a heterogeneous network of companies that focused on their core competencies. Only two companies had developed a completely new business model, which was applied in parallel with the existing model (Schneider, 2018). Created new systems must serve to focus on new trends, keep abreast of improvements. Organizations should try to guess their potential impact of the new systems on their manufacturing system. They also should try to learn quickly how to implement changes to their standard operating and manufacturing procedures (Akkaya, 2020). First of all, customer demands and expectations and competitive conditions should be evaluated in the context of information obtained through external environmental analysis. Within the framework of these competitive conditions and the enterprise's resources, appropriate strategies should be determined to provide products and services that will be able to satisfy customers. A new business model should be created via technologies to allow producing determined products and services and implementing business strategies.

The successes on aforesaid three platforms can provide current enterprises to gain a competitive advantage by growing productivity, improving flexibility, speed, and quality. First current enterprises have to determine the business strategies by considering the informations gained correctly, organization, its culture and processes.

References

Adamik, A. & Nowicki, M. (2020). Barriers of Creating Competitive Advantage in the Age of Industry 4.0- Conclusions from International Experience. In A. Zakrzewska-Bielawska & I. Staniec (Eds.), Contemporary Challenges in Cooperation and Coopetition in the Age of Industry 4.0 (pp. 3–42). Switzerland: Springer.

Akkaya, B. (2020). Review of Leadership Styles in Perspective of Dynamic Capabilities: An Empirical Research on Managers in Manufacturing Firms. Yönetim Bilimleri Dergisi, 18(36), 389–407.

Barney, J. & Hesterly, W. (2006). Strategic Management and Competitive Advantage. Upper Saddle River: Pearson Education.

Farkas, A. (2018). Impact of Industry 4.0 on Robotic Welding. IOP Conf. Series: Materials Science and Engineering (Vol. 448). Kecskemét, Hungary: IOP Publishing doi:10.1088/1757-899X/448/1/012034.

Hadian, A., Vaghasloo, Y. A. & Doroud, R. (2014). The Impact of Knowledge Management System on the Quality of Test Result in Quality Control and Calibration Laboratory. In 2014 IEEE International Technology Management Conference, Chicago: IEEE.

Hecklau, F., Galeitzke, M., Flachs, S. & Kohl, H. (2016). Holistic Approach for Human Resource Management in Industry 4.0. In 6th CIRP Conference on Learning Factories, Procedia CIRP 54, 1 – 6.

Hecklau, F., Orth, R., Kidschun, F. & Kohl, H. (2017). Human Resources Management: Meta-Study – Analysis of Future Competences in Industry 4.0. In M. Rich (Ed.), Proceeding of the 13th European Conference on Management, Leadership and Governance (pp. 163–174). London: Academic Conferences and Publishing International Limited Reading.

Iansiti, M. & Lakhani, K. R. (2014). Digital Ubiquity: How Connections, Sensors, and Data Are Revolutionizing Business. Harvard Business Review, 92 (11), 90–99.

Klein, J. (2002). Beyond Competitive Advantage. Strategic Chance, 11, 6, 317–327.

Koçyiğit, Y. & Akkaya, B. (2020). The Role of Organizational Flexibility in Organizational Agility: A Research on SMEs. Business Management and Strategy, 11(1), 110–123.

Laudien, S. M. & Daxbröck, B. (2016). The Influence of the Industrial Internet of Things on Business Model Design: A Qualitative-Empirical Analysis. International Journal of Innovation Management, 20(8), 1–28.

Lustri, D. M. T. (2007). Knowledge Management Model: Practical Application for Competency Development. Learning Organization, 14(2), 186–202.

Mondy, R. W. & Martocchio, J. J. (2016). Human Resource Management (14th Ed.). England: Pearson Education Limited

Müller, R.,Vette, M., Hörauf, L., Speicher, C. & Burkhard, D. (2017). Lean Information and Communication Tool to Connect Shop and Top Floor in Small and Medium-Sized Enterprises. Procedia Manufacturing, 11, 1043–1052.

Schneider, P. (2018). Managerial Challenges of Industry 4.0: An Empirically Backed Research Agenda for a Nascent Field. Review of Managerial Science, 12, 803–848.

Shamim, S., Cang, S., Yu, H. & Li, Y. (2016). Management Approaches for Industry 4.0. Evolutionary Computation (CEC), 2016 IEEE Congress, 5309–5316.

Skobelev, P. O. & Borovik, S. Yu (2017). On the Way from Industry 4.0 to Industry 5.0: From Digital Manufacturing to Digital Society. International Scientific Journal "Industry 4.0", Year II, Issue 6, 307–311.

Sun, S. & Yen, J. (2005). Information Supply Chain: A Unified Framework for Information-Sharing. In P. Kantor et al. (eds.) Intelligence and Security Informatics. ISI 2005. (Lecture Notes in Computer Science, Vol. 3495, pp. 422–428). Berlin: Springer.

Trstenjak, M. (2018, March 03). Challenges of Human Resources Management with Implementation of Industry 4.0. Retrieved from https://bib.irb.hr/datoteka/956303.IoTSm_2018_paper_87.pdf on the date of 12.04.2020.

Ubud, S. & Nanere, M. (2010). The Role of Supply Chain Flexibility and Its Antecedent Variable in Increasing Competitive Advantage of Manufacturing Industries in East Java. AFBE 2010 Conference Papers, ISSN 1905–8055.

Yukl, G. (2013). Leadership in Organizations (8th Ed.). The United States of America: Pearson Education.

Nuran Varışlı

Importance of Strategıc Human Resource Management in Creating Competition and Innovation Culture

1 Introductıon

It is a fact to say that organizations should be aware of environmental changes. Since the concept of organization emerged as an open system, this claim has become evident. The emphasis on the operational efficiency of organizations led to an understanding of competitiveness based solely on factors related to the technical environment. In this regard, competitiveness will result from business excellence in carrying out activities that can be measured economically or financially. There are also sufficient reasons in the specific literature regarding on this subject to believe that an organization's competitiveness does not depend solely on these factors, especially in the theoretical framework of institutional theory.

For this reason, the aim of our study is to examine the strategic human resources management in creating a culture of competition and innovation. Therefore, the main question is to verify whether the values underlying competitiveness in the environment dominate the technical environment or whether they care about the institutional environment. In the technical environment, we understand the direction of the contextual dimension, which includes factors and indicators of business competitiveness based on economic resources and valuing the operational efficiency of organizations. The institutional environment is understood as the direction of the contextual dimension regarding organizational need to gain legitimacy before its employees.

In terms of the corporate envrionment, competitiveness is linked to the organizaton's ability to understand and manage symbolic resources by adapting to socially valued norms and standards of behavior that correspond to the actors' expectations in the context in which they operate. The organization's interest in these socially structured and established norms and values guarantees its permanence and legitimacy in the environmental context, thereby providing better access to material and economic resources.

The strategies that organizations can develop are related to the possibility of reacting to environmental pressures. In this context, certain strategies may result from institutionalized standards at a certain level in the context of the environment.

2 Conceptual Framework

2.1 Concept of Competition

Competition is one of the most popular terms among entrepreneurs, consultants and government representatives. Porter's understanding of competition is not limited to the consideration of companies competing in a particular industry and their behavior at a given moment, but is much broader in that sector, covering the economic and institutional structure in which competition has developed. The main tool of Porter's method of analysis is a model that represents the structure of competition available in a particular line of business through five forces affecting the company[1]:

1) Threat of new competitors entering the industry;
2) Substitution threat, that is, products or services from other branches that can replace the product or service of the branch in question;
3) The bargaining power of buyers;
4) The bargaining power of suppliers and
5) Competition between existing companies.

According to this model, customers, suppliers, substitutes and potential participants and competitors themselves are putting pressure, which will be larger or less in any case, on the company. In this sense, the competition that Porter draws attention to can be defined as the increase in competition. In addition to the characterization of competition within the five force model, Porter also offers a strategy typology that the company can successfully use to confront the five competitive powers that Porter calls "competitive strategies"[2].

Differentiation, which is a general strategy, is to create something new in the product or service offered by the company, thereby allowing the company to become special, differentiated within its industry. In this way, the buyer may choose this product over the other competitors and may even be willing to pay more for it.

---

1 Grundy, T. (2006). Rethinking and reinventing Michael Porter's five forces model. *Strategic Change*, *15*(5), 213–229.

2 Porter, M. (2012). Micheal Porter's 5 forces. *University of National Economy*.

Finally, a different general strategy Porter focuses on consists of defining a group of buyers, a range of products or a geographic market and devoting the company to serving this target market better than its competitors.

2.2 Concept of Innovation

The need for organizations to innovate is a constant demand from the community. For Schumpeter[3], the invention creates a new idea with potential for commercial exploitation, while innovation is the same idea when it is exploited in any way commercially. While Porter[4], described innovation as a new way of doing something as long as it was commercialized, he also defended the differences between these two concepts. Innovation is the realization of a commercially used invention.

Accordingly, innovation is a modest or revolutionary initiative that appears to be a change for the organization and the market, and is applied in practice, brining economic results to the company. The current context, marked by accelerated social and economic changes, means that public and private sector organizations need to adapt to meet the requirements of the goods and services markets driven by supply, productive globalization and the knowledge economy[5].

Activities focused on innovation become essential for the continuation of economic development in the capitalist system, including the transformation of living standards and the creation of new technologies. Literature in various fields points to innovation as a key element of creating and sustaining competitive advantages, and even as a key element in understanding most of the main problems of society.

As emphasized by Wolfe, it is clear that various theories and concepts related to innovation that can be applied in different situations. At the same time, due to the complex and diverse nature of the phenomenon of innovation, researchers often have difficulty to grasp and systematize innovation. In this context, it is stated that he has difficulty in following the development of the scientific literature on the subject from a theoretical perspective. According to Wolfe, there are four main lines of scientific studies on innovation: the stages of the innovative

3 Hagedoorn, J. (1996). Innovation and entrepreneurship: Schumpeter revisited. *Industrial and corporate change*, 5(3), 883–896.

4 Porter, M. E. (1981). The contributions of industrial organization to strategic management. *Academy of management review*, 6(4), 609–620.

5 Birkinshaw, J., Hamel, G., & Mol, M. J. (2008). Management innovation. *Academy of management Review*, 33(4), 825–845.

process, organizational contexts, the underlying theoretical perspectives and features of innovation[6].

Regarding the types of innovation, it is clear that the authors focus on innovations in products and services, processes and operations, marketing, strategies, organizational innovation, and managerial innovations. In turn, an innovation in marketing is the implementation of a new method with significant changes in design, packaging, positioning, promotion or determination of prices.

2.3 Innovation Culture

Culture is a series of basic assumptions shared among people that can determine their behavior and relationships. Schein[7] examines culture as a result of group learning, external adjustment problems and internal integration problems. In the culture of innovation, these solutions are the result of exploration, creativity, the risk of established and daily rupture and uncertainty. From this point of view, the central element of the culture of innovation is the people and their group work to constantly achieve innovations.

Gandotra[8] has defined the innovation culture as a culture associated with organizational structures and processes that make innovation a daily business. Innovation culture determines the ways regarding how to promote creativity, risk-taking, entrepreneurship and ways of sharing information and ideas. The culture of innovation enables the formation of norms that help members of the organization to develop behaviors that do not hinder their innovation activities but support them.

Russell[9] states these norms as;

- Supporting the creative activities of the members of the organization,
- Seeing innovation as a suitable solution method for strategic organizational problems,
- Ensuring free and open exchange of information within the organization,
- Maintaining close contact with groups outside the business that have knowledge of potential innovations,
- Being open-minded for new ideas,

---

6 Wolfe, R. A. (1994). Organizational innovation: Review, critique and suggested research directions. *Journal of management studies, 31*(3), 405–431.

7 Schein, E. H. (2010). *Organizational culture and leadership* (Vol. 2). John Wiley & Sons.

8 Gandotra, N. K. (2010). Innovation culture for sustainable competitive advantage. *Asia Pacific Journal of Research in Business Management, 1*(2), 51–59.

9 Russell, R. D. (1989). How organisational culture can help to institutionalise the spirit of innovation in entrepreneurial ventures. *Journal of Organizational Change Management.*

- Providing both psychological and financial support to those who bring forward new ideas,
- Promoting a reasonable risk taking for new ventures and
- Supporting an effective change practice.

Among the bibliographic studies regarding expression culture or organizational culture of innovation, it was observed that these studies aimed for definition of the studied elements and thus increase of these elements' understanding. The relationship between organizational innovation and the presence of an emergency in developing an innovative culture is emphasized in these studies. Innovation culture is a concept that takes up more and more space in organizations and it aims to increase competitiveness in a scenario where it is very important to stand out from the rest of the organizations. However, although much has been said about innovations in companies, the concept has not yet been fully defined. It is important to understand what it means to innovate as an organization to stay in full possible growth.

Organizations with innovation as the basis of their development are getting ready to produce more competitive and sustainable products and services. The secret to remaining as a market leader is to invest in innovation culture processes. When an employee's innovative ideas are implemented and returned to the company, it is important to recognize their involvement in the process. The rest of the employees will realize that just like the collaborator, who will be motivated to have more ideas, they may be there just like them in the future. As such, innovation management should aim to provide tools that contribute to employees to have and implement ideas that solve problems in an innovative way.

2.4 Strategic Human Resource Management

Despite their vital importance, material resources are overcome by intangible resources that we find in the knowledge, skills, values and attitudes of people who are part of the stable core of the company. Human resources require experience, knowledge, tendency to accept risk; judgment and wisdom of the people associated with the company. It is important to harmonize the human resources strategy and the company strategy to achieve organizational goals. The human resources department plays an important role in the competitiveness of the most organizations[10].

10 Daley, D. M. (2012). Strategic human resources management. *Public Personnel Management*, 120–125.

New technologies and innovations imply new ways of perceiving organizations, adapting their resources and capacities to production requirements, due to the constant dynamism they are exposed to. Companies require high quality and personal work, with preparation and attitude towards the development and expansion of knowledge and experience, when they are dedicated to complex and changing services, such as companies with constantly new technologies.

Strategies increase the ability to achieve high performance and longevity if they are well matched with the company's general strategy. Researchers collect a list of seven of these practices: job security, selective recruitment, decentralization, decision making, conditional compensation, comprehensive education, few status differences, comprehensive financial status and outcome. Some researchers warn that in order for these practices to be successful, they must first be internally consistent with each other, and secondly, externally with the strategy[11].

It can be said that the strategy looks at the economic impact of managerial decisions, as well as how in-strategy managerial decisions affect the unity level of the company. Since managerial decisions have an impact not only on the economic outcome or profit, but also on the corporate outcome or unit, managers should evaluate their decisions from both perspectives to maintain their competitive position.

Innovation is stochastic, that is, it is not possible to predict when it occurs. However, from an administrative point of view, it is possible to create organizational conditions for the emergence of the organization by creating organizational mechanisms and forms that enable the synergistic interaction of its members to generate new ideas by developing the strength of their relations.

Through delegation and leadership, innovation in the organization is supported through strategic decision-making that supports the integration and combination of the company's dynamic capabilities. Adapting to the pace of change means that all members of the commercial organization are actively involved in the dynamics of the innovation process.

2.5 Strategic Human Resource Management in Creating Competition and Innovation Culture

As a result of globalization, the speed of realization of innovations begins to impose the development of new competencies, skills and attitudes, gradually

11 Schuler, R. S., & Jackson, S. E. (2008). *Strategic human resource management*. John Wiley & Sons.

reducing the response time for the managers of institutions. The growing importance of innovation for competitiveness in companies has been recognized in academic, social and organizational environments. In general, the production of new technological information begins with the perception and identification of technical or economic problems or opportunities. For Porter[12], innovation is one of the foundations of competition and is influenced by the following:

(a) Change of competition rules,
(b) Production of competitive advantages over competitors and
(c) The spread of new jobs to existing foundations, existing companies and markets.

Organization' interest in innovation relates to the need for a competitive position search or defense in the market in which they operate to develop the brand and ensure the satisfaction of its employees, customers and shareholders. Organizations that benefit from human capital begin to place more emphasis on creating innovation and ensure that the results achieved by these efforts become the competitive difference the organization expects. Therefore, strategic human resources management should be implemented effectively for businesses.

Researchers define using strategic planning for achieving innovation in organizations as a structured process that enables determination of the direction that the company will follow in order to achieve some level of optimization in its relationship with the company's market[13].

In addition to being used as a learning mechanism, strategic innovation planning should be used systematically and continuously by the organization to identify and operationalize strategic actions that maximize the resources used, whether technological or human.

What distinguishes innovative companies from others is that they value the potential and exalted knowledge of their employees and transform this difference into business competitiveness, not costs. In recent years, the field of human resources management has been in strong demand to act strategically and in partnership with other areas of the organization. The strategic management of human resources aims to organize their processes according to the company's strategy and the performance of the company and employees, based on classic

---

12 Lanoie, P., Laurent Lucchetti, J., Johnstone, N., & Ambec, S. (2011). Environmental policy, innovation and performance: new insights on the Porter hypothesis. *Journal of Economics & Management Strategy*, *20*(3), 803–842.

13 Dodgson, M., Gann, D. M., & Salter, A. (2008). *The management of technological innovation: strategy and practice*. Oxford University Press on Demand.

HR functions (attraction, implementation, retention, development and evaluation). Therefore, in order to be strategic, strategy, structure, people, processes and skills should be included to be better developed as the roles are presented to their expected actions. As such, it is considered that the integration of a strategic HR field with the company strategy, considering the effects of the external organizational environment, should recognize the impact of competition and the dynamics of the labor market, highlight selection and decision making.

3 Conclusion

The results of this study on the competitiveness factors and the determination of the underlying values allow us to verify that the pressures are driven by the contextual values of the technical environment to maintain change, as well as the strategies, structural forms and procedural features.

The presence of environmental pressures for technical compliance has been found to be similar to institutional compliance, meaning that organizations need to develop capacities to achieve performance and operational efficiency rates that meet the expectations of other social actors. The values that are identified point to the adoption of strategies in line with the need for social legitimacy through actions such as ecological protection and immeasurable quality criteria. This does not mean that demands from the technical environment do not require focused performance on results with increased levels of excellence; however, these results are becoming increasingly easy to be imitated by other social actors in the face of increased business collaboration and the spread of technology. Therefore, competition for a company may come from actions that consider institutional values, such as the establishment of strategies with decisive environmental concerns.

The first conclusion that can be drawn from this study is that organizations should learn to reconcile both competencies by using operational efficiency to support strategies to achieve social legitimacy. Organizations can compete for quality, using their operational efficiency, for example, by offering products and services that meet social needs.

References

Birkinshaw, J., Hamel, G., & Mol, M. J. (2008). Management innovation. Academy of Management Review, 33(4), 825–845.

Daley, D. M. (2012). Strategic human resources management. Public Personnel Management, 120–125.

Dodgson, M., Gann, D. M., & Salter, A. (2008). The management of technological innovation: strategy and practice. Demand: Oxford University Press.

Gandotra, N. K. (2010). Innovation culture for sustainable competitive advantage. Asia Pacific Journal of Research in Business Management, 1(2), 51–59.

Grundy, T. (2006). Rethinking and reinventing Michael Porter's five forces model. Strategic Change, 15(5), 213–229.

Hagedoorn, J. (1996). Innovation and entrepreneurship: Schumpeter revisited. Industrial and Corporate Change, 5(3), 883–896.

Lanoie, P., Laurent-Lucchetti, J., Johnstone, N., & Ambec, S. (2011). Environmental policy, innovation and performance: New insights on the Porter hypothesis. Journal of Economics & Management Strategy, 20(3), 803–842.

Porter, M. (2012). Micheal Porter's 5 forces. University of National Economy.

Porter, M. E. (1981). The contributions of industrial organization to strategic management. Academy of Management Review, 6(4), 609–620.

Russell, R. D. (1989). How organisational culture can help to institutionalise the spirit of innovation in entrepreneurial ventures. Journal of Organizational Change Management.

Schein, E. H. (2010). Organizational culture and leadership (Vol. 2). John Wiley & Sons.

Schuler, R. S., & Jackson, S. E. (2008). Strategic human resource management. John Wiley & Sons.

Wolfe, R. A. (1994). Organizational innovation: Review, critique and suggested research directions. Journal of Management Studies, 31(3), 405–431.

Ilgım Eroğlu & Çiğdem Yılmaz Özsoy & Özge Ceylan Esen

The Expectations of Industries from Designers

1 Introduction

Designers' roles have been discussed by several studies in the literature that have established various positions for designers that can be observed in the work environments (Perks et al., 2005). Some studies provide a theoretical explanation for the emerging roles through design thinking, which, as an approach, underlines the significance of the involvement of designers in management and the participatory design practices (Siu, 2003). Some of these studies also define several competencies that are related to these roles, which were derived from the studies conducted through interviews with companies (Perks et al., 2005).

Variations in the organizations' expectations from designers may emerge due to different product development models. There are studies in the literature that examine the subject through periods, as well as design's possible roles in companies during product development processes (Valtonen, 2005; Perks et al., 2005). Since the literature on designers' roles still needs improvements (Tan, 2012), this study aims to make a contribution by comparing the expectancies from designers within different product development models and evaluate the changes through time. This paper describes the expectations of industries from designers through a thematical analysis of job announcements that are posted to the Coroflot website. The aim is to explore designers' roles on the bases of the company's expectations.

2 Design Thinking and It's Effect on the Expectations from Designers

With the introduction of new communication and information means, the workplace and practices of production and management are expected to change (Castells, 2000). It's discussed in the literature that the understanding of innovation has been altered through time, resulting in more participatory and open processes (Rothwell, 1994). It has been foreseen that the networks are going to be managed to support product management processes and will include buyers and users (Tidd et al., 2005). The emphasizes laid on the inclusion of buyers, and the overall creativity of the organizations hint a tendency toward the application of design thinking within organizations (Dodgson et al., 2008).

The design thinking concept suggests the idea of application of designerly problem-solving competencies to managerial actions, as they can also be applied to user-centered competitive strategies (Brown, 2008). It is suggested that during a design process, designers deal with "wicked problems" (Rittel & Weber, 1973; Buchanan, 1992). The tendency to utilize design in managerial actions can be explained through the idea that problem-solving in business and design environments are both "wicked," therefore, the skills that are needed to deal with them should be similar (Dorst, 2011). It is also claimed that "...the treatment of design as a human-centered, core creative activity in business challenges the overly scientific, rational view of the firm and, with it, many of the standard intervention tools of innovation management" (Hobday et al., 2011). Therefore, it is hinted that the design's solution centered view does not correspond to other user-centered approaches; the economy, society, and industry can all apply design thinking (Hobday et al., 2012).

Cooper et al. (2009) support the application of design thinking in the business environment by claiming that designers have started to be involved in the managerial issues in companies, and their abilities are suitable for strategic actions; thereby companies encourage their administrative staff to employ designers' capabilities. Also Valtonen (2005) hints that the problem-solving abilities of designers may lead them to acquire more involvement with managerial functions in work environments. The study states that designers took a role in the product development process in the past; however, recently they have started to become more involved in this area and management. Valtonen's research includes a quote from one of the design-solution providers claiming that the corporate directors declare that they have a motive to improve their organizations' strategies; since they do not know how to do it, design-service providers deal with their demands (Valtonen, 2005). The quote implies the way design is applied to companies' strategies for value creation.

Along with the aspects that support managerial elements of design thinking, Valtonen's (2005) study defines roles that appear through a time-scale: (1) creator, (2) multi-disciplinary team member, (3) end-user expert, (4) coordinator, (5) experience and brand creator and (6) innovation pusher/champion. Perks et al. (2005) also address the emerging tendency on the utilization of design in product development process leadership, as they evaluate the changing roles of design through time. The spreading of design through disciplines with the inclusion of all stakeholders is also suggested in other studies in the literature (Broadbent, 2003).

The emphasis on designers' function on innovation is also stressed in recent discussions in the literature. Design's role in pushing radical innovation (Verganti,

2009) and empowering of social innovation (Manzini, 2014; Tan, 2012) is frequently emphasized. The emerging role of the designer as a social entrepreneur also is discussed in other studies. Siu (2003) points out the necessity for designers to work with users to understand their social context. Lee (2007) also acknowledges the participation of users in the design process to enable the creation of more socially responsible designs. Muratovski (2015) suggests that the changes in the business context lead designers to adopt skills that are beyond traditional; such as business development and ethnographic research.

3 Roles of Designers within Different Product Development Scenarios

Companies may require designers to acquire different skills according to their business settings (Yang et al., 2005). The diversity can also be seen in other studies that evaluate the problem-solving actions of designers (Adams et al., 2011). Yang et al. (2005) compare in-house design teams and design offices; they suggest that design offices put more focus on overall professional competencies, addressing skills such as managerial experience. The varying demands of different work contexts are understandable, as designers can apply various problem-solving skills (Dorst, 2003).

Even though there is evidence in the literature that different business environments may demand designers' to apply different skills (Yang et al., 2005) the studies that evaluate designers according to job definitions in differing contexts are limited in the literature. In the study conducted by Tan (2012), it is stated that the role of the designers has been discussed in the literature for some period; however, the outcomes are still limited.

Tan (2012) refers to Dott 07 projects, which define designers as a (1) co-creator, (2) researcher, (3) facilitator, (4) capability builder, (5) social entrepreneur, (6) provocateur, (7) strategist. The entrepreneur level is discussed both at social and business levels, and the "communicator" role is also considered in the evaluation of Dott 07 outcomes. The defined roles of the designer as a "social entrepreneur" and a "provocateur" both criticize the influence of industry and market to stress the importance of design activism and critical design. However, since this study seeks the expectations of industries, it is not prospected to observe the clues for these roles in the demands of companies from designers.

One other research on design's roles in companies describes three different roles a designer may conduct in a firm (Perks et al., 2005). This study demonstrates these three roles as "Design as a Functional Specialism", "Design as Part of Multifunctional Team" and "Designer as NPD Process Leader". The first role addresses the traditional designer skills and pure design action, while the second requires interaction, communication, and flexibility as skills to enhance the function of generating interaction between team members and acting as a team member. "Designer as NPD Process Leader" addresses non-functional skills like project management, business analysis and such; demanding designers to get more involved with the overall management of new product development processes and informing other functions.

Since different types of problem-solving types and roles do exist in the literature, it may be beneficial to explore further the effect of product development models on expectations of designers to see if certain work types may be associated with specific skills. In this study, three different product development models will be defined based on previous studies (Eroğlu and Ceylan Esen, 2016) in an effort to differentiate differences among them.

The first group defined is "design houses", which consists of the agencies and other companies which mostly provide design services for other companies (advertising, product design, software, and website design, etc.). This group is can be seen in previous studies on the subject (Yang et al., 2005; Eroğlu and Ceylan Esen, 2016) and outsourcing design is considered as a strategic tool for innovation even for companies with internal design capabilities (Dell'Era and Verganti, 2010) Main concern for this group is inferred to be the designers' obligation to adapt to different brand identities and work paces (Yang et al., 2005; Eroğlu and Ceylan Esen, 2016), along with the concerns regarding marketing knowledge, project management skills and marketing knowledge (Hemonnet-Goujot et al., 2019).

"Own brand manufacturers" consists of the companies which produce tangible products for their brand. Although own brand management term is also used for companies that provide products under their own brand (Hobday, 2003). But since products and services driven by today's computer-led industries such as graphic design and software design are evaluated in a different group, this group is named as manufacturers as they deal with more complex manufacturing processes. Designers in this group have more necessity to work with other departments to manage relatively complex production and marketing processes as frequently described in innovation literature (Trott, 2005). Internal designers of manufacturing companies are claimed to take a role in every step of the product development including identification of the need and launch, while external designers mostly take a role in concept development and design stages (Perks et al., 2005). Therefore, overall management skills may be required by original brand manufacturers.

"Services and graphics" group consists of the companies which produce intangible products (software, etc.), services (finance, banking, leisure, etc.) or printed products (books, magazines, etc.). The items in this group have a shorter path between design and production with fewer pre-production concerns; therefore, designers are considered almost as makers (Raasch, 2011), so they may be differentiated from other groups of designers that deal with more complex development and production processes. Recently, software is referred as a modern craftsmanship environment (Sennett, 2008), as it is easier to develop and alter software products (Raasch et. al, 2009). Since open design is becoming more widespread and encouraged in design education (Phillips et al., 2014), it may be important to understand the current qualifications required for designers that deal with intangible items. Although currently open design and rapid manufacturing of tangible items are not efficient (Philips et al., 2014; Raasch, 2011), upcoming developments may lead to a more software-based design environment for tangible goods. Therefore it could be important to evaluate modern service, software, and graphic designers to understand the future profiles of designers in other groups.

4 The Research

Job announcements on the Coroflot website board were read and coded in the study. A total of 880 job board texts for March and April 2014 were read for this study; for the same period in 2017, the number of the announcements read is 475. Job announcements that do not ask for any specific ability related to basic design functions/related to the basic design function are neglected (positions for sales, buying, engineering, teaching, etc.). Therefore, the purposive sampling method was used for sampling (Robson, 2002). Furthermore, the announcements which did not specify the industry clearly or were written in languages other than English were eliminated. The thematic analyzing method was applied (Braun and Clarke, 2006). Industries were classified into three groups mentioned above to analyze any difference that may be related to the business environment.

Saturation for the codes is reached within the first 50 announcements (Guest et al., 2006). Seasonal differences may change the frequency of some of the announcements, such as internship job texts. Therefore the exact two month period was coded for both years. Multidimensional scaling analysis is conducted for evaluating the codes (de Leeuw and Heiser, 1982); this method is useful for determining tendencies and expectancies, (Cooper and Schindler, 2014) and used to measure the similarities/dissimilarities between pairs of objects.

The codes are; (1) Working in teams/cross-functional teams, (2) Working independently/self-managed/self-motivated, (3) Working closely with executives, (4) Mentoring/leadership, (5) Marketing research, (6) Brand management skills, (7) Business management skills, (8) Multi-tasking/flexibility, (9) Working in a fast paced environment, (10) Project management and organizational skills, (11) Working under pressure, (12) Self-starter/proactive, (13) Problem-solving, (14) Client interaction/management, (15) Communication skills.

5 Evaluation of Groups and Changes through Time

When we look at all six analyzes, three capabilities are considered irreplaceable by firms, which are: "Work in Cross-Functional Teams & Team Work," "Project Management and Organizational Skills" and "Communication Skills." Since these three capabilities are distinguished from others in a meaningful way to be considered irreplaceable, it can be said that companies show a preference towards these skills. These three capabilities may suggest a trend towards designers who can communicate effectively within a team environment and also manage project flows. A tendency towards employing team players and an emerging tendency towards hiring process leaders can be deduced from the overall preferences.

When we look at the year 2014, it can be seen that the companies in Design houses also identify "Working in a Fast-Paced Environment" and "Client Interaction/ Management Skills" as differentiated skills, which represents a propensity to hire designers with these abilities. The companies in design houses work with other companies and have less control over the design schedule, production calendars, and overall workload at a particular moment. Therefore, it can be expected from these firms to prefer designers with the capabilities to adapt to changes and manage their workload. In the year 2017, this preference can be seen more clearly as "Working Independently/Self-Managed/Self-Motivated" and "Multi-Tasking/Flexibility" are also distinguished from other capabilities. These two skills also form a dimension as they are perceived close to each other, hinting that companies expect designers to manage their workload in a constantly changing work environment. The companies in this group show a higher predisposition towards the designer role as a process leader.

For own brand manufacturers, in addition to the features mentioned above, in the year 2014, "Working in a Fast-Paced Environment" is differentiated from other skills. In the year 2017, this skill is replaced by "Problem-Solving" skills, which is not differentiated by other groups. Since the companies in own brand manufacturers produce tangible goods with more complicated production processes, identification of a clear need for troubleshooting skills can be understandable. The companies in the design houses deal with varying production processes, while the ones in Services and graphics deal with much less complicated procedures. Furthermore, in the year 2017, "Working Independently/Self-Managed/Self-Motivated," "Multi-Tasking/Flexibility" and "Working in a Faced Paced Environment" form a dimension which seems to be drifting from other capabilities, but they are not as mandatory as others yet. This new dimension can be followed up further to identify a change in the general competitive environment of industries. This group seems to have an emerging tendency toward employing designers as process leaders; however, currently, they lean to functional designers more than the design houses does.

The companies in the services and graphics show the least differentiation between the companies, as seen both in the year 2014 and 2017, only the skills that are mentioned above as overall tendencies seem to be differentiated from others. The companies in this group have more control over their workload with fewer production and manufacturing issues. Therefore, it can be said that their focus on designers' functional capabilities seems to be in accordance with their industrial environment. Even though being able to work within teams and project management and organizational skills address an environment that is projected by design thinking, there is a seemingly stable description of the designer role in this group.

6 Discussıons and Further Studies

This study describes companies' expectations from the designer through analyzes of job advertisements through a multidimensional scaling analysis. The research hint that an emerging trend towards employing designers as process leaders can be seen in some of the industries, and the preferences of companies may differ according to the industry they operate in. The results are in line with the previous studies which suggest that the expectations from designers in the modern age are compatible with the design thinking context.

Most of the companies require designers to have team working, communication, and project management skills. This tendency is compatible with the roles of designers in management and collaborative design processes. However, when companies are evaluated in three different groups that are formed based on their operating styles, differences can be seen between the groups. The designers that work in design houses are required to manage their work independently while being able to cooperate. The companies that produce their own tangible products require problem-solving skills in addition to basic managerial skills. In both groups, there is a tendency towards employing a designer that fits the environment that design thinking addresses and the tendency seems to get stronger with time. However, the third group doesn't add any more qualifications on the basic organizational skills and there is not much change in the preference within three years. These companies, in which designers' role is considered closer to the functions of makers, want to hire designers with mildly improved functional roles. These designers are asked to be competent in several areas such as publication (graphic design), software (interaction design, graphic design, etc.), where the design and production are finished almost simultaneously. Since the gap between design and production is narrow, the overall product development process in these companies may be more design-oriented. Therefore it can be said that as the production and work pace of companies get more complicated and less foreseeable, companies expect designers to perform more autonomously. This brings an emerging trend within these companies towards planning to hire designers acting as process leaders.

A notable outcome of this study is to invoke a discussion on the roles of designer-makers in the modern industry. Although the designer-maker role can be perceived mainly as small-scale oriented, the change towards wider networks with flexible and rapid production techniques may call for the integration of designer-makers into the industries with wider scales. At this point, the business environment and assumptions about future business environments can be revisited to see if every designer should develop professional managing skills, or the modern craftsmen that are suggested to work through virtual networks (Sennett, 2008) will be demanded by large scale industries.

The discussion of the differentiation of designers' required abilities through business environments may be useful for reforming the design education and understanding the upcoming media for design practice. Today many fields shorten the gap between design and production, and the gap within tangible products may be shortened in the future following the developments in production techniques. Although recent trends show a tendency towards an environment that is described in design thinking literature, changes in means of production may shift the tendency to functional designers in the remote future. Even though these assumptions are not realized in the future, it can be said that the industries with more simultaneous design and production processes require a designer to build competencies that are closer to a functional designer today.

To sum up, regarding the three groups which are studied, the first two groups with agencies and own brand producers seem to have tendencies that are in line with the ideas that are supported by design thinking. However, this tendency declines for the companies in which designers are expected to have a closer role to a maker's role. For further studies, working environments and demands from maker designers might be considered to provide a better understanding of the emerging roles of designer-makers.

References

Adams, R. S., Daly, S. R., Mann, L. M., & Dall'Alba, G.(2011). Being a Professional: Three Lenses into Design Thinking, Acting, and Being. Design Studies, 32(6), 588–607.

Braun, V., & Clarke, V. (2006). Using Thematic Analysis in Psychology. Qualitative Research in Psychology, 3(2), 77–101.

Broadbent, J. (2003). Generations in Design Methodology. The Design Journal, 6(1), 2–13.

Brown, T. (2008). Design Thinking, Harvard Business Review, June, 1–11.

Buchanan, R. (1992). Wicked Problems in Design Thinking. Design Issues, 8(2), 14–19.

Castells, M. (2000). Toward a Sociology of the Network Society. Contemporary Sociology, 29(5), 693–699.

Cooper, D. R., & Schindler, P. S. (2014). Business Research Methods. McGraw-Hill, New. York..

Cooper, R., Junginger, S., & Lockwood, T. (2009). Design Thinking and Design Management: A Research and Practice Perspective. Design Management Review, 20(2), 46–55.

de Leeuw, J., & Heiser, W.(1982). 13 Theory of Multidimensional Scaling. Handbook of Statistics. 2, 285–316, Netherlands.Dell'Era, C., & Verganti, R. (2010). Collaborative Strategies in Design-intensive Industries: Knowledge Diversity and Innovation. Long Range Planning, 43(1), 123–141.

Dodgson, M., Gann, D., & Salter, A. (2008). The Management of Technological Innovation: Strategy and Practice. Oxford University Press, New York.

Dorst, K. (2003). The Problem of Design Problems. Expertise in Design. Paper Presented at the Design Thinking Research Symposium 6. 17–19 November. University of Technology.

Dorst, K. (2011). The Core of Design Thinking and It's Application. Design Studies, 32, 521–532

Eroğlu, I., & Ceylan Esen, Ö.(2016). A Research on Designer Roles in Industries. 6th Forum of Design – Systems and Design, Beyond Processes and Thinking. Universitat Politècnica de València, Spain

Field, J. G. 1., Clarke, K. R., & Warwick, R. M. (1982). A Practical Strategy for Analysing Multispecies Distribution Patterns. Marine Ecology Progress Series, 8(1), 37–52

Guest, G., Bunce, A., & Johnson, L. (2006). How Many Interviews Are Enough? An Experiment with Data Saturation and Variability. Field methods, 18(1), 59–82.

Hemonnet-Goujot, A., Manceau, D., & Abecassis-Moedas, C. (2019). Drivers and Pathways of NPD Success in the Marketing–External Design Relationship. Journal of Product Innovation Management, 36(2), 196–223.

Hobday, M. (2003). Innovation in Asian Industrialization: A Gerschenkronian Perspective. Oxford Development Studies, 31(3), 293–314.

Hobday, M., Boddington, A., & Grantham, A. (2011). An Innovation Perspective on Design: Part 1. Design Issues, 27(4), 5–15.

Hobday, M., Boddington, A., & Grantham, A. (2012). An Innovation Perspective on Design: Part 2. Design Issues, 28(1), 18–29.

Lee, Y. (2007). What Is Designers' Social Responsibility? Investigating New Roles of Designers in Design Participation Processes. Paper Presented at the: IASDR 2007. 12–15 November 2007, Hong Kong.

Manzini, E. (2014). Making Things Happen: Social Innovation and Design. Design Issues, 30(1), 57–66.

Muratovski, G. (2015). Paradigm Shift: Report on the New Role of Design in Business and Society. She Ji: The Journal of Design, Economics, and Innovation, 1(2), 118–139.

Perks, H., Cooper, R., & Jones, C. (2005). Characterizing the Role of Design in New Product Development: An Empirically Derived Taxonomy. Journal of Product Innovation Management, 22(2), 111–127.

Phillips, R., Baurley, S., & Silve, S.(2014). Citizen Science and Open Design: Workshop Findings. Design Issues, 30(4), 52–66.Raasch, C. (2011). Product Development in Open Design Communities: A Process Perspective. International Journal of Innovation and Technology Management, 8(04), 557–575.

Raasch, C., Herstatt, C., & Balka, K. (2009). On the Open Design of Tangible Goods. R&d Management, 39(4), 382–393.

Rittel, H. W. J., & Webber, M. M. (1973). Dilemmas in a General Theory of Planning. Policy Sciences, 4, 155–169.

Robson, C. (2002). Real World Research: A Resource for Social Scientists and Practitioner. Blackwell Publishing., Oxford.

Rothwell, R. (1994). Towards the Fifth-Generation Innovation Process. International Marketing Review, 11(1), 7–31.

Sennett, R. (2008). The Craftsman. Yale University Press, New Haven.Siu, K. W. M. (2003). Users' Creative Responses and Designers' Roles. Design Issues, 19(2), 64–73.

Tan, L. (2012). Understanding the Different Roles of the Designer in Design for Social Good. A Study of Design Methodology in the Dott 07 (Designs of the Time 2007) Projects (Doctoral Dissertation, Northumbria University).

Tidd, J., Bessant, J., & Pavitt, K. (2005). Managing Innovation: Integrating Technological, Market and Organizational Change (3rd ed.). Wiley, Hong Kong.

Trott, P. (2005). Innovation Management and New Product Development. Pearson Education, Essex.

Yang, M. Y., You, M., & Chen, F. C. (2005). Competencies and Qualifications for Industrial Design Jobs: Implications for Design Practice, Education, and Student Career Guidance. Design Studies, 26(2), 155–189.

Valtonen, A. (2005). "Six Decades – and Six Different Roles for the Industrial Designer". Nordes Conference In the Making. 30–31 May, 2005. Copenhagen.

Verganti, R. (2009). Design Driven Innovation: Changing the Rules of Competition by Radically Innovating What Things Mean. Harvard Business Press, Boston.

İsmail Dülgeroğlu

Selling with Neuro Linguistic Programming (NLP)[1]

1 What Is Neuro Linguistic Programming (NLP)?

Neuro Linguistics Programming, or NLP for short, is a field of study that examines the processes of thinking, language and behavior, and teaches how to use them most effectively to achieve goals. NLP is a method that allows to examine and recreate the perfection required to always achieve the desired results (Knight, 2003:xi).

NLP helps to learn how to use our ideas, subconscious, more effectively and as we want, brain is a surprising computer in the human organism, but people do not know how to use it. The brain is like an untouched resource that has not been defined yet. The simulations made, the method of representing the thoughts, attitudes and information in the memories and the storage format are individual. Once the operation of this vocabulary is understood, the brain and experiences can be controlled and integrated with them. NLP stands short for (Aydemir, 2002:89);

- NEURO: Using the feelings of seeing, hearing, taste and smell, it can be defined as neurological processes that transform the experiences about the outside world into conscious or unconscious thoughts. It examines the functioning of the brain and mind as a whole. Neuro is a reference to thinking or perception, that is, to the brain processes and nervous system that form the basis of any behavior. The subject that NLP emphasizes most is to increase the efficiency of neurological processes and gain the ability to manage.
- LINGUISTICS: It is about how language is used to give meaning to experiences and to convey these experiences to the individual or others. The way a person uses language is the way he expresses his identity and way of thinking. It is difficult to envision conscious thought in the mind without language.
- PROGRAMMING: Programming is to examine the experiences, to determine the steps of formation, to reorganize them to achieve the goals. It is the product of personal programming of the results achieved and their impact on people. Each behavior

1 This chapter is an improved English version of oral presentation named "Kişisel Satiş Sürecinde Nöro Linguistik Programlamanin (Nlp) Yeri" which took place at YEBKO Conference in 2009 at İzmir.

consists of a series of thoughts and attitudes. It is possible to code the behaviors that will determine this sequence and define their infrastructure.

The essence of NLP is to increase the quality of life of the individual, to make him a positive, accessible, realistic, beneficial to himself and others, well-structured, balanced, and established and set the roof of his goals and objectives. Therefore, it aims to achieve personal and interpersonal perfection by helping people communicate more effectively. Enables anyone to be successful and strong in the areas of communication, therapy, personal development, success, and mental control (Aytaç, 2000).

Among the uses of NLP are (Gün, 2002:28);

- Education,
- Health,
- Therapy,
- Sales,
- Personal relationships,
- Marriage,
- Communicating with children,
- Work life.

2 Principles of NLP

NLP, which can be used as a means of compliance and persuasion in the personal sales process, has ten basic principles. (Gün, 2002:31–42):

1. The map is not the region itself. In other words, people's behaviour may not always have perceived meaning. Various behaviours can have different meanings according to values and experiences. It should not be biased.
2. Language is the second degree representation of experience.
3. Communication shapes the reaction.
4. Mind and body are part of the same cybernetic system.
5. The most direct information is in behaviours.
6. Every behaviour is an adaptation.
7. Your current behaviour represents your best possible choice right now.
8. If even a person in the world can do something, it is possible.
9. It is the law of flexibility.

3 Sense Channels According to NLP

If you can determine a person's preference for the senses, you can match it, create dialogue and communicate better. But how can you determine a person's preference for the senses? You can watch certain features of the person showing you the favorite or priority perception system (Adler et al., 2001:117). These sensory channels are of three types: Visual, Auditory and Kinesthetic.

People who prefer the visual approach often stand or sit with their heads and bodies upright and their eyes facing up. They do not tend to breathe deeply. In general, they speak quickly with a louder tone than usual, and their thoughts are also very fast during speech. They will sit forward in their chairs and they will look neat, meticulous and careful. Visual people see pictures of things and keep them in their memories, and voices for them do not attract attention or attract attention. They often have trouble remembering verbal directions because their mind tends to go blank. They tend to use visual words or predictions. Visual people will be concerned with the image and how things look (Adler et al., 2001:117). Their pupils move above sides of the eyes.

People who prefer the auditory approach shifts their eyes to their sides when they think. They breathe through the middle of their breasts. Noise can easily distract. They speak to themselves quietly and sometimes their lips move while doing this. They are not as high-pitched as visual people, but they have a reverberant tone when talking. Their voices are rhythmic and even musical. They can easily repeat what is being said and learn by listening. They generally like music and talking on the phone. They memorize step by step and in a certain order. An auditory person likes responses when speaking, a certain tone of voice, or answers that speak of determination. They tend to use auditory loads like "sounds good." Often they are concerned with how things sound. (Adler et al., 2001:117–118). When they inner talk their pupils go left down side of the eyes.

People who prefer the kinesthetic approach breathe in and out of their lungs, and as they breathe in, they see their stomachs go up and down. They tend to look down and to the right while thinking. Often they have a very deep voice. They speak slowly, weighing their words and leaving silent spaces between words. They seem to think and speak more slowly than a visual person. They respond to physical rewards and touch. At the same time, kinesthetic people tend to stay closer to the person they are talking to than a visual person during speech. They memorize by doing or walking towards something. They tend to use kinesthetic feeling verbs. They are concerned with how things feel (Adler et al., 2001:118).

In the table below, there are some examples of words used by people with visual, auditory and kinesthetic sense channels.

Table 1

Visual	*Auditory*	*Kinesthetic*
See	Hear	Feel
Look	Listen	Touch
Appear	Heard	Grasp Firmly

Source: Adler et al., 2001:119–120

4 Personal Sales with NLP

In her book Nil Gün (2002: 19) has defined the sale with an NLP approach as follows; Sales is the ability to change one's perspective with logic, knowledge, emotional connection, language use, and charisma, and the aim is to create the motivation to make the person come true by having a positive dream experience.

Which of the customers' visual, auditory or kinesthetic sense channels are dominant can be understood by following the movements of the pupils, tone of voice and the words they use, so that the other person can be better recognized and the process of harmonization can be initiated. Trust is very important for sales and continuity cannot be mentioned without its presence. Gaining the trust of the other person goes through this harmonization process (Molden, 1996:170–180). The use of words and voice toning can be done as follows. Care should be taken to use visual words if the person is visual, auditory words if auditory, or kinesthetic words if kinesthetic. It is not enough to use only the same words. Sound toning according to the customer's sense channel should be done. Visual people are annoyed by slow talkers and prefer to speak fast. Auditory people prefer to speak melodic and grain and are disturbed by excessive sound. Kinesthetics, on the other hand, hesitate to talk and often hesitate while doing various spellings while speaking. Body language is as important as words and intonations. It is not enough just for the harmony of words and voice intonation. It should also be noted that the body language must be the same (Molden, 1996:145–168).

People like people who look like them. Harmonization can be done with words and eyes. It is possible to adapt to people even without speaking a word. When you adapt to your physical postures and movements, the subconscious person of the other person perceives you as "reliable and similar to me". (Gün, 2002:130). In this context, the body language of the customer can also be imitated. However, this imitation should be done slowly, comfortably and without being felt. Closed body postures will open spontaneously after natural adjustment is achieved.

However, no violation of personal space should be made. Personal space may vary from person to person in one or half meters.

It is possible to create a harmony environment by mirroring the body posture, movements, tone of voice, speech speed and other voice features, language and thinking style, word selection, and breathing exchanges during communication. (Öner, 2001:86).

This whole adaptation process is referred to mirroring in NLP. While mirroring, it is necessary not to disturb the other side and to perceive that the whole process is natural. When mirroring is done, the message that the other side is similar to the subconscious is given. Naturally, people trust that they feel similar. The most important element of effective communication is "harmony". People can achieve harmony by chance during their communication. It is possible to consciously create these coincidences related to creating harmony in communication with modeling and mirroring techniques in NLP (Gün, 2002:54).

While all compliance activities are carried out, a personal sales process integrated with the AIDA process is carried out. This personal sales process consists of finding potential customers, preliminary approach, approach, presentation and implementation, dealing with objections, closing and follow-up and improvement after sales. The proximity achieved with this adaptation process is also not sufficient. In order to persuade those whose visual, auditory and kinesthetic senses are dominant, separate approaches should be displayed within the framework of the personal sales process. Visuals want to see proof that the product or service will be useful to them, audiences want to be told to them, internal speakers need to read and evaluate the information, and kinesthetics are convinced by doing and experimenting (Gün, 2002: 126). After adaptation, treating the dominant sense channels properly can facilitate persuasion and make the closing phase more comfortable.

5 Result

Neuro linguistic programming supports the personal sales process by creating harmony and trust. In this context, the performance of the vendors may increase. However, NLP is not a magic wand. It should be noted that it is a supportive tool in the sales process. In order to increase the sales performance by using NLP more effectively and efficiently, the issues of marketing and consumer behavior must be well known. Because any action to be taken without understanding the psychological and sociological structures of consumers may result in failure.

References

Adler, Harry & Heather, Beryl (2001). 21 Günde NLP, İstanbul: Kariyer Yayıncılık.

Aydemir, Aydem (2002). "*İşletmelerde Çağdaş Yaklaşımlar*", içinde: *Yöneticiler İçin NLP Teknikleri*, (Editör: Zeyyat Sabuncuoğlu) Bursa: Ezgi Kitabevi.

Aytaç, Serpil (2000). *İş Yaşamında Başarının Sırrı: NLP Tekniği*, İş Güç Dergisi, 2:1.

Gün, Nil (2002a). NLP ile Satış ve Pazarlama, İstanbul: Kuraldışı Yayıncılık.

Gün, Nil (2002b). NLP Zihninizi Kullanma Kılavuzu, İstanbul: Kuraldışı Yayıncılık.

Knight, Sue (2003). Uygulamalarla NLP Yaşamınızda Fark Yaratan Yöntemler, İstanbul: Sistem Yayıncılık.

Molden, David (1996). Managing with the Power of NLP, Edinburgh: Pearson Education Limited.

Öner, Mehmet (2001). NLP ve Başarı, İstanbul: Kariyer Yayıncılık.

Didem Göçmen

Using Triz in Management Problems Solving

1 Introduction

The main function expected from the management is to ensure that the organization continues its existence in accordance with its founding purpose and goals. Their organization's capability to maintain its existence is attributed to their ability to adapt to changes, and even to be more of a source of innovation today. Managers are responsible for monitoring the performance of other employees while seeking answers to problems specific to their current management areas within their own line of business. For this reason, they are forced to see problems from different perspectives and to find unusual ways of solving problems from time to time.

Besides the routine problems that are to be answered in the operational activities' fulfillment such as motivation or organizational commitment of employees, customer satisfaction or a new marketing strategy, unforeseen funding needs or catching up with new technological developments, new competitors in the industry, insufficient stocks or not well-run stakeholder relations; It is expected that the problems requiring more creativity, such as the production of a new groundbreaking technology or serving in a new industry, to be solved by the managers.

The need for creative problem-solving skills of managers becomes more evident when different problems arise, which are not previously encountered, and are unforeseen in organizations. New problems can only be solved with new approaches in a healthy way. New approaches arise from the ability to see different extensions of already existing information, rather than completely ignoring the existing information itself. Because in many cases, problem solving comes from the restructuring and development of currently used perspectives or processes.

Problem solving, conceptually, is defined as a process of transforming certain conditions into another preferred state (Stevens, 1998) or a period that requires a series of efforts to eliminate the difficulties encountered in achieving a certain purpose (Bingham, 2004), when the outcome is uncertain, a cognitive quest to reach the correct result (Martinez, 1998), finding the best way to overcome the obstacle encountered (Morgan, 1999), the process of correcting the difference between where something is now and where it should be (Kneeland, 2001).

The increasingly complex structures of organizations, the increased expectations of employees and shareholders from managers, confront managers with the need for more creative problem solving. Creative problem solving is essentially a methodological method that uses creativity to overcome obstacles in its efforts to achieve the goals. Here, success in problem solving depends on being able to apply and use creative techniques to solve problems scientifically and systematically (Marsap, 1999: 64).

The possibility that any organization or a researcher working on management anywhere in the world may have solved the current problem we have encountered before, and the possibility that they have developed a systematic including preventive measures or alternative solutions is perhaps a state that all managers would like to. In fact, all the answers we obtain today come mainly from the cumulative accumulation that several researchers or practitioners have gained as a result of active use of their creative problem solving skills. For this reason, it is important that we think more about problem solving techniques.

There are several methods that make creative problem solving applicable to organizations. In order to creativity to be used better, researchers have sought various ways and it has been generally accepted that creativity can be developed with educational programs and techniques. Examining the application processes of these techniques, which differ from time to time in the fields of management, educational sciences or engineering, will make it easier for managers to use creative thinking and instill in employees. The main purpose in applying these techniques is that employees can develop different perspectives by getting free of ordinary thoughts, and produce new and creative ideas. Despite being born from brainstorming, Gordon Technique (Synectics), Six Thinking Hats, 5N 1K (WH Questions), Reversing and Morphological Method or engineering discipline, TRIZ is also one of the methods used in problem solving.

Many researchers working on creative problem solving techniques have recently been working on the impact of TRIZ on management problems outside of technical fields such as engineering. The main purpose here is to reveal objective universal and ideal problem solutions by keeping the subjective evaluations of the management and the manager as much as possible outside the evaluation.

2 TRIZ (Theory of Inventive Problem Solving)

TRIZ, which means "Theory of Inventive Problem Solving)" in Russian, takes its name from the initials of the words "Teoriya Resheniya Izobreatatelskikh Zadatch". It is a theory put forward by the Russian engineer Genrich Altshuller, who worked in the patent office of the Soviet Navy in 1946. Focusing on the question of how inventions are made, Altshuller has worked on 200,000 patents in different fields and found that there are 1,500 technical contradictions that can be resolved by applying basic principles. Altshuller indicated that 40,000 of the patents he examined have creative solutions; while the rest involves a new use of a previously known idea or concept. Thus, he revealed that the idea of a design solution that can be applied to a new problem can be known in advance (Yang and Zhang, 2000).

Stating that the inventions contain different levels of creativity, Altshuller divided them into five groups according to five levels. The first level contains the lowest and the fifth contains the highest creativity. In general, it can be said that a first level invention obtains solutions by using the "trial and error" method less frequently than the second level. The higher the level of the invention, the more trials are required (Petrov, 2019: 19).

Level	A	B	C	D	F	G
5	New problem is found	New method is found	New data related to the problem are obtained	New principle is found	New design principles are developed	The entire system into which new design is incorporated, is modified
4	New task is found	New search concept is found	New data related to the task are obtained	New solution is obtained	New design is created	The design is applied in a new way
3	Source task is changed	Search concept is modified as applied to the conditions of the task	Collected data are changed as applied to the conditions of the task	Known solution is changed	Source design is changed	New design is implemented
2	One of several tasks is selected	One search concept out of several ones is selected	Data from several sources are collected	One solution is selected out of several ones	One design is selected out of several ones	Modification of a ready design is implemented
1	Ready task is used	Ready search concept is used	Available data is used	Ready solution is used	Ready design is used	Ready design is implemented
Stages	**Selection of the problem**	**Selection of the search concept**	**Data gathering**	**Search for the idea of a solution**	**Developing the idea into a design**	**Implementation**

Table 1. Process of Inventive Creativity
(Petrov, 2019: 19).

While examples such as microscope, steam engine, photocopy machine are shown among level 4 inventions, inventions such as X-rays, penicillin, DNA, laser are examples for Level 5.

The range of Altshuller' invention levels are observed as follows: 32 % level 1, 45 % level 2, 19 % level 3, below 4 % level 4, below 0.3 % level 5. Accordingly, it states that the vast majority (77 %) consist of level 1 and level 2 inventions and that the main creativity belongs to level 3 up to level 5 inventions (Altshuller, 1999).

While quite few ideas are successful in the problem solving process, many ideas are abandoned. Thus, people proceed by learning from their achievements or failures. Altshuller seeks after developing a practical methodology that includes concrete rules, from experiences collected from the best solutions so far, based on the question of whether there is a more logical way to learn from achievements (Orloff, 2006).

Altshuller has developed a number of practical TRIZ usage tools for the solution of problems over a period of about 40 years, and its followers have been adding new techniques to these existing techniques for more than 15 years. 40 Inventive principle, 39 Contradictions, Ideality, Su-field, 76 Inventive standarts, 8 Trends of Evolution, Functional Analysis, S-Cure Analysis are examples of these tools. In this part of the study, some of the tools that can also be used in the field of management are explained.

Ideal Final Result: It reflects the maximum use of available resources inside and outside the system. It indicates that a system should be simple, effective and safe throughout its lifetime, and states that each system has evolved towards an increasing degree of ideality. Ideality is expressed as the ratio of the sum of useful effects of the system to the sum of harmful effects of the system.

$$\text{Ideality} = \frac{\sum \text{useful functions and benefits}}{\sum \text{harmful functions} + \sum \text{costs}}$$

While useful effects represent all the valuable results resulting from the operation of the system, harmful effects mean unwanted inputs such as cost, labor costs, material, cathexis, pollution, and danger. The ideal final result is a practically unrealizable system. However, increase of the useful functions and reduction of the harmful effects bring systems closer to ideal (Şener, 2006).

Contradictions: Problems and solutions developed against them always bring contradictions if there is no perfection in the system. Each action triggers a reaction. Each proposed solution to problems can create new problems with them.

Altshuller identified two types of contradictions; technical and physical. While the technical contradiction expresses that one parameter of a system is improved while another parameter of it deteriorates; physical contradiction indicates that the condition of an object should have opposite requirements. (Technical contradiction – The product becomes stronger, but its weight increases/Physical contradiction – Coffee must be hot for good drinking and must be cold for the customer not to be burned.

Altshuller found 39 technical contradictions that caused contradiction as a result of the patents he examined. To illustrate these contradictions, a matrix of 39 improved and 39 worsening parameters are used. The rows of the matrix express the change that has been made and the columns represent the new problem that has arisen. In the cells where the rows and columns of the matrix intersect, there are 40 ideal solutions, no more than four. These solutions are called "40 Inventive Principles" in the TRIZ method (Altshuller, 1999). The application of these principles takes place in a matrix called a Contradiction Table with 39 lines and 39 columns (Table 2). (Livotov, 2008: 8)

Which properties of the system change for the worse? / Properties of the system to be modified or improved		1	...	27	28	...	39
		Mass of the moving object	...	Reliability	Accuracy of measurement	...	Produktivity
1	Mass of the moving object			3, 11 1, 27	28,27 35,26		35, 3 24,37
...	...						
9	Speed	2, 28 13,38		**11,35 27,28**	28,32 1, 24		
10	Force	8, 1 37,18		3, 35 13,21	35,10 23,24		3, 28 35,37
...	...						
39	Productivity	35,26 24,37		1, 35 10,38	1, 10 34,28		

Table 2. Search for Solution Principles Using the Contradiction
(Livotov, 2008: 8)

40 inventive principles: The solutions stated at the intersection points of the contradictions matrix represent the ideal solution methods that Altshuller obtained by examining the current patent applications. These principles provide clues to attain a quite creative solution to the problem. The contradictions matrix determines which inventive principle to be used to solve the problem. (Mazur, 1995). 40 principles determined by Altshuller are shown in Table 3. (Altshuller, 1998: 268)

Principle no.	Principle title	Principle no.	Principle title
1	Segmentation (Fragmentation)	21	Rushing through(Skipping)
2	Extraction(Taking out)	22	Convert harm into benefit(Blessing in Disguise)
3	Local quality	23	Feedback
4	Asymmetry (Symmetry change)	24	Mediator(Intermediary)
5	Consolidation(Combining)	25	Self service
6	Universality(Multi Functionality)	26	Copying
7	Nesting (Matrioshka)	27	Dispose
8	Counterweight(Anti-Weight)	28	Replacement of a mechanical system
9	Prior Counteraction	29	Pneumatic or Hydraulic construction
10	Prior Action(Do It In Advance)	30	Flexile films or thin membranes
11	Cushion in advance(Cushioning)	31	Porous materials
12	Equipotentiality	32	Changing the color(Color Changes)
13	Do it in reverse(The Other Way Around)	33	Homogeneity (Uniformity)
14	Spheroidality (Curvature)	34	Rejecting and regenerating parts
15	Dynamicity(Dynamics)	35	Transformation of properties
16	Partial or Excessive action	36	Phase Transition
17	Transition into a new dimension	37	Thermal Expansion (Relative Changes)
18	Vibration	38	Accelerated oxidation(Strong Oxidation)
19	Periodic action	39	Inert environment(Inert Atmosphere)
20	Continuity of useful actions	40	Composite materials

Table 3. 40 Inventive Principles of TRIZ
(Altshuller, 1998)

TRIZ was initially seen as a solution tool mostly for engineering and design problems. Today, while many other work areas such as marketing, development, supply chain and production, use highly developed methodologies and data processing methods, it is impossible for management discipline not to be affected by this transformation. The fact that the decisions made in most creative problem solving techniques are still based on the personal decisions and intuition of the managers, and its revelation of the situations like the risk is not evaluated correctly, the resources, information and potentials that are not used as the best solution tool at the right time, have made it essential to examine the approaches to the problems. TRIZ allows managers to obtain systematic and powerful thinking tools that help them process the information and make the right decisions at the right time (Livotov & Ruchti, 2001). Samples that can be adapted to management through TRIZ tools will be mentioned in this section of the study.

3 Examples of Triz Usage in Business Management

The fact that Triz was created by those working in the field of engineering enabled it to be used mostly in problem solving in technical fields. It was perceived as more complicated and difficult as it required much longer processes compared to a technical field, to see practically if it could succeed in management problems. Because, in a management problem, human have played an important role with his individual characteristics and his own personality and dealing with dynamic human characteristics was not so easy (Mueller, 2005).

Literature examples regarding the use of Triz in business, management, marketing and similar fields can be listed as follows; Mann and Domb, 1999, 40 Inventive (Business) Principles With Examples; Ruchti ve Livotov, 1999, TRIZ-based Innovation Principles and a Process for Problem Solving in Business and Management; Filkovsky, 2003, 40 inventive principles with applications in universe operations management; Zhang, Chai, Tan, 2003, 40 inventive principles with applications in service operations management.; Retseptor, 2003, 40 Inventive Principles in Quality Management; Filkovsky, 2003, reverse operation management; Averboukh, 2003; Six Sigma Business Process Management; Dourson, 2004 The 40 inventive principles of TRIZ applied to Finance; Retseptor, 2005, 40 Inventive Principles in Marketing, Sales and Advertising;; Domb and Kling, 2006, How to Reduce Cost in Product and Process Using TRIZ; Movarrei ve Vessal, 2006, Application of Theory of Inventive Problem Solving in Customer Relationship Management; Movarrei and Vessal, 2007, Theory of inventive problem solving (TRIZ) applied in supply chain management of petrochemical projects; Su, Lian, Chiang, 2008, Systematic improvement in service quality through TRIZ methodology: An exploratory study. (Ersin, 2009; Mahmoudi et al., 2012).

Mann (2004), who made the first studies on the implementation of Triz in the field of business, stated that 40 Inventive Principles, although they seem similar for engineering and business practices, contain differences, and at this point the contradictions matrices will be different, and pointed out the subsets of Inventive Principles.

1-Segmentation	1a-Divide an object into independent parts. *"Divide an organisation into different product centres." "Franchise outlets"*
	2b-Make an object easy to disassemble. *"Flexible pensions" "Use of temporary workers on short-term projects"*
	3c-Increase the degree of fragmentation or segmentation. *"Quality Circles". "Empowerment' – segmentation of decision making."*
2. Taking out	1.Separate an interfering part or property from an object, or single out the only necessary part (or property) of an object. *"Breakdown barriers between departments "Eliminate exhortations"*
6. Universality	1.Make an object or structure perform multiple functions; eliminate the need for other parts. *"Multi-skilling of work-force" "Team leader acts as recorder and timekeeper."*
12. Equipotentiality	1.In a potential field, limit position changes (e.g. change operatingconditions to eliminate the need to raise or lower objects in a gravity field). *"Make 'horizontal' career changes to broaden skills" "Team members distribute their own merit award Money (rather than often divisive management dictate)"*

Table 4. 40 Inventive Principles for Business.

In Table 4, there are examples of principles adapted to the field of management. For more samples, the studies of Mann and Domb (1999) can be examined.

Livatov and Ruchti (2001) exemplified the use of TRIZ in a problem they have built on communication problems in businesses as follows: If we assume that there is a communication lack between a technically competent and thus important individual and the rest of the staff, we know the resulting personal conflicts will have a negative effect upon the productivity and the working environment. Suggestions regarding the use of TRIZ principles for the solution of the problem are as follows: "Principle 1. Combination – Separation:

- "Isolate" the person for the staff to avoid direct contact and organize a central counselor.
- Provide the "difficult" person to work at home or have flextime.

Principle 2. Symmetry – Asymmetry:

- Reduce asymmetry in company expertise; train or hire several experts internally.

Principle 3. Homogeneity – Diversity:

- Encourage psychological homogeneity and raise the tolerance threshold of the colleagues.

Principle 4. Expansion – Reduction:

- Reduce the individual's direct involvement with colleagues and in projects.

Principle 5. Mobility – Immovability:

- Reduce the individual's sphere of movement within the company through organizational means..

Principle 7. Standardization – Specialization:

- Use the unique (or specialist) knowledge of the individual to build up the knowledge management system or have them organize this task.

Principle 8. Action – Reaction:

- Arrange a social and psychological guidance program for the individual.

Principle 9. Continuous action – Interrupted action:

- Only involve the individual in a consultative role and in certain phases of a project.

Principle 10. Partial action – Excessive action:

- Reduce the amount of time that the individual spends in projects.

Principle 11. Direct action – Indirect action:

- Provide a mediator or a social buffer for the individual in the team or in the company."

In his study, Ersin (2009), has created a contradiction matrices through 19 contradiction parameters such as employee satisfaction, employee motivation, human capital, management leadership, information sharing, employee loyalty, value compliance, structural capital, process execution, information integration, education, retention, to identify the problems related to Human Capital Management. (Table 5) Also, it has adapted 40 creative parameters together with examples close to the Mann and Domb study, which is an example of TRIZ principles in the field of business management, and gave descriptive metrics for some parameter samples in order to obtain measurability.

improving / worsening	Employee Satisfaction	Employee Motivation	HR System (Human Capital)	Management Leadership	Knowledge Sharing
Employee Satisfaction	+		1, 15, 37		
Employee Motivation		+	1, 15, 20	12	4, 24
HR System (Human Capital)	10, 26	10, 14	+	12	22
Management Leadership	12	14	12	+	10, 22,
Knowledge Sharing	4	4, 5		4, 6	+

Table 5. 19X19 TRIZ Matrix for Human Capital (Example 5x5)
(Ersin, 2009)

Contradiction parameters listed on the left side of the table from top to bottom are the improving features; the parameters listed from left to right represent the worsening features. The numbers in the boxes are 40 creative principles that are adapted. If a feature that is trying to be improved worsens another feature, the numbers at the intersection of these two features can be used to determine the solution principles.

Ersin (2009), stated that the central problem in their studies is subjectivity, and indicated that in order to reduce subjectivity; it can be developed along with the perspective of other researchers. Based on the knowledge that each company has its own "identity" or culture, they suggested that the HR TRIZ matrix should be designed depending on the culture of the company.

4 Result

TRIZ has long been widely used to solve engineering problems. Altshuller, creator of the theory, determined in the process of classifying the inventions that, a large part of the solution of engineering problems existed somewhere as solved.

Because a very small part of the inventions involve an entirely new scientific discovery or an entirely new system. As a result, when the person seeking an answer for a solution to a technical problem starts to look for a solution other than one's own experience, he/she can see that his/her questions are answered in that sector or a similar industry before.

Recently, researchers working on TRIZ are turning to the use of TRIZ in non-technical areas such as management and business problems, and even some researchers express the use of TRIZ in management and business as a new concept called xTRIZ (extended TRIZ).

In the studies focusing on the applications of TRIZ extensionally in non-technical areas, it is evaluated that some TRIZ tools – especially 40 inventive principles – can be as effective as technical areas in solving management problems. The method provides a systematic structure that accelerates the decision-making process of managers in complex and comprehensive problems through well-organized thinking tools. One of the most important features of the theory is to take people out of their areas of knowledge and experience and to refer the information obtained from other disciplines to use, thus preventing time lost in trial and error processes. Another expectation in the application of the method in this area is to take individuals out from the habit patterns created by professional experience, to free them from the narrow patterns of the usual problem solving methods and to free the managers' decision making processes from the intuitive, subjective evaluations of individual experiences.

However, the human factor is at the center of management problems, and it is expressed as a limitation in the observed studies that this factor, which is in continuous transformation, as a fixed element in problem solutions. They emphasize that many of the studies on TRIZ in the field of management focus on the adaptation of 40 inventive principles, and some technical principles seem harmonious for business problems, while others remain ambiguous and difficult to determine which principle is dominant. Another point mentioned as a deficiency is that in this approach arising from patent reviews, the number of cases studied on inventions and the number of cases examined upon the same management problems are much higher than technical studies and therefore the validity of inventive principles cannot be as precise as in the technical area. In line with these suggestions, applications on TRIZ tools are aimed to contribute to case studies in the field of management.

References

Altshuller, G. (1998). 40 Principles: TRIZ Keys to Technical Innovation, L. Worcester: Technical Innovation Center, Inc.

Altshuller, G. (1999). The Innovation Algorithm: TRIZ, Systematic Innovation and Technical Creativity. Worcester: Technical Innovation Center, Inc.

Bingham, A. (2004). The Development of Problem Solving Skills of Children (A.F. Oğuzkan, Trans.). Istanbul: MEB.

Ersin, F. (2009). Implementatıon of Trız Methodology in Human Capıtal, Master Thesis, The Graduate School of Natural and Applied Sciences Industrial Engineering, Bahçeşehir University.

Kneeland, S. (2001). Problem Solving (N. Kalaycı, Trans.). Gazi Ankara.

Livotov, P. (2008). TRIZ and Innovation Management. Available at: https://www.researchgate.net/publication/242219907_TRIZ_and_Innovation_Management (Accessed 14 March 2020).

Livotov, P., and Ruchti, B. (2001). TRIZ-Based Innovation Principles and a Process for Problem Solving in Business and Management. TRIZ Journal, 1, 677–687.

Mahmoudi, N., Nahaeia, V.S., Fahmia, A., and Faridyahyaiea, A. (2012). Application of TRIZ to Eliminate the Contradictions of a System Dynamics (SD) Model to Solve Business Problems Conference Paper Conference: The 9th International Industrial Engineering Conference, at Tehran, Iran. https://www.researchgate.net/publication/259147685

Mann, D. (2004). The Next Common Sense: Philosophy-Level Integration of TRIZ into an Integrated Business and Management Innovation Process, in the ETRIA TRIZ Future Conference, Italy.

Mann, D. and Domb, E. (1999). 40 Inventive (Business) Principles with Examples. The TRIZ Journal September https://triz-journal.com/40-inventive-business-principles-examples/

Marşap, A. (1999). Yaratıcı Liderlik. Ankara: Öncü Publishing.

Martinez, M.E. (1998). What Is Problem Solving? Phi Delta Kappan, 79(8), 605–609.

Mazur, G. (1995). Theory of Inventive Problem Solving (TRIZ). Retrieved March 2020. http://www.mazur.net/triz/

Morgan, C. (1999). Psikolojiye Giriş (Hüsnü Arıcı, Trans.). Ankara: Netekson A.Ş.

Mueller, S. (2005). The TRIZ Resource Analysis Tool for Solving Management Task: Previous Classification and Their Modification. Creativity and Innovation Management, 14(1), 43–58.

Orloff, M.A. (2006). Inventive Thinking through TRIZ: A Practical Guide. Verlag Berlin Heidelberg: Springer.

Petrov, V. (2019). TRIZ. Theory of Inventive Problem Solving Level 1. Heidelberg: Springer.

Şener, S.D. (2006). TRIZ: Yaratıcı Problem Çözme Teorisi Ve Diğer Problem Çözme Yöntemleriyle Karşılaştırma, Master Thesis, Istanbul Technical University The Graduate School of Natural and Applied Sciences.

Stevens, M. (1998). Sorun Çözümleme (A. Çimen, Trans.). İstanbul: Timaş Publishing.

Yang, K., and Zhang, H.(2000). A Comparison of TRIZ and Axiomatic Design, in: Proceedings of ICAD2000—First International Conference on Axiomatic Design (Cambridge, MA), pp. 235–242.

Münevver Bayar

Importance of the Managers Attitudes and Behaviors Against Cultural Differences Observed in Organizations

1 Introduction

All activities in organizations consume resources and produce products and services, regardless of their qualifications or purposes. The business environment demands increased levels of efficiency from organizations, which means continuous organizational change. This demand is met with constant change. The change in the organization is effective only when the change in culture is processed. The cultural beliefs and values of the institution should be carried with the processes, especially in the pursuit of compliance with the external values that customers and resource suppliers perceive more clearly as they are part of the environment close to the organization.

Organizations can be viewed from a partial perspective as a series of activities managed by experts in certain areas. In accordance with this purpose, in our study, the attitudes and behaviors of managers against cultural differences in organizations were examined. Another aspect of the organizational management model and the problematic state of organizational culture is related to the mission of the institutions involved in this process. In organizations, managers and owners have different and conflicting tasks. The biggest contradiction is that the owners focus on the profit margin and the managers concentrate on the organization's functionality. Therefore, managers have to manage cultural differences within the organization without disturbing the organizational climate.

2 Conseptual Frame

2.1 Culture Concept

Culture is a term widely researched by Anthropology, a science that emerges at the same time as sociology and aims to analyze human societies from cultural organizations to the most complex forms of social organization. If the etymologically rooted in the culture, it is seen that it comes from the word Cultura, which means agriculture in Latin. This word, which was later used as Culture in Western languages, is the Ottoman word hars. On the other hand, the British

Anthropologists used the term culture in Europe at the end of the 19th century to describe all the thoughts, actions, beliefs, value systems, symbols and techniques that are specific to the societies studied by ethnography. In sociology, the concept of culture is used as a concept that helps better understand the functioning of the scenarios and roles that guide interactions. British Anthropologist E. B. Taylor, who used the term culture for the first time in this sense, made a famous and valid definition of culture; culture is "a complex whole in its broadest meaning in ethnography, including information, art, law, morality, custom, and all other abilities and habits."[1]

The word culture is a complex concept that assimilates values, norms, beliefs, traditions, or any chosen term from the vast texts of the current anthropology.

In this context, Culture refers to the environment of man established and created by man. It has two aspects, material and spiritual. The material culture, which some sociologists call civilization at the same time, consists of visible material elements such as our structures, techniques, roads, employment and transportation means, and our environmental conditions, which are our own works. On the other hand, spiritual culture is the whole culture that consists of moral elements (i.e. customs, customs, collective behaviors and attitudes) that make a nation a nation and determine its own personality[2].

2.2 Organizational Culture

Researchers have presented one of the newest and simplest definitions, saying that culture means "everything people have, think and do as members of society." According to Beckhard[3], organizational culture means a way of life, a system of beliefs, expectations and values, a typical relationship interaction of a particular organization.

From the formal concepts of culture, from the 19th century to the present day, culture is understood and defined as a series of factors specific to individuals in society. From the definition of culture, we can define the organizational culture, which can be called corporate culture according to Durğun, and represents the

---

1 Tylor, E. B. (1871). Primitive culture: Researches into the development of mythology, philosophy, religion, art, and custom (Vol. 2), London.

2 Bilgiseven Kurtkan, A. (1995). Genel Sosyoloji, Filiz Kitabevi, İstanbul.

3 Beckhard, R. (1972). Optimizing team-building efforts. *Journal of Contemporary Business*, *1*(3), 23–32.

set of habits and beliefs created through the norms, values, attitudes and expectations shared by all stakeholders[4].

The difficulty in defining the organizational culture is that it interacts with social psychology, sociology, political science and anthropology and takes place in an area defined as interdisciplinary, as an important part of organizational behavior[5].

Organizational culture means the system of meanings shared by all members, as well as the factor that distinguishes an organization from others. When establishing relationships with other people in any social group, the characteristics of each individual form the basis of the group's characteristics as a whole. The same corporate culture forms the way of institutionalized thinking and acting in an organization.

The essence of a company's culture is expressed in the way it does business, the way it behaves to its customers and employees, the degree of autonomy or freedom that exists in its units or offices, and the degree of loyalty expressed by its employees. Organizational culture represents the perceptions of the officers and employees of the organization and reflects the dominant mentality in the organization.

In other words, organizational culture represents informal and unwritten norms that daily guide the behavior of members of an organization and direct their actions to achieve organizational goals. Basically, it is the culture that defines the mission and enables the objectives of the institution to emerge. Culture should be compatible with other aspects of the organization's decisions and actions, such as planning, organization, direction, and control, to better recognize the organization.

The background of organizational culture studies can go back to the origins of social sciences. Understanding this contribution is very important because most of the dilemmas and debates surrounding organizational culture reflect differences in the historical tradition of social research. Researchers argue that organizational culture is "a dominant and consistent set of shared values conveyed by symbolic meanings, such as stories, legends, slogans and jokes." Deal and Kennedy[6] define organizational culture as "Here is how business is done."

4 Durğun, S. (2006). Örgüt kültürü ve örgütsel iletişim. *Yüzüncü Yıl Üniversitesi Eğitim Fakültesi Dergisi*, *3*(2), 112–132.

5 Doğanay M. (2019). Örgüt kültürü ile sosyal sermaye arasındaki ilişkinin incelenmesi: özel sektörde bir çalışma. *Journal Of Socıal And Humanıtıes Scıences Research*, 6(43), 2950–2957

6 Deal, T. E., & Kennedy, A. A. (1982). Corporate cultures: The rites and rituals of organizational life (Vol. 2, pp. 98–103). Reading, MA: Addison-Wesley.

Organizational culture, although relatively stable, is not static, but dynamic: it constantly builds on its own mechanisms, even without changes in its components. Change and new experiences fuel the organizational culture with new elements structured with existing subjective content[7].

Culture is an open system, it is affected by other cultural systems. The subject, passively involved in the organization, is considered to accept the existing culture as themselves, but all people join other organizations and even the society, which can be said to have exchanged cultural content[8]. This is illustrated in examples that overlap with the content of the culture of the organizations from which these human resources come from, in new companies where cultural characteristics of other organizations are appreciated.

2.3 Effects of Cultural Differences in Organizations

The feeling that world events, economic, social, cultural, technological and commercial influences as well as other natures unite rapidly to summarize a unique, integrated world in which nations, national cultures, time and space cross traditional boundaries.

Organizations are not only influenced by globalization: the unified activities of all types of organizations encourage, facilitate, maintain and expand globalization. They shape the assumptions that guide and limit future research on what globalization will be, what the other should be allowed to speak or say about it. For example, a sociological approach to globalization represents this phenomenon as the understanding of the world and the growing awareness that it is the whole of the world[9].

As a national "absence of borders", this concept of globalization can conclude that globalization produces a trend of homogeneity and uniformity worldwide. A paradoxical consequence of the globalization process, consciousness, is fineness, the human condition and the connection of humanity to this planet is not the production of homogeneity, but the sharpening of great diversity perceptions expressed through many local cultures. Cultural difference is the sum of a scenario in the transition from the Industrialization age to the Information age. Here, using diversity as a competitive advantage in the company can guarantee

7 Alvesson, M. (2012). *Understanding organizational culture*. Sage.

8 Martin, J. (2001). Organizational culture: Mapping the terrain. Sage Publications, California.

9 Moran, R. T., Harris, P. R., & Moran, S. (2007). Managing cultural differences: Global leadership strategies for the 21st century (7th ed.), Boston.

new forms of interaction and different forms of perception and movement in the market segment[10].

According to the literature, the concept of cultural difference is the representation of people in groups that are clearly different in terms of cultural significance in a social system. Cultural difference is defined as a mixture of people with different identities interacting in the same social system. In these systems, majority and minority groups coexist. Majority groups are groups whose members have historically been advantageous in terms of economic resources and power over others. Broader definitions indicate that the term difference means all individual differences between people, that is, everyone is different.

This conceptualization reflects individualism, which structures most of the ideas about organizations. On the other hand, limited approaches limiting diversity to race, ethnicity and gender are interpreted as referring only to a particular gender or to a minority race-ethnic group in the social system (e.g., diversity refers to white women or racial minorities).

Cultural difference is at the center of understanding diversity in organizations. Therefore, the diversity debate has concentrated around the true meaning of identity and its treatment in the work of organizations. Differences in individual identities (both physical and cultural) interact as a complex range of individuals, groups, and organizational factors to determine the impact of diversity on individual and organizational outcomes. Accordingly, individual results are divided into emotional response variables such as satisfaction, organizational identification and participation, and performance variables such as performance, mobility and wages[11].

It can be said that the management of cultural difference means planning and executing human management organization systems and practices in a way that maximizes the potential advantages of diversity and minimizes its disadvantages.

2.4 Managers' Attitudes and Behaviors towards Cultural Differences

Many of the transfers to the management sciences scope do not have a split between what should be called culture and what should be called the standard of behavior. Culture is not enacted or manipulated. Culture; in anthropological

10 Shane, S., Venkataraman, S., & MacMillan, I. (1995). Cultural differences in innovation championing strategies. *Journal of management, 21*(5), 931–952.

11 Sofyalioğlu, Ç., & Aktaş, R. (2001). Kültürel farklılıkların uluslararası işletmelere etkisi. Yönetim ve Ekonomi: Celal Bayar Üniversitesi İktisadi ve İdari Bilimler Fakültesi Dergisi, 8(1), 75–92.

sense, it is a set of patterns of behavior, belief, knowledge, tradition and value that separates a social group, it is extremely complex and above all unconscious. Culture refers to how individuals in a group act in the face of social stimuli or personal emotions and needs, their uniformity in the behaviors exhibited by them, certain situations within organizations.

Most of the work under the name of organizational culture continues today with the interest of basic instrumentalism. But the incompatibility between different rationalities emphasized by the shock of the "mentality" and the restructuring processes of characteristic companies of the early 21st century, transforms the understanding of culture. Understanding organizational culture as the nature of a closed, homogeneous and permanent universe has turned into a relational concept.

According to some authors[12], the biggest factors of organizational culture are the founders and main leaders of the company. As the descriptors of the management model, they impose their personal beliefs, ways of doing things, as they have maximum power in the company.

The community influences the culture of the company by interacting, providing and acquiring the economic resources necessary for its continuity. The customer has expectations about the quality of the products. The size of the organization affects the culture of delegation and responsibilities. Whether public or private, the legal nature of the owner determines the levels of corporatism and the necessity for effectiveness. The dimensions of technology as a technical system represents the realization of some related values about time, quality, employability, dimensioning of activities etc. For Schein[13], the culture of an organization can be defined as a series of common basic assumptions in which a group of people learn how to solve problems of external cohesion and internal integration. It is considered valid and likewise assimilated by new members as the right way to perceive, think and feel about problems.

Besides the change in organizational culture is a necessity of the society in which the organization is located, it is important that this requirement is based on the correct definition of the characteristics and aspects of the changing culture. In this sense, Deal and Kennedy[14], while talking about organizational or

---

12 Schein, E. H. (2010). Organizational culture and leadership (Vol. 2). John Wiley & Sons, Hoboken.

13 Schein, E. H. (1990). Organizational culture (Vol. 45, No. 2, p. 109). American Psychological Association, Washington.

14 Deal, T. E., & Kennedy, A. A. (1982). Corporate cultures: The rites and rituals of organizational life (Vol. 2, pp. 98–103). Reading, MA: Addison-Wesley.

cultural change, states that it means real changes in the behavior of people in the organization.

Culture is the basis for behavior, to identify challenges, analyze alternatives and make decisions, put people into action. Therefore, it is possible to make inferences about the possible decisions and actions of a certain group of people sharing the same culture, after understanding the basic support assumptions.

The beliefs and values included in the concepts presented as the ideal management model can create a culture in the company that is suitable for adaptation to the external environment, flexibility and challenges, as well as the establishment of goals and results to be achieved by the company.

Accordingly, the effectiveness of the company mainly depends on the satisfaction of people, efficiency, adaptation and development of the decision-making process. At the same time, it should create an appropriate environment for adequate monitoring of the external environment and the participation of participants, as well as for discussions and innovative ideas.

As for the set of principles, beliefs, and values that should characterize the company's culture to produce the best conditions for relationships between people and achieve the best results, it would be very ambitious to associate them as they are infinite. However, they can be defined as culture-specific in which people can participate in the management process without changing the qualifications of managers for the responsibility of final decisions.

3 Conclusions

The current competitive and connected market requires companies to continually develop strategies to separate themselves from their competitors and to attract consumers who are constantly demanding and knowledgeable. As a result, organizations are increasingly investing in the development of strategic management departments that are deeply involved in creating an organizational culture that is compatible with senior management.

Companies are made up of people who bring their roots, personal values, dreams and goals to the office. Therefore, organizational culture will naturally be built by these people for a good interaction between teams and presenting results. However, the manager will be fragile and incompatible with his business strategy, without involvement in this process and without defining substantial foundations that guide culture.

Culture is the DNA of a company. It shows and determines how the employees think and act from the shareholders to the intern. It is important that the company executives together with HR create a culture code that will explain the company's values, goals and tasks and affect the construction of the work teams. Therefore, in order to involve a professional team, it is necessary to align them with the company culture from the selection process to the post-work period. When presented to internal and external audiences in companies, these guidelines are in the form of the company's mission, vision and values. A strong organizational culture is that the company has deeply defined and shared values that have a positive impact on leadership and the behavior of the whole team.

Promoting the formation of organizational culture provides the company with a range of benefits that will help it grow and out of competition. Its development will continue firmly and in a planned manner, at an upward pace that enables the implementation of projections and target planning.

Organizational culture is closely linked to the appreciation of human capital. A company that takes care of its employees, offers growth opportunities and encourages participation in the decision-making process has a good image in the market. One of the main bases of organizational culture is leadership. Managers must comply with the values advocated within the company so that these codes must be followed. The company should lead and develop this issue by harmonizing attitudes and expectations.

Trainings are short-term information processes that involve the transfer of certain information to conduct the business. It can also be applied to develop the basic skills and positive attitudes needed to achieve the goals. Promoting education that focuses on organizational culture will help understand these values and form the basis of this behavioral practice within the company. On the other hand, when corporate culture guides people management policies, employees are proud of their jobs and talent retention is provided much more.

References

Alvesson, M. (2012). Understanding organizational culture. London: SAGE Publications Ltd.

Beckhard, R. (1972). Optimizing team-building efforts. Journal of Contemporary Business, 1(3), 23–32.

Bilgiseven Kurtkan, A. (1995). Genel Sosyoloji. İstanbul: Filiz Kitabevi.

Deal, T. E. (1982). Kennedy (1982). Corporate cultures. Reading, MA: Addison.

Deal, T. E., & Kennedy, A. A. (1982). Corporate cultures: The rites and rituals of organizational life (Vol. 2, pp. 98–103). Reading, MA: Addison-Wesley.

Doğanay, M. (2019). Örgüt kültürü ile sosyal sermaye arasındaki ilişkinin incelenmesi: özel sektörde bir çalışma. Journal of Socıal and Humanıtıes Scıences Research, 6(43), 2950–2957.

Durğun, S. (2006). Örgüt kültürü ve örgütsel iletişim. Yüzüncü Yıl Üniversitesi Eğitim Fakültesi Dergisi, 3(2), 112–132.

Martin, J. (2001). Organizational culture: Mapping the terrain. California: Sage Publications.

Moran, R. T., Harris, P. R., & Moran, S. (2007). Managing cultural differences: Global leadership strategies for the 21st century (7th ed.), Boston.

Schein, E. H. (1990). Organizational culture (Vol. 45, No. 2, p. 109). American Psychological Association, Washington.

Schein, E. H. (2010). Organizational culture and leadership (Vol. 2). Hoboken: John Wiley & Sons.

Shane, S., Venkataraman, S., & MacMillan, I. (1995). Cultural differences in innovation championing strategies. Journal of Management, 21(5), 931–952.

Sofyalioğlu, Ç., & Aktaş, R. (2001). Kültürel farklılıkların uluslararası işletmelere etkisi. Yönetim ve Ekonomi: Celal Bayar Üniversitesi İktisadi ve İdari Bilimler Fakültesi Dergisi, 8(1), 75–92.

Tylor, E. B. (1871). Primitive culture: Researches into the development of mythology, philosophy, religion, art, and custom (Vol. 2), London.

Gülşen Kırpık

Literature Review on "Decision Fatigue": Example of Google Scholar Database

1 Introduction

Person decides millions of times throughout his /her entire life, both in business life and in his /her social life, because he/she is constantly faced with numerous problems both during his/her business life and non-business life. He /she decides for the solution of these problems by choosing one of the available options. A choice/preference and therefore problem solving are at the core of every decision made (Koçel, 2010: 109; Byrnes & James, 2002: 210; Naftel & Driscoll, 1993: 177). According to Barker (1999: 17), decision making makes more sense than choosing what to do. What are we going to do about it? What possibilities do we face? What does it look like? With questions such as, the person determines how he/she behaves in the decision making process (Sperry, 2003: 165).

According to Stretching Theory of Eva M. Krakow a person makes around 35,000 decisions daily (Huang, 2019:7) some of them have an intensive impact on the long run and some do not (Dubey, 2019: 58). There is now significant mainstream media exposure and literature on decision fatigue and the activities to which it applies (Huang, 2019: 4).

Decision making is a demanding process and our brain gets tired every time we make a decision. Mental fatigue in difficult decisions is even more. After getting mentally tired, there is a slowdown in our control level and other mental functions. When people are mentally tired, they continue to make efforts to continue or complete the job. This effort manifests itself as "making quick decisions without thinking too much" (URL-1). Making a quick decision without thinking in detail may be the result of decision fatigue, which reduces the quality of the decision and thus causes unnecessary use of workmanship, time and other resources and can lead to an additional cost problem. Similarly, it was stated by Baumeister and Tierney (2011) that decision fatigue, which occurs when people make efforts for complex decisions for a certain period of time, temporarily reduces the quality of subsequent decisions.

Although several studies have investigated the impact of decision making (Danziger, Levav and Avnaim-Pesso, 2011; Linder et al., 2014; Vohs et al., 2008), there is no clear information that decision making can cause decision fatigue.

Actually, the decisions made do not cause decision fatigue. When a large number of sequential decisions (URL-2) are required during the day, decision fatigue becomes apparent after a certain period of time. The emergence of decision fatigue is when a person's mental resources are exhausted. After decision fatigue appears, each decision is made faster and therefore the quality of the decision decreases. In other words, the situation arises from getting away from analytical decisions and approaching intuitive decisions for solving the problem.

In this study, firstly, information about the concept of "decision fatigue", definitions and explanations, and the effects of decision fatigue from previous studies on decision fatigue are given. Then, in which area the studies in the literature are conducted and what are the important findings about decision fatigue are mentioned. Finally, in line with the information obtained in the literature, the results obtained regarding decision fatigue are discussed and suggestions are made for future studies.

2 The Concept of "Decision Fatigue"

In the literature, decision fatigue is defined as a result of "ego depletion", which is defined as the draining of mental resources (Hirshleifer et al., 2019; Huang, 2019; Reinhardt and Hurtienne, 2018; McAllister, 2017; Baumeister, 2011; Tierney, 2011; Baumeister et al., 1998). The tendency of avoiding to make more decisions because of the mass of the decisions taken earlier is called decision fatigue (Dubey, 2019: 58). According to Liss & Linder (2019), decision fatigue is a gradual erosion of ability, self-control or willpower that occurs when people choose. According to Rao & Nyquist (2018), decision fatigue is defined by psychologists as a disorder of control and decision-making skills as a result of repeated decision-making actions.

Decision fatigue emerges as a concept that causes the depletion of limited resources on decision making, and then defines a phenomenon that is difficult to self-control (Vohs et al., 2008). Simply put, decision fatigue is the deterioration of our ability to make good decisions after a long decision-making session (Mackay, 2018).

It is observed that decision fatigue is also important in major decisions that change life. To the best of our knowledge, the first study to examine the impact of decision fatigue in a professional setting belongs to Danziger, Levav and Avnaim-Pesso (2011). The authors examined the rate of conditional release requests approved by eight parole judges in Israel. According to the study, the ratification rates of conditional release requests dropped regularly for approximately two hours before eating. It was observed that tired and hungry judges preferred to reject the request, which is easier than accepting the request, when evaluating their requests for parole. n the working hours immediately after lunch, the positive response rate of judges to the parole requests increased by approximately 65 %. A similar decision fatigue study was conducted by Linder et al. (2014). In this study, it was observed that after several hours of work, physicians were more likely to prescribe antibiotics due to decision fatigue. As stated by Kouchaki and Smith (2014), when both study samples are evaluated together; It can be said that people tend to make less ethical decisions at the end of the day when the resources for self-control required to make decisions are reduced. On the other hand, in the section titled "Occupational fatigue" of the study by Soukup et al. (2019); It is stated that the task time has a critical effect, but the critical effect depends on the amount of mental effort.

Studies have concluded that decision-making can consume people's self-control resources. In addition, it is stated that when the sources of self-control are exhausted, people will therefore have difficulties in reaching their goals or can make the right decisions later (Tian & Exline, 2017; Vohs et al., 2008). Decision fatigue was handled differently by Polman & Vohs (2016). According to Polman & Vohs, people feel strong when they decide for others. One of the possible reasons why the decision is fun for others is who influences the results of the decisions.

In addition, decision fatigue is a structure that can manifest psychologically and cognitively from working conditions and leads to self-regulation failure and decreased decision-making quality (Hickman, Pignatiello & Tahir, 2018). Data from psychology show that decisions made under more pressure, distraction or fatigue are made more intuitively (Hirshleifer et al., 2019; McAllister, 2017; Kahneman & Egan, 2011; Stanovich & West, 2000).

On the other hand, there are studies related to the deterioration of the performance due to the fatigue that occurs due to the long term task performance (Campagne, Pebayle and Muzet, 2004; Kecklund and Akerstedt, 1993; Torswall and Akerstedt, 1987). In a study by MacDonald, Cohen, Stenger, and Carter (2000), it has been stated that the problems people experience in these conditions are largely due to the fact that they are poorly monitoring their actions.

In the light of the information given above, it can be said that decision fatigue is a psychological condition, and after a series of decisions, the person's limited mental resource is exhausted. In addition, it can be stated that with the effect of decision fatigue, one can make a lower quality decision after each decision. Therefore, due to decision fatigue, the possibility of low-quality follow-up decisions will decrease, and the intuitive feature will increase.

3 Literature Review

In this study, Google Scholar database was used for literature review. Despite its limited software features and quality, Google Scholar service is free and very helpful to users in the process of finding resources, with a huge and diverse, multidisciplinary I/A database and an incredibly fast search engine (Jacsó, 2008: 102). In this context, the studies published in the Google Scholar database constituted the universe of this study because of the reasons such as "home-office" work due to Covid-19, inability to make institutional connections from home, and to reach personal connections and some related studies, especially costly.

3.1 Findings

When "decision fatigue" was written in the Google Scholar database, 1,600 studies were reached (URL-3). However, the studies using the concept "decision fatigue" in its title are as follows; Tierney, 2011; Hirshleifer, Levi, Lourie and Teoh, 2019; Polman & Vohs, 2016; Vohs, Baumeister, Twenge, Schmeichel, Tice and Crocker, 2005; Pignatiello, Martin and Hickman, 2018; Persson, Barrafrem, Meunier, and Tinghög, 2019; Reinhardt & Hurtienne, 2018; Kwan, Stein, Delshad, Johl, Park, Martinez, Topp and Spiegel, 2016; Vohs, Nelson and Rawn, 2009; Mallard, 2016; Allan, Johnston and Powell, 2019; Olsen, Meyerhoff and Mørkbak, 2017; Twenge, Tice and Baumeister, 2000; Robertson & Court, 2018; Vohs, Baumeister, Twenge, Schmeichel, 2006; Stewart, Ferriero, Josephson, Lowenstein, Messing, Oksenberg, Johnston and Hauser, 2012; Vohs, Twenge, Baumeister and Schmeichel, 2003; Vohs, Baumeister, Twenge, and Schmeichel, 2004; Sollisch, 2016; Oto, 2012; Mathew & Joseph, 2014; McAllister, 2017; Howard, 2019; Winkle, 2014; Hughes, Lysikowski, Acharya, Phelps and Kandil, 2019; Le, 2018; Anindya & Psi, 2013; Chen, Liou and Chen, 2018; Lushaku & Lahtinen, 2019; Tian & Exline, 2017; Olsen, 2015; Hunt, Ambrose, Haaland, Hanson and O'Neil, 2020; Zheng, Kwok, Taljaard, Nemnom and Stiell, 2019; Soukup, Lamb, Weigl, Green and Sevdalis, 2019; Huang, 2019; Liss & Linder, 2019; Dubey, 2019; Rao & Nyquist; 2018; Halamka, 2011; Marghoob & Carrera, 2016; Clear, 2013; Denton,?; Petrie, Holschen, Adams and Zelisko, 2019; Cure & Weight,?, Saposnik, Maurino and Jaja, 2018; Birchall, 2012; Barnett, Linder and Jena, 2016. As can be seen, 47 studies using the concept "decision fatigue" were found in the title. However, the content of 16 studies could not be reached. The content of only 31 studies has been reached. Information on both reached and inaccessible studies is given below.

3.1.1 *Information about the Inaccessible Studies*

The study titled “Decision fatigue: Making multiple personal decisions depletes the self’s resources” prepared by Twenge et al. (2000) and the study conducted by Vohs, Twenge, Baumeister and Schmeichel (2003) under the same title and differentiated could not be reached. The study published by Denton, whose field is unknown and the date of which is not known, and the study carried out by Petrie et al. (2019) in the field of health could not be reached. Likewise, the study published by Weight with an uncertain date has not been reached. The study published by Saposnik et al. (2018) could not be reached. The study published by Birchall (2012) and which is in the nature of a magazine has not been reached. The study published by Barnett et al. (2016) in the field of health sciences was also not available.

On the other hand, the study titled “Decision fatigue exhausts self-regulatory resources” conducted by Vohs, Baumeister, Twenge and Schmeichel (2006) could not be reached. The study titled “Decision fatigue: Making multiple decisions depletes the self” conducted by Vohs, Baumeister, Twenge and Schmeichel (2004) and the study titled “Decision fatigue: Choices influence self-regulatory resources” could not be reached. The study titled “The cure for decision fatigue” conducted by Sollisch (2016) could not be reached; The study titled “When thinking is hard: managing decision fatigue” conducted by Oto (2012) in the field of health science has not been reached; The study carried out by Howard (2019) on errors related to decision fatigue in the field of health has not been reached. In addition, the study carried out by Halamka (2011) on decision fatigue in the computer field could not be reached and the study published by Marghoob & Carrera (2016) in the field of health could not be reached.

3.1.2 *Reached Studies and Brief Information*

As a result of the studies on the studies reached, only 1 of the studies on decision fatigue was in the field of human resources (3.2 %), 13 in the field of health (41.9 %), 4 in the field of psychology (12.9 %), 3 in the field of economics and finance (9.7 %), 2 in the field of food (6.5 %), 2 in the field of consumers (marketing) (6.5 %), 2 in the field of informatics and computer (6.5 %), 1 in the field of politics (3.2 %), 1 in the field of sports (3.2 %), 1 in the field of ergonomics (3.2 %). In addition, it has been observed that 1 published study has a magazine content (3.2 %). All of 31 studies are summarized below, as given in this paragraph, taking into account the rankings.

3.1.2.1 *Study on Human Resources Related to Decision Fatigue*

Only the summary part of the study carried out by McAllister (2017) published in HR Future magazine on the concept of "Decision fatigue" has been reached. In this study, it was stated that developing a strategy to deal with decision fatigue is an important part of improving the decision making process. It is mentioned that the person uses his limited self-control and mental resource gradually while performing his duties. In addition, it was stated that the next tasks requiring focusing were getting harder and every decision made during the day made it difficult for the next one.

3.1.2.2 *Studies on Health Related to Decision Fatigue*

1. In the study conducted by Rao and Nyquist (2018) in the field of health, various strategies and system changes and collaborative and versatile approaches were mentioned to increase seasonal flu vaccination rates. In addition, it is stated that it should also deal with decision fatigue. Because, in this study, the reduction of influenza vaccination rates was mentioned as a negative result of decision fatigue.
2. In the study by Tian & Exline (2017), it was assumed that making too many decisions during one day will lead to decision fatigue, which can create negative situations in clinical practice. According to the research result, the assumption has been confirmed. Because, with the reduction of time dealing with problem solving and the decrease in self-control to maintain attention, decision fatigue has emerged.
3. In the study conducted by Liss & Linder (2019) through a literature review, other studies on decision fatigue were examined. As a result of the examination, it was stated that the analysis of Israeli judges who made serial conditional release decisions was mostly defined regarding decision fatigue. The findings in the study are as follows;
   * Probably, as judges get tired more cognitively, they prefer to do something easy and refuse parole.
   * Enterprises other than medicine increase their income by making use of decision fatigue. For example, car dealers offer more expensive and possibly unnecessary options towards the end of the purchasing process. Supermarkets offer sugary, unhealthy foods at the checkout.
   * Decision fatigue in medicine has been associated with increased antibiotic prescribing for respiratory infections, increasing opioid prescribing for back pain, reducing influenza vaccination, and reducing hand washing.

4. In the study by Pignatiello et al. (2018), a research was conducted for the term "decision fatigue" in seven research databases. In this research, 17 related articles were obtained. However, it is stated that the current literature does not adequately describe the consequences of decision fatigue. In addition, it was stated that the concept of decision fatigue is a valid concept for health psychology.
5. In the study by Soukup et al. (2019), while providing practical solutions for improvement, it was discussed how prolonged task period affects performance and what strategies are available to balance negative effects.
6. In a study by Hunt et al. (2020), decision fatigue, a gradual decrease in consistency and quality of choices, was observed with repeated decision-making in breast and colorectal cancer care. When this study is examined in detail, it can be said that people who are not experts in the field are prone to decisions that mitigate cognitive decision making.
7. In the study published only in abstract by Chen et al. (2018), the Chinese version of decision fatigue scale will be confirmed.
8. In a study by Zheng et al. (2019), 87,752 patients were analyzed. As a result of the study, there was no significant difference between the decisions made according to the shift time of the patient (consultation, computed tomography and other decisions). As a result, no evidence of decision fatigue was found among emergency doctors during an eight-hour shift.
9. Hughes et al. (2019) aimed to measure the effect of primary care physicians on the possibility of decision fatigue on prescribing inappropriate treatment. As a result of the research, it can be said that the effect of decision fatigue is very weak, since the effect of decision fatigue on the inappropriate prescription is minimal.
10. In the study conducted by Persson et al. (2019), the exhausted effect of repeated decision making was called "decision fatigue". As a result of this study, fewer patients were planned for surgery by surgeons approaching the end of their shift, and this effect was attributed to decision fatigue.
11. In the study conducted by Kwan et al. (2016) on the journal of health sciences, it was investigated whether decision fatigue could affect the acceptance of the article. As a result, it was decided that the fatigue of the decision had no effect.
12. In the study conducted by Allan et al. (2019), it was concluded that as decision fatigue increases, each successive decision provides a predictable change towards more measured, that is, less risky and less resource saving decisions. It can be said that this is an indicator of decision fatigue.

13. In the context of the fight against decision fatigue whether or not the articles sent to the Annals of Neurology journal will be published, a study was conducted by Stewart et al. (2012). As a result of the study, it was stated that when the workload of the day was high, there was an increase in rejection of the article and this was a symptom of decision fatigue.

3.1.2.3 Studies in Psychology Related to Decision Fatigue

1. In the non-academic study published by Clear (2013), ways to get rid of decision fatigue were mentioned. In addition, it was discussed whether decision fatigue causes bad decisions and unhealthy choices.
2. In a study by Vohs et al. (2005), it was found that people are better at self-regulation (measured in terms of physical endurance and velocity-accuracy changes) after performing a task of their choice. If others chose their task, the measurement results of the study differed to indicate decision fatigue.
3. In the study conducted by Huang (2019), it has been argued that motivation strategies and decision fatigue can be prevented. In the study, three different suggestions are presented to solve the problem of decision fatigue. The first is to reduce decisions. The second solution is to educate people to make decisions. Theoretically, this is a better solution than reducing decisions because it gives the subject long-term flexibility. Accordingly, people can learn to make decisions while using less resources through guided practice. The third solution, very different from the other two, is to increase an individual's base motivation to complete a task. Like training, it is a more permanent and longterm solution than reducing the number of decisions. It has the resilience of the training solution while being practical, as this method is accessible to anyone. However, that is not to say increasing someone's motivation is a simple task. It is sometimes simply not possible to change one's motivation on certain tasks.
4. In the study by Polman and Vohs (2016), it was mentioned that choosing for others is more enjoyable and less consuming than the decision makers are independent. According to this, it can be said that as the person who is in the position of a decision maker becomes more affected by the result of the decision he has made, he will be uncomfortable with this situation and will experience fatigue, that is, it will be exhausted more quickly.

3.1.2.4 Studies on Economy and Finance Related to Decision Fatigue

1. In a study conducted by Le (2018) as a thesis study in the field of economics, it has been stated that intuition promotes egoistic and selfish behaviors in

decision making by using difficult choices to induce decision fatigue and encourage intuitive responses. It was also stated that this was especially valid for men.

2. The aim of the study conducted by Lushaku & Lahtinen (2019) as a thesis study in the field of economics is to test the extent to which the decisions made by the driver's license specialists in the Swedish Transport Authority are affected by decision fatigue. Afternoon decisions were seen as a sign of decision fatigue. However, since it was determined that the sample was not random, it was stated that an exact result could not be reached.
3. In the field of finance, Hirshleifer et al. (2019) examined whether decision fatigue affected analysts' decisions. It was stated that previous decision fatigue studies examined non-professional and first-time or sparse ones. It was also stated that the motivation levels of these people to perform successfully in the task should be investigated.

3.1.2.5 Studies on Food Area in Related to Decision Fatigue

1. In a study by Olsen (2015), decision fatigue was assumed to be caused by mental energy depletion and low blood sugar levels. As a result of the research, it was revealed that individuals with relatively low blood sugar levels regarding decision fatigue showed significantly larger error variations and their decisions were less consistent.
2. In another study by Olsen et al. (2017), it was concluded that the afternoon decisions (responses) were less consistent than at other times of the day. It can be said that this is an indicator of decision fatigue.

3.1.2.6 Studies on Marketing (Related to Consumers) about Decision Fatigue

1. In the study conducted by Vohs et al. (2009) on consumers, it was stated that the choices made by the person for himself/herself were more consumer (exhausting) than the choices he/she made for others. It has also been stated that pleasant choices consume fewer people than non-pleasant choices, but this is limited to only a few. Because, after too many elections, it is stated that the person is exhausted regardless of whether the elections are enjoyable or not.
2. The study by Winkle (2014) is about shopping and decision fatigue due to Christmas. According to Winkle, one has less energy about what to buy. Decision fatigue is an advantageous situation for vigilant marketers who know how to schedule sales steps. Because when people shop when they are tired, they tend to get the recommendation of the salesperson.

3.1.2.7 *Studies on Informatics and Computer in Related to Decision Fatigue*

1. In the study conducted by Dubey (2019) on critical thinking in the informatics field, it was stated that critical thinking is the subject of decision-making and decision fatigue is the case of showing daily interest in the decision-making process. This work is drawing attention towards decision fatigue, which must be taken care of while developing a course content framework adopting constructivism in e-learning.
2. It has been suggested by Reinhardt and Hurtienne (2018) that decision fatigue arises because repeated self-control and acts of will are based on a single limited intrapsychic source. It has been concluded that the concept called "cursor entropy" used in computer science increases in people with higher decision fatigue than those with lower decision fatigue.

3.1.2.8 *Study in the Field of Policy about Decision Fatigue*

The purpose of the study conducted by Anindya & Psi (2013) in this field is to determine whether citizenship and decision fatigue can predict political disinterest among university students. However, since only the summary part of this study can be reached, information about the results of the research could not be obtained.

3.1.2.9 *Study in the Field of Sports about Decision Fatigue*

In a study by Mallard (2016) on the Wimbledon tennis championship, the results suggested that professional tennis players show loss avoidance behavior during the game to combat decision fatigue.

3.1.2.10 *Study on Ergonomics Related to Decision Fatigue*

In the study by Robertson and Kortum (2018) on usability (ergonomics), it was stated that every additional decision after fatigue may become increasingly negative, but more research has been proposed on the subject.

3.1.2.11 *Magazinal Study on Decision Fatigue*

When "decision fatigue" is written in the Google Scholar database, the first study belongs to Tierney (2011). In the study, it was seen that there is a magical study. According to Tierney, when decision fatigue occurs, if people have to make other decisions, they start looking for unreasonable shortcuts. These shortcuts often do not take into account long-term effects. On the contrary, they focus only on short-term benefits. People with decision fatigue tend to make safer or easier decisions, even if they have long-term disadvantages for others.

4 Conclusion

Unfortunately, the most important result of the literature review made in the Google Scholar database is that there are no studies on decision fatigue in areas such as business management, organizational behavior, and management organization. Although decision-making is one of the most important functions for managers to be successful, it is surprising that there has not yet been any study on the concept of "decision fatigue" in the literature, and it has not yet attracted attention.

As a result of the literature study, 41.9 % of the total studies were in the field of health. Psychology follows the field of health with 12.9 %. Therefore, it has been revealed that the most attention to the concept of "decision fatigue" has been given in the last years (especially between 2018 and 2020) in the field of health.

However, the conclusions and suggestions reached in line with the general information obtained as a result of searching the literature on the concept of decision fatigue are as follows;

- As a result of the literature review; it was concluded that after long-term tasks, poor performance and decision fatigue may occur (Campagne et al., 2004; Kecklund and Akerstedt, 1993; Torswall and Akerstedt, 1987). As stated by MacDonald et al. (2000), it is imperative to monitor the actions in order to behave in a consistent and harmonious manner in order to prevent errors due to low performance and decision fatigue. In doing so, information is obtained that can be used to adjust the behavior in progress.
- As stated by Huang (2019), decision fatigue can be prevented by using motivation strategies. Applied research studies can be conducted on this proposal, and motivation tools or strategies that prevent decision fatigue can be shared in the world of science and business.
- Since cognitive capacity is limited, increasing options may cause decision fatigue (Mathew & Joseph, 2014; Olsen 2015). Accordingly, it can be said that it would be beneficial to reduce the number of options to prevent decision fatigue.
- Overloading information about products on e-commerce websites can cause decision fatigue (Mathew & Joseph, 2014). When there is a lot of information, the decision can be troublesome and this leads to depletion of mental resources. When the mental resources are exhausted, bargaining power is weakened, the possibility of making the right decision decreases, satisfaction decreases and more regrets may be experienced due to the choices made.
- In the informatics field, a study by Dubbey (2019) on critical thinking, e-learning and decision fatigue, it was concluded that increasing daily average decisions is proportional to mental fatigue.

- As stated by Hirshleifer et al. (2019), it was observed that professionals went to reduce the number of options especially in their daily decisions in order to eliminate decision fatigue. As also stated by Mathew and Joseph (2014), as the number of options increases, it will be difficult to make decisions and lead to depletion of mental resources. In addition, it may be beneficial to take breaks at regular intervals to employees to get rid of the negative effects of decision fatigue and to rest their habitats away from unnecessary stimuli in order to get rid of the negative effects of decision fatigue.
- In addition, it has been determined that fatigue of decision affects especially financial representatives (Hirshleifer et al., 2019). However, it has been concluded that the studies carried out are limited to very few fields and sectors. It can be suggested that future studies on decision fatigue should be carried out especially in the fields related to business administration and on managers at all stages of management levels. In fact, organizational and managerial can be associated with many concepts and bring more beneficial results to the studies.
- However, the concept of "decision fatigue" can be examined separately on the basis of sectors and professions. As decision fatigue increases, professions in which the cost of error can increase can be determined. What are the administrative actions to reduce the effect of decision fatigue can be researched on the basis of sector and profession. All these applications can shed light on business managers, human resources managers, financial managers and other line managers and other researchers.

This study has its limitations. Although it was published on Google Scholar, even the summary of 16 studies could not be reached. Some of the studies are in a pacified state, while others are available for a fee. Unfortunately, it is an important difficulty for academics to overcome that studies made for the scientific world are available for a fee. The free access of information presented to the benefit of all people, especially other scientists, will make science more important and useful for the entire universe.

References

Allan, J. L., Johnston, D. W., Powell, D. J. H., Farquharson, B., Jones, M. C., Leckie, G., & Johnston, M. (2019). "Clinical decisions and time since rest break: An analysis of decision fatigue in nurses". Health Psychology, 38 (4), 318–324.

Anindya, S. and Psi, S. (2013). Peran Perasaan Kewargaan Dan Decision Fatigue Dalam Memprediksikan Apatisme Politik Pada Mahasiswa. eprints2.binus.ac.id. https://scholar.google.com/scholar?hl=tr&as_sdt=0%2C5&q=%22decision+fatigue%22%2C+Anindya%2C+Psi%2C+2013&btnG=(04.07.2020)

Barker, A. (1999). How better … decision making. Translated by: Ali Çimen, Istanbul: Timaş Publishing.

Barnett, M. L., Linder, J. A. and Jena, A. B. (2016). Day of the Week and Physician Decision Fatigue. https://scholar.google.com/scholar?hl=en&as_sdt=0%2C5&q=%22decision+fatigue%22%2C++Barnett%2C+Linder+and+Jena%2C+2016&btnG=(04.07.2020)

Baumeister, R. F., Bratslavsky, E., Muraven, M., & Tice, D. M. (1998). "Ego depletion: Is the active self a limited resource?" Journal of Personality and Social Psychology, 74 (5), 1252–1265.

Baumeister, R. F., & Tierney, J. (2011). Willpower: Why self-control is the secret to success. New York: The Peaus Press.

Birchall, A. (2012). Decision Fatigue-Choosing the best time to make the right call. Management Today-Australia's Leading Magazine for . . . https://scholar.google.com/scholar?hl=en&as_sdt=0%2C5&q=%22decision+fatigue%22%2C+Birchall%2C+2012&btnG=(04.07.2020)

Byrnes, Ph.D., & James, P. (2002). "The development of decision-making". Journal of Adolescent Health, (31), 208–215.

Campagne, A., Pebayle, T., & Muzet, A. (2004). "Correlation between driving errors and vigilance level: Influence of the driver's age". Physiology and Behavior, 80, 515–524.

Chen, Y. C., Liou, C. F. and Chen, Y. C. (2018). Validating the Chinese Version of the Decision Fatigue Scale. https://scholar.google.com/scholar?hl=tr&as_sdt=0%2C5&q=%22decision+fatigue%22%2C+Chen%2C+Liou+and+Chen%2C+2018&btnG=(04.07.2020)

Clear, J. (2013). The Science Behind Bad Decisions: Is 'Decision Fatigue' Causing You to Make Unhealthy Choices? Access from https://www.huffpost.com/entry/decision-fatigue_b_4044212(18.04.2020).

Danziger S., Levav, J., & Avnaim-Pesso, L. (2011). "Extraneous factors in judicial decisions". Proceedings of the National Academy of Sciences of the United States of America 108 (17), 6889–6892.

Denton, R. (?). "Effects of decision fatigue". https://scholar.google.com/scholar?hl=tr&as_sdt=0%2C5&q=%22decision+fatigue%22%2C+Denton%2C&btnG=(04.07.2020)

Dubey, S. (2019). "Towards Finding Association between Decision Fatigue and Critical Thinking in the Constructive E-Learning Environment". International Journal of Scientific Research and Review, 07 (06), 58–66.

Halamka, J. (2011). Coping with IT decision fatigue. Computerworld, Inc. https://scholar.google.com/scholar?hl=tr&as_sdt=0%2C5&q=%22decision+fatigue%22%2C+Halamka%2C+2011&btnG=(04.07.2020)

Hickman, R. L., Pignatiello, G., & Tahir, S. (2018). "Evaluation of the decisional fatigue scale among surrogate decision makers of the critically". Western Journal of Nursing Research, 40 (2), 191-208. doi: 10.1177/0193945917723828

Hirshleifer, D., Levi, Y., Lourie, B., & Teoh, S. H. (2019). "Decision fatigue and heuristic analyst forecasts". Journal of Financial Economics, 133, 83–98.

Howard, J. (2019). Decision Fatigue. Cognitive Errors and Diagnostic Mistakes. https://scholar.google.com/scholar?hl=en&as_sdt=0%2C5&q=%22decision+fatigue%22%2C+Howard%2C+2019&btnG=(04.07.2020)

Huang, D. (2019). "Where There's a Will, There's a Way: Implementing Motivational Strategies to Combat Decision Fatigue". CMC Senior Theses. https://scholarship.claremont.edu/cmc_theses/2022(17.04.2020).

Hughes, J., Lysikowski, J., Acharya, R., Phelps, E., and Kandil, E. (2019). "A Multi-year analysis of decision fatigue in opioid prescribing". Journal of General Internal Medicine. DOI: 10.1007/s11606-019-05217-x.

Hunt, T. C., Ambrose, J. P., Haaland, B., Hanson, H. A., & O'Neil, B. B. (2020). "MP75-06 decision fatigue in Prostate-Specific Antigen (PSA) testing". The Journal of Urology, 203 (Supplement 4), e1143–e1144.

Jacsó, P. (2008). "Google Scholar revisited". Online Information Review, 32 (1), 102–114.

Kahneman, D., & Egan, P. (2011). Thinking, fast and slow (Vol. 1). New York, NY: Farrar, Straus and Giroux.

Kecklund, G., & Akerstedt, T. (1993). "Sleepiness in long distance truck driving: An ambulatory EEG study of night driving". Journal of Ergonomics, 36 (9), 1007–1017.

Koçel, T. (2010). Business management (Extended 12th ed.). Istanbul: Beta Printing Publishing Distribution Inc.

Kouchaki, M., & Smith, I. H. (2014). "The morning morality effect: The influence of time of day on unethical behavior". Psychological Science, 25, 95–102.

Kwan, J., Stein, L., Delshad, S., Johl, S., Park, H., Martinez, B., Topp, L., & Spiegel, B. (2016). "Does "Decision Fatigue" impact manuscript acceptance? An analysis of editorial decisions by the American Journal of Gastroenterology". American Journal of Gastroenterology, 111 (11), 1511–1512.

Le, C. S. (2018). The effect of decision fatigue on pro-social behavior. Access from https://scholarbank.nus.edu.sg/handle/10635/146964(17.04.2020).

Linder, J. A., Doctor, J. N., Friedberg, M. W., Nieva, H. R., Birks, C., Meeker, D., & Fox, C. R. (2014). "Time of day and the decision to prescribe antibiotics". Journal of the American Medical Association, 174, 2029–2031.

Liss, D. T., & Linder, J. A. (2019). "Decision fatigue, running late, and population health management — screening out of time. BUT Netw Open, 2 (5), e193402. doi: 10.1001/jamanetworkopen.2019.3402 (16.04.2020).

Lushaku, F. and Lahtinen, T. (2019). The Gambler's Fallacy and Decision Fatigue in Decision-Making: A Study on Driving License Examiners. https://scholar.google.com/scholar?hl=tr&as_sdt=0%2C5&q=%22decision+fatigue%22%2C+Lushaku+%26+Lahtinen%2C+2019&btnG=04.07.2020

MacDonald III, A. W., Cohen, J. D., Stenger, V. A., & Carter, C. S. (2000). "Dissociating the role of the dorsolateral prefrontal and anterior cingulate cortex in cognitive control". Science, 288, 1835–1838.

Mackay, J. (2018). Decision fatigue: What it is and how it's killing your focus, motivation, and willpower. [Blog post]. https://blog.rescuetime.com/decision-fatigue/(16.04.2020).

Mallard, G. (2016). "Loss aversion and decision fatigue at the Wimbledon tennis championship". International Journal of Behavioral Accounting and Finance, 6 (1), 70–91.

Marghoob, A. and Carrera, C. (2016). ". . . Seth, Case Western Reserve University School of Medicine; Kord Honda, MD, University Hospitals Department of Dermatology Decision fatigue suggests that over . . .". https://scholar.google.com/scholar?hl=en&as_sdt=0%2C5&q=%22decision+fatigue%22%2C++Marghoob+%26+Carrera%2C+2016&btnG=(04.07.2020)

Mathew, S., & Joseph, J. (2014). Decision fatigue differential impact of information display formats on consumer decision-making. Listening to consumers of emerging markets, Edited by Jain, Dash, Nair, Ali, Goyal, Dasgupta and Maity, Chapter 36, pp. 175–179. IIM Lucknow, First Edition: New Delhi

McAllister, J. (2017). "Beat decision fatigue". HR Future, 2017 (5), 14–16. Access from https://journals.co.za/content/journal/om_hrf_feb_2020(17.04.2020).

Naftel, M., & Driscoll. (1993). "Problem solving and decision making in an eight-grade class". The Clearing House, 66, (3), 177–180.

Olsen, S. (2015). "The influence of time of day on decision fatigue in stated choice experiments". Access from http://www.icmconference.org.uk/index.php/icmc/icmc2015/paper/view/822(17.04.2020).

Olsen, S. B., Meyerhoff, J., Mørkbak, M., & Bonnichsen, O. (2017). "The influence of time of day on decision fatigue in online food choice experiments". British Food Journal, 119 (3), 497–510.

Oto, B. (2012). "When thinking is hard: managing decision fatigue..". Journal: EMS World. https://scholar.google.com/scholar?hl=tr&as_sdt=0%2C5&q=%22decision+fatigue%22%2C+Oto%2C+2012&btnG=(04.07.2020)

Persson, E., Barrafrem, K., Meunier, A., & Tinghög, G. (2019). The effect of decision fatigue on surgeons' clinical decision making. Access from https://onlinelibrary.wiley.com/doi/full/10.1002/hec.3933(16.04.2020).

Petrie, C., Holschen, J. C., Adams, W. and Zelisko, S. (2019). The Impact of Decision Fatigue on Ancillary Test Ordering in the Emergency Department. https://scholar.google.com/scholar?hl=en&as_sdt=0%2C5&q=%22decision+fatigue%22%2C++Petrie%2C+Holschen%2C+Adams+and+Zelisko%2C+2019&btnG=(04.07.2020)

Pignatiello, G. A., Martin, R. J., & Hickman, R. L. (2018). "Decision fatigue: A conceptual analysis". Journal of Health Psychology, 25 (1), 123–135. https://doi.org/10.1177/1359105318763510

Polman, E., & Vohs, K. D. (2016). "Decision fatigue, choosing for others, and self-construal". Social Psychological and Personality Science, https://doi.org/10.1177/1948550616639648. Access from https://journals.sagepub.com/doi/abs/10.1177/1948550616639648(16.04.2020).

Reinhardt, D., & Hurtienne, J. (2018). Cursor Entropy Reveals Decision Fatigue, Access from https://www.researchgate.net/publication/323591748_Cursor_Entropy_Reveals_Decision_Fatigue

Rao, S., & Nyquist, A.-C. (2018). "The power of the nudge to decrease decision fatigue and increase influenza vaccination rates". BUT Netw Open, 1 (5), e181754.

Robertson, I., & Kortum, P. (2018). "Extraneous Factors in Usability Testing: Evidence of Decision Fatigue During Sequential Usability Judgments". Access from https://journals.sagepub.com/doi/abs/10.1177/1541931218621321(18.04.2020).

Saposnik, G., Maurino, J. and Jaja, B. (2018). The influence of decision fatigue on therapeutic decisions in multiple sclerosis care. https://scholar.google.com/scholar?hl=en&as_sdt=0%2C5&q=%22decision+fatigue%22%2C+Saposnik%2C+Maurino+and+Jaja%2C+2018&btnG=(04.07.2020)

Sollisch, J. (2016). The cure for decision fatigue. Wall Street Journal. https://scholar.google.com/scholar?hl=tr&as_sdt=0%2C5&q=%22decision+fatigue%22%2C+Sollisch%2C+2016&btnG=(04.07.2020)

Soukup, T., Lamb, B. W., Weigl, M., Green, J. S. A., & Sevdalis, N. (2019). "Task effects with a pragmatic framework for understanding and improving decision-making in multidisciplinary oncology team meetings". Frontiers in Psychology, https://doi.org/10.3389/fpsyg.2019.01245(15.04.2020).

Sperry, L. (2003). Becoming an effective health care manager: The essential skills of leadership. Baltimore: Health Professions Press.

Stanovich, K. E., & West, R. F. (2000). "Individual differences in reasoning: Implications for the rationality deate?" Behavioral and Rain Science, 23 (5), 645–665.

Stewart, A. F., Ferriero, D. M., Josephson, S. A., Lowenstein, D. H., Messing, R. O., Oksenberg, J. R., Johnston, S. C., & Hauser, S. L. (2012). Fighting decision fatigue. Access from https://onlinelibrary.wiley.com/doi/full/10.1002/ana.23531(18.04.2020).

Tian, F., & Exline, M. (2017). Reduced clinical recall and attentiveness due to decision fatigue, Access from https://www.atsjournals.org/doi/abs/10.1164/ajrccm-conference.2017.195.1_MeetingAbstracts.A7153(17.04.2020).

Tierney, J. (2011). "Do you suffer from decision fatigue?" The New York Times magazine Access from https://www.nytimes.com/2011/08/21/magazine/do-you-suffer-from-decision-fatigue.html(16.04.2020).

Torswall, L., & Akerstedt, T. (1987). "Sleepiness on the job: Continuously measured EEG changes in train drivers". Electroencephalography and Clinical Neurophysiology, 66 (6), 502–511.

Twenge, J. M., Tice, D. M. and Baumeister, R. F. (2000). Decision fatigue: Making multiple personal decisions depletes the self's resources. Manuscript submitted for publication. https://scholar.google.com/scholar?hl=tr&as_sdt=0%2C5&q=%22decision+fatigue%22%2C+Twenge%2C+&btnG=(04.07.2020)

Vohs, K. D., Twenge, J. M., Baumeister, R. F. and Schmeichel, B. J. (2003). Decision fatigue: Making multiple personal decisions depletes the self's resources. Unpublished manuscript. https://scholar.google.com/scholar?hl=tr&as_sdt=0%2C5&q=%22decision+fatigue%22%2C+Vohs%2C+Twenge%2C+Baumeister+and+Schmeichel%2C+2003&btnG=(04.07.2020)

Vohs, K. D., Baumeister, R. F., Twenge, J. M. and Schmeichel, B. J. (2004); Decision fatigue: Choices influence self-regulatory resources. Unpublished manuscript. https://scholar.google.com/scholar?hl=tr&as_sdt=0%2C5&q=%22decision+fatigue%22%2C+Vohs%2C+Baumeister%2C+Twenge%2C+and+Schmeichel%2C+2004&btnG=(04.07.2020)

Vohs, K. D., Baumeister, R. F., Twenge, J. M., Schmeichel, J. M., Tice, D. M., & Crocker, J. (2005). Decision Fatigue Exhausts Self-Regulatory Resources- But So Does Accommodating to Unchosen Alternatives. Access from https://www.researchgate.net/profile/Jean_Twenge/publication/237738528_Decision_Fatigue_Exhausts_Self-Regulatory_Resources_-_But_So_Does_Accommodating_to_Unchosen_Alternatives/links/554b9e40fecurecontroller unchosen-Alternatives.pdf

Vohs, K. D., Baumeister, R. F., Twenge, J. M. and Schmeichel, B. J. (2006); Decision fatigue exhausts self-regulatory resources. Unpublished manuscript. https://scholar.google.com/scholar?hl=tr&as_sdt=0%2C5&q=%22decision+

fatigue%22%2C+Vohs%2C+Baumeister%2C+Twenge%2C+Schmeichel%2C+2006&btnG=(04.07.2020)

Vohs, K. D., Baumeister, R. F., Schmeichel, J. M., Twenge, J. M., Nelson, N. M., & Tice, D. M. (2008). "Making choices impairs subsequent self-control: A limited resource account of decision making, self-regulation, and active initiative". Journal of Personality and Social Psychology, 94, 883–898.

Vohs, K. D., Nelson, N., & Rawn, C. (2009), "Why do choices tax self-regulatory resources? Three tests of candidates to explain decision fatigue". In Ann L. McGill & Sharon Shavitt (Eds.), NA-advances in consumer research (Vol. 36, pp. 172–176). Duluth, MN: Association for Consumer Research.

Weight, B. B. (?). Decision Fatigue and Ego Depletion–Too Tired to Decide. https://scholar.google.com/scholar?hl=en&as_sdt=0%2C5&q=%22decision+fatigue%22%2C++BB+Weight&btnG=(04.07.2020)

Winkle, C. W. (2014). "Decision fatigue: A tired brain and Christmas shopping". Access from https://www.theravive.com/today/post/decision-fatigue-a-tired-brain-and-christmas-shopping-0001782.aspx16.04.2020.

Zheng, B., Kwok, E., Taljaard, M., Nemnom, M-J., & Stiell, I. (2019). "Decision fatigue in the emergency department: How does emergency physician decision making change over an eight-hour shift?". The American Journal of Emergency Medicine, In Press, Corrected Proof. https://doi.org/10.1016/j.ajem.2019.12.020.

Used Links

URL-1

http://changingminds.org/explanations/decision/decision_fatigue.htm(16.04.2020)

URL-2

https://www.dailymail.co.uk/news/article-2612738/How-decision-fatigue-hampering-social-workers-Damning-report-says-employees-rarely-hear-consequences-actions.html(16.04.2020).

URL-3

https://scholar.google.com/scholar?hl=en&as_sdt=0%2C5&q=%22decision+fatigue%22&btn(13.04.2020).URL-3

https://scholar.google.com/scholar?hl=en&as_sdt=0%2C5&q=%22decision+fatigue%22&btn (13.04.2020)

URL-4

https://scholar.google.com/scholar?start=10&q=%22decision+fatigue%22&hl=en&as_sdt=0,5 (14.04.2020)

URL-5

https://scholar.google.com/scholar?start=20&q=%22decision+fatigue%22&hl=en&as_sdt=0,5 (14.04.2020)

URL- 6

https://scholar.google.com/scholar?start=90&q=%22decision+fatigue%22&hl=en&as_sdt=0,5 (16.04.2020)

URL-7

https://scholar.google.com/scholar?start=100&q=%22decision+fatigue%22&hl=tr&as_sdt=0,5 (16.04.2020)

URL-8

https://scholar.google.com/scholar?start=20&q=%22decision+fatigue%22&hl=tr&as_sdt=0,5 14.04.2020

URL-9

https://www.ncbi.nlm.nih.gov/pubmed/22670402 (14.04.2020)

URL-10

https://scholar.google.com/scholar?start=30&q=%22decision+fatigue%22&hl=en&as_sdt=0,5 (14.04.2020)

URL-11

https://link.springer.com/chapter/10.1007/978-3-319-93224-8_6 (15.04.2020)

URL-12

https://scholar.google.com/scholar?start=60&q=%22decision+fatigue%22&hl=tr&as_sdt=0,5 (16.04.2020)

URL- 13

https://www.jaad.org/article/S0190-9622(17)31972-2/abstract (16.04.2020)

URL-14

https://www.airitilibrary.com/Publication/alDetailedMesh?docid=P20181023002-201810-PP201810230001-PP201810230001-1-3-055 (17.04.2020)

URL-15

http://www.diva-portal.org/smash/record.jsf?pid=diva2%3a1348232&dswid=-2560 (17.04.2020)

URL-16

http://eprints.binus.ac.id/28328/1/2012-2-00208-PS%20Abstrak001.pdf (17.04.2020)

www.ingramcontent.com/pod-product-compliance
Ingram Content Group UK Ltd.
Pitfield, Milton Keynes, MK11 3LW, UK
UKHW021846100926
8556IPUK00020B/1088

9 783631 819036